Practical Psychology

Important Knowledge and Useful Exercises for ~~

By Dr. Edward Schellhammer
Founder and President of MARBELLA UNIVERSITY

2nd Edition 2012, revised
© Copyright 2012. Dr. Edward Schellhammer.
All Rights Reserved.

ISBN-13: 978-1478366942
ISBN-10: 147836694X

www.MarbellaUniversity.com
www.PioneeringEducation.com

Table of Contents

Foreword

With the 21st century a new époque of absolutely extreme challenges has begun. Most people know about the big problems of humanity and the earth. Soon the earth's population will reach 7bn and will continue growing up to 9bn, 10bn, and more. Today more than 4bn live in extremely low and very bad conditions.

Never can the entire population of the earth live on the level of the industrialized standards. All limits of balance have already been broken. Famine, poverty, misery, suffering, unemployment, corruption, wars, climate change, pollution, destruction of environment, speculations, economic crisis, rotten societies, a complete disrespect of human values, and a disastrous failure in local, national and global politics. 500 billion Dollars are necessary every year to finance alone the damages of climate change in the developing countries.

Let's forecast: in a year it will be one trillion; and later several trillions each year. It will be globally much worse in 10, 20, 30, 50 years. Humans have created their own hell! And everybody will be sucked in by this nightmare.

Humans around the globe have lost trust in politics, economy, media, religions, justice, and even in education and human values. Humanity has lost hope and love.

Humanity needs a new generation of responsible people with a trustworthy way of living, and especially of leaders and business people with a rock-solid personality integrity acting with knowledge, competences, fairness, responsibility and honesty.

Human life starts with education and with environmental influences already in the prenatal time. A global brainwashing together with all kind of sublime manipulations has produced a humanity living far away from their genuine inner being. 5-6bn humans have become exploited as a sole "human biomass". Where will this lead all of us?

Our program "Practical Psychology" is the powerful answer for real hope with all-sided balanced solutions for everybody: a new education forming humans for the challenges today and in the future in the personal life, in work and business, and in politics and religions. The management of the relevant psychological knowledge and efficient social skills is indispensable for a good personal life as well as for professional success in all fields.

See the facts that politicians and leaders around the globe are not telling you:

- We live in a world where fundamental changes are arising with high speed.
- The world in 20-35 years will bring you unimaginable challenges.
- Everything that seems to be safe today will become completely insecure.
- The entire life frame around the globe will be different from today.
- The huge global problems of humanity will dramatically increase.
- The damages and destruction of nature will affect billions of people.
- Humanity will need 50-65% more resources for industry and living.
- Poverty in the industrialized countries will hit half of the population.
- One must be prepared for the worst living conditions to survive in any way.
- The young people today will inherit the damages from current causes.
- The people in their forties today will be faced with a sad "third age".
- The people in their sixties today will probably die in a disgraceful way.

You want love and happiness. You want food and everything that makes life comfortable. You want a home. You want to create a family. You want fun and entertainment. You want a financially stable existence. You want to live your "third age" in a worthy way. You want to be healthy.

You never want to die or be seriously injured or handicapped through an accident. You want to work and to use your potentials for work and life. You also want to spend good times on weekends and of course you want great holidays every year. You never want war or terrorism.

You never want to suffer from disease caused by contaminations or by suppressing your inner conflicts, pains, and unsolved problems. You want to live yourself authentically and to grow psychologically and spiritually as a person. You want to find your genuine fulfillment.

How can you get all this by ignoring the state of humanity and the earth?

How can you get it if you completely disrespect your inner being?

How can you get it if you don't strongly contribute with your way of living to drastically reduce the damages made to natural resources, the environment, the world of nature and animals, and the climate?

You are the cause for the huge global problems of humanity and the earth! You together with billions of other people! Therefore: you and billions must significantly contribute to avoid the collapse of humanity and the earth in 20-35 years with a new way of successfully living your life.

→ By reading the chapter, new realities will open up to you.
→ By doing the exercises you will acquire knowledge for everyday life.
→ By completing the exercises you will recognize yourself.
→ By contemplating your results you will start changing yourself.
→ By changing yourself you will broaden yourself and grow extensively.
→ By exploring your being, you will find happiness and fulfillment
→ By understanding your being you adapt knowledge about humans.
→ If many people live this path, the global problems can be solved.

There is no better and more efficient path to success in being, becoming, life, job, and business.

There is no higher fulfillment in the truth, not in life philosophy, not in spirituality, not in religion.

There is no salvation and redemption for the entire humanity in the sense of the salvific history without this inner and terrestrial practical path.

Without this path humanity has no future at all!

Dr. Edward Schellhammer

1. Knowledge

1.1. Life Philosophy and Human Values

The core of a positive life philosophy

Searching for the truth has a philosophical, a spiritual and a religious impact:

The truth has got a lot to do with self-knowledge. A person first acknowledges his real face. If a person knows himself completely, he first recognizes his own truth. And he recognizes the truth of other people, because self-knowledge is the foundation of human knowledge.

Now, we have to see that self-knowledge is a process of growing. As a consequence we can say: Awareness of God is finally the result of this growing process.

We understand this in an extensive meaning: The practical psychology leads to the and through the self-knowledge process, and through the following process of growth towards God; or the other way around: Without practicing psychology as a tool for self-knowledge, awareness of God isn't possible. "Practicing psychology" in this context means: self-knowledge, personality education and Individuation. The alternative to life lies is the truth of life.

Is this understanding of the truth useful and right? Do you want to know it? Then, you must start this process of self-knowledge and you must explore your inner world. That's the way to prove it. In any case it is a good start.

The result of personality education is to be classified neither as political, nor religious, nor esoteric nor spiritual. Nobody will become a racist, or a socialist, or a communist, or a Christian-socialist, or a Christian, or a Muslim, or a Hindu. Individuation doesn't guide us to a determined psychological or philosophical position in the traditional manner.

One doesn't become a disciple of a psychological-esoteric movement. The whole theory that involves the psychical organism and the process of Individuation has a binding character; but the models are steadily revised by science, widened and formulated into more practical ways.

What is the right life philosophy? Which institution teaches the right life philosophy? Find it out by asking the following questions:

1. Are the psychical forces of the human being and the whole psychical organism entirely considered, taught, educated and changed (by these organizations)?
2. Do the institutions/teachers practice the methods, which create a holistic self-knowledge, a self-renovation and a self-development for man and woman?
3. Do they practice the inner way, guided and developed through the inner force?
4. Do they reach and form all those psychical forces in the human being, which cause problems, sufferings, damages and wars?
5. Do they guide the human being to the spiritual force, the source of life within everyone?
6. Does everybody receive a deepened psychological consciousness about everything that they experience as 'religious'?
7. Do they build up peace in the world, from the 'roots', namely in the unconscious psychical forces within the human being?
8. Do the heads of all institutions (especially educational institutions/organizations) form their own psychical organism and their acting, considering the deep psychological background?
9. Do the heads of institutions (especially educational institutions/organizations) reflect upon the deep psychological effects of their power behavior on the unconscious life of everybody?
10. Do they make the dynamic of projection clear and the way one can fix (bond) his libido on an institution, person and teaching?
11. Do they love the human being with the psychical life and do they love life as an expression of the psychical life?
12. Do they promote autonomy, self-responsibility, individuality, critical thinking, and the archetypal processes (transformations) of the complete psychical life through Individuation?

The ultimate statement about a positive life philosophy is: Living on this earth is a gift!

The main questions in life touch everybody:

→ Do you want to live?
→ Do you say 'yes' to your life?
→ How do you appreciate your life?
→ What do you do with your life?

→ What do you do with the lives of others?
→ In which practical way do you say "yes" to your life?
→ In which practical way do you say "yes" to the life of others?

The 10 most important human values

Let's explore the human values by looking at simple facts in real life.

1. First of all: you are a human with body and mind (and soul). And this is the first basic human value.

In other words: this first basic human value needs to be formed and cared for. To be a human is in the evolution of life on this earth something like the crown of the creation.

2. To be on this earth as a human, to live and to grow on this earth in manifold ways is an enormous gift.

The possibilities of developing inner life and realizing your genuine self, your ideas, interests, and talents are countless. This is an important human value.

3. Fact is: you have come to this earth which means you need a certain environment to live and grow in a healthy way. The environment gives you everything for life and humanity's evolution.

That means: the earth with all possible resources and conditions for a human life has highest value.

4. As a human being you deserve to be protected and promoted in your development and life; and this from the prenatal time, up to the childhood and until the last moment of your third age.

Education is not only a necessity for living; it is also a chance to form amazing qualities of human being and environment.

The earth has essential human value in manifold variations for humans and their evolution.

5. You have a psychical-spiritual organism, called "mind" or "psyche". This organism has a conscious and unconscious area.

The singular functions are, e.g.:

The "I", the defense mechanisms, the intelligence with a great variation of potentials including language and learning, the feelings (with the well known constructive and destructive spectrum), the psychical needs (security, freedom, autonomy, self-realization, love, care, etc.), the ability to love, the world of dreams give messages created by the inner Spirit, and an unlimited ability to perform.

All these psychical-spiritual functions have to be formed in an all-sided balanced way. These functions with their potentials have highest human value.

6. A human soul, coming to this earth can't decide how parents, people, society, religion, and environment influences it and determines it's forming process. A lot may be wrong.

Very difficult experiences may produce heavy suffering and even traumas. Serious incidents such as an accident or life conditions such as poverty can form a human in a very sad way.

But principally humans can become free from such experiences by transforming the content of the unconscious mind. This chance is a wonderful human value.

7. The exploration of the psychical and spiritual potentials leads to a concept of psychical-spiritual development that includes the following archetypal inner processes:

- Accepting and turning to the whole inner life
- Discovering and forming all inner forces
- Developing the true Self by conscious forming
- Integrating the inner Spirit as guidance
- Proceedings of dying and becoming new
- Unification with the inner opposite gender pole
- Integration of the spiritual principles
- Balance between external and internal life
- Fulfillment of the completeness and wholeness

The following archetypal inner processes go much further in the spiritual state of a person:

- God and his manifoldness;
- God's alliance with you;

- Becoming a specific destination of service in God (e.g. priest, religious leader, supreme teacher);
- The transcendental world of the souls;
- Denomination as a representative of a Messiah or prophet;
- Authorization from the inner Spirit to develop further the original teaching and practices.

Nothing, absolutely nothing on this earth and in the human evolution since ever and for ever can have higher human value than these archetypes of the soul made vivid from humans.

8. Today humans have created and can create an immense amount of different products and technical tools that enormously facilitate human life and management of society. Looking back to the past: How was life 200 years ago without toilet rolls and mobile phones?

We conclude: The products and technical tools humans have created for "a better life" are, considered on an objective view, absolutely enormous. This also has high human value.

9. For a healthy development humans need love and want to love. The manifoldness of love as an active psychical and spiritual potential is unlimited for humans, the world of nature and animals, and the Creator, called "God" (whatever is meant with this word). The power of love is immense and in essence, the power of the human evolution.

10. Another power of the human evolution is the inner Spirit, that creates messages to the dreaming person. Dreams tell the truth about us, others, religions, ideologies, society, the earth, the future and God. The Spirit is an informative, organizing and guiding force.

The Spirit is the principle of acting in the soul. The Spirit is animating, stimulating, and benevolent. The Spirit is the source of wisdom. The inner Spirit is the highest authority and stands above all religions and dogmatic teaching! This is obviously the highest spiritual value for humans. The Spirit also expresses a human value because every human has this inner Spirit.

The state of the formed qualities of the individuals and of humanity in general, and what people do with these human values determines the present and the future of humanity. In other words to humanity in general: ignore these human values and humanity will perish! Respect these human values and humanity will grow evolutionary towards a good future.

Love is the central pillar of human life

Most people rapidly oversee that love is much more than a feeling. Love is a complex performance. Love without reasoning (thinking) has little chance of performing something stable. Love without Spirit is structure-less and has no inner depth. If somebody wants to live with Spirit, he has to learn how to interpret dreams and to meditate correctly. If somebody wants to love, he has to observe with concentration and clear view the inner and external world. Love presupposes a will to act. Living love means to precisely look at the genuine inner needs, to one's own acting, psycho dynamism and all feelings. In a raw state the force of love is archaic, instinctive, nothing more than a physiological (brain) social pattern.

Love is a manifold creative force of life. Love gives meaning and value to life. Love makes life worth living and rich. Love is the key to a lot of apparently unsolvable situations. Love respects life's many-sided balances. Love operates in many directions: for one's own psychical life, for the psychical life of the partner, for living together, for creating a life environment, for political and economical life, for culture, and for the religious (spiritual) life.

The statement "How can you love others, if you don't love yourself?" has been very widespread; however it fails to entail the true essence of life's complexity. What everyone should really be asking themselves is: How is it possible to care for the needs of others, if you reject and suppress your own basic needs and that on a daily basis? How can you disrespect your own feelings, but protect and carefully promote the feelings of others? How can you express Spirit in your life, but disregard your own inner Spirit? How can it be possible to love God, but not turn toward your own inner psychical life? How can a human being love God, glorify him and realize him in real life, but reject his own inner psychical-spiritual life? How can one teach the truth without recognizing one's own inner true life?

Love respects life in many balanced ways. In society, love integrates the world of children and that of the elderly. Ill and disabled people and all people with limited abilities can discover love and learn to live love creatively like everybody else in society. Love operates in diverse directions: for one's own psychical life, for the psychical life of the partner, for the social life, for the environment, for the political and economic life, as well as for the cultural and religious life.

Love is a creative force. The Spirit is the ordering and controlling principle of love. Love is the specific essential human nature: as a potential, a performance and way of living. If this can't be the deepest meaning of life, what else can it be?

Love has a tendency to transform everything that hinders a balanced inner wholeness. Love tends to dissolve "complexes" in the unconscious, to transform thought to external realities, and to openly care for feelings. Love wants to put through its own values and pushes to live meaning and values beyond the individual frame of life.

Transforming means: re-forming psychical forces, growing with spiritual values, as well as creating a way of living with spiritually and with the essential meaning of life and its values. This is the dedication to the real life of human beings and demands the education of the psychical life. Expressions of such a performance are: elaborating one's own inner life, the ability to reconcile and to renounce something in the interest of higher aims in the context of psychical-spiritual development.

To love also means: to understand (to see, to care for, to live) one's own whole being in a network of mankind and the earth. To go beyond one's own unity also leads to the environment: What human beings have inside as an archetypal ideal shall find a real expression in the external world.

→ Thesis: Love is a manifold creative force.

→ Thesis: Love respects life in many balanced ways.

→ Thesis: Love wants to put through its own values.

→ Thesis: Love has a tendency to create a holistic balance.

Abilities are necessary in order to love

Abilities to love are expressed in:

- Having an active interest in the psychical-spiritual life of human beings.
- Giving importance to one's own psychical-spiritual life and to consciously form it.
- Valuing one's own sensuality, to care for it creatively.
- Valuing one's own real resources and to use it for the psychical-spiritual life.

- Searching for the high values of the human being in dreams and contemplations.
- Discovering spirituality in one's own inside and in other people too.
- Being vigilant with the destructive forces of the unconscious and of thoughts.
- Not rejecting (suppressing) the desires, but being more open to live them in a creative way.
- Respecting the healthy needs of the body and consciously taking care of them.
- Regularly and actively experiencing nature and valuing it.
- Caring for the values of living together (family, relationship) and to protect them.

Self-love is the beginning of each and every love. To love has got to do with having interest, caring, dedicating, promoting, allowing to grow, protecting and strengthening. Many people don't do this with their psychical life and with their real life. The reality shows us: People realize very little self-love.

Love has also got a lot to do with authenticity and truthfulness, with understanding and indulgence for all human difficulties. Patience with oneself as an expression of self-love is an uncommon idea. Many people confuse egoism with self-love.

Egoism splits the holistic psychical life. The result is inner disruption and lack of inner freedom. Destructivity is also a result. Hate, greed and envy are the consequences. The denial of the psychical life leads to a disrespect against love and spirituality. That means: The egoistic person doesn't really love life.

Through self-love one is able to live love in real life. One can only consider and promote onto others what one perceives and cares for in himself. If a person perceives his own needs and cares for his own needs with responsibility, he is able to integrate the needs of others.
If a person elaborates his own dreams, he is able to develop interest for the dreams of others. If somebody forms himself in the psychical-spiritual growing process, he can promote others in the same process. If a person loves himself, he loves his partner and others in the same way: with their complete psychical organism.

Love consciously clarifies. Love perceives the future above the fast pleasure. Love understands human beings from an all-sided balanced view, and also performs for others and for the human values. That's the way self-love converts into love for other people. Love also finds expressions in dealing with nature, animals, and plants.

Do you want to be loved? Do you want to love? Are you able to love? How is life without love? How is a person that is unable to love?

Extend and strengthen your ability to love by learning and contemplating about love. And live what you learn about love!

- Attitudes about psychical-spiritual life of human beings. Give two examples:
- Attitudes about respecting the healthy needs. Give two examples:
- Attitudes about authenticity and truthfulness. Give two examples:
- Attitudes about psychical-spiritual human values. Give two examples:
- Attitudes about being loved. Why do you want to be loved? Give some reasons:

Love being on this earth

No matter if you are rich or poor, healthy, ill, or handicapped, young or old, you are on this earth. You have a soul and you came to this earth to grow, to discover yourself with your innermost being and your potentials (talents), to develop your dispositions and to use your capacities, to realize projects, to create culture, and to discover the world of nature and animals. This includes having fun, enjoying sex, creating culture, understanding others, learning from others, and sharing your life path, joy of life and concerns, with others.

To love being on this earth means:

- Value your physical being, your psychological being, your talents, your special character, and your spiritual potentials
- Value everything life offers you to live and to realize yourself, including all little things that can make you enjoy life
- Value all possibilities to learn for your development, for your work, for creating a home, living with a partner, relationships and a family
- Value what your society can give you: a frame for your life, infrastructures, a cultural identity, and much more
- Value the history of your country and culture with all the countless efforts made during centuries by all kind of pioneers for a better and more comfortable life

But also learn from the present situation and the past of your country. Learn from the mistakes! Learn from the dark side of life and human beings in the past and present! Learn for your future!

Even if you are poor and penniless, you can discover the world around where you live: enjoy parks, museums, historic monuments, lakes or the sea, landscapes, hills and mountains. It doesn't matter if you need to walk to every place, if necessary even for hours just to get there.

If you are poor, ill or handicapped and unable to discover the world around where you live – your "earth", you can create your own environment: make it more comfortable and healthy; put things in order and clean everything; put a lot of plants in your living area including on your balcony; if you like, buy small animals such as canary birds, a fish tank, a little tortoise, or any other appropriate animals. Discover the world with books and DVDs! If you can, contribute to making your environment (neighborhood) better! Help others to discover and improve their personal "world"! Don't damage and don't contaminate your "earth"!

Whether rich, poor, healthy, ill, or handicapped, everybody can find and create his environment to enjoy being on this earth. It is a gift being on this earth, and never a punishment! What do you do with this gift?

All women and men are equal

All women and men have:

- A conscious mind with certain content about themselves and their life.
- A unique biography with multiple (good and bad) experiences.
- Feelings in the full positive and negative multiplicity.
- Resistance, defense mechanisms, and abilities to integrate realities.
- The natural force of love in a certain state of personal maturity.
- Natural, psychical, psycho-physical, social, and spiritual needs.
- Talents and potentials that may be suppressed and ignored.
- A "self" ("I") with a specific level of self-esteem, confidence, and control.
- A formed or unformed (in-) efficient self-management in all life issues.
- An unconscious mind, surely with suppressed conflicts and complexes.
- A sexual self-identity integrating or rejecting drive and expressions.
- A unique dynamic of life energy, controlled or chaotic and not calculable.
- Dreams at night, bringing messages: demanding to learn and to grow.
- A vast quantity of opposite images about the other gender.
- A little or a lot of knowledge about inner psychical-spiritual life and being.
- A certain level of one's own psychical-spiritual development.
- A "super-ego" with norms, laws, attitudes, beliefs and punishment patterns.
- A certain way and quality of verbal and non-verbal communication.

- A unique way of dealing with crisis and conflicts (which may be efficient or not).
- A pattern of reactions to distress, disagreement, and misunderstandings.
- Certain models of resolving critical life situations, efficient or not.
- A unique expression as a whole being and person (nature, character).

Both partners have a complex psychical life. The biography of both contains a lot of disorder, not worked out, and fixed on many things. Both have habits, talents, and reluctances to many things. Both have a physical self-relationship, a special way of experiencing pleasure, a way of nourishing, a style of clothing, special expressions of movements, a style of body care, and a relationship to nature and animals. A multitude of attitudes, beliefs and values form a contradictory wholeness. Also the kind of emotions, the psycho-energetic dynamism, and the biorhythm are different.

Both can remain in stagnation or in a development of their potentials. Both partners also have inappropriate formed psychical functions. Finally there are inextinguishable essential natural differences between a woman and a man.

If a person can't manage all these realities or ignores these realities, a code program is formed: disappointments, neurotic developments, arguments, conflicts, and often psycho-somatic reactions.

Simple but clear: a woman is never a man and a man is never a woman!

- Female psychological attributes are:
- Female ways of caring are:
- Male psychological attributes are:
- Male ways of caring are:
- Female ways of understanding humans are:
- Male ways of understanding humans are:
- Female ways of creativity are:
- Male ways of creativity are:

Live a genuine spirituality

You can find a million books about spirituality and esoteric exercises; most of them are total rubbish for children and naïve people. Our understanding of spirituality is on the ground; based on real life with effects on real aspects of human beings, and not something intangible in the air.

On the one hand spirituality has got a lot to do with human values, in first instance with love and everything that love includes. All human values are in a certain sense "spiritual". Love is a quality, expressed in attitudes and certain behaviors. For example, "truthfulness" is a spiritual value which at the same time includes a pattern of real behavior. Behaviors expressing essential human values demand a moral effort from a person, sometimes including an abdication. In that sense certain ethical character traits are also "spiritual". "Spirituality" as a dimension of living can be understood as the opposite to "physical reality". The entire psychical organism (mind) is in that sense "spiritual" because we don't refer to the brain, but much more the singular psychical forces such as psychical needs, dreams, force of love, suppressed conflicts and painful experiences, etc.

As dreams are messages created from the inner Spirit, we can also understand dream interpretation as a "spiritual" activity. The characteristics of this inner Spirit also express aspects of spirituality. One of the essential characteristics is that this force supports and promotes psychical-spiritual development, allowing one to become aware of suppressed matters, and growing towards an all-sided balanced person. Such qualities are spiritual and bound to each person – not imposed from outside intrusion such as myths, dogmas, or any kind of superstition.

Therefore, living spirituality means:

- Living human values with one self, others, nature, animals, etc.
- Having and expressing a character with moral traits
- Going the path of psychical-spiritual process (Individuation)
- Forming one's own inner (psychical) forces, being responsible for
- Living love or oneself, a partner, children, others, nature, etc.
- Resolving suppressed conflicts and painful experiences
- Interpreting one's dreams and living the conclusions
- Meditation and Mental-Training with all its variations
- Forming one's psychical energy with specific techniques
- Being responsible in general for the effects of one's own acting
- Understanding the meaning of life in relation to the inner Spirit

The state of humanity and the earth shows us that the spirituality of all religions and spirituality-concepts together are unable to provide mankind with a dignified life! That's because they exclude in their teachings and practices the psychical organism with all its potentials.

What is a "human being"?

Today we determine a human being with the entire mind (psyche, inner life) as a whole. We call it "the psychical-spiritual organism".

Many non-physical functions determine a human being: the "I" (self), the control and decision making instance, the defense and projection mechanisms, the intelligence, the ability to think and learn, the feelings, the capacity to love, the psychical needs, the memory, the unconscious, the ability of visualization (imagination), the dreams (at night) with the "inner Spirit" creating dream messages, the conscious and unconscious conscience (with ideals, values, norms, attitudes), the consciousness (its content), and some more supportive functions. All these functions can be formed in countless ways, with constructive and destructive results.

The inner Spirit is the anchor and the most powerful "absolute intelligence" that every person has in their mind. The principles of this inner Spirit give us the normative orientation for education, life, and also for a new policy in general:

- ☐ All functions have to be formed (trained) and this is a natural need of every human being.
- ☐ The forming of a function must be in an adequate relation to the other functions.
- ☐ The most valuable aim of life is an all-sided balanced state of all functions.
- ☐ Suppressing and neglecting singular functions always has a destructive effect.
- ☐ The inner Spirit is informative, corrective, educative, supportive, and normative.
- ☐ The most essential meaning of life is forming the psychical-spiritual organism.
- ☐ Love is as essential as intelligence for living and realizing the meaning of life.
- ☐ Ideals, values, and norms must be in an appropriate network with these functions.
- ☐ Everything excessive and over-dominant by ignoring other functions is destructive.
- ☐ The unconscious world is more powerful than the conscious mind and Ego.
- ☐ An unelaborated unconscious means disequilibrium and is always destructive.

- [ ] An unelaborated collective unconscious produces wars and world destruction.
- [ ] Real life today demands extensive formation processes of all psychical functions.
- [ ] A claim to power by ignoring the aim of an all-sided balanced being is destructive.
- [ ] Ignoring authentic and genuine growth and living ends in illness and destructivity.
- [ ] The qualities and values of all the functions must be higher than external values.
- [ ] There is no peace, no happiness, and no fulfillment without this formation process.
- [ ] The state of humanity and the earth is an expression of the results of wrong formation.
- [ ] Giving priority to fun, assets, reputation, prestige, and power destroys humanity.

This is the chance for the most advanced NEW AGE in the history of mankind: People around the world adapt this new understanding of human being as described above – or humanity will perish.

What is a human being without this psychical-spiritual organism? He is a human biomass!

Do you really want to be a human biomass and to understand people as a mere human biomass?

The psychical organism	Describe the deficits of forming you can identify:
the self "I"	
the control and decision making instance	
the defense and projection mechanisms	
the intelligence	
the ability to think and learn	
the feelings	

the capacity to love	
the psychical needs	
the memory	
the unconscious (suppressed matters, unsolved past and present conflicts)	
the ability of visualization (imagination)	
the dreams (at night) with the "inner Spirit" creating dream messages	
the conscious and unconscious conscience (with ideals, values, norms, attitudes)	
the consciousness (its content)	

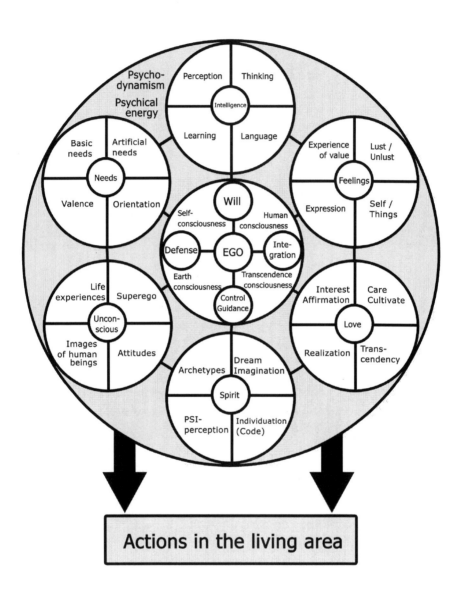

Psycho-dynamism
Psychical energy

Perception | Thinking
Intelligence
Learning | Language

Basic needs | Artificial needs
Needs
Valence | Orientation

Experience of value | Lust / Unlust
Feelings
Expression | Self / Things

Will
Self-consciousness | Human consciousness
Defense | EGO | Inte-gration
Earth consciousness | Transcendence consciousness
Control Guidance

Life experiences | Superego
Uncon-scious
Images of human beings | Attitudes

Interest Affirmation | Care Cultivate
Love
Realization | Trans-cendency

Archetypes | Dream Imagination
Spirit
PSI-perception | Individuation (Code)

Actions in the living area

Global Individuation

Create your own new world and you will change the world! Spirit, love, and self-fulfillment are the indispensable solution for humanity and the earth!

- The irreversible breaking point for humanity and the earth is very near!
- Everybody sees the huge problems of mankind and wants a new world!
- Evolutionary human life includes collective self-knowledge & self-fulfillment!
- Spirituality and religions must integrate the vivid archetypes of the soul!
- The collective nightmares about humanity and the world are horrifying!
- A new global Spirit for peace in the world is necessary for human evolution!
- Dreams & the inner Spirit are the most valuable source of human life!
- The ultimate solution for humanity and the world is Global Individuation!

Individuation has a strong focus on humanity and the earth:

- Openness to learn & readiness for changes in the personal and collective interest.
- Flexible integration of life realities respecting social networks and conditions.
- Living with social skills, life techniques, responsibility for health and the environment.
- Forming an efficient self-management for life issues, also in matters of health.
- Liberation from the generation-destiny for an evolutionary future.
- Establishing a harmony between the inner and external life to reduce egoism.
- Consciousness about the inner world and the network with external realities.
- Understanding humanity as a community on a collective spiritual path.
- Solidarity with the human community in all human basic needs.
- Respecting all human beings in the spiritual view of the collective evolution.
- Self-control within the inner and external world for constructive interactions.
- Cleaning the subconscious for inner peace and peace in the world.

- Dissolution and balance of all contradictory inner forces for peace on earth.
- Relevant knowledge about the complexity of inner and external life.
- Many-sided consciousness about mankind and the state of the world.
- Differentiated perception of one's own reality as well as the reality of others.
- Strengthening life energy, using it aim-oriented for a better life and world.
- Living consciously with responsibility and love for humanity and the world.

A Global Individuation which follows the path of the archetypal processes of the soul is the incredible solution for humanity and the earth!

⇒ Individuation is the ultimate understanding of human beings and life on this earth for politics.

⇒ Individuation includes the spiritual understanding of human beings and meaning of life for all religions.

⇒ Individuation is the indispensable psychical-spiritual path for all officials in all religions and every concept of Spirituality.

⇒ Individuation is the collective path of salvation! A concept that can be lived in all cultural expressions.

Not much years are left to collectively start the Global Individuation. If 500 million people go this path, then the world will see that this is the only chance to save humanity and the earth. Another 20 years will follow to entirely renew the world. Then the global evolution of humanity will lead into a good future for the following generations.

The alternative is to continue living as until today, then humanity and the earth will be lost forever.

1.2. Renewal and Transformations

Archaic human being

The "archaic human being" is characterized by the negation of the psychical life, by neglecting the psychical organism as well as suppressing love and Spirit. At the same time this kind of human being is more or less completely tied to the unconscious psychical life.

The consequences are disruption (inner conflicts) and decomposition, lack of inner freedom, and infantile dependencies. Such an unformed and wrongly formed psychical life is expressed in greed, envy, hate, destruction, exploitation, violence, unscrupulousness, ignorance, arrogance, belief and dogmas as well as in ideologies, despotism and egocentrism.

The essential characteristics of an "archaic human being" are:

- Ignoring the psyche as the genuine life; therefore no holistic development.
- Rejecting the inner Spirit and the performance potential of the power of love.
- Pushed from suppressed burdens and in the tendency projecting strongly.
- Not living with dreams, imagination, contemplation, and introspection.
- Only partially conscious forming of the psychical forces – if at all.
- Defense from and suppression of all uncomfortable, weak and different realities.
- To a large extent an unconscious way of living without being aware of the psychical life.
- Personal and life culture are rooted in ideologies, dogmas and fundamentalism.
- Extensively being fixed on material goods, events (fun), and external securities.
- Undifferentiated unilateral experiencing of love, lust and sensuality.
- Performances with increase of gain and the extreme have highest value.

If a society is created by archaic human beings, then one can see the result in the environment.

In which way do you see yourself as an "archaic human"? Give some examples:

Evolutionary human being

The essential characteristics are:

- Accepting the psychical life and a conscious forming of all psychical forces.
- Liberation from inner burdens of the biography and becoming free from projecting dynamics.
- Elaborated images in the unconscious constructively and progressively promoting life.
- Continuous inner orientation through dream interpretation, imagination and contemplation.
- Integration and elaboration of all the uncomfortable, weak and different "things" in life.
- Creating relationships, politics and economy (etc.) from the understanding of Individuation.
- Dealing with nature and the world of animals, and the environment with Spirit and love.
- Differentiated development and use of the power of love and the Spirit.
- High flexibility and inner freedom towards material goods and external values.
- Psychical-spiritual performances, characterized by love and Spirit have highest values.

If a society is created by evolutionary human beings, then one can see the result in the environment.

In which way do you see yourself as an "evolutionary human"? Give some examples:

Care for that which makes you a human being

"PSYCHICAL ORGANISM": What do you associate with this term?

The single psychical forces can be put together into "classes" or "sub-systems".

The different sub-systems of the psychical organism are:

- Action (behavior) in the external world
- Psycho-dynamism and its psychical energy
- The ego with its auxiliary functions (will, defense mechanism, integration, guidance)
- Intelligence (from the perception of thinking and learning)
- Feelings (the whole spectrum from love to hate)
- Needs (psycho-physical, psychical)
- The unconscious (with the conscious)
- The "Spirit" in dreams, imaginary and contemplation
- The force of love with all its performances
- Would you add a further system? Which?

The mutual influences of the singular psychical forces are manifold; some examples are given (you can add more):

- Feelings influence thinking
- Needs drive perception and actions
- Perception is influenced by wishes
- The unconscious acts on feelings and on thinking
- The capacity for love forms feelings and thoughts
- Dreams activate moods
- Psycho-dynamism is formed by thoughts and experiences
- Actions are produced by different inner psychical forces
- What we have in our consciousness, influences our self-being
- Suppression and oppression make our psychical energy tense

Describe the qualities of your formed psychical organism:

Give yourself a chance now

A life without love and Spirit is characterized by ego-centrism, narcissism, self-satisfaction and arrogance. Where there is no love, there is emptiness, sadness, pain, rejection of life, greed, lack of Spirit and ultimately no balance. Narrow-mindedness, naivety, ignorance, blindness and showing off are incredibly dangerous for an individual.

What is a human being without love and Spirit? It is a biological organism. Don't be surprised if world-leaders in politics, military, industry, trade, economy, religions and sects also see you as an organism to be raised for their (own) interests. Be a mental slave. Or find yourself! Live a life pushed by your drive, coded by your non purged unconscious, or live a life with love and Spirit. Live life lies. Or work on your self-fulfillment!

What is a human being that doesn't live on the path to self-knowledge and self-fulfillment? Such a person lives in chaos and unconsciousness. Nothing can be further away from the Spirit than a human being which lives beyond the process of self-fulfillment. Without Spirit the path is an endless meander. The market offers you over 10,000 meanders!

Maybe you want to be part of this:

- Most people know themselves on a level of 3-5 %; the rest they avoid to see.
- Most people don't think about their tomorrow and the inner network of their living.
- Most people believe that they are totally right with the way they think and judge.
- Most people have no idea about their unconscious inner world – their true being.
- Most people believe it is enough what they learnt; but that is only blind obstinacy.
- Most people cannot distinguish between infatuated appearance and realities.
- Most people want to be cheated spiritually, religiously, ideologically, or esoterically.
- Most people don't want to learn for love, Spirit, joy, happiness, peace and balance.
- Most people don't have the necessary knowledge and skills for their self-fulfillment.

You will never find your happiness and your self-fulfillment without love and Spirit!

The humanity and the world will never have a future without love and Spirit!

You have several options to let yourself be guided mentally, spiritually (religiously) to be a follower:

- Follow dogmatic and fundamentalist religious teachings and practices from ancient times.
- Follow fanatic preachers, self-designated prophets, or psychopathic spiritual shows.
- Follow scurrile spiritual masters or sects, practice a New Age life style, or fulfill 1,000 rules.
- Follow the manipulating adverts of consumerism, fun, money, competition, power, success, etc.
- Follow that and you can throw away the inner Spirit in your soul and you will never find fulfillment.

Or what could be your alternative path from today on? It's your Individuation!

Produce your turning point in life

The first big turning point in life is given by the following acknowledgement: "I have a psychical inner life". The second turning point is based on a profound self-contemplation: "I don't want to continue living like I do! I want to do more with my life!" and the third turning point is the big enlightenment that is expressed by the first touching self-knowledge: "Now I must work for a long time with myself in order for a new life to grow."

What does such a "new life" bring? For example, you live more and more your own life instead of the life of others. Your way of living and your entire dealing with life and the world starts from inside; and is in that sense an authentic self-expression. Your self-esteem grows. Your Ego-strength comes from inside. With that you expand your self-image and on top of that your perception will also become more realistic. Obviously all this happens only in small steps. That's the genuine life!

In the "new life" the inner life gets organized. Thinking becomes clearer, more free and over all more creative. It becomes easier to bear frustrations and anger and the capacity to assimilate increases. The inner balance can be found faster, also during turbulent times. The inner complexes that produce depression or compulsion or fear or any other disturbance can be reduced, even eliminated. The biographical elaboration becomes a psycho-catharsis with the effect to be freer (completely free). Another result is the renewal of the inner and real life. This frees up new energies. Transformations (changes) produce a turning point!

During the course of these changes, one's own life path becomes clearer. From there one can begin to form new life perspectives. New realistic visions become a drive for new life projects. At the same time new life knowledge is built up, dormant abilities can come to action in real life, and new life forces begin to strengthen. With a newly created life culture (way of living) one can realize his authentic human being.

In the middle of this working process another turning point follows: You will find your inner center. The all-embracing inner renewal is achieved. The hunger of the soul can be satisfied. The relation to one's own body and to lust (of living) becomes positive, in essence, accepting life. A relationship with true love can be established. Interests, tendencies, needs, and wishes are all-sided balanced. The "I" can manage its psychical life and also be sustained by it. Once the aim is achieved, the completeness of the new being and life is achieved.

What more do you want from your self-fulfillment in your life?

Always remain in a process of change

You can develop yourself and grow, renew yourself from your innermost being, and in that sense you can change yourself whenever you want. Do something for this purpose!

15 theses that found the basis for a good life:

1. You can change your expectations by adapting them to realistic opportunities.
2. You can change the image you have about yourself by changing your self-perception.
3. You can realize your talents and potentials, depending on the opportunities your environment offers you.
4. You can resolve the conflicts with yourself, with your life partner, and with life in general.
5. You can find a higher satisfaction with yourself and with life through learning processes.
6. You can clarify your feelings and attitudes that hinder changes, and dissolve them.
7. Your honesty and truthfulness towards yourself produce processes of changes.
8. You can change rigid attitudes and beliefs that are inapplicable for life.
9. You can transform ego-centrism, narcissism and false pride through self-reflection.

10. The more you accept yourself, the more you produce changes if you want to improve yourself.
11. You can change exaggerated ideals and illusions about yourself, about God and life.
12. Your critical reflection about the content of your consciousness is the engine of all changes.
13. You can elaborate your biography, in turn producing changes towards freedom and authenticity.
14. You can change your destructive behavior through self-reflection and psycho-catharsis.
15. You can elaborate most difficult and intricate situations in your inner life (psyche) and in your life.

You can change yourself and your life towards more authenticity, more love, more satisfaction, and more happiness. But you also must want change and motivate yourself. Good aims cannot be achieved by doing nothing. Changing your human being and your life into the direction of more quality at the same time leads to a genuine self-fulfillment. Everybody can activate hope, flexibility and initiative.

If you don't want to change yourself, you will remain in stagnation and fall into regression!

15 tips to make changes possible

1. A person can change his expectations relating to himself, others and the world; he can adjust his expectations more and more with realistic possibilities.
2. A person can change the image he has about himself in the same manner he perceives and develops himself truthfully.
3. A person can realize his dispositions, talents and possibilities as far as the frame of his life allows him to do so with self-education.
4. It is effectively possible to resolve conflicts with oneself, with the partner and with life in general. In this process the person is changing himself.
5. A deeper satisfaction with oneself and with life in general is possible if the person learns to live more and more authentically with himself and together with others.
6. Emotions hindering changes – e.g. envy, greed, hate, self-doubt, etc. – can be resolved to make the process of change possible.
7. A higher sincerity and honesty toward oneself is possible, if the person wants it. The process of change starts.
8. Rigid limitations, narrow attitudes and unbalanced beliefs can be dissolved (changed), thereby the psychical life can grow (develop).

9. Ego-centrism, narcissism and false pride reject contemplation and hinder systematic and profound changes.
10. Accepting oneself more and more is a pre-condition for change. Accepting the individual being one is, is at the beginning of each change.
11. A person can reflect his exaggerated ideals and illusions about himself and about God and life. And with that he can change it to authentic and realistic images.
12. A critical reflection about the content of our consciousness (of what we have in this screen) about ourselves, others, life, transcendence) is the engine for changes.
13. The elaboration of the biography is the daily work of substantial changes to a renewing of our being for inner freedom, with dignity and humility.
14. A destructive behavior of all kind is mostly influenced by the environment and by the subconscious of the person.
15. We can explore, elaborate and resolve even very difficult and muddled situations in the inner and external life with the purpose of producing changes.

Conclusion: A person can change himself and his life toward an increase in; sincerity, love, satisfaction, fulfillment, and happiness. But he must contribute by being willing and motivated.

Valuable aims are not achievable if we do nothing. Changes of the psychical-spiritual being toward more and more quality at the same time lead to a genuine fulfillment of life. Everybody can activate hope, movements and initiatives. Each person has the freedom to choose to live with life lies or in the truthfulness of the psychical-spiritual evolutional human being.

You are formed and can further form yourself as a person:

● Negative forming:	● Positive forming:
▪ Inhibited, blocked to learning	▪ Open to learning
▪ Undifferentiated	▪ Differentiated
▪ Unconscious	▪ Conscious
▪ Disordered, chaotic	▪ Ordered, structured
▪ Not or badly controlled	▪ Controllable
▪ Unbalanced	▪ Balanced

▪ Unpredictable	▪ Predictable
▪ Destructive	▪ Constructive
▪ One-sided	▪ Manifold
▪ Suppressed	▪ Developed, considered
▪ Defensive	▪ Integrated

Describe the positive forming you have experienced up to today:

Describe the negative forming you have experienced up to today:

Describe your desirable changes in the actual forming state:

28 positive attitudes towards life

Wrong attitudes towards life are:

- To think too much only creates problems. The future is unimportant today.
- To contemplate about one's own way of living is unimportant.
- With positive thinking one can resolve nearly all problems.
- The church teaches the path. All life is in the hands of God.
- Politicians can and will solve the problems of mankind.
- Sex is for people that need it. Everything producing pleasure is allowed.
- Politics has got all the problems under control.
- Work and performance have highest priority.
- Only the objective reason is important. Feelings hinder life.
- Life is like it is. To live as it arises in the moment is right.
- The past has passed. Why should I think about the past?
- Being stressed is quite healthy. It's good to accelerate sometimes.
- Scientific research produces progress.
- To wallow in vice is allowed as long as it doesn't disturb others.
- If you are ill, you just had bad luck.
- The law is the salvation of the people.
- Psychology is for weak people. Dreams are unimportant.
- People with problems are simply problematic people.
- There have always been wars and there will always be wars in the future.
- What people say about damages caused to the environment is exaggerated.

Describe in an overview why these attitudes towards life are not efficient and even absolutely not acceptable:

Positive attitudes towards life are:

1. When I have a problem, I deal with it systematically.
2. I think about what is the right moment to go into pending difficulties.
3. When I relax to reflect, I reduce noise and other disturbing factors.
4. I relax myself with methods.
5. I apply a technique to clear my thoughts.
6. When I am occupied with memories, I try to understand them.
7. I keep a diary/dream diary/working diary.
8. I have my "tricks", how to deal with myself when I am in a bad mood.
9. I know what time of the day I am available for specific work.
10. I interpret my dreams.
11. I meditate according to clear rules and working steps.
12. I regulate closeness and distance to the facts of my daily life.
13. I have meditation music at home and I use it.
14. I formulate my inner difficulties and emotions.
15. I have a place in my home, where I can write and study.
16. I regularly buy books to broaden my knowledge and open my mind.
17. I have a good self-control when I talk on the telephone.
18. I control myself consciously in conversations with others.
19. When I am preoccupied with something, I deal with it systematically.
20. I can accept when I have difficulties with myself.
21. I take my time to overview the way I create my life.
22. I keep a list about the small things I have to do.
23. I meditate about archetypes of the soul.
24. I care about my self-identity and I explore it as a man/woman.
25. I consciously take time to be alone.
26. My physical (body) self-experience is important for me.
27. I look for variety in my leisure and free time.
28. I have a good overview about what my life contains.

Describe in an overview your needs for improvement in your attitudes towards life:

Practice Individuation

Mark what you agree with and wish to live:

☐ Systematic and extensive self-knowledge, especially internally oriented.
☐ A firm, dynamic, positive self-experience in daily life and in social interactions.
☐ Being free from rejection and projection; objective perception and information.

- [ ] Consciously formed and integrated willpower related to firm purposes.
- [ ] A unique biography with well elaborated experiences, wisdom & skills for living.
- [ ] Controlling feelings in the full positive & negative multiplicity for a creative life.
- [ ] Integrating suppressed and ignored potentials for self-realization & other aims.
- [ ] Forming a "self" with a specific level of self-esteem, confidence, and control.
- [ ] Not living life lies: giving attention to the inner life; with predominant values.
- [ ] A creative & constructive thinking with a clear use of words aiming for good results.
- [ ] Flexible & vital psycho-dynamism; free from tense opposites for success.
- [ ] Daily behavior which is consciously connected with the psychical organism.
- [ ] Differentiating the quality of verbal and non-verbal communication.
- [ ] Achieving a unique expression as a whole person (nature, character, strength).
- [ ] Ability to love and to be loved; ready to act with love in all matters of daily life.
- [ ] Realizing well-balanced psychical needs and the demands from life and the world.
- [ ] Personal development with intelligence, love and the Spirit considering the frames of life.
- [ ] Forming the psychical forces to a constructive ability in order to master life.
- [ ] Psychological unification of masculinity & femininity to become integrated.
- [ ] Living the natural force of love in a certain state of maturity in all life areas.
- [ ] A sexual self-identity integrating sexual desire, living with intelligence and love.
- [ ] Knowledge about the other gender's psychological characteristics.
- [ ] Self-reflection aiming for a completely understood and liberated subconscious.
- [ ] To grow towards the highest archetype of mankind: the fulfillment of the soul.
- [ ] Understanding the psychical inner world as the essential part of our being.
- [ ] Aiming for self-renewal: the rebirth of the inner being for a new life.
- [ ] Accepting the inner Spirit as one's spiritual guidance and authority.

- ☐ Fulfillment of the wholeness of all psychical and spiritual forces as a meaning of life.
- ☐ Promoting one's own psychical-spiritual (inner) development as a daily matter.
- ☐ A well-balanced development of all psychical forces towards fulfillment.
- ☐ Realizing an authentic life-culture with love, Spirit and multicultural attitudes.
- ☐ Transformation: from the old archaic principles to the new evolutionary ones.
- ☐ Constructive dealing with weaknesses, also with conflicts and challenges.
- ☐ Well-balanced integrated emotional life for a more cooperative way of living.
- ☐ Exploring one's own biography until the prenatal time aiming for a total renewal.
- ☐ Transforming the inner contradictory forces with tolerance and flexibility.
- ☐ Respecting natural, psychical, psycho-physical, social, and spiritual needs.
- ☐ Communication with the inner Spirit (dream interpretation, meditation).
- ☐ Learning the many-sided language of dreams and meditation.
- ☐ Contemplating the archetypes of the soul for a vivid spirituality.
- ☐ Taking realistic measures and consequences from dream messages.
- ☐ Practicing mental-training and imagination for a balanced way of living.
- ☐ Acquiring knowledge about the focused values in dream messages.
- ☐ Understanding the inner Spirit's way of communication.
- ☐ Not suppressing realities; elaborating them with competences & measures.
- ☐ Forming useful norms, laws, attitudes, beliefs, and ideals.
- ☐ Learning about effective models of resolving critical life situations.
- ☐ Constructive reactions to distress, disagreement, misunderstandings.

Individuation is a life project for those who appreciate being on this earth and want to achieve their personal fulfillment.

1.3. Social orientations

Always ask questions

The most critical question is: Who am I? The most useful question is: What are the motives of my actions? The most delicate question is: Who speaks the truth? The most essential question is: What are the most vital characteristics of all human beings? And the most important question is: What am I on this earth for?

Not asking these highly relevant questions means being ignorant, disrespectful, irresponsible, indifferent, dumb, regressive, and lazy. The behavior of such people is inefficient and thoroughly destructive towards humanity and the earth. Such people live like a human biomass and are brainwashed and manipulated during their whole life. As a consequence such people must also entirely suppress their own being, and reject every possible serious answer from such questions.

There are and always will be people on this earth that never ask such questions. But what will happen in the future if billions of people are not asking such questions? They will all be brainwashed, manipulated and slaves of their social environment. Or what will happen if billions ask such questions, but receive the wrong answers? Then, they will also all be brainwashed, manipulated and slaves of their social environment.

Therefore, the first question above all other questions is: How can I find the right answers to my essential questions by myself?
Here are the indispensable orientations:

- Acquire as much knowledge as you can about possible answers.
- Your dreams tell you the truth; the inner Spirit knows it all.
- Understand your feelings: they all contain a meaning.
- Be decisive in searching, honest and critical with yourself.
- All answers start with the reality of your psychical organism.
- Your psychical-spiritual development leads to the right answers.
- Follow the archetypes of the soul to get on the right path.
- With correct meditation you discover inner worlds and meanings.
- Critically control your way of perceiving, thinking, judging and evaluating.

- Always look behind the scenes, games, façades and masks.
- Always identify the effects that something has for life and people.
- Multiply a fact, effect, or action by billions and you see the value.
- Close your eyes and you can see the real reality and the truth.
- In the result you see the qualities and motives of behavior.
- Recognize your entire inner life, and compare with answers.
- Find out if it is comprehensible what others say and teach.

Now you can find your correct answers, take the conclusions, and evade from the state of an archaic human being.

Don't let yourself be blinded

Fact is the archetypal experiences in the process of psychical-spiritual development (Individuation) do not transmit "enchantments", or "ecstasies", or "beatitude". A lot of terms exist in the spiritual, transpersonal and transcendental scenery of enlightenments that are hollow and pompous: the "all-awareness", the "essential of beatitude", the "essential of a miracle", the "transcendence process of the 'I'", the "sanctification of the everyday life", and the "highest enhancement of sensual perception". Such terms are very emotional, vague and therefore also dangerous. They pretend to be something with these forms of superlatives. They activate diffuse dispositions of expectations. They are not linked with the psychical organism (the totality of the psychical forces).

In the esoteric world, God and spirituality are key words used in manifold ways. "Spiritual masters" talk about the "divine soul", the "divine awareness", the "divine visions", the "mergence with God" and the "paths towards God". The esoteric market is full of "paths of salvation", of exercises for the "big enlightenments" and of "wonderful spiritual insights", for "transcendental experiences" until the inaccessible allure of people with children's mind. Paths of initiations up to highest grades are purchasable with weekend courses. With all kinds of pieces of jewelry, tubular-pyramids, gems and scents they make the "wonderful intervention of God" possible. The "world of angels" helps with all kinds of sorrow. The "envoys of the light" make nearly everything possible: perfection, perfect freedom, eternal redemption from karma and a potpourri of other blessings.

The esoteric concepts of self-knowledge are psychologically meager, their occupation with the unconscious mind dilettante, their dream theory a confusing game with the motto "spiritual is what is spiritual". They meditate the way they talk: language in general allows nearly any construction of a sentence, and anybody can always interpret any meaning – the main point is: it must sound "spiritual". In the same way one can meditate: Everything can be visualized by meditation, and one can always say "this is a spiritual experience", even if it is thoroughly absurd.

All professionals in such esoteric and spiritual scenes have little knowledge about depth psychology. They have no idea about all the defense mechanisms and projections, especially not about their own ones. Their introspection ends where it should start: with their own narcissism, neurosis, romantic images about God, infantile masters, Messiahs or Christ, their sexual repression, their mother or father projections, their longing for mergence, their libidinous bonds, and their lack of self-critical thinking.

The spiritual illusion is: they think that they can find God and enlightenment without any inner fulfillment of the archetypal processes of Individuation. They want "salvation" by evading from their unconscious complexes and shadows. They separate the inner psychical world from the spiritual world. They negate the (universal) inner Spirit as the force creating dreams, or they interpret their dreams based upon their interests.

That's why spiritual masters are seducers of people, always with soft, lovely and spiritual words. In the end all this is nothing more than commerce, nowadays hidden behind concerns such as "holistic education", "environmental problems", "living healthy", "wellness", "anti-stress program", etc. And apart from that they teach: "Kill your ego!" What a murderous lust! Certainly, the ego is a real problem! But we can't solve any problem by killing! Spiritual salvation teachings are as dangerous as fundamentalism.

→ Genuine spirituality is efficient for human's life!

Take political responsibility into your hands

"Political" first of all means: the community of a folk and the citizens of a state. For example, at the beginning of a constitution (industrial state in Europe) you can read: "In the name of God the Almighty in the responsibility for the creation ... and in the responsibility for the future generations ..." and: "... the strength of a folk is measured by the wellbeing of the weak people."

About responsibility for the creation: Environmental destruction, deforestation, contamination of the air, the soil, and the groundwater, etc.

About responsibility for the future generations: For centuries people have to live with the environmental destruction and with the contamination of air, soil and groundwater. For millenniums up to one million years the following generations have to pay for then maintenance of the waste of nuclear power stations. And the national debt: a burden for future generations!

About responsibility for the weak people: 10% live in poverty and another 20-30% live on the verge of poverty. Environment and social life is not made for the world of children and the world of elderly people ("third age").

About the strength of the folk: Immense amount of money is wasted for the maintenance of the army and the (re-)armament, for luxurious services in favor of politicians, for questionable projects, for prestigious buildings, etc. – Is this to weaken (exploit) or to strengthen the folk?

In the name of God: Which God? The God of the capital, the career, the Catholic Church, the zeitgeist, the consumption, the power, the economic growth, the rich people, the greed, the life lies, the narcissistic people, the unscrupulous managers...?

Do you know the time use of politicians? Think about this: 35% for establishing and reinforcing power, reputation, prestige and career; 20% for traveling and gossiping, 15% for idle acting and idle projects, and the remaining 30% for substantial political matters. Hard workers have another 10 hours a week left for fights, quarrels, and insulting other politicians. They don't care about the inner life. They don't care about financial losses. They are chained to lobbyism and varied hidden interests and personal agendas. They act for their ideology and not for the human beings. Probably most of them are sexually unsatisfied. Is that the main cause?

The folk demands from politicians: money, a home, consumer goods, cheap nourishments, fast streets (highways) and fast trains, financial security for retirement, good education from the early childhood on, work for everybody, a stable economy, a trustworthy and safe financial system (banks), working time of 35 hours/week, cheap electricity and cheap petrol, 6 weeks holiday per year, many special holidays, a lot of dole; and nearly everybody wants a car, etc. Such demands from people today have become too expensive to finance! The time of being verbally pampered by politicians has come to an end. Everyday, more and more people are confronted with reality.

What about the wellbeing of the inner life of people? What about the wellbeing of love and truthfulness? What about the inner Spirit (instead of this "God")? What about the wellbeing of the world of nature and animals? What do you contribute to the wellbeing of the creation, the human beings and the future generations?

As long as politicians are unable to integrate their own inner life, including their inner Spirit, they will act like the authorities did 1000, 500, 300, and 70 years ago collaborating "behind" the scenes with the Christian authorities (in the mutual interest), and leading humanity and the earth to perish, either through climate change, through contamination, or through nuclear wars.

Contribute for a better humanity and earth

With your contribution, you save money every month. But you also create more balance in the industry. With your contribution you reduce contamination of the air, the sea and lakes, the animals, the soil and nature as a whole. You especially reduce the amount of chemical substances people around the world already have in their body. Nobody knows the multiple effects this chemical mixture will have in the human genes and body. But fact is, in the future this will become more and more an intrinsic chemical bomb worldwide!

The following suggestions are ways in which you can contribute to a better state of humanity and the world and at the same time improve your own quality of life:

- Use electricity efficiently
- Use petrol carefully
- Reduce the use of ink (printers)
- Reduce garbage: packaging, bottles, plastic, synthetics, cans, paper…
- Use detergents intelligently
- Use chemical products carefully
- Don't exaggerate the use of medicine
- Reduce traveling around with the car "just for fun"
- Eat balanced healthy food instead of taking vitamin & mineral supplements
- Buy quality products to last for a long time (e.g. car, furniture, electronics)
- Don't buy useless, ridiculous, and senseless products
- Buy bio-products and in general focus more on natural decorations
- Buy reasonable insurance from experts with extensive experiences
- Be well informed by consulting consumer information (TV, internet, etc.)
- Buy agricultural products from your area (local markets)
- Before procreating a baby, learn about caring, health, budgets, education…

- Before getting married, participate in seminars about love and relationships
- Don't buy a home with more than a 50% mortgage
- Don't buy a holiday home with more than a 35% mortgage
- Never accept a mortgage with an interest rate over 3.5%, fixed for at least 20 years
- Invest your money in 100% secure offers and avoid speculations
- Invest some money in quality products you can use for 20 years or more
- Invest every two years in further education for personal life and for work
- Invest money in buying books and DVDs with high learning potentials
- Support local businesses by using their services and buying their products
- Go back to the old times and always pay everything you buy in cash
- Don't use consumer credit for more than the amount of one salary
- Buy your car with at least 65% cash, and maximum 35% credit
- At least every second year go on holiday in your own country
- Never sign any contract you have not read carefully and slept over
- Never accept a contract with any condition you don't really agree with fully
- Don't live empathizing the life of people you see on TV; live your own life
- For small shopping trips go on foot, even for one kilometer or a bit more
- Walk to school with your kids, if it's less than one kilometer
- Consume tobacco, alcohol, medicine in moderation
- Eat consciously with time and style, and celebrate eating with others
- Decide what you want to buy and don't let yourself be seduced by something useless

If you disrespect such suggestions and if everybody disrespects such suggestions, you can be sure the collapse of humanity will happen. Comment:

Stop with the hype and with speculations

Lottery, betting, and similar public games are games of speculation. A huge amount of the participants will always be the losers – their whole life. This is a dirty game!

All kind of shares, profit margins, and other types of financial papers are gain-oriented and do not express the value of possessions (land, premises, machines, stock). There are always losers that are paying for the speculation gains, for the winners. This is a very dirty game!

The real estate sector is a field made up of tremendous hype and speculation: Buy today and in one year, two or some more years you can sell it for a much higher price; you can gain up to 30%, 50%, or even 100% in the long run.

On the one hand this is in many cases not even true. On the other hand nobody knows how this sector will develop in the next 20-35 years. Buyers may think: "I can sell it in 20 years and with the gain I will have back all the money I spent for my life in the last 20 years."

Another game is the contests on TV: "Call us and tell us if A or B is true. You can win 10,000€. One will win; the rest will lose. Deducing the costs and the prize, the rest is the gain for the TV-channel.

The global financial crisis, which exploded in 2008, shows us where such speculation businesses lead: millions lose money, millions lose their existence, millions more become unemployed, and millions fall into poverty and even into the deepest level of poverty. The global damages today are already in the trillions of Dollars! And on top of it all there are a billion people who will pay for these damages with their taxes! Confidence in the world economy has vanished! A very dirty game!

The attitude which all this was built on has three components:

1) Earning as much money as possible
2) Earning without doing anything
3) Accepting that anyone can lose (a lot) of money

And the winners are always guaranteed to be the institutions which offer this kind of "money making" (Banks). On a spiritual level this is worse than 5,000 Hitler and Goebbels!

Behind all these speculation businesses is greed, lies, cheats, unscrupulousness, disrespect, manipulation, and abuse of trust. The main character traits of the people responsible for these games are psychopathic. The power of all the responsible people is immense: 5,000 managers have been able to produce the worst economic catastrophes of all times around the globe. The results of what they have done are unfolding non stop: millions of job losses, trillions of dollars vanished, a billion people thrown into poverty levels, total collapse of countless businesses, and a terrible misery and suffering for all those involved! Countless millions of individuals have contributed to that disaster with their own greed for money, with an exaggerated life on consumer credit, with huge expectations of (monetary) gains by doing nothing or investing very little!

Give some examples of constructive and evolutionary attitudes:

The problems of the religious thinking

First of all every Christian must know the truth about the Holy Bible: over 2000 diverse text variations and 250,000 variations of reading.

The Bible's texts in a rarely accountable manifoldness are simply mission letters, mythological tales, religious edifications, legends, with a lot of anecdotes and fictional stories.

The texts in the Bible: countless copywriting, new additions and eliminations, smaller and bigger changes. All texts are made by unexampled lies, falsifications, and displacements. In the Gospels you can read: And Jesus said: "..."; or: "I am ..." Fact is: Nobody knows what Jesus said! The Old Testament and the New Testament are full of legends, myths, sagas, fictions, superstitions, anecdotes, full of manipulation and deceit. The Bible is a chaotic and corrupted collection of texts. There is practically no real historical substance. The four Gospels are never a biography of J.C.!

Critically we have to reveal the truth about some essential teachings:

- Spiritual procreation of J.C. is a fairy tale
- Physical resurrection of J.C. is an old myth
- Physical resurrection of the mother of God is an infantile fantasy
- The miracles of J.C. are absurd tales from the oldest times
- The story about Adam and Eve is never real
- The natural death of human beings as a punishment is perverse
- Baptism is a baby abuse (child abuse)
- Baptism guarantees memberships and taxes
- The son of God, savior, messiah is a myth without authentic documentation
- J.C. died for the sins of mankind is a sick understanding of men and history
- The promise to come back with 10,000 angels is fiction solely for triumph
- The last supper is a farewell celebration and never a spiritual celebration
- The dogma of the trinity is a game with words and categories of qualities
- Hell is fiction, and completely totalitarian, undifferentiated and unbalanced
- Consecrated wafer (to be body & blood of J.C.) is a cannibalistic idea
- Getting the consecrated wafer with open mouth shows: self-lowering
- Folding the hands for praying is often an expression of hypocrisy
- Giving blessing in the sign of the crucifix is a magic way of binding people

- Making the crucifix on one's body means identification with the death penalty
- The crucifix of Christianity: death penalty, hopelessness, suffering, guilt
- To knee in front of the priest expresses: humiliation, putting down
- Ecclesiastic teaching about sexuality is ignorant, neurotic and psychopathic
- No original from the Gospels texts exist, not even first transcripts
- The authors of the original Gospels are unknown
- No apostle has ever written a Gospel
- Nobody has written down what Jesus said

Final conclusions: All the Christian dogmas, teachings and practices have got absolutely nothing to do with any part of the psychical-spiritual life (the inner life) of a person, of psychical-spiritual development, and of a constructive process of self-forming for living and growing with love and the inner Spirit. Christian dogmas, teachings and practices completely ignore what makes a person a genuine human being.

→ Do you want to be paralyzed in the use of your intelligence, reason and spiritual power of living?

→ Do you want religious practices that are meaningless and an inefficient way of magical self-protection?

→ Do you want a religious practice that totally ignores the psychical organism?

Work is a basic and essential human need

All women and men have an inner drive to work, to transform talents and dispositions into activities, to earn a living, or to contribute for living in any way. Work is a basic need of the human soul. Work is also a call from the real life. This need doesn't end with the official regulations of retirement, but is expressed in a lower energy level corresponding the age and state of health of a person.

Today, especially in industrialized nations the government is responsible to provide people with possibilities to satisfy their basic human needs. This includes education on all levels, from primary school up to university and professional education; why not for people in their "third age" as they also have to face special challenges? Take note: Work is also a basic human right!

High rates of unemployment are a shame for a state, especially considering the highest incomes and additional benefits of hundreds of thousands of managers and members of board of directors and management! Reorganizing responsibilities and work of this group of managers could give five times more jobs paid with the same amount of income and benefits.

Big companies are great in the sense that they give tens of thousands of people work. But at the same time they are also a serious danger: they lay off thousands and put most of these people in a dramatic disaster with unemployment. The main cause is the theory of capitalistic growth. A new way of understanding could be: The aim is to achieve an optimal balance of a company with let's say 5% fluctuation. Another orientation could be: it is better and more stable to have one million very small companies (with each employing 2-3 people) and one million self-employed people than an endless increase of big companies with one million or more employees each.

Of course many unemployed people are not aware of their responsibility to actively search for work. Many are simply lazy. Others can't find work because of the age limit many companies have set, or because of a lack of professional further education. Individual initiative is demanded! Get out of unemployment:

- Move to another location where jobs are offered, if necessary.
- Learn as much as you can for better professional qualifications.
- Improve your personality and skills, including general behavior.
- Fight hard, every day, and never give up finding any work.
- Prepare yourself with business skills for your own business.
- Be very flexible and find totally new options / visions for work.
- Adapt yourself to local conditions and contribute with new ideas.

Distance yourself from life lies

Many people claim: "I have no problems." That is because a reality charged with problems should not exist. What else should not exist in the social network of a person? A person is always exposed to certain expectations from his social environment (attitudes, norms, belief, and behavior). If a person fulfills such expectations from his social environment, then he tends to live life lies, and at the same time becomes more and more alienated from himself. As a consequence he fails to authentically live himself. This happens with clothes, goods, cars, career, money, and with adjusting one's own attitudes. The reality of one's awareness also determines the social pressure. That's how life lies arise. The supporting function has got a lot to do with: negating, distorting, glossing over, repressing, and suppressing.

Most people don't want to precisely look how their "I" masters life. The tendency to external harmonization ("all this can't be that important and bad") might relax in the moment of a situation. But life lies grow and grow.

One cannot build up constructive solutions on life lies as the non-perceived reality still exists and continuously produces effects: from the inside and outside, from oneself and from others. The non-perceived reality submerges individuals and the collective like a flood: in suffering, in conflicts, in climate change, in the financial crisis, in poverty and misery, and in wars.

The life lie is a self-negation, a repression of one's own and of other people's psychical life. People don't want to know their own suppressed true psychical being. They repress their inner being and consequently also their real problems. Life lies are always an escape from oneself.

Life lies force people to suffer, to a kind of self-plague; because the separation from the inner psychical life produces tensions and always also neurotic conflicts. So life lies in a way lead to an artificial balance in narcissism, greed, excessive consumption and ego-centrism.

Life lies are a form of self-deceit with which a person doesn't live himself, and doesn't go his own path. People are permanently forced by a need to be loved, recognized, and admired. They cannot live from their inner source, but only from the value others and society as a whole gives them. They live that which is given to them from outside, but never their authentic self-realization. This again includes an enormous potential of conflicts and it makes life really difficult and complicated.

Imagine your last day on earth: You become fully aware of the fact that you have lived a life filled with life lies, but never your authentic inner being! How will that feel?

Love the world of children

All adults were once a baby, a child, and then an adolescent. Around 33% of the world population is in this age! But this world is not made for these 2.25 billion young people! Babies, children, and adolescents have special needs. Too many parents are not prepared to give an adequate education. The environment is not made for the needs of these very young human beings.

It is absolutely wonderful to create a baby, a human being; but it is also absolutely disgraceful that we created an environment worldwide that is not made for these young people.

We put trillions of Dollars in constructing cars worldwide for the interests of adults and their "freedom", but not half of this money in a child-friendly environment and educational system, in the children's world, including their feelings, their thinking, and their needs for love.

Babies, children and adolescents need love and care in manifold ways:

- If you have a baby or want to create a baby, learn how to care for it in all matters: love, nutrition, playing, talking, entertaining, etc.
- Children want to discover, to learn; and they need to learn. State schools can't do this job all alone! Parents have to contribute daily! Human evolution and life in general demands learning!
- Learning includes: giving support and stimulations, understanding and strengthening, being accepted in their needs and wishes, including weaknesses and mistakes.
- Children also need moral education. First of all children copy their parents and people in their environment. If the adults are amoral, liars, cheaters, unscrupulous and disrespectful, then children copy such behavior and character traits.
- Children need protection in physical matters, but also in psychological aspects: e.g. with the media they are exposed to uncontrollable influences – not only good ones for life.
- Parents are a role model: if they communicate badly, or live an archaic relationship, children will copy it. If parents resolve conflicts by ignoring and suppressing, children copy it.
- The best education parents can give to their children is simply to live an all-sided balanced role model by living genuinely from their own well formed inner being.

Disrespect children's needs and these children will disrespect your needs when you will be old and ill.

If you contribute in the destruction of the world, the children today will never love you.

Today, creating a baby makes you responsible for the future of your kid. Esteem the values of being a father or mother!

And be appropriately responsible!

Respect the "third age"

There are men and women in their forties and fifties, but they are mentally and some even physically like many people in their sixties. There are also men and women in the sixties and seventies, but they are mentally and some even physically like others in their forties and fifties!

Elderly people can have positive and hopeful perspectives for a long and interesting life. If you are in this age: Train your mind by reading and learning. Expand your knowledge and skills. Make order in your mind about your past. Improve your personality and character. Be open for new experiences and challenges. Grow spiritually through contemplation. Find the meaning of life inside!

Especially in industrialized nations, people above 48 are understood as "old" and not demanded anymore in the industry and economy. But these people are the source of knowledge, life experiences, and professional skills. Many of them are also a great source of wisdom and role models with high spiritual qualities. It's a disgrace how these people are excluded from the working field and social life in general. Fight to get work if you want to work! People in the "third age" also need affection, tenderness, and joy of life just as much as young people do.

The "third age" is your great chance for a new active life with manifold perspectives! You may live another 20-35 years or more! But you must do something for physical, mental, social, and spiritual health. Work if you can! Have pleasure, entertainment, and fun.

You are not too old for a romantic dinner with your actual partner or a new partner! Sex is not only for young people! In a new way learn to discover a wonderful sexual life with a lot of love. With love and good sex you remain young in mind and body!

Find new friends for going to the countryside, the mountains and the beach somewhere! Share leisure with new friends going to museums, cinema, concerts, parks, and expositions. Explore new places as well as historic monuments.

If you are single, find an interesting, understanding person to talk to without reserve. Find a good person to contribute mutually for a meaningful and interesting life. Be open for possible true love and even a future with a new partner.

If you have a partner; refresh your love and daily life with new undertakings.

Nothing can give you more happiness than friendship, love, care, and your personal fulfillment! But you have to learn a lot, every day!

At least 75% of all elderly people enter more and more into a process of regression because they don't learn anything. They don't want to renew themselves. They prefer to be become child-like, stubborn, inflexible, and spend their life time like children spend their holidays.

1.4. Personality development

Discover and live your interests and talents

The functions of interests:

- Interest is a basic condition and motivation force for the daily functioning of humans.
- Interest is a positive motivation.
- Interest forms an important motivation for the development of abilities, social competences (skills) and intellectual performances.
- Interest is a unique motivation to keep up with the daily work in a healthy way.
- Interest is indispensable for each creative work.
- Interest provides a person with a sensation of being challenged by the matter of the interest.
- If the feeling of the interest includes a visual perception, then the eyes tend to fixate and explore the object of interest.
- The perception of changes (transformations) and the newness of an object (matter) activate interest.
- What is new and different produces interest.
- The imagination of a possibility (opportunity) activates interest.
- Daydreaming and fantasizing arouses an interest, especially if the interest is related to something new, a change or an aim.
- Interest gives the feeling to be engaged, enchained, fascinated, and curious.
- Interest is a desire to explore, to be demanded, or to extend one's self-identity and life through new information or experiences.
- Interest plays an important role in increasing lust (sexual lust), also to maintain the sexual relationship.

For self-discovering:

- Talent means an outstanding ability for certain mental or practical performances.
- Skillfulness, effortlessness, and agility are attributes of a talent.
- A talent needs to be developed, trained, and refined.
- Behind a strong interest there is often a disposition of a talent.
- Without a personal interest, a disposition of a talent can never be performed in its full capacity.
- A talent can be part of a self-identity.

Practicing and developing a talent can also give, within a certain limit, a meaning of life as well as a certain level of self-fulfillment.

- What are your talents?
- What do you do to qualify (develop) your talents?
- What is hindering you to develop and practice your talent(s)?
- How can you to develop and practice your talent(s)?

Discover your personality qualities

Self-discovering is the chance of life for all men and women because the process is progressive, constructive and evolutionary when thoroughly applied. With education of the psychical forces many risks of life are reduced to a minimum.

Life always conceals risks. But many people guide themselves with their unconsciousness and their chaotic inner world, with high probability toward certain suffering and conflicts.

The pressure of the unconscious inventory alone creates a large scale of destructive potential which in most people one day breaks through.

We also have to take into account the collective consequences. The force of a suppressed unconscious (that means the unconscious inventory which is not integrated into consciousness) is always stronger than the conscious ego with the will to reject and suppress.

Find out the components of your strength:

- ☐ I integrate my psychical life entirely.
- ☐ I am open to discover the reality and to see how it is.
- ☐ I live connected with my inner process of development.
- ☐ I live with a high consciousness about my inner life.
- ☐ I care about orderliness and a balanced structure in my inner life.
- ☐ Dreams and meditation are a superior instance for my life.
- ☐ I have a high level of inner liberty (unconscious, thinking, attitudes).
- ☐ I think, feel and mostly live constructively (realizing a "tree of life").
- ☐ I experience myself and my life entirely conscious.
- ☐ I expand my knowledge and my abilities, my life in general, with quality.
- ☐ As far as I have power, I use it for promotion and guidance.
- ☐ I am positively dedicated / orientated to life with my whole being.
- ☐ In strong human bonds, I live this bond progressively and constructively.
- ☐ I totally accept the psychical-spiritual life.

- [ ] I am open to learn about the psychical life.
- [ ] My inner life (unconscious) is easily controllable, calculated and balanced.
- [ ] The more I elaborate my biography, the more I feel a new life.
- [ ] The force of love is elemental in everything that I live, also professionally.
- [ ] I have clearly experienced inner transformation in small aspects of life.
- [ ] My inner opposition changes more and more to an equilibrated wholeness.
- [ ] I live in harmony between my inner life and my external life.
- [ ] In meditation I have experienced what the fulfillment of the circle-cross-Mandala means.
- [ ] My psychical forces are entirely and widely developed.
- [ ] I care about my feelings and needs.
- [ ] I come across on all well formed psychical life with respect.
- [ ] I feel myself as an inner totality.
- [ ] I confront myself with the transcendental dimensions with reason and realism.
- [ ] Veracity is something very important in my life.

→ Describe the weak aspects of your personality:

→ Describe your personality strengths:

→ What are the conclusions about the state of your strength? Comment:

Organize your qualitative self-forming

We can define and plan aims, what we want to do with whom: with the life partner, with the children, with a friend, with parents, with colleagues, with neighbors, etc. This way everybody can meaningfully take his own wishes into his own hands.

We can take our destiny into our own hands.

It doesn't matter if we have to postpone certain important wishes for months or even for a couple of years. It is only important, that you follow the path of your planning, without losing flexibility.

It is for certain that we cannot completely plan our life with thinking and with a 'mechanical' guidance. It also may be that for high aims we have to prepare ourselves during a long time: sometimes we have to first reach the steps in-between. Therefore: plan your "one day I will..."!

With planning you achieve your goals more efficiently:

- Make a list of books for your further education.

- Consumption needs and time can be planned within a family and in a 'single' household.
- You can plan and consciously create your relationships and leisure contacts.
- Leisure activities shouldn't always depend on your lust and mood.
- If you want to give a deeper sense to your leisure activities, draft and plan them.
- If something doesn't contribute to reaching certain aims, put it back in the right place.
- Your weaknesses can be systematically dealt with to reach specific aims.
- Goals and plans are only effective, when you write them down and take them seriously.
- The more precisely you define your aims, the more securely they can be reached.
- Some subjects can be postponed, others you should do straight away.
- Discuss your wishes and expectations with the people concerned as soon as possible.
- Revise your checklist on a daily basis and mark the finished points with "success" or "failure".
- It won't do any harm, if you create order in your private life, in relationships, and activities.

A checklist for a critical view of the situation. Give key words about what there is to do:

- Casual acquaintances
- A 'possible' intimate relationship
- Unspoken subjects in marriage
- Heaps of paper on the table and in the drawer
- Needs and wishes of consumption
- Ideas for further education
- Wishes for weekend amusements
- Hobbies (starting or neglecting)
- Difficulties in relationships
- Concerns of friends and acquaintances
- Little vices and tics
- Habits
- General education (courses, reading)
- Order around the living area
- Attic and cellar (clearing out)
- Old clothes and other unused possessions
- Suppressing annoying subjects

- To speak about wishes (not suppress them)
- No folder, no place for files
- No desk, no place for studying and writing

Forming a strong personality for success

Forming your personality is the foundation of success.

- Personality education is the key-qualification for personal and professional life.
- Personality education is an indispensable part of every further education in the future.
- Personality education creates the competences (skills) for constructive relationships.
- Personality education reduces many risks during life and in the social network.
- Personality education is useful; has practical importance, stabilizes the self-identity.
- Personality education contains life knowledge and daily behavior.
- Personality education qualifies for leisure and for dealing with lifetime.
- Personality education produces inner security and trust into one's own forces.
- Personality education leads to an all-sided balanced well formed psychical organism.
- Personality education is necessary for a self-fulfillment during all life phases.
- Personality education integrates ethical responsibility for oneself, for others, etc.
- Personality education is an investment for a future with huge challenges.
- Personality education is a condition for responsibility in many professions.
- Personality education reaches a person in his deepest psychical-spiritual being.

The self-image is the result of one's own self-knowledge. In the self-image a person in essence, constructs his own value with a varied fantasy, based on the superficial external being; oriented in the zeitgeist: money, properties, reputation, power, status, clothes, consumption, etc. Today one's own esteem isn't based on one's own potentials, talents, dispositions and skills; neither on creativity, mind capacities, abilities to love, etc.

Stand in front of a mirror, look at it and contemplate your face. What do your eyes tell you? And what does your mouth tell you? Contemplate yourself completely naked in front of a mirror and feel: Do you like yourself? And then, explore around your life a bit: What do you want to change? What should you do? Think about your future: What are you looking for? What do you want to achieve and live?

Finally have a look through your past: Let your life go through your mind in a short overview back to your early childhood. How do you feel with your biography? What do you feel about your past?

The realistic self-image is based on:

- Wanting to widen one's self-image
- Acquiring knowledge and willing to learn
- Consciously recognizing feelings
- Flexibility in social adaptation
- Exploring and elaborating rejected matters
- Clarifying the content of the subconscious
- Taking responsibility for one's own "destiny"
- Giving the necessary importance to the psychical life
- Prepared for self-education
- Openness for a self-critical perception
- Practicing contemplation as a method
- Wanting development and growth

What do you like doing a lot? First go through a spectrum about daily life: shopping, cooking, house-work, body care, creating your living environment, eating, drinking, smoking, etc. Secondly go through your leisure time: watching TV, reading, making or listening to music, doing handicrafts, painting, garden work, going to the cinema or theatre, surfing on the Internet or chatting, doing some sport, walking around, writing your diary, interpreting your dreams, meditating.

Self-contemplation: Some questions for a systematic self-contemplation:

☐ Do you practice methods that are well-aimed for relaxation?
☐ Do you know a meditative technique to strengthen your life energy?
☐ Do you reflect upon your state of psychical energy?
☐ Do you meditate about your daily way of living?
☐ Do you contemplate about how you are and feel?
☐ Do you understand your feelings, its causes and effects?
☐ Is it important for you to reconcile painful experiences?

- ☐ Do you seriously consider your physical state (e.g. afflictions)?
- ☐ Do you know your genuine inner (psychical-spiritual) needs?
- ☐ Have you already meditated about your projections?
- ☐ Do you know the way you deny (ignore) your inner life?
- ☐ Have you ever searched for the so-called "Spirit" in yourself?
- ☐ Do you practice self-management also for your inner life?
- ☐ Do you meditatively deal with your conscious mind?
- ☐ Have worked out your life experiences with meditation?

Transform your weaknesses into strengths

The 13 aspects of forming humans are the frame for a genuine strength:

1. Widening perception of reality.
2. Growing acceptance of oneself, of others and of nature.
3. Increasing spontaneity.
4. Better focus on problems.
5. More distance and longing for retreat.
6. Growing autonomy and resistance against acculturation.
7. Greater freshness of understanding, of richness of emotional reactions.
8. Higher frequency of transcendental experiences.
9. Growing identification with the human species.
10. Deeper understanding of humans.
11. Increasing responsible democratic character.
12. Strongly increasing creativity.
13. Human values rooted in the genuine inner human being.

Give some keywords with regard to your weaknesses and strengths:

- Changing mood:
- Sociability:
- Cheerfulness:
- Passion:
- Restlessness:
- Feeling of inferiority:
- Vivacity:
- Nervousness:
- Excitability:
- Sensitivity:
- Ego-strength:
- Tendency to dominate:
- Joy for expressions:
- Ego-strength:

- Social courage:
- Suspicion/distrust:
- Being carefree:
- Keen perception:
- Tendency to feelings of guilt:
- Independence:
- Power to assert:
- Agreeable nature:
- Emotional instability:
- Helpfulness:
- Being unhappy:
- Need for acceptance:
- Self-confidence:
- Masculinity/femininity:
- Coolness:
- Objectivity:
- Nonchalance:
- Shyness:
- Thoughtfulness:

Describe what aspect you need and wish to strengthen:

Now find out how to strengthen your weaknesses! Write down some ideas:

Love yourself with your inner life

Maybe you have experienced a lot of love in your childhood and life in general. Develop this gift, love yourself und give this gift to others! You have not experienced any love in your life?
Even if your parents did not love you, and even if you have experienced a total lack of love, start loving yourself! Or stay at home in your bed and dwell on it or whine until your last day – which would be very stupid! What makes you a human being? It's your mind, your inner life, your soul!

Loving yourself has many practical aspects:

- You have feelings: understand these feelings and transform them into a constructive power for living and growing! It's stupid and meaningless to indulge in all kind of (negative) feelings!
- You have psychical needs: love, understanding, being accepted, promoted and supported, living relationships, experiencing intimacy, etc. Start by accepting, understanding and promoting yourself!

- You have an ability to perceive; in general with your five senses. Identify what you perceive! Interpret and understand what you perceive! Look behind the façades! Control your perception!
- You have intelligence and the ability to think. If your information (perception) is wrong, rudimentary, one-sided, superficial, or even a big lie, the result of your thinking will be of the same quality. Think in the network of the qualities and the time (past-present-future).
- You have an inner source of love, the power of love: Even if you have never experienced true love, you have the source of love in your soul! Search for it and you will find it! Connect yourself with this source of life! And transform this power into something real in your life!
- You have life energy: Everybody radiates his psychical energy depending on his emotions, thoughts, suppressed conflicts, and physical state. Discover your energy and the inner dispositions that form this energy! Improve its state to get strength!
- You have a personal biography: All experiences, especially the emotional ones, are engraved in your unconscious mind. You are programmed by your life experiences! You copy these patterns! Elaborate your codes carefully and revise what is necessary for a better life!
- You have an inner Spirit, giving you messages with dreams and in meditations: Use this spiritual power! Learn to interpret your dreams and to meditate correctly!

With his self-image a man gives to himself in the core a fanciful own value through physical expressions corresponding with the zeitgeist: money, goods, prestige, power, status, clothes, consumption, etc. His own value is not founded on his potentials, disposition and abilities, and not on thinking creatively, or on his ability to love, etc. This mandatorily leads to life lies. That's why the self-image is mostly an illusion.

Accept what you are and also your life conditions! Don't let yourself be paralyzed, not even by the worst state! But analyze yourself and understand your life conditions!

Love yourself means: Revise what is not efficient! Improve what is weak! Learn from your mistakes! If you don't love your being, you must know that you remain a mere human biomass!

Live your development as a path

Do you feel bored?
Do you live in loneliness?

Does your life seem to be meaningless?
Do you not know what to do with your life time?
Do you want a rich and exciting life?
Do you want to live with all your forces, abilities, talents, and potentials?

Here you get many tips for your life path that will certainly not be boring.

Mark what you feel is important to you today:

☐ Learn to know the essential psychical forces and discover them by yourself.
☐ Understand your biography and find access to this past.
☐ Become aware of the complexity and the network of your acting.
☐ Constructively handle your psychical energy.
☐ Find clarity about your awareness and become able to manage these realities.
☐ Build up knowledge about the "I" and its control mechanisms.
☐ Discover the objective knowledge about the intelligent functions on yourself.
☐ Understand the world of feelings as manageable and find access to it.
☐ Acquire knowledge about the manifoldness of needs through self-reflection.
☐ Understand the unconscious as a reality you can transform.
☐ See the importance of your dreams and try to find access to it.
☐ Understand love as a constructive life force that also promotes your growth.
☐ Comprehend the importance of the psychical life for all human beings.
☐ Recognize the interconnection between life and psychical inner life.
☐ Discover the basic values of human being from the perspective of the psychical life.
☐ See the difference between the unconscious and conscious way of living.
☐ Contemplate your relationship life from the perspective of the mutual psychical effects.
☐ Evaluate the importance of the senses, also in the context of the psyche.
☐ See the importance of sexuality and its manifold creative ways of living it.
☐ Evaluate your way of living from a practical view of self-management.
☐ Practice your learning for self-education intelligently and in an exciting way.
☐ Determine the bigger and smaller aims of your self-education.
☐ Understand how images about human beings can be created and judged.
☐ Interpret and practice health from a holistic perspective.
☐ Apprehend a partnership-like relationship by integrating the psychical life.
☐ Discover masculinity and femininity in a new way as roles and ways to be.

- [ ] Understand and practice the methods of self-knowledge.
- [ ] Build up competences for intuition, introspection, imagination, contemplation.
- [ ] Understand and practice the first practical steps of dream interpretation.
- [ ] Meaningfully handle the basic techniques of relaxation.
- [ ] Formulate positive values of living and realize them for yourself.
- [ ] Discover the ways of operating of the inner Spirit, and take them seriously.
- [ ] Take responsibility for your acting, life, and use of life time.
- [ ] Experience your human being in the real and transcendental network.
- [ ] Competently handle your meditative and analytical way of dealing with questions.
- [ ] Build up lust for life, love for life, hope and confidence in life.
- [ ] Reflect, ask, discuss, and argue with substance about inner life.
- [ ] Localize the religious (spiritual) dimensions of the inner realities.
- [ ] Take a critical view about the psycho-spiritual offers available today.
- [ ] Understand the actual ways of living with objective distance and differentiation.
- [ ] Experience your growth, development, extension of awareness inside and outside.

Nobody is interested if you are hanging around lazily at home doing nothing with your life.

But in the last hour of your life you will experience your truth: You either achieved your fulfillment – or you failed in everything which is really important!

Discover your unconscious being

It's well known that people can repress their thoughts, feelings, and wishes. Later they can't remember them; but what they repress continues being active in their unconscious.

In the same way one can eliminate critical (conflictive) experiences from one's awareness; e.g. embarrassing, painful and "forbidden" experiences.

Meditative regressions clearly show that those past moments which were significantly negative or positive, produce the same emotions in the remembrance.

Joy and pain, embarrassing situations, intensive thoughts, threatening moments, problems and conflicts, moods of the environment, etc., are obviously still vivid in the unconscious mind.

The code program of the actual life lies herein because these images also generate psychical energy. Therefore, the past is always vividly present. With meditative regressions one can change these "codes".

Furthermore, we can mention the manifold painful experiences, starting often even in the early childhood, first in the family, then in school, and later in life.

The list of such experiences is very long: rigid father, rude patterns of punishments, emotionally overcharged mother, principles of performance in the school with all kinds of failure and mockery, devaluation of the person, disregard of the creativity, lack of dialogue and understanding, religious moral from old times, the hate of the collective against all weak and alien, professional failure, all kinds of breakdown, ignoring feelings and the individual psychical needs, being exposed to people with moral defects, illnesses, death of a beloved person, etc.

It's an easily proven fact that a fetus "thinks", feels and experiences in manifold ways what goes on in his environment.

The entire life book in the unconscious mind can be revealed meditatively back to the moment of procreation.

The qualities of a person are also a field where nearly everybody represses (ignores) a lot. People don't want to be aware of what they really are.

Examples are:

The "shadows" (often breaking through and forming the character from t
he background) such as defiance, rage, violent temper, greed, instability, indifference, control, sadism, blind confidence, egoism, good faith, naivety, laziness, opportunism, eagerness for power, moral indifference, lies, etc.

There are also the inappropriately formed psychical forces which nobody wants to see because they are too embarrassing: weak will, laziness to think, defiance, bad discipline, not reflected talking, an emotional chaos, and an inability to love, lack of knowledge, superficial perception of life, misanthropic attitudes and beliefs rejecting life.

Patterns of punishment such as "if you are not what I like, then fuck off!" People want to keep their unconscious inner world secret from themselves and from others at any price.

And above that they negate their defense mechanism, also at any price.

The unconscious (mind) is something like a "reservoir". Everything that a person experiences and holds in images can come into that reservoir; and it remains vivid.

Generally we can also observe that the inventory in the unconscious consists mainly of images. To elaborate the unconscious, to clarify, to make order and to transform it, is the indispensable essential duty for any serious psychical-spiritual development.

Close your eyes for 5 minutes and try to visualize the content of your "reservoir". What do you see?

Be aware of the collective network

- You think love isn't important? Others also. Everyone thinks the same. What then?
- Professors don't want wisdom; students don't want wisdom. The consequences?
- Some think self-knowledge is nonsense; others too; finally everyone thinks that. And now?
- Some say, only money is important; others also. Finally everyone says that. What then?
- One says: you have to be faster than others; everybody says that. What does that turn into?
- First, one wins with lies; then several; then many; then all. What remains?
- Many people go as far as to say "feelings are not important". What comes after that?
- Weak and ill people are ostracized. Imagine: from 58-85 you are weak and ill. Painful?
- Men haven't got any psychical needs; women neither. What would this look like?
- In 30 years 100 times more nuclear waste has to be administered for 10,000 and more (up to 1 million) years? And who pays for these bills?
- All Europeans are 50% healthier, drive 50% less. The consequences?
- All households and enterprises consume 50% less electricity. Why? How?
- 50% of all Europeans pursue 1 hour of self-knowledge every day. Consequences?

- Second question of an interview for a 'top-job': How well do you know yourself?
- If only people that have worked through their biography can teach? How would schools be?
- Every European reduces his waste by 50%. What kind of consequences would that have?
- European politicians don't lie and don't distort anymore? What happens then?
- Priests of all religions are "individuated men". What then?
- Statesmen and ministers are "individuated men". How would politics be then?
- 50% of all adults in Europe reflect on their leisure life. What changes?
- Nobody is a fan of high-performance sport, but still of sport. What causes does that have?
- 10 million people demonstrate because nobody takes love seriously anymore. Imaginable?
- 1 hour daily self-knowledge at the work place. Would everyone do such a job?
- Nobody wants to learn anymore after school and professional school. The consequences?
- If life-lies would stink like sewage. How would people treat each other?
- All adults read 12 books every year about psychical life. What could change?
- The newspapers report daily about dreams from readers. Exciting reading?
- Centers for self-education are put up everywhere. Everybody goes. Consequences?
- Anyone can only get married if he/she has thoroughly practiced self-knowledge. Advantages?
- It is forbidden to have children without a thorough self-education. Who protests?
- Only people who strengthen themselves by self-education can become a boss. Bad luck?
- 75% of adults train daily 2 x 10 minutes psycho-hygiene. How would this influence society?
- Earnings are linked to the status of the personal Individuation. Why not?
- Everybody writes on their door, what makes them happy. How would people communicate?
- Change your ways of living

Concrete suggestions for a new way of living:

- Looking for positive images.
- Constructive thoughts in daily life.

- Calming thoughts; daily 2-3 times.
- Meditate with releasing and deliberating images.
- Creating mental distance, especially if thoughts are too cramped.
- Dissolving opposites with active meditation (visualization).
- Getting rid of inner suffering by working it out.
- Becoming free from conflicts by clarifying them, with the right attitude.
- Exercising and fitness.
- Considering the reality of meanings.
- Accepting life positively; taking this attitude seriously, even with unimportant things.
- Living needs with a clear mind; that means: balanced and at the right moment.
- Controlling perception; not too much wandering around with the eyes.
- Reducing stimuli; do not focus and empathize too much.
- In some moments becoming free from space and time through meditation.
- Thoughtful life rhythm, also in hectic professional moments.
- A healthy and holistic way of living, psychologically and physically.
- A rational and intuitively balanced understanding of one's own existence.
- Dealing with life in a combination of analytical, artistic and creative ways.
- Thinking in an integrated combination of logic and spirituality.
- A networked dealing with language and images in life issues.
- To elaborate in line and synthetically at the same time. (Networked thinking).
- Considering a personal biorhythm especially for specific work.
- Continuously taking a certain distance from others and life themes.
- Consciously creating and enjoying lust.
- Containing themes during conversation, and guiding the communication with the participants.
- Don't produce too much pressure.
- Living in a permanent learning development.
- Holding discipline: emotional, social, mental, moral, etc.

Life is beautiful. Living a life with knowledge and skills is amazing. To benefit from all inner sources gives man a priceless gift!

Find self-esteem and self-confidence

A lack of self-esteem and self-confidence has manifold consequences:

You start neglecting yourself and disrespect for others starts to emerge. You ignore your social life and your environment. You permanently expect others to give you self-esteem and confidence. You eat too much; or you don't care about healthy food, you even refuse to eat enough. You drink too much alcohol or you take too much medicine. You get constipation, chronic headaches, depression, fear, migraine, and you can't sleep well anymore. Various serious psycho-somatic diseases can arise as a reaction. You also lose control over your daily life, relationships and family. With a high probability the quality of your work will also be affected.

A lack of self-esteem and self-confidence can be a result of having lost the self-control. The content of one's subconscious is highly burdened with unsolved problems and conflicts.

Of course real problems and conflicts people are fully aware of also lead to a lack of self-esteem and self-confidence, especially if one can't resolve them.

Most people with low education, very small economical dispositions, and in a situation of unemployment will also find themselves in a state of low self-esteem and low self-confidence.

People above 48 and many retired people are also affected by this lack of self-esteem and self-confidence.

People that have no self-confidence have in essence, a fear of themselves:

A fear to do everything wrong; fear to show weakness; fear to fail; fear to make themselves ridiculed; fear to make themselves unpopular; fear of quarrels and conflicts; fear to lower one's guard. Impatience is often an expression of a lack of self-confidence.

The causes are manifold: lack of self-management; inability to deal with quarrels and conflicts; a need for social harmony; an unstable psychodynamic; little self-knowledge; an exaggerated sensibility; being overly dependent on the opinion of others; a tendency to hide realities from oneself; not much self-love; a conflict with authorities; lack of skills for analyzing, planning and realizing; an attitude which in essence says: "I can't"; strong defense from one's own as well as alien realities; a tendency to be forced to live with life lies.

Many people in such a state compensate with narrow-minded attitudes, intolerance, and aggressive behavior. Or they become followers of a sect or any religion with strong fundamentalist teachings and rules for living. Self-esteem and self-confidence is not given by birth.

One has to build up such inner strength.

Consider the following:

- Self-esteem needs substance: perform something important.
- Self-confidence needs facts: discipline, reliability, self-control.
- The better you know yourself, the more you build up strength.
- The more you know about mankind and life, the stronger your self becomes.
- The more you live human values, the more you get power.
- Find out if something in the past happened that reduced your self-esteem.
- Improve your personality qualities with "self-education".
- Learn more about how to deal with critical incidents, life, feelings.
- Give yourself esteem, acceptance, support and care in daily matters.
- Build up life energy: go for long walks or do any sport activity.

1.5. Become a strong personality

Power and Methods

Your journey of self-discovery can start: the plan, the instruments and the aims are determined.

Live with efficient methods!

Self-education and training of life is the ultimate key for success, happiness, and fulfillment.

POWER means: drive, force, ability, energy, strength, performance, potency, authority, eligibility, qualification, rights, mightiness, mastery, and disposal. – How much power do you have to master your life, to live true love and a real relationship, to genuinely develop yourself, to achieve your aims, and to authentically realize yourself?

You can live a genuine life with true love! Truly live yourself! You can find your happiness. You can have success. But you need POWER to get it!

POWER = Knowledge + Methods

What is the difference between a person that has a lot of knowledge about life, human beings and the inner life – and a person that does not know anything essential about life? What is the difference between a person that knows the methods for living, understanding, growing, and managing life and one's inner life – and a person that doesn't know anything essential about this?

No Knowledge + No Methods = POWERLESS LIFE

How will your life be in 5, 10, 15 and 30 years if you learn nothing essential about yourself, human beings, inner life, life in general, and if you don't know the right methods to deal with this or to manage all this efficiently?

Take down the artificial façades! Become authentic! Become your complete Self! Get rid of your expensive life lies! Truly live what you are inside! Quit the stupid superficiality! Find the valuable Self you have inside! Stop looking away and ignoring it! Live from your full healthy forces! Take distance from the stupid manipulated life! Use your life forces for a genuine life! Forget the disdainful illusions about happiness! Build up genuine fulfillment from inside!

With the right POWER you achieve more with your being and life!

Stop with the alienating brainwash! Find your true being and live it! Put away that which hinders you on your path! Develop all the good and positive in you! Don't run away from yourself anymore! Realize your potentials and talents! Change the ineffective mental coding! Modernize everything there is to revise! Stop lying to yourself! Convert your life into your genuine happiness! Say goodbye to stupid ways of living! Find a new orientation! Change yourself! Renew yourself! Get rid of the self-suppressing ways that make you sick!

Of course you can do it!

Live with intelligence, love, Spirit, wisdom, knowledge, skills and methods!

Knowledge means power. Having and using the right methods means power! Power for living! What is the life of a completely powerless person like?

How is your life with intelligence, love, Spirit, wisdom, knowledge, skills and methods?

Life: Live what you truly are inside

Evolutionary human life includes self-knowledge and self-fulfillment.

No life without risks. No life without problems. No life without critical challenges. Some look away. Others repress everything. Many fiddle around. Nearly everybody only wants to "have" and not to give higher value to the being. Bank loans, speculation, unemployment, poverty and insufficient private retirement arrangements destroy the majority of all well being. The value-orientation "the biggest", "the best", and the "fastest" transform most people into a small endlessly frustrated "worm".

The collective epidemic: most people permanently look at how others live, and at the same time forget to live their own life. Most people are never trained to completely and truly live themselves. The risks accumulate to a collective breathtaking adventure. Not resolving one's own problems, crisis and difficulties with mastering life, produces enormous long-term suffering. Most people avoid professional help because they exorbitantly overrate their objective knowledge, life knowledge, and their own skills – or they feel ashamed within our zeitgeist to do so. You are not guilty if you have problems with yourself and your life. But not dealing with such problems makes you guilty towards yourself.

Maybe you enjoy being part of this:

- Most people know themselves on a level of 3-5 %; the rest they avoid to see.
- Most people don't think about their tomorrow or the inner network of their way of living.
- Most people believe that they are totally right with the way they think and judge.
- Most people have no idea about their unconscious inner world – their true being.
- Most people believe it is enough what they have learnt; but it's only blind obstinacy.
- Most people can't distinguish between infatuated appearance and realities.
- Most people want to be cheated spiritually, religiously, ideologically, or esoterically.
- Most people don't want to learn for love, spirit, joy, happiness, peace and balance.
- Most people don't have the necessary knowledge and skills for their self-fulfillment.

That's life: To correctly deal with life is an art. The circumstances in life are not always as simple and clear as most people like to have it. Knowledge, skills and life techniques are necessary to get success with oneself and with life. Some decisions in life are very important and logically demand life competences. In such cases one must see clearly through life, especially in "critical situations". It is important: to efficiently and correctly recognize and balance the facts, and to act accordingly. You want a good life. Take note: without a solid effort you will never find the really good life!

You need more life energy, strengthened and centered energy? You want the special joy of life and the creative pleasure to live a fulfilling day to day life? You strive to find your breakthrough to a fulfilled being and life? You think (more) success, (more) satisfaction, (more) balance is important? You wish to resolve an apparently unsolvable personal critical situation? You want to feel good (better) with self-esteem, self-confidence and self-strength? You want to gather more from life and more from your potentials? You want to build up your new happy life with the correct strategies?

Ignoring the psyche is indeed a piteous intention of self-escape. And not systematically forming these psychical forces is an expression of ignorance, arrogance, and complete unscrupulousness against humanity, love and the Spirit. The way people deal with each other is collectively characterized from a secret solidarity: Hold the unconscious being unconscious; hide the inner psychical life; don't look at the manipulations and life lies: "Ignore your unconscious burden!" – Do you want to escape this collective misery?

The external world of each person and the collective is an expression of the psychical inner life of the people in general: disrespecting the world of nature and animals, ignoring our natural resources of life, damaging the climate conditions, polluting the environment, and much more. That means: people live alienated from themselves. The way people treat each other, they treat themselves, especially their inner life. What people are inside, we see it outside in the world and society.

What is a human being that is not living on the path of self-knowledge and self-fulfillment? Such a person lives in chaos and unconsciousness. Nothing can be further away from the Spirit as a human being living beyond the process of self-fulfillment. Without the inner Spirit the path is an endless meander. The market offers you over 10,000 such meanders!

Constructive orientations for life:

- Become authentic, completely yourself!
- Live what you truly are inside!
- Find the valuable self that you are inside!
- Modernize everything there is to revise!
- Live from your healthy forces!
- Use your life forces for a genuine life!
- Find your true being and live it!
- Build up genuine fulfillment from the inside!

Questions of self-knowledge	Give answers:
On which level do you know yourself?	
How do you think of your tomorrow and the inner network of your way of living?	
How do you think about what you think and judge?	
What do you know about your unconscious inner world – your true being?	
How do you see everything you have learnt up until today?	
How do you distinguish between infatuated appearance and realities?	
How do you want to be treated spiritually, religiously, ideologically, or esoterically?	
What do you want to learn from love, spirit, joy, happiness, peace and balance?	
How do you judge necessary knowledge and skills for your self-fulfillment?	

The truth about the world of love

Each woman and each man has varied psychological qualities in many aspects: way of thinking and expressing feelings, character traits, attitudes, spiritual values, reliability, honesty, faith, moral behavior, communication and understanding, knowledge and wisdom about life and love, ability to express affection and love, readiness to get love, skills for living relationship (e.g. making compromises) and dealing with life (misinterpretations, disagreements, etc.), manifold character expressions, and an unconscious mind (often full of unsolved conflicts, traumas, and complexes from the past).

All these psychological realities work as a "coding" in the unconscious mind for finding a partner, for living love and relationship. In the cyber world of love there are a lot of people with low qualities!

→ Most people know themselves on a level of 3-5 %. On that low level love and a relationship can never achieve great success!
→ Most people want love, happiness, and a better life, but they don't want to learn anything! No chance to get great success!
→ Divorce rate: 30-50%. Separation rate: 50-75%. Cyber love failure: up to 95%. Better you first learn how to get great success!

The main causes for failure are:

Ignorance, arrogance, narcissism, superficial attitudes, stubbornness, laziness, rudeness, vanity, dogmatic thinking, negation of living spiritual values, focusing too much on appearance or on cheap fun and not enough on inner life, trying to create an illusionary harmonic relationship, rejection to learn about love and life, lack of knowledge and skills for living a relationship, unsolved traumas and serious conflicts from the past, unconscious inner tie to a previous partner, rejecting importance and care for personal development, disinterest in contemplative self-reflection, lack of understanding and communication, suppressing emotions and desire, not mutually accepting weaknesses and sexual needs. – Nobody is perfect.

It is not necessary to be free from all this. But it is absolutely essential to learn about everything, to improve and to strengthen whatever is necessary, and to grow towards becoming an all-sided balanced person.

There is no love without risks. No life without problems. No love without critical challenges. Exaggerated narcissism is the collective illness. Here there is little or even no ability to love. Narrow-mindedness, stubbornness and narcissism are the main causes for failure of love. The inability to understand sexuality as the normal hunger, and living sex creatively in a corresponding way is another essential cause of failure. The inability of women to live sex with their partner in a selection of what the sex-industry offers, and the inability of men to give to their partner daily signs of love as well as to regularly create romantic events have made the sex business to a super-industry. Obviously love and spirit fall on the hard shoulder. People don't bother about it: a boring life! The endless fight of the genders is the most stubborn fight ever to exist! Some look away. Others repress it all. Many fiddle around. And the majority avoids professional help because love and sex are actually not so important to them.

To understand your partner is difficult and demands a lot of communication. How will you understand your partner if you don't even understand yourself? How will you find the right partner if you do not prepare yourself inside? In a relationship and living together many people are in certain critical situations. Love does not grow by itself. Happiness does not arise "simply like that". One has to learn how to live love, sex and romanticism correctly, and to care for it. One has to acquire knowledge and skills to clarify and efficiently resolve, with competences and balance a critical situation of love and relationship. You want to be happy with yourself and with your partner. You want to finally find and to live the great love in a partnership-like relationship.

- Love is a many-sided creative force of life. Love gives meaning, quality, and value to life.

- Love makes life worth living and rich. Love is the key to a lot of apparently unsolvable situations.

- Love is much more than just a feeling. Love is a complex performance. Pure love is a rarity on earth!

- Love without reasoning (thinking) has little chance of performing something stable in real life.

- Love without the Spirit is structure-less and has no inner roots. How can you live love without contemplating?

- Love demands observation of the inner and external world with concentration and a clear view.
- Love presupposes a will to act. Living love means to look at the genuine inner needs.

- Love in a raw state is archaic, instinctive, nothing more than a physiological social pattern.

- Love is powerless and unstable if your unconscious is full of suppressed traumas and unsolved conflicts.

- Love operates for one's own psychical life, for the psychical life of the partner, and for living together.

- How can you love others if you don't even love yourself? How do you love ignoring your inner being?

Humans:

Qualities for love and a relationship	How do you see it?
Ignorance and superficial attitudes	
Arrogance	
Narcissism	
Rejection to learn about love and life	
Stubbornness and rudeness	
Laziness	
Vanity	
Dogmatic thinking	
Negation of spiritual values Disinterest in contemplative self-reflection	
Focusing too much on appearance or on cheap fun and not enough on inner life	
Trying to create an illusionary harmonic relationship	
Lack of knowledge and skills for living	
Unsolved traumas and serious conflicts from the past	
Unconscious inner tie to a previous partner	
Rejecting importance and care for personal development	
Lack of understanding and communication	
Suppressing emotions and desire	
Not mutually accepting weaknesses and sexual needs	

The basic needs:

Your basic needs	Describe your deficits of satisfaction:
You want to have and live human qualities. How then, without self-knowledge?	
You want to live your genuine true being. What then is your genuine inner being?	
You want to live meaning and values. What then are your values and your meaning?	
You want to realize your inner potentials and talents. Do you even know them	
You want to grow and to develop as an authentic person. How do you do that?	
You want to live and receive love. Do you actually know what love really is?	
You want to perceive, know, think, and correctly conclude and judge. Do you do that?	
You want to live a relationship honestly and constructively. Can you really do that?	
You want to be and to remain psychically healthy. How can you do that with all the life lies?	
You want wellbeing and health. How then considering the rejection and suppression?	
You want to act efficiently in daily matters. How then, without learning life techniques?	
You want balance and stability in life. How then, if stubbornness hinders you?	

You want to perform as an authentic expression. How, if you don't know your Self?	
You want autonomy and self-determination. How, considering the collective brainwashing?	
You want good sex with inner fulfillment. How then, if you are only able to love very little?	
You want joy of life and to be happy. How then, if you ignore your inner being?	
You want to experience God and the transcendence. How then, without inner growth?	
You want to be guided by the Spirit. How then, without dream interpretation and meditation?	

The feelings:

Your feelings	**Describe your deficits of forming:**
You want to understand your feelings? This is only possible with reflection and meditation.	
You want to be able to deal with your feelings? Then first you have to understand them.	
You want to be free from inner disruption? Then understand that which is disrupting you inside.	
You want to have positive feelings towards life? Then, make a move towards the real life.	
You feel an inner burden? Then search for that heavy burden from inside.	
You feel depressed? Then there is something inside that is depressing (suppressing) you.	

You feel sadness inside? Then mourn and feel; later find your way back to life.	
Your state is stressful, moody, and nervous? Analyze exactly what pushes you to this state.	
You lack true hope and confidence? Then, build it up within you.	
You are unsatisfied with yourself? Then, do what is necessary to find satisfaction.	
You don't feel "complete"? Then, find your fulfillment with Individuation.	
You are unhappy? One can only be really happy with love and Spirit.	
You feel a lack of inner peace? Then, make peace with yourself in your mind and your life.	
You feel a diffuse guilt? The biggest guilt is to refuse oneself.	
You think everything is meaningless? The deepest meaning of life is to find one's Self and to live it.	

The "I":

Your "I" (ego)	Describe your deficits of forming you can identify:
You feel inferior? Then give yourself value with self-knowledge and self-education.	
You feel very little richness? Then discover your inner values and treasure.	
You hide, project and suppress? Then, simply stop with all the life lies.	

Your will is weak? Then, become a strong person and clearly determine small aims.	
You live rather little in a conscious or differentiated way? Then learn to observe.	
You experience your self-identity as diffuse and ill-formed? Then, form it meticulously.	
You feel a lack of motivation for daily matters? Then, be thankful that you can be on this earth.	
You are struggling with yourself and your life? Then, learn the efficient self-management.	
You lack firmness when taking decisions? Then first decide, what is really urgent and important.	
Your past is constantly preoccupying you? Clarify and understand what you lived in the past!	
You have little knowledge about the psychical life? Then, read about it and practice what you learn as much as possible!	
You don't really understand people? Then first very precisely begin by understanding yourself.	
You don't reflect yourself in the dimension of time? Meditate about yourself in the network of time.	
You don't feel as being part of the network of humanity? Then, think about the climate change.	
You simply believe what others taught you? Then, discover the lies and manipulations.	
You don't believe in religious teaching? Then, find God and Spirit through your Individuation.	

Love:

Your ability to love	Describe your deficits of forming:
You don't develop all your psychical forces. You don't love yourself!	
You live with high risk of accident and illness. You are unscrupulous with yourself.	
You don't care for yourself. You are ignorant towards yourself.	
You are not open to learn in order to grow and change. You are blocking yourself!	
You have little inside-oriented meaning of life. You strongly devaluate your being.	
You rarely care for your inner life. You are arrogant against yourself.	
You don't feel responsible for inner values. You are a mass human being.	
You don't develop your life from your inner being. You are a shopping human being.	
You don't see the inner life from your partner? Your love is superficial.	
You give little signs of love to your partner? Then your love is dying.	
You are rarely cooperative with your partner? Then you are rigid and inflexible.	
You permanently focus on external values and appearance? You are unable to love.	
You judge and react with little understanding and love? You are not reliable.	

Psychical-spiritual performances have no importance to you? You are a human biomass.	
You can only integrate very little from the other gender? You are very unbalanced.	
You don't care about the protection of the world of nature and animals? No existential love!	
You are not rooted in the inner Spirit? Your love has only got a very small stable structure.	
You ignore the challenges of inner values. You have an extremely reduced ability to love.	
You contribute nothing for a better state of humanity and the earth. Very dumb person!	

The intelligence:

These contemplations here have not got much to do with IQ (the intelligence quotient); but much more with the practical use of the intelligent functions that everybody has and can use.

Your intelligence	Describe your deficits of forming that you can identify:
You don't look behind the masks and façades of others. You don't want to see what there is.	
You don't like to read texts with serious content? You are a lazy and dull person.	
You can't express yourself well? Then, read a lot and participate in seminars.	
You can't really decompose complex matters. Then, make an effort!	
You don't consciously control what you want to perceive. You are very suggestible.	

You are superficial in analyzing a problem. Then you will never achieve success.	
You don't have a good retentiveness. You are charged with problems or you are disinterested.	
You fix your thinking in dogmas and ideologies. This is archaic and inefficient!	
You don't reflect upon your values and norms. You are a robot and only live what you have learnt.	
Your attitudes are not thoroughly reflected. This can't lead to good aims.	
You don't examine your beliefs. You only copy what others forced you to adapt to.	
You don't think before you judge. You are and live full of prejudgments:	
You don't justify your demands. You are driven by (sexual) drive, desire and ego.	
You are not flexible in integrating something new. This expresses stubbornness and blindness.	
You don't think in complex networks. You have little good chance in your life.	
You rarely perceive with the perspective of time. You don't understand anything about life.	

The unconscious:

Your unconscious	Describe your deficits of forming:
You have a lot of unresolved life experiences? You repeat old patterns.	

Many memories are still painful when they come into your mind? Resolve them!	
You don't like people that have problems? You simply evade your own problems.	
You like images such as mother of God, holy people or heroes. You are a naïve "dreamer"!	
You don't scrutinize religious authorities. You are childlike naïve and easily cheated!	
You have inexplicable remorse. You have a real or suggested guilt in your inside.	
The laws and norms from your childhood still activate emotions. Revise everything!	
Sometimes you punish like your father and or like your mother. You copy your parents.	
You have vague vegetative disturbances or sleeping disorder. A problem is nagging you!	
You are extremely overweight. You have a greedy complex in you that totally dominates you.	
You have agoraphobia (tunnel, elevator etc.). You are extremely confined inside yourself, in your life	
You have sexual disturbances. The relationship doesn't work well. Something is wrong with "love".	
You have constipation. Causes are: Stress, weak self-confidence, being determined by others.	
You think: "The churches show the path to God." You are dazzled, arrogant, and obsessed.	
You think: "There will always be wars over and over again." You promote motives for wars!	

You think: "Environmental damages are not dramatic." How can you be so blind?	
You think: "Traffic accidents are destiny." You are unscrupulous and a danger for others.	
You think: "Better not to think too much about myself." You reject responsibility.	

The psychodynamic:

Your psychodynamic	Describe your deficits of forming you can identify:
You are repeatedly feeling tense. Clarify and free yourself from inner and external pressure.	
You feel disharmony inside. Create a balance between the psychical forces.	
You feel inner pressure. Then, take away the real pressure even if it's strenuous.	
You are easily angered. Everything has to go the way you like it. And you are discontent.	
You are rather depressed. There are preoccupations. Or your inner being can't live.	
You feel corseted. Values, norms, attitudes, beliefs, thinking and life circumstances corset you.	
You are unsettled, unsteady. You don't have inner foothold, no clear values and no good aims.	
You easily feel insecure. There is lack of knowledge, abilities, self-esteem, and self-confidence.	
Your inner life is rigid (inflexible) and armored. The rejection and suppression is total.	

You can react very rigidly even in simple situations. You are not well formed as a person.	
You only have little life energy. The unconscious eats energy away; there is a lack of aims.	
You don't have a zest for being active. Something that is suppressed paralyzes you. You are unhappy.	
You chronically react with a bad mood. Your personality and your life do not have inner structure.	
You can be inexplicably destructive. You have a lump of unresolved conflicts in your subconscious!	
You are easily infected by the moods of others. You are not well structured in yourself.	
Being together with others easily makes you lose your energy. You are not set in yourself.	

Describe your general psycho-energetic state and dynamism:

The acting (behavior):

In which life themes do you consider your acting as "critical"? Mark with a cross.

"Critical" means: unable to act, unfortunately no skills to act, the result of the action is not good, your acting is uncontrolled, others act inappropriately (against you in a specific matter), the matter produces preoccupations or fear, etc.

▪	Relationship, marriage, friendship	▪	Politics, Parties
▪	Kid's education	▪	Economy, Business life
▪	Colleagues, acquaintances, family	▪	Art, Culture in general
▪	Free time	▪	Institutions of the religions
▪	Holidays	▪	Traffic, Transport
▪	Intimate living area	▪	Atomic waste, nuclear power stations

• Personal environment (living location)	• State economy, taxes
• Nutrition, eating	• Environmental pollutions
• Health	• International conflicts
• Alcohol and/or tobacco	• National, regional conflicts
• Medicaments	• Constructed living areas
• Consumption in general	• Destruction of nature (climate change)
• Doing the domestic work	• Animal welfare
• Conflicts with the boss	• Criminality
• Divorce/Separation	• Pornography, Prostitution
• Illnesses	• Foreign infiltration
• Psychical suffering/disturbances	• Banks, Insurances
• Life crisis (abouto whatever)	• Public authorities
• Religions practices, belief	• Marginal groups
• Self-experience (fear, inferiority)	• Extremism, Fundamentalism
• Education, further education	• Waste, sewerage
• Sexuality	• Destruction of environment
• Day planning	• Poverty (in your country)
• Media consumption (TV)	• Wars, genocide, suppression of people
• Money, life costs, petrol & gas price	• Elderly people, getting retired
• Furniture, equipments, car, clothes	• Communication between people
• Leisure activities (hobbies)	• Situation of drug abuse
• Victim (burglary, cheat, etc.)	• Unemployment
• Work/Working place	• Death

The dreams:

About attitudes, knowledge, and skills.

Your dreams	Describe your deficits in dealing with your dreams that you can identify:
You can rarely remember dreams. You are not interested in dreams.	
You don't bother about your dreams. Dreams mean nothing to you. Open your eyes!	

You don't know that a spiritual principle is acting in dreams. You can learn it today.	
You don't form your personality with your dreams. You can't become a complete person.	
You don't try to meditatively understand yourself. You avoid feeling who you are.	
You don't elaborate your life themes with your dreams. You are missing the best solutions!	
You don't orientate yourself around dreams when you have problems. You only see the external.	
You don't meditate about your unconscious. Complete catharsis is never possible.	
Your way of living doesn't allow you to meditate regularly at all. You are avoiding yourself.	
You don't meditate about symbols and archetypes. You don't have a spiritual orientation.	
You don't take extra-sensorial perception serious. You don't understand a lot about human beings.	
You don't feel any solidarity with psychical-spiritual values. There is no vivid Spirit inside of you.	
You can't distinguish between belief and experiencing. Just to believe is very cheap.	
You don't accept your dreams as your advisor. You may think that you know everything better.	
You think: "Dreams are nonsense". That's what you have heard (read); you learnt wrong!	
You don't think that dreams want to tell you something. You don't want to know.	

The psychical-spiritual development:

The process of the psychical-spiritual development contains a multitude of small steps and can be interpreted as a "path".

Mark with a cross where you feel that you already know a lot, have learnt and done a lot and still practicing regularly:

- [ ] I regularly practice techniques for relaxation
- [ ] I know my projections and their causes
- [ ] I know my defense mechanisms and rejection (tendencies to suppress)
- [ ] I regularly practice Mental-Training
- [ ] I practice contemplation, deep meditation about basic values
- [ ] I interpret my dreams with competences and do so regularly
- [ ] I integrate my weak psychical forces
- [ ] l know the interactions (interplay) of my psychical forces
- [ ] I have extensively elaborated my biography
- [ ] I can entirely accept the psychical life
- [ ] I have the overview of the interplay between inside and outside
- [ ] The power of the Spirit is an important root for me
- [ ] I have inner footing through forming my psychical forces
- [ ] The archetypes of the soul give me orientation in life
- [ ] I live values and meaning from inside and with Spirit
- [ ] I profoundly elaborate my inner life (feelings, complexes, etc.)
- [ ] I practice psycho-catharsis and Mental-Training
- [ ] I feel responsibility for love and an inner bond to live it
- [ ] I accept the Spirit as the inner principle of guidance
- [ ] I extend my knowledge about human beings
- [ ] I experience the essential inner needs more clearly
- [ ] I give special attention to build up my power for love
- [ ] I can easily distinguish between masks and the realities behind them
- [ ] I clearly experience what freedom and duty from inside means
- [ ] Spirit and love are very dominant and determining forces in my life
- [ ] I feel free inside. I know that I am completely free inside
- [ ] I know the collective unconscious and its way of acting
- [ ] I feel firmness inside even in very difficult situations
- [ ] I have differentiated experiences with the archetypes of the soul
- [ ] I am completely reliable in my inner bond to Spirit and love
- [ ] I am able to live the transforming power of love
- [ ] My life is an extensive expression of my elaborated self-education
- [ ] I experience more and more being an all-sided balanced totality
- [ ] I am very formed through life, and with dreams and meditation
- [ ] I experience the positive images I have in my subconscious as supportive

1.6. Practical self-management

Succeed with self-management

1. You need time for yourself; that means: nobody has to be reachable and accessible at every time of the day. Everybody needs their calm moments, with their mobile phone switched off. Relax every day for 5-10 minutes.
2. To say "no" without frustrating the other person, is an art. On the other hand one has to be able to say "yes" as well. In either case one has to account for such a "yes" or "no". It is recommendable to precisely think how and why one has to say "yes" and "no".
3. Identifying troubles gives us a clear orientation. Strategies for problem solving make life easier. Noise and clutter produce troubles and disturbances. Difficulties in any activity produce disturbances. Motto: Daily life contains troubles and disturbances that need to be managed. They are part of life.
4. Think and act with an aim in mind: In daily life, plan and act in the perspective of long term personal aims. To practice this, one needs to keep a journal or diary.
5. Aspire for your determined aims with a timetable and with working methods. For that, one sometimes has to read a book to get new suggestions and inspirations. Or ask others about their experiences. Never be afraid of asking for advice.
6. Divide high aims of life into small constructive steps. Each life phase has its own goals. And don't miss out on living the present!
7. Prestige, money and success are not the highest aims of life! Reflect upon your consumption, especially your compensating behavior. Search for your meaning of life inside in your soul.
8. Concentrate on the use of your energy. Don't dissipate your forces in chaos and lack of planning. Recharge your energy on a daily basis. There are various techniques for relaxation.
9. Ascertain priorities, which lead to determined aims. The truthful life is the essential aim of life. Working is also living. Never forget: Life lies don't lead to a good and fulfilling life.
10. Not everything is equally important and urgent. Importance means: aim and success. Urgency means: time and fixed date. Urgency goes before importance. Start every week with the question: What is important and what is urgent this week?
11. Deal with daily matters, but also with long term aims. Where do you want to be in 1-3 years? Check every few months if you can achieve your determined aims with your way of living.

12. Regularly control your use of time. Make a day to day plan for the week, integrating your use of time. Then analyze: your life time is your capital; have you invested this capital well this week?
13. Control your stress factors in order for them not to control you. Plan your mobility. Caution: even people, TV-news, advertisements, articles in newspapers, etc., are often stress factors.

Bear in mind: Nobody is interested if you live a good self-management with success. Nobody is interested if you psychically and physically ruin yourself or if you live in a healthy way. Nobody cares if you have a happy relationship or if you are lonely. Nobody is bothered if you find the meaning of life, or if you lead an enslaved and manipulated life such as the one represented in our zeitgeist.

> **Success with self-management is simply the call from life itself for success, happiness, and personal fulfillment.**

The ultimate ways to deal with stress

→ Stress is an unspecific physical reaction of each given requirement.
→ Stress isn't just a nervous tension.
→ Stress isn't always the unspecific result of harm.
→ Stress isn't something which must be avoided.
→ Stress is the spice of life.

Thus 'stress' means a 'burden', while 'distress' works negatively because of its disharmony and dissonance. Stress is the response of the body - and linked with that also the psyche - to burdens of all kind.

💣 Stress causes (= "stressors") among others:

💣 noise	💣 traffic
💣 advertisement	💣 bad air
💣 worry	💣 conflict, quarrel
💣 sitting	💣 lack of movement
💣 success-push	💣 haste, speed
💣 population	💣 challenges
💣 driving	💣 emission
💣 prestige thinking	💣 wrong nutrition
💣 violence	💣 ambition

- religious norms
- poison
- diffuse anxiety
- money problems
- narrow places
- artificial holiday
- lying
- working with a PC
- wrong authority
- moral attitudes
- frustration
- new technologies
- distrust
- swindle

Physical stress reactions are (among others):

- breathing difficulties
- shooting pains (heart)
- nervousness
- urge to eat and drink
- diarrhea
- irritability
- rashes
- shake (tremor)
- cancer
- urge to pass water
- smoking, drinking
- stuttering
- gastric ulcer
- vague anxiety
- stomach pressure
- undue sweating
- lack of appetite
- constipation
- migraine
- depression
- asthma
- shivering
- dizziness
- sleeping troubles
- stomach pain
- circulatory disturbance
- consumption drive

"Healthy" dispositions are:

- Mostly I am aware what sensual feelings I have.
- I can stand up for my opinions and interests.
- I can speak about anger, rage and temper.
- I can accept strong and also unsettled feelings.
- I like new and uncommon ideas.
- I can 'do nothing' without losing the floor under my feet.
- Sometimes I like being alone and I can occupy myself.
- I can spoil myself now and then.
- I don't feel forced to always solve every problem immediately.
- I can live well if things don't go well.
- I occasionally walk (instead of taking the lift or going shopping by car).
- I often like going out into the fresh air.
- I regularly let fresh air into my home.
- I consciously avoid noise and bad air, if possible.
- I don't always need background music.

- ❏ I switch off the television if the program bores me.
- ❏ I ensure that I have a regular life pattern.
- ❏ I am moderate in my consumption of cigarettes, alcohol, coffee, sweets and eating in general.
- ❏ I enjoy eating with time and calmness.
- ❏ I often enjoy my work.
- ❏ I can manage time pressure without 'swerving'.
- ❏ I see sense in my work as well as in my leisure.
- ❏ I am content with my life situation, I feel good and comfortable.
- ❏ I like the environment around my living place.
- ❏ I handle electricity, petrol, detergent, medicine etc. with discretion.
- ❏ I experience and treat waste ecologically.
- ❏ When driving I respect others, and I drive sensibly.
- ❏ I take interest in the biographies of others in my leisure environment.
- ❏ I often visit cultural, social and political events.
- ❏ If necessary I forcefully put my interests on the table.
- ❏ My life makes sense and has value.
- ❏ The basic values of human beings are very important to me.
- ❏ I can accept suffering in life.
- ❏ I don't think that I missed important things/events in my life.
- ❏ Today I can accept difficult life phases from my past.
- ❏ I am confident about how I create and master my life.

The basic theses about stress:

1) Stress as a reaction to overstrain is a complex phenomenon that we have to consider and to judge in the frame of a holistic image of the human being.

2) A healthy behavior, as prevention and mastering of stress, has to be developed and practiced also with a holistic understanding of human beings.

3) A healthy behavior is indeed simply a healthy life practice considering the permanent and largely oriented education of human beings.

4) We should give a life-philosophical foundation to the individual life style with values and attitudes which accept life in its biological and psychical-spiritual entirety.

Time management for a better life

With most people, time runs away: 15-20 hours a week on watching TV; 10 hours and more on talking without a content of individual interest; more than 10 hours hanging around doing nothing, plus the varied time-consumers such as phone calls, reading newspapers, short visits here and there, small quarrels in relationships without any result, waiting in a traffic jam, lack of personal organization, etc. All this added up over the years of one's life equals years of life time that simply gets lost!

A constructive control of time usage:

- [ ] recognize time wasters
- [ ] plan the day in the morning
- [ ] weak planning
- [ ] check through daily aims
- [ ] communicate awake
- [ ] organize dossiers
- [ ] prepare telephone calls
- [ ] define small aims for the day
- [ ] regulate stress
- [ ] start acting slowly
- [ ] make checklists (e.g. travel)
- [ ] say "no"
- [ ] recognize urgency
- [ ] recognize importance
- [ ] quarrel constructively
- [ ] don't always hesitate
- [ ] make a shopping list
- [ ] reflect on mobility
- [ ] concentrate during meetings
- [ ] take breaks
- [ ] overview courses

Use of time: Note the daily use of time <u>in minutes</u> (taking a weekly average):

... getting to work	... haste	... listening to music
... reading books	... buying without a plan	... hobbies
... going to the toilet	... paperwork	... decorating rooms
... getting dressed	... searching for something	... buying small things
... housework	... visits	... health

... chatting	... visiting pubs/bars	... psychical reinforcement
... making phone calls	... false planning	... searching for information
... curiosity about events	... discussions	... doing things for others
... searching for objects	... eating	... dream interpretation
... listlessness, lack of drive	... cooking	... keeping a diary
... watching television	... dish-washing	... meditation
... waiting	... playing	... adventures
... restless	... reading a newspaper	... body experience
... taking a decision	... professional reading	... preoccupation
... traffic jams/stop lights	... further education	... relaxation
... not clearly listening	... hanging around	... love and relationship

Working and living effectively to achieve success. Respond with a short sentence:

- How do you concentrate on results of your doing?
- How do you invest time and work for your wishes?
- How do you investigate your thinking and judging (evaluating)?
- Which own small but essential aims have you determined for yourself?
- How do you try to objectively and reasonably solve problems?
- Do you distinguish between urgent and important problems?
- Have you calculated your need of time for a determined concern?
- Does your time planning give some space for unexpected things/facts/events?
- What should you generally leave off in important situations?
- How do you clarify your time and forces for an optimal use?
- Which priority of values do you give to your needs?
- How do you take responsibility for your emotions?
- How do you care for your strengths and weaknesses?
- Where do you have courage to act and risk something new with calculation?

10 critical points about cars

The entire traffic system:

1. kills hundreds of thousands of people every year.

2. causes millions of heavily injured and handicapped people.
3. produces immense suffering and stress in general.
4. produces immense lateral and interconnected damages.
5. produces very dangerous illusions to individuals.
6. creates an absolute disequilibrium in the system of industry.
7. charges people financially in an unbalanced dimension.
8. can never be an ideal for other countries worldwide.
9. is one of the main causes of climate change.
10. is in its current situation an evil madness and absurdity.

The fixed costs of a car include: amortization of the paid price, interest of a loan, administration fees to get a loan, insurance (third party insurance and comprehensive insurance), taxes, official inspection (MOT), and license number. The costs for maintenance include: servicing, repairs, new tires (summer and winter), etc. The running costs for petrol, toll, etc. Additional costs also worth considering: fines, cleaning, aluminum wheels, snow chains, parking (garage) at home, parking outdoor, child car seat, small damages (own car) or franchise (comprehensive insurance), and individual improvements or additional equipment.

A small car costs a minimum of 300-500€ monthly (15.000 km p.a.). For a middle class car one has to calculate with an average of 1,000€ per month. And for a top class car one has to pay around 1,500 to 3,500€ per month. Around 60% are fixed costs. Depending on the car model after 4-5 years up to 60% of the car value is lost.

You earn 1,000€/month: whatever the model, you have to calculate with a minimum 250€ for a small car. For your life you have 750€ left. Absurd! How do you live with such a small amount?

You earn 1,500€/month: you spend 300€ for a small car. For your life you have 1,200€ left. You have no single tiny financial flexibility and you are forced to live very modestly! Spend 100€ for public transport and think of some creative ideas on what you could buy every month with 200€: every month a present for your partner, every month something that will make your children happy, accessories, books, CD's, etc.

You earn 2,000€/month: you spend a minimum of 600€ for a simple normal car. For your life you have 1,400€ left. You are crazy to spend that much for a car! Spend 100€ for public transport or buy a car with a monthly budget of 300€; and think of some creative ideas on what you could buy every month with 300-500€: every month a present for your partner and something to make your children happy, accessories, books, CD's, concerts, quality clothes, luxurious bed linen, Gym, seminars for personal development, courses for further education, etc.

You earn 3,000€/month: you spend 1,000€ for a good middle class car. Your life may be comfortable, but rather limited with a disposal of 2,000€. Buy a car with 400-500€ monthly budget and dream about what you can buy every month with the rest of the money for yourself, your wife, and your kids.

You earn 5,000€/month: you spend between 1,200€ and 1,500€ which means that for your life you have 3,500-3,800€ at your disposal. Not bad, but have you ever thought if it's worth it? Buy a car for a 600-750€ monthly budget and you can fly with your dreams about the most wonderful things you can do with 600-750€ every month for yourself, your wife, and your kids.

The costs for economical damages (through victims of traffic accidents) and for lateral damages (environmental damages, street and highway repairs, the damages of climate change, etc.). The maintenance of streets, roads and highways are not included in this list of costs, you pay for that with your taxes!

Now, calculate how much you spend directly for your car and indirectly with your taxes.

Make your leisure perfect

A basic question about consciously guided time organization is: "What do I use my free time for?"

Some examples:

☐	getting to work	☐	impatience
☐	reading newspapers	☐	taking decisions
☐	going to the toilet	☐	traffic jams
☐	putting on one's clothes	☐	not listening carefully
☐	doing house work	☐	haste
☐	chatting to friends	☐	unplanned shopping
☐	talking on the phone	☐	paperwork

☐	curiosity for events	☐	unorganized documents
☐	searching for things	☐	visits
☐	un-lust/lack of drive	☐	short visits to pubs and bars
☐	watching TV	☐	wrong planning
☐	waiting	☐	discussions

Self-education and self-management in one's leisure is desirable:

Positive aspects of leisure are:

- joy
- revitalization
- distraction
- dreams
- fun
- relaxation
- experiences
- personal development
- interests
- recharge one's batteries
- being free
- being understanding

Negative aspects of leisure are:

- frustration
- loneliness
- destruction
- trauma
- un-lust
- exhaustion
- resignation
- illusions
- lack of ideas
- waste
- boredom
- lack of comfort

The experience of after work-time can make you ill and lazy:

- The same rhythm as at work continues: one stays in routine with body, mind and soul. Consequences are: rigid structures, subdivision in fixed points, inability to let things go.

- Tendency to passivity and susceptibility: just relax from the working day until the next working day ...

- Tendency to ritualize: The after-work time goes more or less on uniform schemes ... to be fit for the next day ...

- Alone in the community ... in the family ... being with others; but each one stays broadly isolated. The contacts are superficial ...

● Poor "after-work-sexuality": large discrepancy ... between expectation and fantasies for erotic events and real practice ... small quality of the "short-standard program"

● Bad mood: ... rather negative, easily irritable. Physical and mental tiredness and feelings of failure and excessive demands play a role, caused by an unrealistic self-expectation...

Stress in leisure time is caused by:

- crowds, narrowness, queuing
- being disturbed by others
- family meetings, visiting relatives
- traffic jams (waiting)
- shopping for presents
- noise pollution
- being in boring company
- always taking others into account
- constant background music
- making too many plans
- boredom during weekends
- being completely alone

Reactions are:

☐ Inner restlessness: nervousness, lack of concentration
☐ Over-sensitivity, dissatisfaction with oneself
☐ Feeling unwell: physical uneasiness, lack of appetite, pressure in the stomach...
☐ Being aggressive: to slam the door, lack of order, swearing, quarrelling...
☐ Calming down: sportive performances, going to the pub (bar), shopping...
☐ Distraction: watch TV, eat chocolates, have a glass of wine...

Mental fitness for a long and powerful life

Being mentally fit means that the brain-functions work well. The right hemisphere contains the emotional images. Here you find artistic, spiritual and intuitive forces. The left hemisphere works logically, analytically, and rationally. This part of the brain also processes language.

We can train mental fitness in both parts of the brain. We keep thinking fit by: reading, analyzing, doing memory exercises (e.g. remembering names), clearly defining goals, practicing self-control, making daily plans, etc. Imaginative abilities that we train, for example, with: contemplating pictures (museums), listening to music, expressing feelings, considering intuitive impulses and of course with methodically handled imagination (for psycho-hygiene, to work out experiences) and through dealing with dreams.

Mental training is much more than 'positive thinking' and 'positive imagery'. The singular forces are trained in their capacity and are kept fresh to master life, to efficiently treat problems and to work out new creations. This is positive and constructive!

Mental fitness can be trained in life. Our suggestions are:

- Write down what you said and what the other said after a phone call
- Go through the previous day and experience the situations again
- Preview the day and plan the coming day imaginatively and by thinking
- Consciously decorate your living room with pictures and change them every now and then
- Leisure activity with pictures, colors, forms, music, movements and nature experience
- Work through difficult situations thoroughly and write down the key elements
- Keep a diary about your experiences, about others and all kinds of subjects
- Write down your dreams, work through them, draw diagrams, and play with sceneries
- Communicate feelings; express them physically and with constructive actions
- Handle and plan creatively: visits, festivities, presents, being together

Mental training happens through confrontation with life:

- Elaborate precisely on conflicts and guide them to competent solutions
- Formulate precisely your own values, revise them if necessary
- See through masks and facades; find a clear view for deepness
- See everything in a complex network and don't naively simplify things
- Learn new things steadily through systematically aimed reading
- Consciously deal with your life-time and your forces

Mental fitness means on the one hand thinking, including perception and watchfulness. On the other hand intuition, imagination and spiritual experiences are also part of mental fitness.

Mental fitness has a decisive function in all personal and professional areas for satisfaction, success, fulfillment and happiness. Mental fitness is open for all challenges of life, from inside and also from outside.

Mental fitness: Rate the options below: 4 = total/very 3 = preponderant 2 = moderate   1 = limited

1) I am mentally fit ("cognitive"):

☐ ... clear perception
☐ ... differentiated use of words
☐ ... precise thinking
☐ ... analyzed aims
☐ ... objective order
☐ ... logical thinking
☐ ... precise facts
☐ ... reasonable planning
☐ ... the right succession
☐ ... good time organization
☐ ... high concentration
☐ ... a fresh memory

Total points: …..

2) I am mentally fit ("emotional-imaginative)":

☐ ... interest in images
☐ ... remembering dreams
☐ ... sensation of colors
☐ ... experience of form
☐ ... spontaneous associations
☐ ... creating inner images
☐ ... experience of beauty
☐ ... imaginary of experiences
☐ ... clear body sensation
☐ ... good feeling for time
☐ ... feeling for balance
☐ ... sensation of holiness
☐ ... interest in creating
☐ ... ability for observation in life
☐ ... practicing intuition

Total points: ….

3) Mental fitness in life:

… After phoning I remember exactly what we have spoken about
… In the imagination I can go through the past day without difficulties
… I can easily go through past situations with all my feelings
… I can preview a day in my imagination
… I can plan a day with thinking and imagination
… I decorate my living area and I change it sometimes
… I care about images, colors, forms, music, movements, nature experiences
… I can elaborate difficult situations in my thoughts
… I keep a diary about events, other people and all kind of subjects
… I note down my dreams and interpret them
… I can communicate emotions and express them with constructive acts
… I consciously plan and realize visits and being together with others

Total points: …..

4) Mental-Training happens also when one confronts life:

☐ Thoroughly elaborate difficulties and go forward to competent solutions
☐ Formulate own values (attitudes) precisely and, if necessary, revise them
☐ To critically see through the masks and façades, clear until the depth
☐ To see everything in the complex network and not simplify naively
☐ Always learning something new by systematically reading with an aim
☐ To consciously deal with the own life time and forces

Total points: …..

Top 10 techniques for a better life

1. The principle of small steps

- The principle of small steps aims to reduce your goals into rough goals that fit into more precise goals, thus effectively splitting your goals into micro-goals.
- A long path consists of many little paths, these again of many smaller paths.
- You can achieve your goals with this principle: working 1 hour per day = 365 hours a year = 48 days and 7.5 hours = 10 weeks.
- Concentrating on the micro-level allows you to reach your main goal without losing focus.

- Instead of carrying a big stone, break it up into smaller ones!

2. How to efficiently process information

- Don't read or listen to that which you already know.
- Concentrate on new things, things you don't know yet; and learn to manage them.
- Give a certain weight or importance to every piece of information (understanding, actuality) and then assign a priority.
- Put information into context (also the background of interests).
- Ensure you process information is not only rationally, but also with intuition.

3. Manage your strengths

- Someone who is tired achieves little.
- Overeat and your work will go bad.
- That which is too heavy, reduce it into smaller pieces until it can be carried.
- Plan your day the evening before, but finish the previous day first.
- Always leave some space for free time when you plan your day.
- A daily routine helps with tedious work.
- Recognize the inner and outer forces which produce pressure.

4. Learn the secrets of self-management

- If you learn, you will manage a better life.
- Learning is necessary for survival.
- Learning starts with a precise perception and a correct interpretation.
- High aims always contain little steps of new learning processes.
- Disturbances are a call for learning, and therefore also an opportunity. Recognize your biorhythm by writing a diary.
- Regularly check your timetable/agenda/schedule.

5. Use the power of intelligent (!) positive thinking

- Only naive people say "from day to day everything will get better and better".
- You can only achieve a better life by intelligently defining what "better" means.
- Only an ignorant person thinks that suffering doesn't contain something positive.

- Happiness is never a durable state. Search for the "positive" in the real life.
- The "positive" is first and foremost simply life itself; so: live life!

6. Performance as the start to every success

- From nothing comes nothing.
- The more performance, the more substance you produce.
- Increase self-confidence consciously on the basis of the facts of your performance.
- Take another train if the actual train doesn't take you anywhere.
- A lot is important and urgent; a lot is banal, but nevertheless important.
- A perfect job doesn't exist.
- Always reflect on your performance critically within the context.

7. Apply perception to gain valuable insight

- Always add a grain of perception to everything you do, think, and look at. Involve biographical dimensions in self-perception.
- Scrutinize everything which seems clear and obvious.
- If somebody tells the truth, you will see this from his moral performances and never solely from what they say.
- The content of perception is not your life, so keep your distance!
- Never measure your life on momentary self-perception.

8. Learn to use lateral thinking to "go the distance"

- Take sentences apart, divide thoughts and put them together in a new way.
- Put a question in another way and divide it into a variety of smaller simpler questions.
- Change the sequence; put all your thoughts in a new order.
- Make a detour, the shortcut is mostly the longer way.
- Go the distance with time and area, this way you can change the dimensions.

9. Re-framing situations to make the best of the worst

- Many uncomfortable facts become a positive function when looked at from another point of view.
- Put the subject in another context, this way you may find a positive understanding to it.

- Change a negative experience into a constructive philosophical understanding.
- Take action to avoid worrying and start to experience new things in life!
- Everybody has problems; you don't have to solve all your problems alone.

10. Live the ultimate Golden rules of life!

- It is better to make love on a stack of hay, than to make love with lies in a golden bed.
- To live without wisdom is something millions of people can easily do.
- To maintain your health, yes, but: there are higher values than physical health.
- Success without love and spirit has got very little to do with human being.
- Live with a certain distance from others and from all levels of hierarchy.

Strengthen your psychical health

What is health?

1. Health is defined according to the World Health Organization (WHO): "... as a complete bodily, psychical and social well-being and not only as the absence of illness and disease."
2. A definition about 'health': "Health is a culture of all life means; health is assimilation of body and environment through social actions; health is a path which is formed by going along it.
3. Factors of health are also methodical principles as 'aspire for appropriateness', 'respond to feelings', 'nearness to life'....
4. Seven activities for health promote health and avoid illness: "no smoking", "moderate alcohol", "moderate fat with the right composition", "calculated need of calories", "moderate salt (5-6 gr.)", "managing stress" and "balance the lack of movements".
5. Self-responsibility and self-determination are valued as an important part of a healthy personality development.
6. Health is understood as a part of the individual life course development, as a process which is only possible, if an individual flexibly manages at the time the best reachable state of coordination of inner and external requirements, ensuring a satisfactory continuity of the self-experience (self-identity). Health is related to a high capacity of adaptability of human beings to physical, psychical and social burden and the whole way of living.

Factors that form psychical health; the following statements are summarized and freely formulated.

- Productivity, creativity, being active, working interest
- The objective-rational contact with the reality
- Adaptability
- Internal balance, ego-integration
- Ability to satisfy needs
- Genital sexuality
- Being free from (or limited) use of defense mechanism
- Tolerance of frustration, control of impulses, strengthened against stress
- Power of resistance against psychical illness
- Being free from symptoms
- Realistic definition of aims
- Balance between dependency and independency
- Balance between stability and flexibility
- Basic confidence
- Ego-identity
- Realization of individual potentials
- Autonomy and resistance against enculturation
- Self-responsibility
- Autonomous morality
- Self-understanding
- Realistic self-image
- Self-acceptance, self-esteem, and self-confidence
- Naturalness, spontaneity, sociability, genuineness, being free from facades
- Openness for experiences and feelings
- Experiences of transcendence, 'positive feelings'
- Mind-expanding
- Acceptance of one's own body
- Aiming at the 'good', the truth, the beauty
- Humor
- Democratic character-structure
- Need for privacy
- Orientation in meaning and values
- Ability to a constructive mastering of suffering
- Will-power

This list makes it obvious that health means much more than the "absence of illness". Health isn't something someone has or not, that we can lose and gain back. Health also isn't something, that is added to the human life and that can make life more beautiful and more comfortable.

Health is a way of living, is realization of life, and is a way of mastering life.

Care for a good relationship with your body

The state of the body and the relation with one's own body decisively contributes to psychical well-being; characteristics of this are, for example:

▪	creative forces	▪	stability
▪	realistic aims	▪	balance
▪	humanistic values	▪	interest in life
▪	fulfillment of basic needs	▪	social openness
▪	adapting to stress	▪	dealing with aggression
▪	healthy self-acceptation	▪	autonomy
▪	Self-respect	▪	Stress management
▪	Meditation, Mental Training	▪	Reduction of quarrels
▪	Control of emotions	▪	Clarifying conflicts

What to do with feelings and emotions?

The idea that a person can always dominate his feelings or must always control his feelings with intelligence, and to live as much as possible stoicism and not to be moved and affected by highest and deepest feelings, is completely wrong. To care for one's own feelings is indispensable. Feelings and emotions (meaning: strong feelings) are a part of life, an aspect of life per se, the positive feelings as well as the negative ones.

Practical suggestions for dealing with feelings and emotions are:

❑ Thoughts you suppress become especially active and will eventually break through. Therefore: deal with "what it is thinking about".

❑ Sorrows are a part of the "normal" life. If you suppress your sorrows or trivialize them, then the emotions of the sorrow will unexpectedly break through. Therefore: Take your sorrows seriously!

❑ With time even the smallest general fears can lead to a state of inability to take any decision. Therefore: Search for the reasons of the feelings of fear!

❑ Sometimes feelings and emotions are difficult to control. Mostly the approach is wrong. Therefore: If you identify the factors that produce a feeling (emotion), then you start understanding these factors!

❐ Unfinished matters or activities produce inner tension and an inner restlessness, and often fear. If you complete a matter or activity, you will find satisfaction and inner calm. Therefore: On the one hand learn to postpone (e.g. by setting priorities!) certain matters; and on the other hand finish what has to be done (e.g. with a timetable!).

❐ Some feelings of insecurity arise because you don't clearly see the methodical tools or there is a lack of competences (knowledge, skills), e.g. ability to communicate the right way. Therefore: Clarify what you need to learn about knowledge and the right tools (skills); and learn them!

❐ If you wrongly explain and incorrectly reason an incident, then the wrong feelings arise (e.g. seeing the causes on yourself, and accepting causes as unchangeable. Therefore: Be careful and precisely examine your explanations – and pay special attention to the appropriate style of communication (e.g. accepting a conflict as a positive chance)!

❐ If you think that at home or at work everything has to correspond with your ideas, then you produce a lot of inner pressure (and stress). Therefore: In such a case, examine and change your corresponding attitudes!

❐ It may be right to do some matters in a "perfect" way; but mostly you overcharge yourself, others and the matter itself. Therefore: A personal satisfaction with a work you have done on a level of 90% quality (e.g. cleaning), is mostly enough.

❐ Images enormously influence humans and create corresponding feelings, even strong emotions. Fantasies can activate unconscious inventory. Fantasies can also produce feelings simply by visualization. Therefore: Care for a certain psycho-hygiene with your feelings and do not let all kinds of arising images flow without limit!

❐ Everybody must learn to live with deficits. Ideals can often create a massive inner pressure and with that also feelings of dissatisfaction. Therefore: on the one hand accept the positive challenge and on the other hand adapt the appropriate attitudes!

❐ A too strong feeling of success often leads to similar demands for success and high measures in the relationship. As a consequence critical emotional incidents arise. Therefore: It is wise and intelligent, not to place too much weight on financial and business success.

❐ People who are too strongly work-oriented, based on an exaggerated sense of duty produce feelings of frustration because the "inner being" can't live ("breath") under such pressure.

❐ Greed for recognition and avarice produces as much suffering as physical violence! Therefore: practice critical self-reflection and allow yourself "to live"!

💣 A disproportion between social status and psychical-spiritual development destroys every healthy emotional life!

Efficient reading, writing and learning

1. Efficient reading strategy

First of all you need to get a general idea about the content of a book and the text of your interest. You do not start reading every word. You first need to adapt the text material to your purposes and interest. Read through the table of contents (chapters), the foreword and the index. You can then read the first and last paragraph of each chapter. Also take a look at any diagrams and figures included in the book. From all this you may get about 20-30% of the meaning.

In the next step you find out specific details of the topic of your interest. There is no need to read a whole book for this purpose. Identify the key words covering your subject or questions. Main step: Some subjects require a very detailed understanding. Now your selected reading becomes more time consuming. Underline, highlight and use the margins for your comments.

Go through the texts again and summarize the essential content onto small cards with a keyword each. You need to understand the essential terms, facts, theses, and theories. You also need to understand the course of arguing and the network of the knowledge and theories. Always read critically, ask questions, compare facts with other facts, and especially contemplate the given conclusions.

2. Strategy for writing essays

First of all you need to understand the essay topic and the corresponding given questions. It is recommendable to carefully determine the meaning of each given term in the context of the questions. Analyze the parts of the questions and first make a structure of the key terms of the given subject.

Your own points of view (free thinking, judgments) form part of the conclusion, and not of the analytical part of the essay. You can of course bundle several small fields of the subject giving to that an argument for your selection or for the priority you give in the essay. Once you have made your mind-map, you bring the ideas into a course of elaboration. Close the essay with some conclusions and a personal statement.

3. Learning methods

Learning is something very human and normal. Everybody learns and has started learning since the prenatal time.
Learning means acquiring new knowledge (terms, theories, and facts), behaviors and skills, values and attitudes. Learning starts with understanding words, terms, theories, and networks of facts. Adapting new behavior and skills may need special training.

Human learning forms part of education. Personal psychical-spiritual development is a learning process. Learning can be goal-oriented or can happen by accident in any life situation (habituation or classical conditioning). Learning occurs by studying, copying, playing (not only for children!), or simply through an unaware adaptation or by "trial and error". Motivation and positive learning attitudes enormously facilitate the learning process.

Organize your learning: What do I want to learn? What do I want to achieve? Why do I want to achieve this determined goal? Where do I have to collect the learning subjects? – Then you need to make your timetable: set the main goal into parts and small goals; learn with the corresponding small steps. Give the necessary priority and appropriate study time to this learning in your daily life. Consider your biorhythm for learning! Make a weekly and monthly study plan.

Do not learn with noise and other distraction. If you learn on your PC, do not check your incoming emails every 5 minutes. While studying do not surf around the Internet for interests other than those of the study purpose. Make your notes and revise the entire work periodically, every week. Always stay aware of the purpose of your reading. Write down graphics (diagrams, tables, mind-maps, etc.) and summaries of the parts of the subject on small cards. Add to the summaries new content, ideas and connections that occur to you in the process.

Always organize the content with questions: Why? What? What for? Relevance? Importance? Facts? Judgments? Personal comments? Conclusions? Interpretations? Arguments? Framework? Network of terms and theories? Logic? Comprehensible? Implications? Perspectives?

Distinguish between case study, research result, development of a theory, reflective journal, critical review, literature review, adaptation of a theory and concept, developing a new research or practical project for the future, etc.

Always read, learn, and organize your knowledge, your questions, your drafts, and the learning plan with a note book (size A4 or A5)!

1.7. Rules for efficiency in life

Learn every day and never stop learning

Learning doesn't happen by itself. We summarize the central ideas of 25 learning principles which can help you to improve your learning:

- Behavior of adults is changeable; learning throughout your whole life is possible.
- Self-concept (self-identity) and self- esteem influences learning.
- Early learning experiences promote or hinder learning.
- Early learning experiences should be valued and respected.
- New learning should be bound up with early learning experiences.
- Past experiences become more important with increasing age.
- A positive self-concept and an optimistic self-esteem support learning processes.
- Being endowed with learning strategies and learning abilities improves learning.
- Changes in values, attitudes, abilities etc. destabilize at the beginning.
- Needs and feelings influence learning processes.
- Referring to actual developments, life crises etc. activates motivation.
- Learning is always connected with expectations, value systems and life style of the person.
- Needs of learning and alternatives must be taken into consideration.
- Self-chosen directions of development support the learning progress.
- Free decision to learn reduces anxiety and feelings of threat.
- Feedback is a basic precondition for learning success.
- Learning success motivates.
- Stress reactions through learning activities have to be considered.
- Stress through learning isn't the same as 'difficulties in learning'.
- Being flexible with the learning pace; because rigid time organization inhibits learning.
- Learning without referring to life is experienced as 'lost time'.
- Being healthy and rested are basic conditions for successful learning.
- Use listening and seeing for learning, and don't hamper it.
- Every adult has his individual style of learning.
- Learning activities should be organized in sequences and cycles with a purpose.

Our thesis: Regular new learning in all areas of life is a basic condition for personality education and psychical-spiritual development. A person, young or old, who doesn't regularly learn new subjects, loses himself, wastes his potentials and his self-realization.

Perceive in multiple networks

You excessively consume electricity; electricity from nuclear power stations. Do you ever stop to think that the future generations for centuries and countless millenniums will have to pay for the maintenance of the nuclear waste you and everybody else produced?

You have a heavy quarrel with your partner and you start to think about separating or even getting a divorce. Do you ever think about what is behind such a quarrel? It can be a misunderstanding, lack of love and respect, lack of flexibility, lack of understanding, the energy of suppressed old conflicts or frustrations, unclear communication or wrong interpretation. It can be that you started discussing at the wrong moment and in the wrong place. It can also be that you and your partner simply reproduce the patters which you learnt from your parents.

You buy a car. With that your monthly budget is fully on the limit with the monthly rate you have to pay. Now you don't have money for books, CDs, DVDs, visiting museums, excursions on Sundays, nice clothes or shoes, buying flowers for your loved one, going out with your other half for a romantic dinner, participating in a seminar for personal development or professional further education, etc. Visualize what you can do with the money you save, and what positive effects this could have on your life and relationship, if you buy a car 20-30% cheaper!

If one person throws away batteries into the garbage and one billion people do the same, then the contamination around the globe kills people. If one person contributes to climate change, and if 4 billion do the same, then that's the beginning of the end. If you want a car and to be able to drive around for fun whenever you feel like it and if 3 billion people want the same, then the climate change will come to a total collapse – and this very fast.

If one doesn't think about the consequences of his actual behavior in 10, 20, and 35 years, then everyone can be sure that the end result will be a disaster full of misery and suffering. If one believes in the myths and dogmas, and if everyone believe in myths and dogmas, then mankind will never find God and never find peace and complete fulfillment.

If you think that the daily news on TV and in the newspapers informs you about what is essential and really important, and you think it reflects the state of humanity and the world, then you have a very narrow-minded understanding of human beings and life.

The 15 rules of effective communication

A constructive mastering of life includes the top 15 rules for a partnership-like communication:

1. Don't humiliate, don't hurt, don't depreciate, and don't sneer about the partner.
2. Don't horn in, don't exaggerate, don't play down, and don't lose the 'tone'.
3. Talk together about matters cooperatively, mutually, complementary.
4. Speak definitely, clearly, objectively, distinguished, open and direct.
5. Listening, understanding, giving importance, selecting, letting the other speak.
6. To allow problems, wishes, questions and over all feelings.
7. To keep and allow limitation and autonomy.
8. Respect the partner as an independent person.
9. Pay attention to spiritual rootedness (e.g. dreams), to intuition and inner resonance.
10. Responsibility for place, room, time, course, duration, aim, choice, termination.
11. Keep away from external influences (television, other people).
12. Consider one's own physical state and also the state of others.
13. Being persevering but still flexible; keep an eye on the course of communication.
14. Understand things from the past as a challenge to work them out, not as reproaches.
15. Periodically reflect upon values, norms and attitudes; revise them if necessary.

This is the way I care about my communication (process, sale, control, care, advice; and the discussion in the family, the relationship, the leisure):

Chose a person/a group of people:

Mark with an "X" and give an example you remember about:

☐ Objective:	☐ Concentrated:
☐ Original:	☐ Competent in objectives:

☐	Slow-heavy:	☐	Tricky:
☐	Honest:	☐	Informative:
☐	Transparent:	☐	Flexible in aims:
☐	Volatile:	☐	Fearful:
☐	Conscientious:	☐	Consciously controlled:
☐	Open:	☐	Actively adapting:
☐	Impulsive:	☐	Not engaged:
☐	Efficient in time:	☐	Planned:
☐	Organized:	☐	Prepared:
☐	Exact:	☐	Harmonizing:
☐	Profound:	☐	Simple in tendency:
☐	Asking questions:	☐	Stimulating:
☐	Mandatory:	☐	Undecided:
☐	Cautious:	☐	Adequate timing:
☐	Cooperative:	☐	Seriously:
☐	Chaotic:	☐	Indifferent:
☐	Well listening:	☐	Well ordered:
☐	With constancy:	☐	Short/concise:
☐	Restless:	☐	Directive/controlling:
☐	Business like:	☐	Visualizing:
☐	Aware of the right moment:	☐	Emotional:
☐	Without a tie to the matter:	☐	Without questioning:

How do you treat your partner, acquaintances, customers, colleagues, clients, patients...?

Chose a person/a group of persons:

Mark with an "X" and give an example you remember about:

☐ Friendly:

☐ Dominant:

☐ Diplomatic:

☐ Directive:

☐ Talkative:

☐ Aggressive:

☐ Obliging:

☐ Polite:

☐ With inner limitation:

☐ Impatient:

- [ ] Objectively:
- [ ] With distance:
- [ ] Without distance:
- [ ] Carefully:
- [ ] Flexible in style and theme:
- [ ] Cheerful:
- [ ] Emotionally:
- [ ] Adaptable in style/theme:
- [ ] Serving:
- [ ] Appreciating:
- [ ] Breaking resistance:
- [ ] Loose contact:
- [ ] With masks:
- [ ] Deceiving:
- [ ] Ego-centric:
- [ ] Adapted on the person:
- [ ] With companion style:
- [ ] Cooperative:
- [ ] Helpful:
- [ ] Reinforcing:
- [ ] Waiting:
- [ ] Fair:
- [ ] Authentic:
- [ ] Mutual:
- [ ] Attentive:
- [ ] Provocative:
- [ ] Dynamic:
- [ ] Reliable:
- [ ] Informal:

Efficient attitudes for business and work

The social life is considerably directed by norms, rules, customs, regulations, and laws. The whole life – e.g. work, contacts, self-presentation, relationships, all kind of activities, dealing with money, businesses, purchases and sales, etc. - is full of norms, founded in individual and collective judgments: "That is good", or "That is bad" and consequently: "You are allowed to do that" or "You must do that". We can't live without social norms and rules. Everybody adopts such norms and rules already from the early childhood. Autonomy increases with the beginning of the age of 9-12. Children ask: "Why do I have to do that?" Norms represent values and rules organize daily life and social groups. Norms, values and rules are embedded in arguments, in a system of philosophical, spiritual or religious attitudes and beliefs. Attitudes direct behavior and give practical orientation in all life issues.

Therefore, attitudes principally can be changed through persuasion depending on the grade of willingness to learn or the intensity of stubbornness with a rigid general rejection of a person. Any kind of fear, jealousy, indignation, disgust, and anger can hinder changing an attitude because attitudes have an emotional component and give a certain orientation and footing in behavior. Neuroticism, strong emotions behind attitudes (greed, hate, fear, etc.), ignorance and arrogance, and deep religious (fundamentalist) roots highly hinder possible changes.

Changing attitudes also depends on the intelligence, self-esteem, self-confidence, personality strength, the target of an intended change, etc. The lateral influences that support possible changes are interest, attractiveness, trustworthiness, social environment, expertise (e.g. science) and interpersonal attraction.

There is an optimal emotional and intellectual level in the possibility of changing attitudes. Other components of supporting changes are: efficiency of the result, accessibility, self-efficacy, and matters that are involved, furthermore the message sources (the "authority" demanding or offering a change). Practical efficiency and emotional components are the most important factors for change. It allows a person to deal, both with the targeted situation and the specific emotion. If there is not enough emotional and practical motivation, changes are not possible. If the emotional appeal is inappropriate or exaggerated, the motivation can be blocked and attitude changes are not possible.

Attitudes are the result of life experiences and education, of the social environment, of personal conclusion, of "trial and error", or simply of copying. The nature and practical relevance of the attitude for a person plays an eminent role in readiness for changes and in the process of persuasion.

Attitudes include a value and a judgment. Attitudes are a construction of several components and include a positive or negative view of a person. Attitudes always reflect an affective response which marks the intensity of rejection or acceptance. Attitudes also express an expectation about a certain behavior in certain situations or about ways of thinking and believing. Attitudes always include values or judgments such as:

- This is good or bad.
- This is right or wrong.
- This is efficient or not efficient.
- This is beautiful or ugly.
- This is positive or negative.
- This is appropriate or inappropriate.
- This is correct or incorrect

Examples of attitude construction:

1. Politicians are
2. Somebody who is educated is
3. He, who performs something, is
4. Money and properties are
5. As a good Christian I do
6. Life is
7. In life the most important things are
8. To parents one should
9. Teenagers should
10. Pupils should
11. When making love you must
12. When dealing with people you should
13. When facing your boss you should
14. Women should take care of
15. A real man has
16. When facing strangers you should
17. The kitchen must always be

Build up some attitudes for specific situations and explain:

1) Consumption:	
2) Communication:	
3) Business:	
4) Sex:	
5) Healthy life:	
6) Environment:	
7) Relationship:	
8) Self-presentation:	
9) Dealing with money:	
10) Having fun:	
11) Women:	
12) Men:	
13) Working discipline:	
14) Car:	
15) Service oriented job:	
16) Speculations:	

Efficient self-presentation in life, business, work

Self-presentation is the way a person expresses his entire being in a specific social situation; this includes the way somebody is dressed, the tone of voice they speak in, the gestures and mimics they make; the facial expressions they put on, the way of talking, vocal changes, raising eyebrows; the glance of the eyes and the expression of the lips; the squeeze of the hand; the body posture and movements of the arms and hands; the energetic dynamics of the body and voice, etc. Consumption is also a way of self-presentation. Self-presentation is the image – the self-identity – a person shows to other people.

The self-presentation creates a message and due to that has a certain influence on others. In most cases consciously or unconsciously intended: to impress, to gain rewards, to express the own importance, to get a benefit, gain, advantage, or to control the scene, etc. With the self-presentation a person is "selling" an image also to win over other people, to intimidate, to influence, to control, to make them feel subordinate or superior.

On the one hand most people are not aware of their self-presentation and have no idea how it influences their social environment. On the other hand there is a management of self-presentation with clearly determined aims to performing success. There is a way of identifying strategies of self-presentation to achieve certain goals. A wrong self-presentation produces obstacles in whatever aims one has.

Management of self-presentation attempts to control self-relevant images. Strategic factors to influence people in a desired way are: attractiveness of the self-presentation to produce favorable first impressions on others, the congruence between the intended and expected value expression (for an identification), the hidden ties between self-presentation and the aimed behavior (e.g. buying a certain product, entering into a more serious relationship, committing to a contract, following a new life style behavior, etc.), or any self-promotion. Strategies of self-presentation, self-monitoring, and impression management vary with the nature of the field in which an individual performs.

Self-presentation also intends to avoid social disapproval. Positive actions and outcomes demand accommodation and adjustment to the values and behaviors of others. Giving the right impression increases the probability of being accepted as part of a social group.

Self-presentation can make or break a career, or a relationship, or a business, or any social situation. The self-presentation is not important. The effect one produces on others with his self-presentation is what is important. Narcissism with an inflated self-image and exhibitionistic behavior can lead to success if it is addressed to neurotic people; and will fail if it is addressed to psychologically and spiritually mature people.

Self-presentation enhances or produces a determined image perceived by others:

- to make oneself appear experienced and competent.
- to create an impression of moral superiority and integrity.
- to show oneself as an authority (science, politics, business, etc.).
- to intend being likeable by understanding and smooth talking.
- to produce an impression of being helpless, weak, in a need.
- to avoid a negative interpretation and an undesired outcome of others.

Most social interactions can be analyzed and interpreted in terms of a concept of self-presentation. Only a few social behaviors can be considered as not having any intentionally or unconsciously constructed self-presentation.

A self-presentation that is not completely rooted in the character, in integrity and qualities, in knowledge and competences (skills) of the person is a lie and destroys the character of the person itself, the addressed people's natural trust and genuine inner being, and the society's life in general if it becomes a collective "game" of cheating, brainwashing, and manipulating.

There are many "stages" where people express an intended self-presentation.

Give four positive reinforcing characteristics you wish to see (experience) in the self-presentation of a person:

1. Political fields
2. Show Business
3. Business world
4. Industry
5. Science
6. Sale
7. NGOs for humanity
8. Religion
9. Spiritual centers
10. Education
11. Peer groups
12. Sport
13. Dating
14. Neighbors
15. Curriculum for a job

How can you improve your self-presentation?

Think carefully before talking

Talking is a very easy going activity. You can talk about anything without thinking. You also can talk in a chaotic way. But talking means: "giving a message". And the general question is always: Why do you give this message to another person? And: What do you want to achieve with giving out this message? From a practical point of view you should ask yourself: Is the message you want to give or you have given clear and understandable?

The problem of talking starts with the question: what is your message which you are giving to another person based on? You have seen something. You have read something. You have heard something. You feel something. You remember something you experienced. You have made some interpretations about something. You feel something about whatever.

The main problem starts with the fact that most people only have reduced selected, manipulated, wrong and superficial information. Most people are unable to see their perceived information in its network of time (past, present, future), of qualities, of psychological background, of hidden interests, and of related objective facts. Most information that people get from other sources also include interpretation, judgment and emotional components which then, once perceived, become an "objective fact".

What people perceive (read, hear, experience, feel, etc.) is immediately integrated under the disposition of the learnt vocabulary of a person, including the patterns of past experiences about the matter, with patterns of interpretation and judgment, and also with an emotional reaction. Perceiving also goes along with the defense mechanism: people don't see what they don't want to see; or don't register what they don't agree with or with something that they are not comfortable with.

Therefore, the message will never be better than the information they have about what they are talking about and the way how the disposition, patterns, and defense mechanisms of the person work.

People often talk without giving a message. They talk merely to make themselves important, to get attention, or to avoid talking about what would be really important to talk about. Or they say it in such a way that the conversation leads to unexpected or undesired effects. Sometimes it is absolutely not important what they say; they simply want to provoke or to get rid of their bad or aggressive mood.

It's really necessary to clearly look and to think carefully before talking! It is equally necessary to also improve the way of talking by thinking about your way of thinking!

The 2 Euro (Dollar) effect

With one single suggestion you can save on average €2 (2$) per month, in total per month easily €100 (100$) if not up to €300 (300$) or much more!

Find out how much you can save every month:

Mark!	Potentials for saving money	€ or $
	Reduce the time spent showering (all family members)	
	Take a shower instead of a bath full of water	
	Only use the dishwasher if full and necessary	

	Put a brick in the toilet water-tank	
	Turn off the tap when brushing your teeth	
	Turn off the light if you don't need it	
	Use energy efficient light bulbs	
	Reduce the amount of TV you watch by 1hr /day	
	Don't use the washing machine only half full	
	Switch off the computer when you don't need it	
	Reduce the time you spend surfing the internet	
	Cook more strategically by coordinating	
	Use the air conditioning (A/C) sparingly	
	Don't use the vacuum cleaner everyday	
	Control the temperature of the fridge	
	Don't iron every piece of clothing	
	Drive your car 20% less	
	Drive carefully; pay attention to speeding/breaking	
	Don't use the car for less than 1.5 km. Walk!	
	Organize your shopping when you go by car	
	Use public transport whenever possible	
	Smoke 5 cigarettes less per day	
	Drink water or tea instead of sodas	
	Reduce your alcohol consumption by 20-50%	
	Reduce the amount of meat consumed by 20%	
	Reduce the amount of fish consumed by 20%	
	Buy local vegetables from the market	
	Reduce the amount of chocolate you eat 20-50%	
	No need to eat dessert everyday; Sunday is enough	
	Don't eat a lot of chips while watching TV	
	Reduce the amount of snacks you eat by 50%	
	Cook yourself instead of buying pre-prepared food	
	Use detergents carefully, at least 20% less	
	Use perfume and beauty products moderately	
	Don't exaggerate when using butter	
	Go to supermarkets which have moderate prices	
	For lunch and dinner sometimes drink water	
	You don't need to wash your car every week	
	Use credit cards only to take out cash from the ATM	
	Don't use your credit card for monthly payments	
	Reduce the use of your phone/cell phone	
	Reduce the time of your phone calls	
	Moderate the temperature of the central heating	
	If you go to bars, drink in moderation	

	If you go for a coffee, choose a cheaper place	
	If you go for lunch or dinner, chose cheaper places	
	TOTAL:	

Don't say that you can't save a considerable amount of money every month!

The 20 essential questions to ask yourself in order to succeed

There are hundreds of recipes for success and finding happiness. You can find countless books that offer the "silver bullet" for a fast and very easy fulfillment of any desires. Some business people say anybody that doesn't want this "silver bullet", is responsible for their own failure.

There is even worse: some promise the 'egg of Columbus' wrapped in hype, all this without even having to learn anything, only to be open for the secret key. The slogan: You haven't got to do anything! Everything is easy and success is guaranteed. Now the fulfillment of all wishes is ready. From the moment you realize this, success is achieved in all life areas.
Trust in the omnipotence of the magic words about success, and you are a good person. Subordinate yourself under the genial program of success, and you are awarded with success. Yield to the authority, and you get the fast happy life. If you get it, you are a better person. And only such supermen can be winners. All others are losers; they are the people on the lower level; they are guilty, because they failed.

Therefore: Be a millionaire! Win!

The external success is well known and socially appreciated, because it reflects the social collective neurosis: money, properties, career, reputation, power, appearance.

The inner success is difficult to show, and doesn't produce more money or social recognition: fulfillment of life, self-realization, performance as an expression of talents, psychical freedom, love, security, etc.

But the inner success also demands commitment of forces and resources, hard and thorough work, endurance, will power, social competences, self-management, abilities to think and judge, ability for making compromises, understanding, etc.

The following questions essentially concern professional activities. But all self-critical aspects have a high importance also for the personal life.

1. Do you concentrate on your thinking and acting?
2. Are you ready to invest 'work' in your life wishes?
3. Have you searched your mind for old patterns which persist?
4. Do you know that efficiency is more an art than a technique or science?
5. Have you defined your aims and taken full responsibility to reach these aims?
6. Do you try to solve problems simply and reasonably?
7. Do you distinguish between urgent and important problems?
8. Have you ever made an inventory about your time usage?
9. Do you have space in your time planning for unexpected events?
10. Do you know what you should stop doing?
11. Do you ask yourself before you start a task: "Is this the best use of time and energy?"
12. Do you have a healthy self-consciousness and self-confidence?
13. Do you concede the first place to your own needs?
14. Do you take responsibility for your feelings?
15. Can you count on your own forces, skills and character?
16. Are you aware that perfectionism can hinder your effectiveness?
17. Do you have courage to act and can you deal with calculated risks?
18. Do you consciously try to improve your style of communication?
19. Do you try to work together with others or against them?
20. Did you take steps, to limit interruptions to the necessity? (Not only in professional life but also in your leisure!)

The 20% rule to save money

First of all you have to focus on your personal expenses. Deal intelligently with your expenses and start saving money! All solutions start with an effort by individuals to save money in their personal life without losing quality of life, freedom or satisfaction.

Not all of the following suggestions are applicable to everyone and some suggestions can be considered on a level of 5-20% and others on a level of 30-80%. During some months it will be easier to save 20% or even more, and other months not. On average if you follow as many of the following suggestions as possible, it should allow you to save at least 20% in total per year of your personal expenses as well as your business costs.

The result can be seen like this: With a very small income you can save $10 per month and $120 per year. It's good to have $120 at the end of the year! A higher income may allow you to save $600, $1,200, $1,800 or even much more per year. It's cool to have this money at the end of the year. It's also very intelligent if you can live a well balanced life even if you can't save any money! Or in the worst case you can at least survive without any financial drama.

General suggestions for saving money:

- Smoke 20% less
- Drink 20% less alcohol
- Consume 20% less petrol (by driving less, driving slower)
- Use 20% less electricity
- Reduce 20% the amount of meat and fish that you consume
- Buy products that are 20% cheaper
- Use 20% less water (when you shower, wash clothes, etc.)
- Reduce heating and A/C costs by 20% (don't use over long periods of time, and don't create extreme temperatures)
- Use your credit/debit card only when you really need it; at least 20% less
- Get cash from the bank or the ATM of your bank (not the ATM of a competitor bank!) and save the fees, minimum 20%
- Pay all or at least 20% of what your credit card is charged every month
- Eat 20% less snacks & drink 20% less beer while watching TV
- Buy 20% less soda/beer/wine (alternatively drinking tea at home)
- Go shopping to your local market or local shops
- Reduce your monthly pocket money by 20%; also that of your kids
- Buy 20% less newspapers and magazines
- Get a holiday package that is 20% cheaper than the one you had last year
- Purchases: spend 20% less money (20% less goods/20% cheaper goods)
- Perfume/Toiletry: use 20% less or buy 20% cheaper
- Buy 20% less prepared meals (cook your own meals)
- When going out, spend 20% less (choose 20% cheaper menus, wine, etc.)
- Use detergents sparingly and you easily save 20%
- Use medicine when it is really appropriate and save 20%
- Go to a hairdresser, beauty salon, gym that is 20% cheaper
- Turn off appliances at home (TV, PC, Radio, etc.) when not used
- Watch 20% less TV every day
- Use your mobile phone 20% less and / or reduce talking by 20%
- Use your computer (e.g. surfing the internet, chatting) 20% less

Don't fail with your responsibility!

The state of humanity and the earth shows us: globally most politicians have failed outrageously. NGOs could not avoid the dramatic increase of the global problems of humanity and the earth. The five big religions have failed in an incredible way to bring forward humanity's evolution. The public education has also failed to prepare people with relevant knowledge and skills for their life and future. See the facts that politicians and leaders around the globe are not telling you:

- We live in a world where fundamental changes are arising with high speed.
- The world in 20-35 years will bring you unimaginable challenges.
- Everything that seems to be safe today will become completely insecure.
- The entire life frame around the globe will be different from today.
- The huge global problems of humanity will dramatically increase.
- The damages and destruction of nature will affect billions of people.
- Humanity will need 50-65% more resources for industry and living.
- Poverty in the industrialized countries will hit half of the population.
- One must count with the worst living conditions to survive in any way.
- The young people today will inherit the damages from current causes.
- The people in their forties today will be faced with a sad "third age".
- The people in their sixties today will probably die in a disgraceful way.

You want love and happiness. You want food and everything that makes life comfortable. You want a home. You want to create a family. You want fun and entertainment. You want a financially stable existence. You want to live your "third age" in a worthy way. You want to be healthy. You never want to die or be seriously injured or handicapped as a result of an accident. You want to work and to use your potentials for work and life.
You also want to spend good times on weekends and of course you want great holidays every year. You never want war or terrorism. You never want to suffer from disease caused by contaminations or by suppressing your inner conflicts, pains, and unsolved problems. You want to live yourself authentically and to grow psychologically and spiritually as a person. You want to find your genuine fulfillment.

How can you get all this by ignoring the state of humanity and the earth? How can you get it if you completely disrespect your inner being? How can you get a good life and future if you don't strongly contribute with your way of living to drastically reduce damaging the resources, the environment, the world of nature and animals, and the climate?

You too are the cause for the huge global problems of humanity and the earth! You together with billions of other people! Therefore: you and billions must significantly contribute with a new way of successfully living your life to avoid the collapse of humanity and the earth in 20-35 years.

Therefore: Learn now and every day to create a good and happy life!

Give concrete examples how you can contribute with your responsibility:

Living:
_____

Car:
_____

Shopping:
_____

Food:
_____

Electricity / Gas:
_____

Heating / AC:
_____

Health:
_____

Media:
_____

Information:
_____

Life style:
_____

Living human values:
_____

Accidents:
_____

Money management:
_____

Leisure:
_____

Holidays:
_____

Further education:
_____

Detergents: _____

Medicine: _____

Alcohol: _____

Smoking: _____

Eating habits: _____

Water: _____

Spirituality: _____

Insurances: _____

Internet: _____

Social networking: _____

Nature: _____

Animals: _____

Just do it!

Just do it because nobody will do it for you!

→ Do you really want a new world, but without renewing yourself and without the necessary knowledge and skills for self-renewal and a successful life?

→ Do you really think a new world and a good future for you and humanity will be possible without any contribution from your part?

→ Do you really think that science, politicians and authorities in the Churches will resolve the huge global problems of humanity and the earth?

→ Do you really believe that a Son of God will descend from heaven and resolve your problems and all the huge global problems of humanity?

Fact is: If you have the necessary knowledge, skills, and personality qualities you can successfully:

- Live a healthy life and resolve problems with your inner and real life.
- Live your relationship, your love, and your family life with kids.
- Deal with the critical aspects of belief, religion, and the meaning of life.
- Develop yourself towards a new all-sided balanced unity and totality.
- Interpret your dreams and meditate correctly for the right orientation.
- Understand yourself and other people, including the unconscious life.
- Resolve your suppressed conflicts, suffering, and biographic burdens.
- Find trust, peace of mind, satisfaction, happiness and self-fulfillment.
- Lay a stable foundation for your future, especially for your "third age".
- Realize your talents, potentials, qualities, aims, dreams, and visions.
- Manage the complexities and interconnections that you depend on.
- Find and benefit from your inner source of life and your inner Spirit.
- Contribute with your way of living to humanity and the earth.

If you don't have all the necessary knowledge and skills, and you don't develop yourself psychologically and spiritually, your life will end in chaos. If you continuously suppress and ignore; you won't be successful in life! You will fail!

If you don't have all the necessary knowledge and skills, and you don't contribute with your personal development, life style, spiritual attitudes, and engagements for a better state of humanity and the earth, your life will end in the collective global nightmare. You will fail!

What you have to do for a successful and happy life, nobody will do for you! No politician, no spiritual master, no priest, no monk, no bishop, no cardinal, no pope, no holy man, no prophet, no messiah, no king, no emperor, no state president, no millionaire and no billionaire will do for you what your inner life, your real life, and the life in general demands from you for a successful and happy life! If you don't take the necessary steps you will fail!

Now you want to start a powerful personal development and to powerfully live with your authentic Self. You can achieve a successful and happy life for your self-renewal, for your health in the future, and for an all-sided balanced personal development.

You can achieve highest aims with yourself and in your life, especially achieving all precious psychological and spiritual levels, complete happiness and highest personal self-fulfillment.

Describe your aims and what you do (action) to achieve these aims.

Aim and action: ....

1.8. Ways of living

Best ways to live life creatively

We can also treat and solve problems with creativity. Intuition, inspiration and imagination (also fantasy) are a source of this creative force. Being creative means being capable of restructuring knowledge and experiences; it also means being capable of discovering new relations between elements with spontaneity and flexibility. This includes interpretation and understanding.

Dealing with subjects of daily life demands an active critical confrontation with oneself, with others and with the environment. An unprejudiced perception of problems and a freedom to act are preconditions for creative problem solving. The quality of any solution considerably depends on information, however common the problem may be. To collect information is a creative activity. On a trial basis, we can play through each variation of a solution with sufficient information. This way we can widen the narrow limitations of the information previously given. The "sudden idea" (aha-experiences, the "I've got it") doesn't come by accident, it comes through thoroughly thought out and creatively prepared processes.

New learning processes automatically follow, embedded in the elaboration and evaluation of new solutions. Creative forming also demands questions such as: Can I apply it? Can I use it? Can I carry it through? How does it work? What is the 'price' of the effort? How can I discuss this with the people involved? Thinking processes, memory, valuation and behavior contribute to this.

Creativity conditions and promotes (in daily life): psychical health, ego-strength, delight in discovering, energy potentials, tolerance for frustration and conflicts, acceptance of complexity of everything, open mindedness and courage for autonomy for an individual life style.

How can I be more creative? We summarize some proposals:

- Take time to understand the problem before you start trying to solve it.
- Keep all facts clear in your mind.
- Identify the facts that are especially important.
- Prepare a list of questions to deal with the problem.

- Try to be consciously original and to find new ideas.
- It isn't ridiculous if you say anything uncommon or if you are wrong.
- Rid yourself of cultural taboos that could undermine a solution.
- Draw a diagram in order to visualize the problem.
- Write down your ideas to retain important facts and to find models.
- Imagine how you will solve the problem.
- Go through the real elements of the problem.
- Divide the problem into parts: solve a part and continue like that.
- Use analogies (similar situations), examine the possibility for transfer.
- Keep your mind open, if an attempt doesn't work, examine the presumption.
- Use different strategies: verbal, visual, calculating, action.
- If you are stuck in an attempt, try another way to go ahead for the solution.
- Be watchful of strange situations. You could be near a solution.
- Search for connections between different facts.
- Trust your intuition. Approach a way and look where it leads to.
- Try to guess the way for a solution, more and more until achieve it.
- Think about an uncommon manner to use things and environment.
- Making a fuss about a problem may cause a delay, but can finally lead to the goal.
- Jump over common things, try to invent new methods.
- Try to be objective; evaluate your ideas as if they were alien.
- Activate your delight of discovering through variable interpretations.
- Limit norms and 'zeitgeist', which over all support the pressure for 'belonging'.
- Search uncommon places for more information about the facts.
- Daydream a 'successful story' about the problem.
- Ask your dreams for explanations and solutions.
- Widen the problem with new elements that you can perhaps live with.
- Enlarge or decrease certain elements, this helps to find solutions.
- Strengthen the weakest parts of a solving strategy and of an effort.
- Search complementary parts and thus widen the picture of the problem.

Make your life much easier

The daily life as a self-expression.

- [ ] Irregular daily rhythm
- [ ] Noise in the environment
- [ ] Watching too much television
- [ ] No work contentment
- [ ] Negative inner bond with the parents
- [ ] Guilty feelings
- [ ] Existential fear
- [ ] Unsatisfied sexuality
- [ ] An unelaborated past suffering
- [ ] No professional future
- [ ] Unstable life partner
- [ ] Stress at work
- [ ] Concern about the own children
- [ ] No spirituality
- [ ] A lot of sad memories
- [ ] No/not enough love experiences
- [ ] No aim for life
- [ ] Drive of perfectionism
- [ ] Mistrust
- [ ] Forced to play a 'theatre'
- [ ] No partnership in the relationship
- [ ] No basic confidence in life
- [ ] No own clear values of life
- [ ] Fear of big challenges
- [ ] Fear of unemployment
- [ ] Ignoring one's own problems
- [ ] Suppressing annoyance and anger
- [ ] Always putting aside own interests
- [ ] No time and no calm to eat
- [ ] No inner orientation (dreams)
- [ ] No efficient mastering of suffering
- [ ] Predominant rigid psycho-dynamism
- [ ] Low tolerance of frustration
- [ ] Letting yourself overstrain
- [ ] Letting your mood be influenced
- [ ] Unilateral image of the opposite sex
- [ ] Only small experiences of faithfulness
- [ ] Un-reconciled abortion
- [ ] Not enough movements (sport)
- [ ] Strong inhibitions
- [ ] No regular work
- [ ] An unsatisfied relationship
- [ ] An unelaborated biography
- [ ] Fear of life
- [ ] An unorganized life
- [ ] Tensions in the relationship
- [ ] Financial problems
- [ ] Conflicts of separation/bonds
- [ ] Lack of self-confidence
- [ ] Frustration with housework
- [ ] Boredom in leisure time
- [ ] Lack of profound sense of life
- [ ] Unable to say "no"
- [ ] Strong religious norms
- [ ] Strong old-fashioned norms
- [ ] A lot of frustrations
- [ ] Lies of the human beings
- [ ] Delicate sexual experiences
- [ ] Unable to enjoy lust
- [ ] Too much absence of laughing
- [ ] Bad feelings about a neighbor
- [ ] Negative attitude about the body
- [ ] Discontent with living situation
- [ ] Strong need for harmony
- [ ] Unable to be alone with yourself
- [ ] Exaggeration in taking regard
- [ ] Ignoring the own feelings
- [ ] No clear and real self-image
- [ ] Diffuse and weak will force
- [ ] Fear of illness
- [ ] Not much inner flexibility
- [ ] Doing too much what others say
- [ ] Constant drive to consume
- [ ] Jealousy (own, from the partner)
- [ ] Repressed sexuality
- [ ] Ignoring responsibility for life

- ☐ Unsatisfied wishes
- ☐ No profound (self-) reflections
- ☐ Disagreement with others
- ☐ Constant grief
- ☐ Excessive hunger for experiences
- ☐ Small personal autonomy
- ☐ Not living authentically
- ☐ A lot of failure
- ☐ An unstable self-esteem
- ☐ Not enough inner distance

Live with your inner rhythm

The inner rhythm is the result of a complex network of living:

- Be aware of what sensual feelings you have
- Stand up for your opinions and interests
- Speak about your anger, rage and temper
- Accept strong and also unsettled feelings
- Appreciate new and uncommon ideas
- Try to 'do nothing' without losing the floor under your feet
- Learn to like being alone and to occupy yourself
- Spoil yourself now and then
- Don't feel forced to always solve a problem immediately
- Live well, also if things don't go well
- Occasionally walk (instead of taking the lift; going shopping with the car)
- Go out into the fresh air as often as you can
- Regularly ventilate your rooms with fresh air
- Consciously avoid noise and bad air, if it's possible
- You don't always need background music
- Switch off the television if the program bores you
- Take care to have a regular life pattern
- Be moderate with consuming cigarettes, alcohol, coffee, sweets and eating in general
- Enjoy eating with time and calmness
- Enjoy your work by focusing on the 20% you like doing
- Manage time pressure without "swerving"
- See sense in your work as well as in your leisure
- Be content with your life situation, feel good and comfortable
- Like the environment around your living place
- Handle electricity, petrol, detergent, medicine, etc. with moderation
- Be aware of waste and treat waste ecologically
- When driving, respect others and drive sensibly
- Take interest in biographies of others in your leisure environment
- Regularly visit cultural, social and political events
- If necessary forcefully push for your interests
- Your life shall have sense and values

- The basic values of human beings are very important to you
- Accept suffering, problems, and conflicts in life
- Don't think that you missed important things/events in your life
- Accept difficult life phases from your past
- Be confident about how you create and master your life

Think about the following facts:

1) Stress as a reaction to overstrain is a complex phenomenon that we have to consider and to judge in the frame of a holistic image of human beings.

2) A healthy behavior, as prevention and mastering of stress, has to be developed and practiced also in a holistic understanding of human beings.

3) A healthy behavior is indeed simply a healthy life practice considering the permanent and largely orientated education of human beings.

4) We should give a life-philosophical foundation to the individual life style with values and attitudes that accept life in its biological and psychical-spiritual entirety.

Avoid the risks of an accident

You pass by a traffic accident. You see a man, dead behind the wheel, additionally two people heavily injured. Then you feel sad. Do you ever think that this happened because the driver was not concentrated, was quarrelling with his wife, was too tired, occupied with a serious concern, was extremely drunk, or something similar? Do you ever think that they left home saying 'bye my love, I will be back soon', and now they never come back home; or they have to start a completely new life as a handicapped person when he they come back home after six months in the hospital? Do you decisively learn from such an experience for yourself?

Millions die in traffic accidents; millions are injured, and hundreds of thousands become handicapped. The monetary damages of hundreds of millions of dollars and more in car damages and lateral damages are not even accounted for. The result of this is worse than a world war! And it is extremely expensive for all car owners. Everybody pays a lot for this suffering and these damages! The car repair industry with billions of dollars in turnover is not a productive working field. This situation can and must be changed within years. It all depends on every single individual – also on you!

Around the globe we have even more accidents in people's homes: injured or killed because of electricity manipulations, falling from a ladder or a chair (serving as a ladder), accidents working in the garden, accidents when cooking (e.g. hot water accidents), accidents from manipulating machines, accidents with knifes, accidents from children ingesting detergents or medicines, accidents from a fire, etc. Ignoring safety rules also cause millions of accidents at work.

The costs of such accidents are immense! Doctors, clinics and hospitals are overcharged by huge waves of injured people every single day. Countless people around the globe are suffering from the consequences of such accidents! Everybody pays for this with health or car insurance. This situation can and must be drastically changed within years. It all depends on every single individual!

The main causes are also the solution:

- Get informed about all possible causes of accidents.
- Always be concentrated on what you do (when there is a risk of accident).
- Never let yourself be in a hurry doing what you want or must do.
- Take all possible measures to avoid the risk of an accident.
- Do everything with the appropriate skills and precaution.
- Get help from a professional if you are not sure about the "how".
- Always observe the environment for possible risks.
- Improve your use of time, self-management and self-control.
- Be responsible for yourself and others: respect the human values!

Traffic accidents, home accidents and work accidents around the globe produce more suffering, more damages, and more costs than 100 tsunamis per year!

Home staging for a life style with well being

What is home staging? It is all about dressing a home for sale; and also for rent (furnished). Home Staging can provide many suggestions about how to manage a home for well being.

Many aspects (components) of a home can be a real turnoff to a person's well being. Staging is identifying negative aspects of the home. At the same time staging identifies positive aspects of the home by perfecting them with the art of creating good moods. The tenant's emotional reaction must be: "I like to live here!" Or: "I am excited; this is really my home!" The tenant must feel at home and feel in accord with the ways of living in it.

Home staging uses the most efficient ways to create a balance between the negative components (furniture, decoration, painting, possibilities of use of space, etc.), the critical structure of the home (size, division, windows, etc.), and the manifoldness of possible improvements. Home staging aims to improve a home and make it more appealing, by transforming it into a welcoming, appealing, and attractive home for living.

Aims of Home Staging …

- Makes a home look bigger, brighter, warmer, and cozier.
- Creates scenery that appeals to all five senses.
- Spruces up the home by also giving attention to bathrooms.
- Allows all rooms and areas to show themselves.
- Draws attention to predetermined areas.
- Makes rooms look open, airy and delightful.
- Creates a nice, easy room-to-room balance.
- Shows off the home to its fullest potential.
- Brings the outdoors (nature, space, light) inside.
- Builds emotional connection points in every room.
- Creates a clean and ordered impression.
- Marks a home personality and easy going life style.
- Focuses on emotion, light, balance, and flow.
- Creates warmth and not sterility and soullessness.
- Underlines living qualities like a 4-5* hotel.
- Creates an impression of openness and comfort.

Cleaning and organizing:

Basic: If a home is unorganized, messy, untidy, and dirty, then the tenant and his/her partner or family unconsciously feels that this expresses a bad atmosphere. Give attention to:

☐ dirty windows
☐ an unclean bathroom

- [ ] the kitchen in a mess
- [ ] disorderly cupboards, packed full of clothes
- [ ] smelly curtains (from smoking)
- [ ] ashtrays full of smoked cigarettes
- [ ] hairs from a cat or dog everywhere
- [ ] dirty brass door handles
- [ ] bad odors
- [ ] half dried plants
- [ ] overgrown plants
- [ ] the beds are not done and clothes everywhere
- [ ] the kids room with a chaos of toys on the floor
- [ ] the home's flaws
- [ ] dust balls and cobwebs hanging around the baseboards
- [ ] unusual knickknacks everywhere
- [ ] full wastebaskets
- [ ] disorderly hand towels in the bathroom
- [ ] dripping faucets
- [ ] caulking cracks
- [ ] driveway and sidewalk not swept clean
- [ ] garage and basement full of unused old stuff
- [ ] broken gutters and shutters
- [ ] broken woodwork
- [ ] worn carpets
- [ ] loose planks
- [ ] creaky stairs
- [ ] burned out bulbs
- [ ] old doormat

The principle of a personalized home: Very special items related to the biography of the owner or tenant make the home special. Examples include: Awards and certificates; Religious items; Cultural items; Paintings; Extraordinary tastes; Dramatic artwork; Family photos; Trophies; Posters; etc.

The principle of creating a general ambience: The general impression about the ambience influences the well being. Strong patterns don't animate a feeling of well-being.

Examples:

- [ ] Dark and tight spaces
- [ ] Old stylish and cheap furniture
- [ ] Excess of big furniture
- [ ] Too many accessories on the wall and bookshelves

- [ ] Boring cheap accessories
- [ ] Too many rugs
- [ ] Unnecessary extra chairs
- [ ] Very unusual wall paintings (dark blue, bold brown, strong red, etc.)
- [ ] Non-essential items
- [ ] The furniture clustered on one side of the room
- [ ] Grooming items here and there
- [ ] Home office crammed with books and clutter
- [ ] Areas of excess furnishings
- [ ] Not well clipped yard; Rooms obscured by plants or furnishings;
- [ ] Full hangers

There are many possibilities to refresh the home for a better well being:

General:

- [ ] New floor coverings (in neutral shades) on kitchen and bathroom floors.
- [ ] Repair what's necessary: nobody likes a home that needs structural repairs.
- [ ] Consider: New paint indoors and eventually outdoor.
- [ ] Rugs and curtains are in a solid neutral color.
- [ ] A blanket can help disguise any furniture faults, rips or scratches.
- [ ] Don't block windows. Let the light in.
- [ ] Trim large bushes and hedges.
- [ ] Make the rooms look bigger than they actually are (with furnishing, light).
- [ ] Create space by storing appliances, dish racks and washing up soap.
- [ ] Increase the wattage of the lights in the laundry room.
- [ ] Put the lights on where you have dark furniture and poor light.
- [ ] Clear away cluttered spaces.
- [ ] Clean windows to brighten and enlarge rooms.
- [ ] Clear away any unused furniture or storage containers in all rooms.
- [ ] Arrange knickknacks in a pleasant way.
- [ ] Make the rooms alive with light, plants, chair pillows, candles.
- [ ] Plug in lamps to illuminate dark corners.
- [ ] Hide the tangled mess of cables and wires with plants.
- [ ] Artful placement of mirrors adds depth and dimension.

Living room:

- [ ] Add unique elements to shelving, bookcases and fireplace mantels.
- [ ] Use plants.
- [ ] Create crisp spaces.
- [ ] Arrange furniture.

- [ ] Give attention to spaciousness and light.
- [ ] Open curtains and blinds to let natural light in.
- [ ] Wall treatments and flooring in neutral colors and subtle patterns.
- [ ] Paint colors should be neutral whenever possible, and bright.
- [ ] Make the fireplace the focal point of the room.
- [ ] Put brightly colored pillows on the sofa.
- [ ] Add complementary accessories.
- [ ] Living room: if possible make separate areas (sitting, reading, and writing).
- [ ] Arrange furniture to create conversation areas.
- [ ] If needed: Use smaller sofas and chairs to make the room appear larger.
- [ ] Use soft fabrics (silk, lambs wool, satin) by throwing blankets over a chair or sofa.
- [ ] Highlight the fireplace by adding something nice on the mantle.
- [ ] Make the living area homey and appropriate for the time of day.

Kitchen:

- [ ] Coffee tables, kitchen counters and tables should be well organized.
- [ ] Place a nice looking candle on the kitchen table.

Bedrooms:

- [ ] Use folded quilts and blankets.
- [ ] Nice little lamps that give a warm light.

Bathrooms and toilet:

- [ ] Add baskets filled with spa treatments: scented soaps, creamy lotions.
- [ ] Put some quality lipsticks, mascara, and perfume next to the sink.
- [ ] Coordinate the colors of the towels.
- [ ] Fold and display bright towels on the dryer.

Entrance, porch, outside, garage, storeroom:

- [ ] A dark entrance needs a warm light put on.
- [ ] Place potted flowers on the front porch / entrance.
- [ ] The garage and storeroom are always in perfect order.
- [ ] Organize the space for car, bicycles, and other stuff.

Care for a healthy life style

How much do you pay for your health insurance? How much does your government contribute to maintain all the hospitals? How much do you consume and pay for medicine and medical services? Do you know that others also pay for you in case of irresponsible and self-destructive ways of living and behavior?

You have a huge amount of possibilities to consider many positive ways of living in all kind of situations. Contemplate about the components and your chances for health:

- Being active, having an interest in working, being productive and creative
- Having an objective-rational contact with reality
- Being able and flexible to adapt to realities
- Building up an internal psychical balance
- Ability to satisfy needs, also sexuality
- Being free from (or limited) use of defense mechanism (rejection, suppression)
- Tolerance of frustration, control of impulses, strengthened against stress
- Power of resistance against psychical illness
- Being free from psychical and physical symptoms
- Realistic definition of aims and goals
- Balance between dependency and independency
- Balance between stability and flexibility
- Basic confidence
- Self-identity
- Realization of individual potentials
- Autonomy and resistance against enculturation
- Self-responsibility
- Autonomous morality
- Self-understanding
- Realistic self-image
- Self-acceptance, self-esteem, and self-confidence
- Naturalness, spontaneity, sociability, genuineness and being free from façades
- Openness for experiences and feelings
- Experiences of transcendence (and its limits), "positive feelings"
- Mind-expanding: knowledge, experiences, reflections, and contemplations
- Acceptance of one's own body

- Aiming for the "good", the truth, the beauty
- Humor
- Democratic character-structure
- Need for privacy
- Orientation in meaning and values
- Ability to a constructive mastering of suffering
- Will-power

Health is much more than merely the "absence of illness". Health isn't something someone has or not, that can be lost and gained back. Health also isn't something, that is added to the human life and that can make life more beautiful and more comfortable. Health is a manner of living, is realization of life, and is a way of mastering life.

Key orientations for a holistic life style

<u>The essential questions about my life style are:</u>

- Do I feel well in (with) my body?
- Can I accept body experiences? Can I enjoy and create lust?
- What do I think and feel about housework; and how do I practice it?
- Am I aware of how I dress myself and how I buy clothes?
- What are the purposes of and how do I create (decorate) my living area?
- How do I care about my body? What is my attitude towards my personal hygiene?
- How do I make use of the media? How do I behave in front of the TV?
- How have I furnished my bedroom? How do I feel in my bedroom?
- How do I care about food? How do I choose my nourishments?
- What do I indulge myself into? When? Why? How?
- How do I deal with other people?
- What has high importance for me in my very intimate daily life?
- Which values do I live with concentration, well aimed and decisively?
- How do I confine myself against others? (e.g. visits)
- How do I let myself get stimulated with new ideas for my life?

<u>Way of living – Concrete suggestions:</u>

- ☐ Looking for positive images.
- ☐ Constructive thoughts in daily life, even with small things.
- ☐ Calming thoughts; daily 2-3 times.
- ☐ Meditate with releasing and conscious images.
- ☐ Creating mental distance, especially if thoughts are too cramped.

- [ ] Dissolving opposites with active meditation (visualization).
- [ ] Getting rid of inner suffering by elaborating it.
- [ ] Becoming free from conflicts by clarifying them with the right attitude.
- [ ] Practicing fitness.
- [ ] Considering the reality of meanings.
- [ ] Positively accepting life; taking this attitude seriously, even with unimportant things.
- [ ] Living needs with a clear mind; that means: balanced and at the right moment.
- [ ] Controlling perception; not wandering around too much with the eyes.
- [ ] Reducing stimuli; not focusing and emphasizing too much.
- [ ] In some moments becoming free from space and time through meditation.
- [ ] Thoughtful life rhythm, also in hectic professional moments.
- [ ] A healthy and holistic way of living, psychologically and physically.
- [ ] A rational and intuitive balanced understanding of one's own existence.
- [ ] Dealing with life in a combination of analytical, artistic and creative ways.
- [ ] Thinking in an integrated combination of logic and spirituality.
- [ ] A networked dealing with language and images in life issues.
- [ ] Elaborate in line and synthetically at the same time. (network thinking).
- [ ] Considering a personal biorhythm especially for specific work.
- [ ] Continuously taking a certain distance from others and life themes.
- [ ] Consciously creating and enjoying lust.
- [ ] Containing themes in talks, and guiding the communication with the participants.
- [ ] Not producing too much pressure.
- [ ] Living in a permanent learning development.
- [ ] Keeping discipline: emotional, social, mental, moral, etc.

Suggestions for the practical work. Mark what you already do:

- ➔ Writing down your dreams daily; preferably immediately after waking up
- ➔ Systematically relaxing twice a day (10 min.)
- ➔ Emptying your mind every evening with a short mental-exercise
- ➔ Keeping a rough timetable for the day with some keywords
- ➔ Practicing a short imaginary exercise on any theme every day (15 min.)
- ➔ Regularly reflecting on the past week for an hour over the weekend
- ➔ Regularly participating in training courses
- ➔ Making notes about the experiences in training courses
- ➔ Reading a book for a few hours a week about related subjects
- ➔ Meeting new people for discussions, who also practice self-education
- ➔ Try to do new things and then to evaluate the result
- ➔ Summarizing the work done and the results every few months

➜ Tackling in regular rotation every week another subsystem and theme
➜ But: continuously working is not always possible
➜ Short courses, every 3-4 months, can always be an option

Drastically reduce risks in your life

You want to have success in your life and to be happy. You love the zeitgeist of the industrial nations. You expect happiness with money, consumption, your own home, and a family or at least a partner. You believe that what you think and judge is efficient for your life aims. Your attitudes and your religion are "holy" for you. Then, take a look at what you have to expect in your life (the figures vary depending on the country):

- 50% grief over sleeping disorder
- 40-60% are overweight or even obese
- 35-45% are tantalized by constipation
- 50-70% suffer from backache or have problems with their spine
- 35% of all women in a relationship are sexually unsatisfied
- 50% of people in the medium age are endangered by alcohol consumption
- 35-50% of all marriages will end in divorce
- 9-12% suffer from migraine or daily headache
- 8-10 % suffer from depression
- 5-12% stutter, have text blindness and writing difficulties
- 7-9% have social phobia
- 6-8% have chronic fears
- 8-9% drink too much alcohol
- 0.7-0.9% suffer from cardiac fibrillation
- 1.5% occasionally have thoughts of suicide
- 11-13% suffer from chronic pain
- 0.8% suffer from impotence and many other from sexual frustrations
- 10% of children are victims of violence in their own family
- 35% of all violence happens in marriage and family
- 35% of relationships experience physical violence: 50% from women & 50% from men
- Up to 35% live in poverty or at the existence minimum
- 6-12% are unemployed, in certain areas up to 25% (or much more)
- 7-15% are under the burden of the consequences of bankruptcy
- 25-60% of retired people live in poverty or near the existence minimum

Furthermore: a great amount of people consume cocaine and many more are addicts (nicotine, alcohol, drugs of all kinds, medicine, games, consumption, chocolate, pornography, eating, watching TV, mobile phone, etc.) and additionally a lot of people can be categorized into: lonely, neglected, victims of the economy, victims of therapies (medicine; also of judiciary and administration), damaged from environmental catastrophes, ill from stress through noise and contamination – and finally there is a need to mention all those people (each third person once in their life time) suffering from psychical disorder because of their life conditions, their biography, their social environment and economic situation. The percentage of people who can't pay their debts anymore is also huge.

Politics failed! Religion is inefficient! The Zeitgeist is a circus. The economic damages are colossal! Every person has to give away 45-60% of his salary for taxes, health insurance and credit interests. The causes are essentially: Nobody bothers anymore about human values, about the psychical-spiritual (inner) life and about the interconnected responsibility of the individual actions. – Or perhaps you from today on?

Life expectancies:

Low education: reduction 7-9 years
Unemployment: reduction 12-14 years
Divorce: reduction 9-10 years
Smoking (a lot): reduction 18-22 years
Alcohol (a lot): reduction 16-23 years
Diabetes: reduction 21-31 years
High blood pressure: reduction 7-12 years

(Be careful with statistics: already today and more and more in the future, people will die from a cocktail of contamination!)

We assume: A high amount of suppressed inner conflicts and unelaborated painful experiences can reduce life expectances by up to 25 years! A chaos in the unconscious mind and not well formed psychical forces in general lead to serious psychical disorder and with that either to a significant reduction of life expectancy or to a sad life with high risks of a serious psycho-somatic disease.

Care for your psychical energy (life energy)

Sorrows and preoccupations often give a feeling of heavy weight. Negative and also positive thoughts significantly influence one's attitude towards life. Many people experience a telepathic phenomenon:

You think about somebody or you want to call a friend, and some minutes later the phone rings; your friend is on the phone. You are invited to someone's house and on the way you have a strange feeling in your stomach, something like a premonition that something will not be good there. On a public bus, you look at the neck of a person, standing 10 meters away, and suddenly this person turns towards you or starts scratching their neck.

Nervousness and inner tension infects others energetically. Empathizing the suffering of another person produces the feeling this person has. If somebody suddenly starts whining over something after having repressed it for some time, then one can feel the energetic radiation with its full intensity.

Also the mood you are in produces an energetic atmosphere. In a room where people have been with strong aggressive feelings, one can later feel the aggressive atmosphere in the air in that room.

Images and colors not only have an effect on the eyes. They activate psychical energy. Visualizing inner images (with closed eyes) lets you experience the energy of the images in the form of their meaning; e.g. a sun, a dark forest, a deep blue sky with stars, or whatever. TV advertisements with images and colors, including music, have the sole purpose of activating psychical energy in the observer. An exciting novel and an action movie can produce a very tense psychical energy. Watching wrestling or boxing passes on an energetic feeling: a feeling of being boxed, agitated, or even knocked. A movie about love certainly produces a completely different energetic wave.

Many terms in psychology and psychoanalysis are used for such experiences: Libido, Orgon-energy, drive for life, vital strength, life power, drive power, bio-energy, Eros-strength, etc.

Esoteric teachings talk about a cosmic universal energy, the emanation and the aura-energy. Magnetopathy (Mesmerism) teaches a magnetic energy, speaks about fluidum and mediumistic energy. Spiritual healing and diverse para-psychical therapies are also based on an energetic concept, interpreting a spiritual energy reality. The "Prana" in the Far East, have in their vocabulary also other terms such as "mana kundalini" and "kundalini".

We simply call this energy: the "psychical energy".

Facts about psychical energy:

→ There is energy in the human body that is not biological: the psychic energy.
→ The psychic energy is formed by thinking, experiencing, feeling, etc.
→ The psychic energy is influenced by people and the environment.
→ The psychic energy has an effect on behavior and can make psychically ill.
→ Corporal states form the psychical energy and influence the psychical energy.
→ The psychic energy can also make physically ill.
→ Through mental-training one can clean this energy state, and balance it.

There are para-psychical methods that can clean, center, strengthen the energy state, and contribute to healing processes. We have thoroughly explored this energy and its methodical potential; and we have discovered possibilities that no one up to today knows.

Give 5 examples of how you experienced the psychical energy in your daily life:

How can you improve the state of your psychical energy in your daily life?

Meditate correctly and with an aim in mind

It is easy to pray. But God cannot do anything! We are responsible to find the right transcendental access and to do what is right from the power of the inner Spirit. But one has to learn how to meditate correctly.

The fields of application are:

1. To center life energy and to relax energetically.
2. General psycho-hygiene (e.g.: Mental-Training).
3. Liberating one self from suppressed painful experiences.
4. Reflection about one's own way of living.
5. Extension of perception.
6. To understand other people.
7. Finding solutions for conflicts and problems.
8. To understand psycho-somatic disturbances.
9. Finding the meaning of life and how to live it.
10. Identifying one's state of Individuation.

It is not possible to thoroughly explore, or to transform or to communicate with the inner Spirit without meditation. Experiencing God happens by inner elaboration of the archetypes of the soul, and therefore also with meditation.

1. Concrete Imagination (visualization): Life situations from the past and present can be seen with closed eyes. The images can be interpreted psychologically and practically.

2. Symbolic Imagination (visualization): A tree means growth of life. During imagination one calls the image of a tree which shall demonstrate the state of one's own growth; or: In a store room one can find the complete inventory of the unconscious. Imagination reaches psychical realities; for example: a dry tree and the inventory in the store room reflect the state of one's own psychical-spiritual being; and with that also the content in the unconscious.

3. Contemplation: Visualizing the archetypes of the soul; e.g. life symbol, a mandala, a pyramid, the old wise man (or a wise woman), the sun, etc. Experiencing archetypes of the soul promotes the psychical-spiritual development.

4. Combination of the three ways of meditation is also possible. There are two variations one can practice: a) Active Meditation: The images and sceneries can be actively controlled and managed; either by the meditating person or by an expert. b) Passive Meditation: The meditating person lets the images go their course without influencing anything. After a few minutes such meditations should be finished (to avoid an incontrollable flood of images).

Proceeding:

Step 1: Sit or lie down comfortably.

Step 2: Determine the aim: What do you want to know? What do you want to meditate about? For what purpose?

Step 3: Determine the way of visualization: concrete, symbolic, archetypal.

Step 4: Create relaxation and be concentrated towards inside.

Step 5: Call images about your concern. Be concentrated and aim-oriented.

Step 6: Slowly let the images and sceneries proceed. At the same time, try to understand the meaning of them.

Step 7: End the meditation after 3 - 5 minutes. If you have a lot of experiences you can meditate up to 10 minutes.

Step 8: Write down the experiences of your meditation and also the feelings you had (have).

Step 9: Elaborate your experiences by interpreting it like a dream.

Step 10: Put everything which you have interpreted into the context of yourself and your real life. Formulate the appropriate conclusions.

Elaborate your transcendental experiences

A first essential experience is becoming aware that you have a spiritual intelligence (Spirit) in your psychical system (organism) that works through dreams and meditations. Only this force knows how the process of your psychical-spiritual process must proceed. This Spirit has his own values and language. The Spirit surpasses the terrestrial life and has access to the other (transcendental) world.

A second transcendental experience results from the growth of the power of love. Love surmounts the thinking by utility and balance. Love transcends the logic and the dynamic of the psychical forces. Love is first of all targeted on integrating the psychical life and on forming it to a unity and completeness. Through all evil, love is able to protect, manage and develop human life. In that sense love is a transcendental force.

A third transcendental experience can be named with "experiencing the archetypes of the soul". The path to that is contemplation, and sometimes also dreams. Archetypes are the door to another reality: the spiritual reality and the reality of meanings.

A fourth transcendental experience is the main process of Individuation. Proceeding such experiences is not only a psychological experience, but much more experiencing another reality. The process of Individuation lets a person experience the "mystery of human life", revealed through the inner experiences of the process of Individuation.

A fifth transcendental experience is the aim of Individuation. Experiencing this aim means experiencing a new human being. Through Individuation a person becomes something like a vivid copy of the Circle-Cross-Mandala. This archetype is on the other side also a copy of God.

Only by achieving the aim is it possible to experience what God is and to be close to God (by being and not simply by meditating). The new human being, having achieved the aim of Individuation, is part of the transcendental divine being.

→ How do you want to authentically and genuinely experience the transcendence with a religion that is founded on myths and dogmas?

→ How can you get access to the "truth" of the inner being, if you absolutely don't bother about your inner being?

→ The idea that one could experience the transcendence of human being and God through praying and believing is very stupid and brainsick.

1.9. Resolving Problems and Conflicts

Resolve problems and conflicts

How can you be more creative in resolving your conflicts and problems? We summarize some proposals:

- Take time to understand the problem before you start solving it
- Keep all facts clear in your mind
- Identify the facts which are especially important
- Prepare a list of questions to deal with the problem
- Try to be consciously original and to find new ideas
- It isn't ridiculous if you say anything uncommon or if you are wrong
- Get rid of cultural taboos which could undermine a solution
- Draw a diagram so you can visualize the problem
- Write down your ideas to retain important facts and to find models
- Imagine how you will solve the problem
- Go through the real elements of the problem
- Divide the problem into parts: solve a part and continue like that
- Use analogies (similar situations), examine the possibility for transfer
- Keep your mind open, if an attempt doesn't work, examine the presumption
- Use different strategies: verbal, visual, calculating, action
- If you are stuck in an attempt, try another way to go ahead for the solution
- Be watchful of strange situations. You could be near a solution
- Search for connections between different facts
- Trust your intuition. Approach a way and see where it leads to
- Try to guess the way for a solution, more and more until it goes ahead
- Think about an uncommon manner to use things from your environment
- To make a great fuss may delay, but can finally lead to the goal
- Jump over common things, try to invent new methods
- Try to be objective; evaluate your ideas as if they were alien

And never forget: Everywhere you will find people with very bad personality qualities which produce serious problems and conflicts: ignorant, dumb, arrogant, aggressive, violent, vain, greedy, despotic, dazzled, unscrupulous, disrespectful, envious, false-players, liars, hypocrites, big-mouths, cheaters, intriguers, egoists, morbid narcissists, psychopaths, and criminals.

It's really very useful to learn about these kinds of people, to protect yourself from such people, and never to let yourself be affected by such "qualities". The more you know about human life and inner life, the better you are prepared to deal with such people in a self-protecting way. Learn from life and from books!

Overcome the hard blows of your destiny

Many people experience a hard blow from destiny in their life:

A beloved person doesn't come back: traffic accident, death; another person is paralyzed caused by a traffic accident; early death of the parents; or one's own kid dies in a traffic accident; a breakdown of love; separation, divorce; unexpected unemployment; the state of the economy forces a company into bankruptcy; private bankruptcy because of manifold causes; medical diagnosis: cancer or an illness with serious consequences for rest of your life; a storm destroys homes, no insurance; drought or flood destroy professional existence; victim of robbery or murder or rape; abuse of a child or teenager; victim of all kinds of violence; victim of calumny and misuse of reputation with the consequence of destruction of existence; loss of saved money through amoral (criminal) activities of banks; victim of terrorism and war incidents; falling into poverty; and much more…

Have you already had a hard blow from destiny? Now, during your whole life you can lament, whine, rage, give up, become an alcoholic, swear vengeance, fall into depression; and as a broken person continue living in some way or form. For a certain time such a reaction is understandable, partly even necessary. But to spend the rest of your life as a broken person is never necessary! Furthermore, nobody is interested, if you succeed in finding a new life, or if you spend the rest of your life in pain and self-pity. Act now and elaborate:

- Deeply mourn for a certain time. But then: STOP!
- Reconcile with life over what happened to you!
- Find back to the high values that you can live on this earth!
- Elaborate everything that is related to the past event!

- Start finding yourself again! Discover your inner life!
- Determine new life aims that are strongly oriented to your inner life!
- Search inside for the archetypes of the soul and grow with them!
- Bid farewell from the past in very small steps!
- Organize yourself with new furniture, clothes, and everything!
- Learn a lot about the human being and become a wise person!
- Go your own path, given by your inner life!
- Fight hard, every day and this for many years in order to succeed!
- Keep a journal; find orientation in dreams and meditations!
- Your values lie in your inner being: search and live them!
- You are allowed to find back to 100% joy of life and happiness!
- Love yourself, your life; be thankful for finding your new path!
- It is not worth it to remain in defiance for the rest of your life!

Understand the source of your aggressions

The less a person knows himself and the more a person suppresses himself, the higher is his aggressive potential. It is a proven fact that frustration produces aggression, and that aggression also produces aggression. The aggressive dynamic of a person wants to infect others. The "bad" wants to force the "good" one by means of aggression to also become a "bad" person.

Fact is:

- If one has been cheated heavily, he wants to also cheat others.
- If one has experienced hate, he tends to hate too.
- If one has been humiliated, he tends to humiliate others too.
- If one has been deeply hurt, he tends to hurt others too.
- If one has never been loved, he can't love others either.
- If one has been strongly suppressed, he suppresses others too.

Variations of compensations are for example:

- Greed for money, property, power, prestige, being "Nr. 1"
- Exploiting and abusing people: work, money, sex, etc.
- Sadism in the private and business life (work).
- Belief in a Savior coming from the transcendental world.
- Believing and devoting oneself to a Fuhrer.
- Placing all hope and all happiness into the netherworld.
- Binding oneself to fanaticism and fundamentalism.

- Self-abandonment by ignoring one's own inner being.
- Self-sacrifice through suicide bombing.

If one doesn't go his path of solution by elaborating his inner conflicts and problems, he becomes ill.
Psycho-somatic diseases are complex expressions of experienced aggressions (or of one's own aggressions); in the core of the emotional energy of aggression. Such emotions activate psychical energy and this energy radiates in relation to the meaning (e.g. aggression).

Constructively dealing with aggressions (words, thoughts, emotions, actions) demands for an elaboration and resolution of the causes. Sometimes one has to change certain causal conditions. Analyzing the situation and problem further helps and demonstrates where new patterns of acting are necessary. Sometimes a new attitude about the situation of the causes and effects can help. Constructive talking is an essential instrument to resolve aggressions in a relationship.

Profound self-knowledge must also integrate the rejected and repressed realities of one's own being and biography.

Give 5 examples of how you compensate your inner state of aggression:

Give 5 examples of how you constructively deal with your aggressions:

Overcome your psychical suffering

The most increasingly widespread psychical sufferings are: depression, fear, phobias, compulsions, etc. Even more widespread are psycho-somatic disturbances and in that sense also psychical suffering: sleep disorder, headache, migraine, diffuse corporal pains, many forms of allergy, etc. In a psychical suffering we can discover a variety of aspects: unelaborated bad experiences, lack of meaning in the zeitgeist, suppressed rage, self-rejection, disappointments, frustration, repressed sexuality, depressiveness, sadness, passivity, isolation, feelings of deficiency, paralyzed will, feelings of dependency, feelings of inability, minimal self-respect, little assertiveness, feelings of not being good enough and much more.

Over 80% of people in the industrialized nations experience psychical suffering, albeit on a level that is not understood as a psychical disease. An important characteristic is that a solution cannot be found by dedicating more to a lust- and consumption-oriented life.

Animating words that are well known in life support-style groups with prayers and "take courage" support cannot change such suffering. Simple positive suggestions like "I feel better every day, more and more" is only a stupid and empty word game leading to zero effective results.

In a certain sense all these people are "healthy", but they suffer from a state that is not good all around. We could even say: the person who doesn't suffer from the absurdity of the zeitgeist, the delusion of consumption, the greed and unscrupulousness, the barbarity of the state of humanity and the earth, is really ill! And people want to fight against their inner suffering with medicines! That's really very stupid and ignorant! There are much more efficient ways for a definitive success:

- Become aware of what depresses you from inside and from your life.
- Elaborate with the right methods what is your burden.
- Give yourself self-esteem through small activities on a daily basis.
- Turn towards the hidden dominant forces.
- Find your self-esteem and your self-confidence.
- Form ego-strength through self-knowledge and self-education.
- Concentrate on the important values of your human being.
- Reconcile your past and your experienced pains.
- Clarify your repressed problems, difficulties, and conflicts.
- Find yourself; become entirely yourself with the inner Spirit.

There is nobody that doesn't have problems, difficulties or conflicts! A person that is free from that, has either elaborated everything, or is repressing everything and with that contributing more inhumanity to the world!

Organize your unsolved problems

The psychical forces start to get formed during the prenatal time. These forces later determine the course of life. The fetus reacts to the voice of the mother, of the father and the emotional environment of the parents. First patterns of reaction are formed during this time.

The baby inside the mother's body is capable of communicating kinetically. The course of the birth has a decisive psychological influence on the new-born baby: From the sensual joy to the uterine contraction, then through parturition into the glaring light.

Then the "reception": welcome? Or not welcome? This leaves traces on the memory. Reactions to the stimuli from the environment start to form. Reflexes are built up: screaming, sucking, sleeping, scrambling, withdrawing, clasping, being attentive, moving and interpreting signals.

In the early childhood the following is formed: active searching, discovering, crying, smiling, assimilating stimuli from the environment, reactions of separation, being shy with strangers, playing, patterns of behavior to activate interesting reactions and many more. Experiences of lust start to form patterns: drinking, eating, touching, sexual pre-lust, punishing, etc. These are the basic biographical experiences, the psychical foundation of the development of life. During childhood the forming of the concrete-operational and formal thinking starts. This goes on until the end of youth.

Find out your unsolved problems from the past and your current critical life concerns:

☐ Family: Parents, Stepparents, brothers and sisters, relatives, style of education, formation, work, social conditions, absences (separation, death)

☐ Relationships out of the family environment: acquaintances, neighbors, work colleagues, priests, doctors, counselors, teachers, ethnic groups

☐ Friendships, love relationships, marriage

☐ Own family, children, the family of the partner, patterns of relationships

☐ Living, living atmosphere, quality of living and the environment, moving

☐ Body, sexuality, sex education, being man / woman, the culture in the bathroom, pregnancy (course, termination), menstruation

☐ Nutrition, culture of eating and drinking

☐ Illnesses, disturbances, suffering, operation, therapy, addiction (alcohol, tobacco, medicines, drugs, eating, gambling)

☐ Pre-school, primary and secondary school, further education, learning, education, subjects, certificates, change of school

☐ Professional formation, working, work activities, workplace, unemployment

- [ ] Leisure places and activities, hobbies, holidays, weekends, mobility

- [ ] Religious practices, belief, philosophy of life, esoteric, sects, psycho-religious movements (organizations)

- [ ] Political socialization, political events, activities, ecological movements

- [ ] Cultural life, reading (newspaper, magazines, books), music, art, film, theatre, television

- [ ] Objects, articles of consumption, clothes, money, items of values

- [ ] Psycho-social Institutions: unemployment insurance, public welfare, counseling, social work centers, homes, insurance benefit

- [ ] House work, life administration (e.g. taxes, insurances)

- [ ] Sleeping (environment, habits, dreams)

- [ ] Criminality (victim, actor)

- [ ] Ecological environment: air and water pollution, traffic, noise, overpopulation, poverty, rubbish, cruelty to animals, consumption of energy, catastrophes, violence, riots, war

The 6 strategic steps to solve problems

Mastering problems and difficulties requires a plan and a strategy. That means: a systematic, open and transparent planning of possible solutions. Few people do this in their daily life. The effects are evident: bad solutions, no solutions at all, endless trials without any success and a tormenting increase in more and more problems.

The 6 strategic steps to solve problems are:

1st Step: Analyzing and classifying the problem.

- What is the problem? How did it come about? How important is the problem?
- What is part of the problem? Which institution is involved? Who is involved?
- What is my ideal? Which possibilities are given?

2nd Step: Identifying the deficit of information, life-knowledge, theories, and ideas.

- What is the lack of facts, knowledge, theories and ideas?
- Which connections do I not understand?
- Structure ideas and facts, then define the problem in a new way.

3rd Step: Constructing theories and procuring the necessary material (information).

- Search for connections and explanations (causes-effects; networking).
- Construct a diagram (draw, course-diagram, mind-mapping, etc.).
- Managing a problem is always also a learning process for all people involved.

4th Step: Draft a possible solution on the basic of theories (X is because of Y).

- Examine if a solution is feasible. Define the standards of the solution.
- Prepare the decisions. Analyze the concomitant phenomenon and effects.

5th Step: Realizing the plan of a solution.

- Action!

6th Step: Evaluation and examination of the success.

- If necessary, make corrections and try again in a new way.

Everybody has their own individual capacity to solve problems, their own specific factors that hinder a solution as well as their own special abilities to solve problems. Creativity is decisive. Motivation is essential. Mental fitness is a precondition.

The essential question is:

Do you want to solve the problem, or do you prefer to live with it for the next few years, until one day it disappears – or perhaps until it increases dramatically?

The destructiveness of exaggerated narcissism

Exaggerated Narcissism is a type of neurosis; characteristics are:

1. A self-image that is in its tendency grandiose, infantile, archaic and overvalued.

2. Performances serve as a compensation for a weak ego. Performance tends to increase the ego and not the performance of a task. The world of the objects serves for the increase of the ego; this can be for example a car, money, furniture, clothes, properties, and jewels. Other people are perceived in the interest of a personal need / satisfaction; become objects in that context.

3. The identification with a leader figure and the "best of the world" in politics, economy, sports, show business, etc., serves to increase the ego. Narcissistic people admire and idealize highest performances, the "number 1", the best, the most powerful men, the most beautiful women, and the richest in the world, etc. Identification with a football club or other clubs with special highest performance demands and also identification with esoteric or religious communities serves to increase the ego.

4. The increase of the ego is also a fact in exaggerated self-perceptions and self-representations. Such an ego demonstrates itself on the one hand as huge and strong and on the other hand is mostly weak and very vulnerable. Another indication for narcissism is an exaggerated and inappropriate care, protection, fusion, indirect control and a tendency for harmonizing with other people or groups.

5. The identification with objects, people or institutions in most cases, has a background tone of sexualizing an object or person – as if it would have to do with sex or being enamored.

6. Furthermore we can acknowledge: a deficit of ability to accept anxiety, an insufficient drive control, inaccessibility as a mask, a deficient relation to the reality (perception and dealing with), a lack of outpace, partial excess, over idealizing father and mother and often teachers or priests.

7. Finally we can identify narcissism behind an identification with a religion or a religious community promising salvation, denying that a person has to elaborate his salvations himself, e.g. with personality education and Individuation.

Causes of exaggerated narcissism include:

- [ ] A deficit of love, warmth, goodness and human attention during childhood.
- [ ] A strong determination through others with rigid roles during the educational phase.
- [ ] Repressing genital lust through educational norms and control
- [ ] Experiences of loneliness, abandonment, separation and exclusion.
- [ ] Deficient positive esteem as a person during childhood and youth.
- [ ] A strong tendency to underestimate one's own values, forced through education.
- [ ] Repression of feelings, of problems with trust and dedication.
- [ ] A very strong super-ego, coercing to suppress and with that to life lies.
- [ ] Emotions of powerlessness and ego-weakness (etc.) caused by education.

The more a person is ready to accept his psychical-spiritual organism (the psyche) and to understand it as his being, the more he is ready to form it into an all-sided and well-balanced organism. Self-education and Individuation change the relation to oneself, to others, and to the elements of the real world, to God and his institutions on earth.

How to protect yourself from online scammers

Fact is: No man has the time to check 20-100 blacklists or more to find out if the girl he is corresponding with online is already blacklisted somewhere; especially considering that most men are corresponding with several girls at the same time.

Therefore, each man that wants to find love in the cyber world must first inform himself about this disaster and especially about how scammers act.

To give a clear orientation about how to identify scammers, we give the necessary insight and criteria. We also give some very important rules to help avoid becoming a victim of a scammer. The most important rule is as simple as this: Never send money to a person you have not met before! Unfortunately, once in love and excited, men (sometimes also women) forget about this principal rule very fast.

General advice to avoid scammers:

1. Use "free" dating sites very carefully and overall only nationally.
2. Ask specific questions and scrutinize her answers as well as everything that she writes.

162

3. In general, always read letters very carefully: identify the "Red flags" and don't get carried away before you feel safe.
4. Hire someone to do a background check: identity, address, education, profession, etc.
5. Check with search engines: scammer + blacklist + Name + email address.
6. Get support from a confirmed service firm when the time arrives for a visit.
7. If she sends very hot photos don't get crazy about her and don't lose your mind.
8. Wonderful words of love, trust and promises are never enough to fully trust someone!
9. Never forget: Until her identity is verified you never objectively know what is real!
10. Do not visit a girl if you don't have her identity verified by a professional service.
11. Be informed: Regularly read websites about scammers and consult online blacklists.
12. Get informed about her documents, visa, residence, and the marriage paperwork.
13. Never say how much you earn; don't speak about your possessions.
14. Give your love safety with a professional service for her to travel to your country.
15. Do you feel uncomfortable? Do the correspondences make you stressed? End it!
16. Don't use your personal email address. Create a special email address.
17. Never use a password that you also use for other purposes.
18. Be careful with international cell phone numbers; it can cost you a lot of money.

Special advice:

If you use a paid website where you can contact standard-members with or without a special additional fee, do not contact standard-members from abroad! Such websites promote the scammer pest for their own sake.

More and more scammers and gangs are acting on paid websites, even paying for premium membership. They assume that on such dating websites they can find wealthier men than on free websites where the penniless men prefer to search for their love.

Reasons behind online dating failure

The rate of success in finding love in the cyber world is estimated as very low in relation to the amount of correspondences (mails/chats) that end in failure. The main reasons for failed online dating attempts are not simply given by the cyber world of love as a greatly reduced reality, the absence of the "right partner", or a lack of serious attitudes from one or both sides.

One fundamental reason is that countless scammers poison the cyber world of love and produce a disaster in general. Many men are totally desperate after making experiences with scammers, having wasted a lot of time and lost a lot of money, and therefore also lost their hope to find love in the romance cyber world. We know that a lot of men only want to receive hot photos, have sex-oriented chats, and abuse women. There are also a lot of women which send hot photos and engage in hot chats or emails: in most cases these are scammers! Many men (in the online dating world) are married and have a family. They are looking for a sexual adventure or for a lover in a foreign country – not for true love!

Another reason that many online dating attempts fail, is that a huge number of men and women are simply not prepared for love and a real relationship; they solely like corresponding online, experiencing it as an entertainment. In general, a lot of men and women merely create an illusionary dream world with "cyber love". There is very little hope for an ever lasting love in such cases.

Significant reasons for cyber love failure include:

- The person doesn't see the one from 50-100 possible partners "made" for him / her.
- The person misinterprets important components from his / her letters.
- The person feels doubt and nobody helps him / her to clarify the concern.
- The person gives up because he /she can't get professional support.
- The person doesn't see the psychological and spiritual potential of the woman / man.
- The person is too focused on his / her illusionary "dream love".
- The person is a victim of self-infatuation.
- The person is stubborn and doesn't want to learn, change, or grow.
- The person is unconsciously not prepared and not ready for love and a real relationship.
- The person doesn't listen to his / her intuition.
- The person doesn't give attention to his / her body reactions (emotional intelligence).

- The person doesn't identify any kind of hints that show success is not possible.

Many men and women are impatient, give up with the first little disagreement or uncomfortable "problem" in the cyber relationship, still weak and easily breakable. The fact, that a person has a thousand and more other options in the cyber world of love, is great – but it is also a dangerous trap. When the first small "problems" arise while corresponding with someone, then they break it off! It is so simple to just jump from one candidate to the next and even switch dating website if need be.

Top 5 essential rules to avoid scammers

Fact is: In today's world, wherever you turn and regardless of what you do, you face the danger of being confronted with scammers and people who want to cheat or deceive you. Whether it is in your private life or social environment, at work or in your business life – scammers can be everywhere.

ANTI-SCAM RULE 1: Never take everything at face value

A person you have just met may overwhelm you with love and friendship. Never base substantial decisions on such "love" and "friendship". Love, friendship as well as any partnership in business must always be based on trust, and trust in turn should be based on factual experiences. There is a saying that goes: "When the going gets tough, the tough get going". Translate this to your life.

ANTI-SCAM RULE 2: Always double check everything when money is involved

Wherever there is money involved, you are in danger of falling victim to a scammer, be it on a small or big scale. The cashier at the supermarket may cheat you with the change. The sales person may deceive you with the small print in a contract. The real estate agent may scam you into purchasing illegal property. Whatever the situation, always double check everything when money is involved.

ANTI-SCAM RULE 3: If it sounds too good to be true, it most probably is

In today's fast moving world, one is often confronted with "opportunities" or with fast impulse decisions over a great deal. Whatever the situation (private or business), if it sounds too good to be true, it most probably is. In any case, check everything twice and "sleep over it" before taking a decision unless you are confident and experienced in the situation.

ANTI-SCAM RULE 4: When signing any contract, always envision all possible outcomes

A contract can be great but it can also result in a complete drama. Always read the fine print and take into account any possible scenarios and see if you feel ok about the results. If you don't, then don't sign! Whether it is your mortgage or a telephone contract, always beware of the fine print.

ANTI-SCAM RULE 5: Guarantees are always as worthy as the company or person behind them

This one doesn't need a lot of explanation. If the company offering a guarantee is a fly by night operation, then your guarantee is worthless. If the person guaranteeing you something is not trustworthy, then the guarantee isn't trustworthy either.

1.10. Love, Relationship, Sex

Prepare yourself for love and a relationship

Ask yourself if you are able to say to your partner:

"I give my best for you and our real life together; see it as a guarantee from my mind and soul".

This promise includes:

- to understand you in your verbal and non-verbal expressions,
- to support you,
- to not abuse your weaknesses,
- to find compromises,
- to constructively deal with disagreements and arguments,
- to be a "strong shoulder" for you when you need it,
- to console you in sad moments,
- to encourage and assist you,
- to satisfy your needs and desires in a way you feel comfortable with,
- to balance my interests with your interests,
- to respect your feelings and emotional limits,
- to clarify misinterpretation and misunderstanding,
- to care for you and your being (mind, soul, heart, desires, body, health),
- to promote your psychological and spiritual development,
- to respect the rules of partnership,
- to communicate constructively,
- to understand your dreams and thoughts and opinions,
- to objectively discuss based on correct information,
- to always give you the utmost attention,
- to give you opportunities to realize your talents, visions, self-expressions,
- to elaborate important decisions with you in a democratic way,
- to never blackmail or force you against your soul,
- to respect and integrate all your qualities as a complementary part of me,
- to stay with you in good and bad times,
- to give highest priority to our love and always to take care of this love.

However the character of the nature of a woman (man) you have chosen is formed, and however the multicultural differences will manifest themselves in daily life, she (he) is as well as you, a human being with psychical functions and dispositions as we all are! Are these functions and dispositions well formed for love, relationship and life?

Love starts with the complete dedication to one's own psychical life and fully integrating it. Accepting, caring, and letting one's own life grow consciously with Spirit and responsibility is genuine self-love. This occupation with one's self leads the person to a unity and wholeness, and to inner freedom. Self-love promotes this freedom. Human life is first of all what a human being is with his life energy, his feelings, his thinking, his needs, his intelligence, his will, and his inner Spirit. Acting is also an expression of life. Love is essential in daily acting. A person turning towards all these forces, building them in a balanced way, and realizing life rooted in this life, loves himself in a genuine and evolutionary way.

Prepare yourself for love

You want to know if you are able to love and to live a relationship. You want to know what is hindering you in developing a serious relationship, maybe even with an aim to getting married. You want to know the risks on your side for friendship, love and relationship failure. You want to know what and how you can improve your personality qualities to achieve success in friendship, love, relationship and sex.

This self-analysis-guide is for personal reflections with an aim to achieve the best preparation and foundation for friendship, love and relationship. Choose from the following list, the subject that concerns you. Write down your reflections, thoughts, feelings, facts, and the answers to the given questions. Then start to understand the psychological pattern of your concern.

1. Concern subject 1: Describe your experiences with cyber love. What have you done? What did you not like? What went wrong? What did you like? Which was your worst experience? What do you expect about the proceeding of your cyber love correspondences?

2. Concern subject 2: What are your 3 most wonderful wishes you want to have fulfilled in your life? Give 3 concrete wonderful experiences you have lived in the past with a partner. What does your future partner need in order to be able to live with you such wonderful experiences again?

3. Concern subject 3: How should your first meeting with a possible partner proceed? What do you expect from your partner during this meeting? What will you want to talk about? Give 5 questions you will ask your partner. What will you absolutely not want to talk about?

4. Concern subject 4: Give 10 personality qualities your partner should have for you to feel safe with him / her. What convinces you that you can fully trust in your partner? Describe 5 behavior patterns your partner must express in daily life that show that he / she loves you.

5. Concern subject 5: Try to remember your early childhood. What are your 3 earliest memories that come to your mind? Describe your mother in your childhood with 5 words. Describe your father in your childhood with 5 words. What have you missed in your childhood and youth?

6. Concern subject 6: Describe with some keywords the 3 worst experiences you made in your life. Give 3 examples you never want to experience from your partner. What will you do so that such bad experiences will never happen to you again?

7. Concern subject 7: Imagine you are 80 years old and you roll up your past. What do you wish to concretely see about the relationship you have lived? What do you concretely wish to see about your personal life and development you have lived?

8. Concern subject 8: What do you think are the qualities you and your partner need to make love and relationship work? Give 10 keywords. Give some ideas of how you can improve your qualities. What will you suggest to your partner to improve his/her qualities?

9. Concern subject 9: How do you react in situations of misunderstanding, quarrels, and disagreements with your partner? What do you concretely expect from your partner in such situations? Give some "rules" about how to efficiently and constructively deal with such situations.

10. Concern subject 10: What do you absolutely not like in the sexual behavior of your partner? How do you tell your partner about your secret sexual dreams that you want to live? How do you react if your partner starts telling you about how he/she would like to make love to you?

11. Concern subject 11: What is important to you in your daily life together with your partner? Give 5 values that you want to live in your life and relationship. How will you contribute to live everything that is important to you for happiness with your partner on a daily basis? Give 5 examples.

12. Concern subject 12: What are your difficult (critical) character traits? What are your weaknesses in relationship matters? What makes you easily nervous or angry about your partner? Give some concrete keywords. How can you improve? Make suggestions.

How would you tell people that they need to prepare themselves for love?

Success in looking for a partner

Some suggestions to consider:

- Choose a really good person to be with for yourself; "the best" doesn't exist!
- You decide with whom you begin a relationship and who you will marry.
- Don't have unrealistic expectations; these will lead to serious conflicts.
- 10 qualitative similarities have higher importance than one hundred minor differences.
- Cultural differences enormously enrich relationships, life, and expressions of love.
- Be very sensitive and see what your partner is unhappy about.
- You want this person as your partner? Do as much as you can to love him/her!
- An open communication every day and always in any situation is the key to success!
- Always live and protect the good human values and above all: love and trust!
- Mutual care, support, understanding, and help whenever needed are expressions of love.
- Your partner's culture is never the center and source of life. The inner being of both partners is the source of life!
- For both: Make your partner happy every day – mutually! That's wonderful!

- Learning from each other and together in every day life is the power of love!

Success in finding the right partner depends on much more than feelings of love and being excited about the other person. If your aim is marriage, then it's also about sharing the existence on earth. This is a life project! You should also consider that you and your partner will both grow psychologically and spiritually. With the years your personality and that of your partner will differentiate and change.

You will have to face many challenges during your life together. It is important to find the right partner for such a life project. But much more important will be the way of taking the daily relationship and life in general into your hands. To succeed in the varied challenges life will pose you, you need to learn about human beings, about inner life, about many fields of life, including dealing with money, education of children, managing family life, balancing all interests, changes of working situations, etc.

Therefore, the foundation of true love and a real relationship in the first 2-3 years is primordial. Some attitudes are essential and indispensable to succeed: honesty, trust, faithfulness, understanding, cooperation, complete transparency, a satisfying sexuality, and always a fair and open way of communication about everything. Both partners must contribute in creating a stable and secure foundation on a daily basis.

You can choose the right partner and start with true love. But you may fail if you don't learn about love, relationships, sexuality, inner life, personal development, family life, children's development and education, dealing with money and insurances (with contracts in general), and about life in general.

How do you build up the foundation of true love? Give examples:

33 principles to make a relationship work

A relationship includes everything: real life, inner life, character, life aims, work, money, environment, as well as a whole lot more. The abilities to manage all life issues and respecting certain rules with the partner are an indispensable condition for a successful relationship. Comment on the state of your current relationship or your experiences in the past to each statement:

1. Partnership is something especially valuable.
2. Mutual interest in the daily reality.
3. Accepting conflicts and mastering experiences.

4. Respect for differences (Character, gender).
5. Mutuality and equality (of rank).
6. Alternating closeness and distance in living together.
7. The biography of both as a part of the self-identity.
8. Understanding the differences and mutuality.
9. Respecting the limits of the partner and the partner's "world".
10. Daily life as a space of conscious communication.
11. Permanent animation and formation of love.
12. Daily discussion of all common questions.
13. No mutual balance of errors (mistakes).
14. Self-realization as a dedication to one self.
15. Reason and intelligence are basically supporting functions.
16. Eroticism and falling in love have their place in the normality of daily life.
17. Both with a high level of self-management.
18. Accepting moments of symbiotic emotions.
19. Accepting tensions and risks.
20. Mutual acceptance and satisfaction of sexual lust.
21. No mutual demand on possession of the wholeness of being.
22. Seduction and lust as animating forces.
23. Mutual sexual satisfaction without reduction of autonomy.
24. Capacity and effort for understanding.
25. Mutual constructive dealing with the inner child.
26. Periodic experiences of transformation of the self-identity.
27. Mutual support on the ego-feeling and the sexual experience.
28. Mutual realization of the femininity and masculinity.
29. Common solution in objective questions.
30. Partly common elaboration of the unconscious (biography).
31. Common orientation on dreams, intuition and meditation.
32. Mutual enrichment with a creative use of the leisure time.
33. Discussed and accepted distribution of roles.

The golden rules of a constructive partnership

The expectations of a relationship are enormous. On the other hand the sufferings and difficulties in many relationships speak volumes. Humans long for harmony, love, happiness, tenderness, joy, fulfillment and peace through being together.

Longing for love, for being in love, for eroticism and for lust experiences causes a quantity of illusions and hopes that nearly all crumble away over the years.

There are many 'arrangements' that sometimes appear as the only solution. The right understanding of a modern partnership can solve most critical collisions and make a great relationship life possible. Create success with your relationship by always considering the golden rules...
Look at the golden rules in the following context:

Both partners have a complex psychical life. Both have a biography with nearly infinite conditioned experiences. The life history of both contains a lot of disordered, unelaborated and connected life issues.

Both live in a social system - family, acquaintances, and friends, colleagues -, in a specific cultural environment and in a working world. Both have their habits, their patterns of behavior, their talents, and their antipathies towards things, human beings and attitudes.

Both have an individual body experience, an individual lust-experience, habits of eating and clothing, habits of movements, a kind of care for the body and a relation to nature and animals.

A huge amount of beliefs, attitudes and small "values" stay combined or in contradiction. Feelings, psycho-dynamism and biorhythm are also different.

Ultimately there is also an indissoluble genuine difference between man and woman.

Live the golden rules of a constructive partnership:

1. A partnership is not equal to a relationship, but contains specific characteristics.
2. Mutual interest for daily reality is essential for both partners.
3. Openness for the real life of both partners always also contains conflicts.
4. Partners respect each other in their different being (character, gender).
5. Reciprocity (reversibility) and thus equal standing are considered to be principles.
6. Closeness and distance periodically, form a normal part of being together.
7. The biography of each partner is as important as the respective identities.
8. Love promotes Individuation, and thus the individual human creation.
9. Partners communicate about their differences and the things they have in common.
10. A partnership is not a static state according to a contract, but a process.
11. Partners respect the limitations of each other and the "world" of the other.
12. Partners know that limits can't be crossed at any time.

13. Daily life takes up a central space that has to be organized by talking about it.
14. Love in the partnership must be regularly stimulated and formed.
15. A partnership regulates the common things by communication.
16. The power-situation is balanced, and has to be worked at, daily.
17. In the partnership the mistakes of both partners are not calculated.
18. Self-realization (forming of the identity) implies self-devotion.
19. Reason and intelligence are basic functions, but they don't guarantee love.
20. Eroticism and being in love have their place in the normality of daily life.
21. To live in a partnership is strenuous and demands a qualified self-management.
22. Moments of symbiotic feelings may have a place in the normality of the daily life.
23. Partnership-like love isn't possible without tensions and risks.
24. The partners don't "possess" each other with their whole being.
25. Seduction and lust are a natural joyful need and creative drive.
26. The mutual dependence of sexual satisfaction is not against autonomy.
27. The ability to understand belongs to the ability for love; sometimes this is strenuous.
28. Partners can deal with the "inner child" of each other.
29. The parallel development of identity stands in a reciprocal dynamism.
30. Both partners know that every few years the self-identity changes.
31. In a partnership ego-feelings and sexual experiences are encouraged.
32. Both partners mutually create their femininity and masculinity.
33. Both are a "team", also by solving objective questions.
34. Working out the unconscious life (the biography) is partly a shared activity.
35. Both partners commonly orientate themselves through their dreams, intuitions and meditations.
36. Both partners mutually enrich each other with creative actions during their leisure.
37. In a partnership a role division can be accepted.

Create a constructive relationship

- Each person continuously and profoundly practices self-knowledge and personal development. Each person tries in his own ways to realize his inner evolutionary human being.
- Regularly giving effort to understand oneself and the other. To do so we need the ability to communicate, to listen, and to express ourselves in many ways.
- Seriously dealing with one's own dreams. Both mutually promoting this effort. The power of dreams (the inner spirit) shows us what to say and

what to do for the relationship to grow and strengthen itself constructively.

- Accepting the complexity of the psychical life. This implies that both partners acquire practical knowledge; and maybe sometimes participate in a course / seminar.

- Steadily discovering the partner, explaining oneself and accepting the partner in a permanent development of his evolutionary human being – all life long!

- Mutually promoting the all-sided development of becoming a man (respectively a woman) allowing for the inner-psychical opposite gender pole (Anima, Animus) to be formed.

- Elaborating the basic values together, talking about and clarifying attitudes and beliefs, revising all this if desirable (necessary) or simply balancing them.

- To understand self-management as a partnership matter; means: finding rules for living together, e.g. order, punctuality, housework, areas of responsibility, the time for serious talks or for relaxation, making lists for purchases and shopping, distraction (activities) in leisure, and holiday plans, etc.

- Create a cozy home where both feel comfortable and each one has his space for reading books, writing, computer, administrative paperwork, etc.

- Forming one's own self-identity always oriented towards the partner (the opposite gender).

- Using free time for other contacts, a hobby or engagements; but not to compensate for something missing in the relationship and / or personal life (e.g. understanding).

- Regularly creating common experiences for enrichment and joy. That can also mean relaxing together or simply being with the partner and expressing: "It's wonderful to be with you and have you in my life."

- Talking about everything, also small matters and finding understanding. To be transparent about activities concerning both; to prepare such activities and to talk about them before and after. Both promoting each other in all life skills.

- To understand and work out the common biography of the relationship with the biography of each other. The common biography and the common future plans form a common couple-identity.

- To respect that each one always remains a unique person in becoming and growing; never can a person "dissolve" himself in the partner. Both partners know, respect and promote the understanding that both have to learn about the psychical life, love, feelings, and sex all their life.

- To promote and use creativity in all areas of life, also in sex. Talking about it without being ashamed or making one self ridiculous.
- To learn to argue without controlling each other with life lies or games of rejection (manipulations). Respecting the rules of communication and learn the strategies of problem resolving makes it efficient.
- Not to balance the mistakes of each other. Learning to forgive and to reconcile, also after a heavy quarrel. This demands developing and strengthening the ability to love.
- To reduce life lies without reproaching each other and giving higher importance to the psychical life than to the external values.

➔ What is your partner in your relationship without his / her inner psychical life?

➔ What are you if your partner doesn't love your inner life?

The top 20 tips to strengthen a relationship

1. There are a lot of starting possibilities, how to avoid a relationship with quarrels and conflicts. The top 20 tips for strengthening a relationship are:
2. Each partner thoroughly practices ongoing self-knowledge and Individuation in his own way.
3. Each partner regularly makes efforts to understand themselves and the partner.
4. Each partner seriously deals with his or her own dreams. Both promote these efforts. Thereby, the power that creates the dreams – the inner spirit – perfectly knows how to guide each one (with dreams) to aim for a constructive growth of the relationship.
5. Both partners accept and integrate the complexity of the psychical life. This presupposes that both acquire knowledge, e.g. through courses.
6. Each one explores the other regularly, explains oneself clearly and accepts the partner as a human being in a permanent evolutionary process of growth.
7. Both partners mutually promote each other in the all-sided development of being a man / a woman, considering the inner images about the other gender, called "anima" and "animus" that also have to be formed.
8. Through dialogue, exploring and forming the basic values, both partners clarify the attitudes and beliefs, and in case working out in common a revision.
9. Both partners understand self-management as a matter of partnership, forming roles for the daily living together: order, punctuality, housework, responsibilities, moments for serious discussions and relaxation, lists for shopping, ideas for leisure and holidays, etc.

10. Both partners create a "home" atmosphere to feel well and a place for each one for reading, books, writing, administrations, etc.
11. Each one forms his self-identity with a strong focus on the partner (the other gender), being aware of this reality, talking about and differentiating it.
12. Both partners have some contacts in their leisure; have a hobby or a cultural (social) activity. But this life area shouldn't be an area of replacement for an unsatisfied relationship.
13. Both partners regularly create common experiences to enjoy life. Part of that are moments of common relaxation and of a non-verbal being together in the sense of: "It is beautiful, that you are here in my life!"
14. Both partners talk about everything concerning life, also about petty matters. Acting in the interest of both has to be transparent, prepared and discussed (before / after). Both partners promote the other in his life skills.
15. Each partners talks about his personal biography and the common history of their relationship; both try to understand and to elaborate these experiences. The common history of a relationship and the common plans for the future also form a sort of partner-identity.
16. Both respect that each partner stays for ever in his own being and development as an individual; and that they can never become a symbiosis. Both partners know, respect and promote the attitude that each one has to learn a lot during their whole life about psychical life, love, emotions and sex.
17. Both partners regularly stimulate creative activities in all life areas, also in the sexual life. Both can talk about everything without feeling ridiculed or being ashamed.
18. Both partners learn how to argue without controlling each other with life lies and defense games. Both consider the communication roles and the strategies for problem solving.
19. Both partners do not mutually balance their errors. Both learn to forgive and to reconcile, also after a heavy fight. The ability to love with its development and reinforcement demands this.
20. Both partners reduce their own life lies without reproach and give higher importance to the psychical life than to the external values.

Resolving relationship conflicts

Relationship conflicts are frequently caused by the unconscious psychical life. Ideals, experiences with the parents, fears, norms and a whole lot more influence the everyday life of a relationship. Deficits in the childhood long to be satisfied later on in life. But the partner can never fill such a deficit.

If a person has not learnt about his own psychical life and how to form it, he can not acknowledge nor form the psychical life of the partner or promote a constructive forming way.

That's why the psyche produces complex conflicts in a relationship. The inevitable result is divorce or a life long of disrupted relationships.

The chosen partner often shows one's own natural aspects, patterns of values and attitudes. Furthermore each one identifies the partner with his own ideals. He ignores the reality until it breaks through. Then both reproach each other with: "I suffer because you ...", "You reject me because you ...", "You dominate me ...", "You are tyrannical ...", "If you would be more mature we could ...", "If I would not have married you I would be happy ...", "Go away, I don't need you ...". Both partners displace the real reality with that because in such accusations one is, in most cases what the other one has in himself (psychologically).

Quarrels in a relationship are certainly normal. But even minor nagging about meals, clothes or punctuality can grow with time to a serious conflict. If a couple doesn't learn how to deal with tensions and conflicts by talking about them, the relationship life feels more and more like a burden and both tend to withdraw. There are always little things that can be annoying more and more as time passes by. If partners don't communicate, they will find themselves in a cul-de-sac without a way out anymore.

Conflicts in a relationship are often also a conflict with oneself. The "bad" in the other is the own unseen "bad" (aspect). Hostile images grow and get projected. The own dark shadows (aspects of the personality) reflect on the partner. The own super values and ideals of perfectionism destroy a relationship and the partner. Human encounters convert into life lies.

The path for a solution is clear:

➜ If you want to understand your partner and relationship, you must first understand yourself.

➜ If you don't see your own psychical life, you can't see the psychical life of your partner.

➜ One's own self-relation is reflected in all relationship conflicts.

Willingness, readiness, and ability to work out any and every issue and difficulty that will come up, expressed as a mutual life long commitment, is much more important than "high match" in interest, hobbies, tastes, and all the wonderful feelings of being in love.

Describe a relationship conflict:
The "critical" aspect of the conflict is:
Describe how to successfully deal with this conflict:

The main causes of love problems

Without psychical education, every relationship will sooner or later be confronted with the repetitions of the individual experiences from the childhood (mark what you have experienced):

- ☐ Imitating mother (as woman)
- ☐ Imitating father (as man)
- ☐ Repeating parental patterns of quarrelling
- ☐ Repetition of parental punishing patterns
- ☐ Effects of super-ego, formed in childhood
- ☐ Linked to familiar patterns of value
- ☐ Repetition of typical daily patterns
- ☐ Imitating the language of the parents
- ☐ Reactivation of early relation to the parents
- ☐ Making up for earlier trials to break free
- ☐ Trying to satisfy deficits from childhood
- ☐ Making up for unfinished puberty
- ☐ Anxiety about being separated from parents
- ☐ Style of parental talk at the table
- ☐ Patterns of conflict concerning house work
- ☐ Escape to mother/father (as protection)

Varied situations arise in the daily life of a relationship, which can cause a quarrel:

- ▪ Not clearly and concretely expressing one's own needs, also for leisure.
- ▪ Misunderstandings (e.g. expected behavior) because of unclear communication.
- ▪ Ignoring something with the purpose of avoiding arguments.
- ▪ Not giving importance to one's own feelings and to the one's of the partner.
- ▪ Excessive preoccupation with oneself, instead of being concentrated on the present

- To feel excellent by being stressed and in the meantime giving low attention to the partner.
- Starting an important communication at an inappropriate time and frame.
- Planning and taking decisions about what is important and urgent too late.
- Eating and drinking, also watching TV, because of frustration and boredom.
- To please the partner in a way one basically doesn't want to.
- Not admitting to be deeply preoccupied with one self.
- To behave aggressively in order to create distance or to suppress something.
- To behave affectedly, to play the offended and annoyed person.
- Not being punctual as a hidden way of manipulating the partner.
- Making a mess as a form of a strike or protest in relationship matters.
- Being unsatisfied as a result of a deficit of common life aims.
- Problems with money and disagreements about dealing with money (consumption).
- All life lies create arguments as soon as the partner refuses them.

To find new views and new attitudes:

- Talking to each other is a learning process; e.g. contemplating about talking.
- Every partnership is sometimes faced with strong arguments.
- Some quarrels may cover deeper emotions; e.g. about love and trust.
- To have a strong confrontation with the partner is sometimes necessary.
- With the duration of a relationship differences may grow too.
- Arguments about banalities are normal; e.g. organization, house work, cooking, etc.
- The total harmony doesn't exist; this is a life lie.
- If one creates a baby, one must know: The sex life will change from that day on.
- A humiliating criticism at work often affects the life at home.
- Frustration at work sometimes rapidly converts into a frustration in the relationship.
- Good friends can sometimes produce even more problems in a difficult situation.
- Dogmas and ideologies are poison for a partnership with Individuation.

> → **Sometimes one has to contemplate: "Do I really want to destroy my relationship?"**

Resolving conflicts in a relationship demands an ability to love, also to acknowledge that the destiny of a relationship depends on how the partners deal with polarities: the space they want to give for experiencing, passive enjoyments and activities; mutual interplay with a more active and passive role; the limits they give to exploring and acting or suppressing, etc.

*The inner system of values of both partners, even if it is subliminal over a long period of time can sometimes push itself more and more into the daily life. Aspects are: ideological, philosophical and religious ideas. If these values can't be communicated, reflected and revised, severe tensions and conflicts start arising.

Some values and attitudes include:

- Order in the household. My solution is:
- Distribution of work and roles. My solution is:
- Sexual experience and behavior. My solution is:
- Organizing meetings and visits. My solution is:
- Fidelity and adultery. My solution is:
- Masculine and feminine emancipation. My solution is:
- Judging aggression. My solution is:
- Adaptability and being creative. My solution is:
- Termination of pregnancy. My solution is:
- Needs for autonomy and freedom. My solution is:
- Religious and spiritual practice. My solution is:
- Importance of personality education. My solution is:

Hidden realities of a new relationship

All men and woman have varied psychological qualities in many aspects: in their way of thinking and expressing feelings, character traits, attitudes, spiritual values, reliability, honesty, faith, moral behavior, communication and understanding, knowledge and wisdom about life and love, ability to express affection and love, readiness to receive love, skills for living a relationship (e.g. making compromises) and dealing with life (misinterpretations, disagreements, etc.), manifold character expressions, and an unconscious mind (often full of unresolved conflicts, traumas, and complexes from the past).

All these psychological realities work as a "coding" in the unconscious mind for finding a partner, for living love, sex and a relationship. In the world of love there are a lot of people with very low qualities!

→ Most people know themselves on a level of 3-5 %. On that low level, love and relationships can never achieve great success!

→ Most people want love, happiness, and a better life, but they don't want to learn anything to achieve it! No chance to succeed!

→ Divorce rate: 30-50%. Separation rate: 50-75%. Cyber love failure: up to 95%. You are better off learning how to succeed first!

The main causes for failure are: Ignorance, arrogance, narcissism, superficial attitudes, stubbornness, laziness, rudeness, vanity, dogmatic thinking, negation of living spiritual values, focusing too much on appearance or on cheap fun and not enough on inner life, trying to create an illusionary harmonic relationship, rejection to learn about love and life, lack of knowledge and skills for living a relationship, unresolved traumas and serious conflicts from the past, unconscious inner tie to a previous partner, rejecting importance and care for personal development, disinterest in contemplative self-reflection, lack of understanding and communication, suppressing emotions and desire, not mutually accepting weaknesses and sexual needs.

Nobody is perfect. It is not necessary to be free from all this. But it is absolutely essential to have a positive attitude towards learning about it all, to improve and to strengthen whatever is necessary, and to grow to an all-sided balanced person. We guess that more than 90% of all people have an important burden of such critical components. You lose enormous time and even a lot of money by searching for serious aims, if you ignore these facts! Consider these circumstances if you want success in real friendship, true love, harmonic relationship, and a great life! Learn how to deal with such burdens and weaknesses.

The better you are prepared when you start searching for a leisure partner, friendship, relationship or true love, the more time, energy, and money you will save! You will search much more efficiently! You will avoid mistakes with heavy damages! You will create a good friendship, a real relationship with knowledge, skills, strategy, and good personality qualities.

Satisfy your desire for sex and tenderness

Making love is a human encounter. Sex gives strength, hope and new life forces. Good sex makes positive, peaceful, and happy, and also strengthens self-esteem as well as self-confidence.

Making love also means learning about the partner's individuality and expressions, learning about what each one likes and dislikes, and learning about tenderness with its manifold ways. Sexual encounter with a lot of tenderness is a precious language of love. Sexual encounter is a wonderful human gift!

There are many sexual practices. But it can't be an aim to engage in acrobatics or to try it in every strange possible way. Certainly a bit of variety cannot harm. Practicing the same pattern during years, kills all eroticism, becomes boring and reduces pleasure and joy. That's not the way to stay "young". Interest and curiosity are valuable drives in life as well in experiencing the partner in many new ways.

- All past experiences remain in the memory and operate unconsciously in our present life. They bind, chain, and annoy.
- Creative and playful discovering and creating ways of sexual experiences produce joy. Sex and sexual pleasure have a lot to do with love.
- Sexuality is always a self-expression of a person. Living sexuality reflects the whole human being.
- Expressing tenderness always also includes a message. Being intimately close can transmit something vividly important: "I want you to feel safe with me.", or "I accept you fully for what you are."
- Tenderness is much more than a unity of caresses. Intimate tenderness aims to give and to get more pleasure with a message: "I love you".
- Every sensual experience reaches the whole person and is an experience of being and nature, never "just sex" as usual.
- This demands concentration and dedication, understanding physical and mimic reactions of the partner, also one's own motives.
- Discovering creatively and playfully each other creates joy of life.
- Couples loving each other in a real relationship should give a lot of signs of love everyday; e.g.:
- giving a little kiss, a tender caress, a loving word, often a little gift
- emotional words of attention even in unimportant moments
- appreciating the other's presence with a smile
- showing interest in all that the partner may think, feel, and wish
- giving a small support even if it is not necessary
- pampering (spoiling) each other with all kinds of giving
- expressing respect, understanding, and cooperation
- satisfying the partner's need and desires as much s possible
- creating small events for new experiences

The soul of human beings needs a lot of signs of love, to give and to receive. A relationship dies from inside without a lot of signs of love.

Mind and soul become very rigid if the sexual desire of both partners is not sufficiently satisfied. Our body can easily get sick if we suppress our sexual drive. If you want sex only once or twice a week and always only with a romantic prelude or never with romantic settings then your expressions of love is very low. Sometimes an erotic massage or making love smoothly helps to sleep, to calm down, to find peace, to relax, to reconcile, to get rid of nasty thoughts in the mind, to find distance from daily life matters, to find strength, to become motivated, to get new drive for daily issues, etc. And: boring sex kills love! Living a relationship together will entail many situations when the desire arises to make love "just as it comes".

→ The source is always LOVE!

Increase sexual pleasure

There are many forms of sexual unification, objectively classified as 'techniques'. Everybody can discover many of those techniques with playful delight for himself. Other things we may learn from books and magazines.
It should not be an aim to act acrobatically and neither is it vital to do extreme eccentric "exercises". Nevertheless, variation may be necessary. To always act out the same pattern over years kills eroticism, causes boredom and dampens delight and joy. This way sex can't keep "young".

Interest and curiosity are valuable drives that allow a person to experience themselves and one's partner anew from time to time. Creating the frame is also part of this. With time the anonymity of the cities, the well-organized daily world and the offers for consumption a lack of creativity in the sexual experience and actions has a paralyzing effect. We don't see this simply as a stimulant, but more as a conscious care for intimate encounter, as a consciously created variety of experiencing, the way we do it with eating, clothing and leisure activities. Of course problems will arise; but this is normal.

Understand sexual encounter as a complexity of human factors between a man and a woman:

1. Most people believe that sexual desire is bonded with love, so they assume erroneously, that they love each other when they want to possess each other.
2. Sexual attraction momentarily produces the illusion of a unity, but without love after this "unity" they remain aliens.
3. Tenderness is the immediate expression of loving others.

4. If it is really about love, erotic love implies a precondition: that my love expresses my (deepest) being - and that I experience the other in his being.
5. To love a person isn't only a feeling - it is a decision, a judgment, a promise; and much more.
6. The idea of a relationship that can easily be broken off, if it isn't successful is just as wrong as the idea that a relationship cannot be broken off under any circumstances.
7. People, who meet each other lustfully, accept themselves as man and woman and strengthen their sexual identity.
8. In the sexuality one encounters the other through the means of the body, and the experience of nearness and coziness.
9. Happiness has got to do with delightful and loving engagement for others. This also always implies suffering.
10. For most people love remains the centre of their life-project. Sexuality is a biological expression of love.
11. The spiritual part of life can only be divided at the risk of destroying the unity and integrity of the whole human being.
12. Many women consciously or unconsciously reject their sexual nature because they think that this would force them into a subservient attitude.
13. No woman wants to have the feeling of being a sexual object.
14. Searching for lust is an expression of the vitality of orgasm.
15. Excitement and movement are energetic phenomenon. Sexual drive is also an energetic phenomenon.
16. Love and sexuality belong to the innermost core of every living organism. These give a meaning to life and produce the strongest motivation.
17. The ability to reach satisfaction is a characteristic of a mature, integrated and realistic personality.
18. Nothing is more interesting for a child from birth on and during long periods of the child's development than sex.
19. Babies can experience sensual lust trough their body already from the first hour of their life. By no means only through their sexual organs, but also through them.
20. The way to deal with sexuality during the whole childhood has a decisive influence on the later life of a child.
21. The real life, the friendships of the adolescents, the relationship of the parents, their dealing with their children, the emotional atmosphere in the family - all that in the end has more weight on the sexual behavior than what adolescents may see on any screen.
22. There is a form of love that slowly arises from eroticism and friendship. Thus, a love that doesn't appear as a unique immediate explosion between two unknown, but where two human beings firstly meet on a sensible terrain of mutual estimation and confidentiality.

23. Sexuality and love are in interrelation with the whole a person.
24. The idealized presentation of love in the media doesn't prepare couples to deal with disappointments, frustrations and frictions.
25. Specific individual attributes are decisive for a happy relationship: engagement, sensibility, generosity, consideration, loyalty, responsibility, trustworthiness.
26. A decrease of sexual desire is caused by: changing of roles (to secure the income), stress at the work place, problems with health and misuse of stimulants.
27. The most important factors are, however, of a psychical nature: self-doubt, feeling of insufficiency, wrong ideals about one's own body, and fear of sexual performance, general interpersonal problems, and the different preferences about where, how, how long and how often. Self-love enables to love

Identify the causes of your sexual difficulties

Today sexual lust is certainly more accepted than 20 years ago. Many people can live with intimate tenderness, intercourse and masturbation free from moralizing and attitudes that are hostile to life.

But there is more: Sex-shops and sex-services of all kinds are expanding more than ever. Some offers may be helpful, also for learning.

But many of these "offers" hinder a man and a woman to profoundly love sexuality. Some say that in sex life everything is allowed, others experience sexuality with vulnerability, with most intimate sensibility, with values and limits. Reproduction is one aspect. Self-experience, lust, relaxation and intimate experiences of the partner allow for a deep, enriching acceptance of life. Consumption and "free love" appears to break all limits; a reaction against centuries-old hostile attitudes about sexuality! In earlier times sexuality was burdened with guilt and shame. Today lust and joy are in unlimited expansion. Is this "bad"? Human beings satisfy themselves with eating, drinking, cars, clothes, amusements or a foam bath and much more. A wide sensual experience has become a daily aim. Bodily experiences and sensuality are a central part of our life.

Human beings bring into the sexual play their psychical-spiritual wholeness and more than just a lustful acting; many elements are possible, for example:

- Unconscious barricades and blockades
- Daily worries and sorrows
- Ego-control and compulsion to hold back

- Romantic expectations
- Saying "yes" or "no" to one's own body
- Inhibition of movements
- Earlier experiences with men/women
- Unconscious parental control
- Conditioned masks (to be attractive)
- Blocked self-expression
- Expectations about life and partner
- Rejection of feelings
- Experiences about love and lack of love
- Undeveloped sexuality (e.g. identity)

To the sexual biography we can formulate questions for self-reflection:

1. Which partner (man, woman) mainly influenced my life?
2. What did I learn from my earlier partner(s)?
3. Which experiences are still in my memory as being embarrassing?
4. Which conflicts did I have in earlier relationships?
5. How did it come to separations?
6. How did my parents educate me to see men and women?
7. Which masculine and feminine aspects did my parents like especially?
8. How have I been enlightened on sexual matters?
9. How did I realize the sexuality of my parents?
10. How do my memories about my first sexual experiences still affect me?
11. Which attitudes about premarital sex did my parents have?
12. What did I like most about my partner(s)?
13. What other sex-aspects do I see in myself when looking at my past?
14. How did I react to having children?
15. How did I experience jealousy (of my earlier partner)?
16. How did I experience my jealousy?
17. What hurt me especially about sexual experiences and activities?
18. How did I experience seminal fluid and ejaculation?
19. What importance did fidelity and "being together also in difficult times" have for me?
20. What do I especially like about the masculine/feminine body?
21. How did I experience menstruation as a woman? (Man: What did I feel about it?)
22. What didn't I dare to talk about with my partner?
23. What did my partners expect from me?
24. How did I speak with my partners about conflicts?
25. Which attitudes, norms and prohibitions did I experience about sexuality?
26. Which feelings and experiences did I have about masturbation?
27. Which was one of the most beautiful sexual experiences in my life?

28. In case of abortion: How have I reconciled myself with that experience?
29. Which sexual prejudices did I have about men/women?
30. What was (is) the ideal about the body of women/men?
31. Which were the most embarrassing sexual experiences?
32. Which characteristics did I wish for in my partners?
33. Which were the most beautiful non-sexual experiences with earlier partners?
34. How did I feel about my body during my youth/young adulthood?

Top 20 solutions to a sexless relationship

The lack of sexual drive many women feel can have very different roots. Here is a checklist you can use to find out where the roots are:

The partner (friend, husband) is rather rude, unable to create romantic moments, not really tender, mostly in a rush to copulate. With the time a woman gets bored of it and feels like a toy for the man.

Friend (husband) has an unconscious rejection of the woman's body and woman's desire to make love. As a result of his religious education he associates a sexually active woman with a prostitute.

The partner rejects the woman's desire to have sex; he even has a fear of a female orgasm. He is still tied in a mother-bond and forces his woman to become a woman with "mummy-like attitudes".

The friend (husband) may have a reduced ability to feel, to show feelings, and may not be able to communicate about his feelings, sexual wishes ("I want sex right now"), and sexual desires or fantasies.

The woman has had a religious education rejecting sexual lust and valuating a woman solely in the role of being (becoming) a mother. Unconsciously she feels like a prostitute if sexually she behaves "wild".

There is no mutual love in the relationship. Both may reject the partner; or one of both negates the partner for whatever reason in the past (un reconciled conflicts) or in the present (ignored concerns).

Both partners do not really understand the inner life of the other partner. They both refuse to discover themselves and their partner's inner life. The love of both is very superficial and not "touching the soul".

The woman has experienced sexual traumas (abuse), maybe already in the early childhood; or she has heard in her childhood about "bad men" wanting to "touch". The past is always the code for the present!

The woman has never learnt to accept her body, to explore her body or her sexual drive. The source is the religion that still teaches that masturbation is something "sick", "dirty" or "evil", or even a "character weakness".

The woman, in the role of being a mother, has lost her interest in sex as she is overcharged by the daily commitments with children and housework. Having given life, she has lost her sexual desire.

The biography of the woman is overcharged with conflicts, problems, feelings of being lost in a brutal world. There may be a lack of self-confidence and self-esteem, compensated by tyrant-attitudes.

The woman does not love the man or the man doesn't love the woman. She doesn't trust him; she even fears him. She is unable to "open" herself up and to let him come close or even "enter" into her body.

Sexual desire is part of a zest for life. This includes the desire to build up an interesting life, to develop talents, and to discover the world. A lack of sexual desire is also a lack of zest for personal fulfillment.

Men and women are exposed to countless daily stimuli and difficult circumstances forcing to them to live an artificial life and self-presentation. A destroyed natural rhythm of life kills spontaneous sexual desire.

Security and closeness play a decisive role for the quality of the "pure" sexual sensation. Men and women practice sexuality in a blind and unconscious way, with feelings of guilt or embarrassment.

"Do you love me?" does not only concern love in the childhood. For a woman it means asking her partner: "Do you love me, especially me, me exclusively?" A lack of love kills a women's sex desire.

Sexual drive itself produces an energetic tension, excitable through thoughts and fantasies, with external stimulus and contacts. The culminating sexual energy (called "libido") pushes to increase the lust-sensation and "explosion". A woman can be scared to get this "explosion" due to a lack of self-confidence.

Women experience sexuality more holistically and more orientated towards the relationship. Men are more genitally oriented. Both partners must learn to find a mutual balance in their focus.

Men and women must learn to talk, even about their most secret sexual fantasies; or to say: "Go and take a shower first!" The more man and woman avoid talking, the more a woman is at risk to freeze.

1.11. Marriage, Family, Education

The power of love

A relationship needs continuous self-education to stand a chance to succeed. The man as well as the woman should find and form their self-identity. Both can do this "work" together. "The golden rules of a constructive partnership" can give an orientation. This is a true and genuine partnership between man and woman.

Love is a many-sided creative force of life. Love gives meaning and value to life. Love makes life worth living and rich. Love is the key to a lot of apparently unsolvable situations. Love respects life's many-sided balances. Love operates in many directions: for one's own psychical life, for the psychical life of the partner, for living together, for creating a life environment, for political and economical life, for culture, and for the religious (spiritual) life.

Most people rapidly oversee that love is much more than a feeling. Love is a complex performance. Love without reason (thinking) has got a very small chance of developing into something stable. Love without spirit is structure-less and has no inner roots. If somebody wants to live with spirit, he has to learn how to interpret dreams and to meditate correctly. If somebody wants to love, he has to observe with concentration and clear view the inner and external world. Love presupposes a will to act. Living love means to precisely look at the genuine inner needs, to one's own acting, psycho dynamism and all feelings. In a raw state the force of love is archaic, instinctive, nothing more than a brain (physiological) social pattern.

How can a person love others if he doesn't love himself? How is it possible to care for the needs of others, if the person rejects and suppresses their own daily basic needs? How can a person disrespect his own feelings, but carefully protect and promote the feelings of others? How can people express, spirit in their life, but disregard the own inner spirit? How can it be possible to love God, but not turn toward one's own inner psychical life? How can a human being love God, glorify him and realize him in real life, but reject his own inner psychical-spiritual life? How can one teach the truth without recognizing one's own inner true life?

Through self-love one is able to live love in real life. One can only consider and promote to others what one perceives and cares for in himself. If a person perceives his own needs and cares for his own needs with responsibility, he is able to integrate the needs of others. If a person elaborates his own dreams, he is able to develop interest for the dreams of others. If somebody forms himself in the psychical-spiritual growth process, he can promote others in the same process. If a person loves himself, he loves his partner and others in the same way: with their complete psychical organism.

Love consciously clarifies and perceives the future above the rapid pleasure. Love understands all-sided balanced human beings, and performs for others and for the human values. That's the way self-love converts into love for other people. Love also finds expressions in dealing with nature, goods, animals, and plants.

Love respects life in manifold ways. Love integrates the world of children and old people into society. Ill and disabled people and all people with limited abilities can discover love and learn to live love creatively, just like everybody else in the society. Love operates in diverse directions: for one's own psychical life, for the psychical life of the partner, for the social life, for the environment, for the political and economic life, as well as for the cultural and religious life.

Love is a creative force. The spirit is the ordering and controlling principle of love. Love is the specific essential human nature: as a potential, a performance and way of living. If this can't be the deepest meaning of life, what else can it be?

Love has got a tendency to transform everything that hinders a balanced inner wholeness. Love tends to dissolve "complexes" in the unconscious, to transform thoughts to external realities, and to openly care for feelings. Love wants to put through its own values and pushes to live meaning and values in the individual frame of life.

Transforming means: re-forming psychical forces, striving for spiritual values, to follow a spiritually rooted way of life, observing and living meaning of life and values. This is the dedication to the real life of human beings and this demands the education of the psychical life. Expressions of such a performance are; elaborating one's own inner life, the ability to reconcile and to renounce something in the interest of higher aims in the sense of psychical-spiritual development.

Transcendental process also means to understand (to see, to care for, to live) one's own whole being in a network of mankind. To go beyond one's own unity also leads to the environment: What human beings have inside as an archetypal ideal shall find a real expression in the external world.

What importance and meaning does the power of love have for me?

Love your partner

It's of enormous value to have a best friend, a lover, a partner! The potential for a great personal development and life is manifold. But one needs to consider several facts and realities:

- Understand your partner! You need to integrate and understand the inner world. If you ignore your inner life, you also love your friend, lover and partner excluding their inner life!

- A man is always a man and a woman is always a woman! Men and women are not only physically different! There are many natural differences in the inner world and its expressions that complement each other.

- Living in a partnership-like relationship has countless potential and makes life exciting and worth living! Consider the partnership rules: cooperation, equal in decision making, understanding, communication, etc.

- Share your thoughts, feelings, wishes, desires, visions, and concerns. You can enrich each other. You can balance one-sided and wrong thoughts. You can resolve much better any difficulty and conflict by doing so.

- Satisfy your partner's needs and desires. Integrate the genuine differences and be flexible. Give space to each other for living individual interests.

- To love a person includes also: care, support, help, respect, participation, creative common activities, promoting interests and capacities.

- A relationship always forms a relationship-biography! It depends on both how this biography will develop. And each one should know: one can destroy this relationship even if the other partner gives endless effort to make the relationship and love work!

- There is no love and no relationship without misunderstanding, disagreements, conflicts, problems, weaknesses, mistakes, etc. Learn how to efficiently deal with such concerns!

- There is no human being without weaknesses, mistakes, problems, conflicts, bad habits, or undeveloped inner forces. Love always integrates these realities!

- Living together and sharing being and life is a life project! Man and woman agree to share the existence on this earth and to make the best that is possible for growth and a good life.

Sharing being and life with love always includes learning processes. Not wanting to learn or to change is being stubborn and totally inefficient! It is normal that many relationships fail because every human being is in a psychical and spiritual development. To learn from success and failure, from life in general, is the ultimate principle in managing relationships and life.

Almost everybody is longing for a partner, wants to love and to be loved. Human beings wish for harmony, happiness, tenderness, joy, fulfillment, and peace in a relationship. Yearning for love, being in love, eroticism and lust experiences create an immense amount of illusions and hopes. Many relationships fail as a result of the reality.

30 aspects that show if you match with a partner

Don't say to your partner: "Don't ever try to change me!" If your partner says to you "Don't try to change me!", then he/she is wrong and stubborn.

Living together always entails learning from each other and together, adapting oneself to the other, finding compromises, and integrating the partner's psychological gender qualities. Learning from mistakes and improving imperfect aspects (qualities and behavior) is a key for success. To find a common balance in interests and a way of life means learning. Living together in love also means growing together psychologically and spiritually.

1. In my life I cannot do without:
2. In my life in general, I will really never want:
3. I like when people are:
4. I don't like when people are:
5. The way I do my daily/weekly shopping is:
6. I don't like if my bathroom and bedroom is:
7. If I would be an animal, I would like to be:

8. My 3 most important wishes for my life are:
9. The 3 most important aims I want to achieve in my life:
10. My 3 worst experiences in my life are:
11. My 3 most wonderful experiences in my life are:
12. My significant fears in life are:
13. My strengths to make a relationship and love work are:
14. The importance I give to sexual satisfaction is (importance, frequency):
15. Making love with my partner means (to me):
16. When making love I really don't like if:
17. In a relationship I like to be active for myself in:
18. For my self-realization in a relationship, I need:
19. On a sunny Sunday I like to do with my partner:
20. On a rainy Sunday at home I like to do with my partner (3 examples):
21. Living love in a relationship means to me concretely:
22. In relationship situations of misunderstanding I react:
23. Communication with my partner; importance, ways, critical matters:
24. I feel and think about my last relationship(s) / partner(s):
25. Self-knowledge and psychical-spiritual development mean to me:
26. I am very flexible in the following points about life and relationship:
27. My physical health is:
28. My psycho-somatic reactions in stressful situations are:
29. My mental strengths / weaknesses are:
30. If I could meet God, I would say to him:

Now, ask your partner or try to find out the answers of a person you want to know if you match!

Praise the bond of marriage

"Marriage" is a term with the core meaning: Going through the process of psychical and spiritual growth as man and woman to achieve the balanced union of the masculine and feminine archetypes, and in the mutual participation of this process. Making love is also a symbolic expression of this meaning. "Marriage" in its core, focuses from the psychical-spiritual view on these inner processes; and the meaning is "unimpeachable". Only through the aspect of "marriage" as a ritual celebration and realization does it have its full legitimacy. The homosexual "marriage" has got nothing in common with that meaning; the term "marriage" is not justified with any argument and as an archetypal meaning absolutely not legitimate; it's nonsense!

A marriage is not simply a living-community with its own private interests. Marriage is not a mere realization of love; and the meaning includes more than a human and legal space to procreate and educate children. A marriage is more than a common mastering of life. Marriage is from its own genuine and psychological meaning the process of self-growing with and through the opposite gender - cogent with the biological and psychological gender.

There are countless reasons for failure, for instance:

- Unable to show one's own feelings; unable to solve problems.
- Unable to argue and quarrel constructively.
- The motivation to marry was out of fear of living alone.
- A conflict of mutual role expectations: e.g. care.
- Unable to listen and to talk (lack of ability to communicate).
- Lack of self-love and therefore inability to love the partner.
- The illusion that marriage – a relationship – works by itself.
- Unable to realize oneself genuinely (self-realization).
- Being victim and actor of life lies and illusions of our zeitgeist.
- Professional and economical changes character and interests.
- Infidelity as a result of a stagnating or superficial relationship.
- A personal life crisis that the person doesn't want to master.
- A critical and impeding development of the character.
- Inability to live sexuality and to deal with all its conflicts.
- Running away from one's self and from one's responsibility.
- Life circumstances can destroy love and relationship.
- Other people can destroy the love between both partners.

Learn to avoid such risks of failure! Learn to live love and a relationship! Understand the essential meaning of marriage and learn everything that is necessary and useful to get life long success. Marriage needs to be protected and developed in all its capacities by both partners. Creating partnership-like an interesting life strengthens marriage.

Homosexual Marriage: There are definite psychoanalytical explanations for homosexuals that unconscious drive conflicts are always caused by experiences in their relationship with mother and father, and these can be found (except in definite physiological cases). Unfortunately, these people don't want to see their own inner true reality.

The consequences today are: they disgrace the archetype of marriage abusing this term for their homosexual relationship with their neurotic conflict. Their demand is like a dogma and in this sense fundamentalist. They can get their rights on the level of law regulations, but never by desecration of the "marriage" archetype. This kind of law regulations could at the same time regulate the cohabitation of two brothers, or sisters, or elderly people, and of any couple wanting to live together with special legal protections and rights.

You decide about divorce (or separation)

The divorce rate in industrialized nations is, as it is well known, very high. Nowadays divorce is "normal", that means, socially accepted and even promoted. There are many reasons that can force people to file for a divorce, for example:

- Being unable to solve one's own problems.
- Unable to quarrel constructively.
- Having married out of a fear to be alone and lonely.
- Conflict with the mutual role expectations: to provide and protect.
- Unable to listen and to articulate (communication abilities).
- Lack of self-love and with that an inability to love the partner.
- Illusions such as thinking that marriage (relationship) functions by itself.
- Not building up one's own happiness with thinking and "Spirit".
- Inability to genuinely realize oneself (self-realization).
- Victim and actor of life lies and with that of illusions of the zeitgeist.
- Games: power and revenge games, rejection games, hide-and-seek games.
- Unable to show one's own feelings; and to constructively deal with them.
- Infidelity as a result of stagnating & superficial relationship life.
- Personal life crisis that the person cannot or does not want to master.
- Difficult in development of (neurotic) character of one or from both.
- Unable to live sexuality and to deal with the conflicts about sexuality.
- Fear to make oneself ridiculous, to be vulnerable and get manipulated.

That means: Divorce does not really solve any of these causes. People run away from these causes by filing for divorce, and in the end from themselves and from responsibility.

One abandons his partner and at the same time all his own inabilities. On top of that one must know: divorce contains an enormous risk for your health.

In approximately 7 out of 10 divorces a solution would be possible if both partners would face up to their own personality education and Individuation. At the same time that includes renouncing life lies.

The first basic rule for a constructive path is: each partner has to face his self-being, without being influenced or abused by the other. Dreams tell each one what he has to do and how he can progress in his personality education and Individuation. There is no constructive solution without dreams.

The second basic rule for a constructive path is: Love demands Individuation: the personal psychical-spiritual development. Only if one partner entirely refuses this call from love, and the other partner goes this path with responsibility, is divorce appropriate.

The third basic rule for a constructive path is: One partner must first go the path of his Individuation alone – if the other partner doesn't follow. By doing so he has to demonstrate to the partner that this path is a genuine alternative to life lies. One has to learn how to love, so that the other partner can be convinced with facts, which show it's worth going this path of learning and growing.

If the partner disrespects these rules and doesn't want to live them, divorce is appropriate, even necessary. Not to divorce can paralyze the entire still open life of a person and definitively block any development and self-fulfillment. The consequences would be: getting a rigid character, escape into religion or into alcoholism, psychical suffering, psycho-somatic disturbances or illnesses, also cancer, in the end a bitter and sad old age.

Decide carefully about abortion

First of all, it is your absolute duty to thoroughly think with your partner if you want to procreate a baby; and if you are ready together for the responsibility of educating a child, including all financial consequences this entails. In this sense it is also your duty to take appropriate measures so that you do not create an un-desired baby. It is definitely not advisable to procreate a baby if you are not educated for this responsibility. A child needs a lot of love and support from the father and the mother!

A person who finds herself in the situation to decide about abortion must know and consider the following facts:

A woman, that has aborted without elaborating this event thoroughly, will even in ten, twenty or more years have tears in her eyes; tears of pain and guilt. This will also happen if the abortion later seems to be rationalized and forgotten. The event of an abortion and a repressed guilt always creates a new destiny.

Meditative regressions into the prenatal times clearly show us that with the procreation at the same time a soul is bonded to this biological being that will become a human being. This soul has a paranormal consciousness, a paranormal perception, and a corresponding emotional experiencing. This soul experiences that it is not accepted and has to go back to the transcendental world. (I have done such meditative regressions hundreds of times in seminars with people; and there is no doubt about this fact!)

Men in general like to leave the emotional and moral problem of abortion to their woman. But men also unconsciously feel a certain responsibility for the new life of a human being that is beginning to grow, even if they rationally repress this. Repressing this responsibility makes them become rigid in their character. Men too can be pursued during decades from the nagging question: "What kind of daughter or son would it be today?" Such a question can sink down in the hectic everyday life. But the importance and seriousness of this possible human being and life has deep effects, more intense that any other repression of wishes or feelings.

The decision for abortion is indeed humanly a very difficult challenge. In all cases professional advice and support is appropriate. Because once aborted, the decision cannot be revoked. The procreated baby and the rejection to accept it, forms a person.

A sole technical way of dealing with this decision (in the sense of "this is anyway only a first development of human body cells that can be removed") makes a person (in his character) rude, brutal, hard, cold, and aggressive towards all sensible human beings.

The other attitude that condemns abortion to be murder is also inappropriate. The technical attitude, if we consider the critical consequences of bearing a child; for example: humanly and economically very difficult circumstances of the woman, highly burdened with psychical and physical dispositions, a creator that is for the woman an unacceptable burden (e.g. in the case of rape), and more.

The enormous consequences of such a moral and human decision should at least lead to responsible attitudes in one's own sexual life, fully considering such a risk.

Furthermore such a challenging life situation (abortion) can also be a destiny opportunity to thoroughly think about the psychical-spiritual human being. Part of such reflections should be one's own inner life and the inner life of other people. This at least gives oneself a chance to promote one's own evolutionary human being (and its development).

Efficient family management

Nowadays we observe many different forms of family and many different styles of family life. A family is a social institution, and if we talk about family management, then before we do so, we have to underline: a family starts with love, a man and a woman loves each other, want to live together and procreate a baby. The most essential and deepest core of family management is LOVE! Love between the man and the woman, and between the parents and the child / children. Living love without intelligence, knowledge and skills will fail. Management is a pattern of skills. In the management of a family, love holds everything together.

Family management is also based on the human longing for having a home with the partner, growing together with the partner and with children. Living together always includes giving appreciation, showing affection, and encouraging each other. Love accepts the differences in each person during the entire life course where all members are growing. Spiritual and general human values, as well as beliefs, hold the family together. All members of a family need to be loved and valued. Positive feedback, encouragement, and signs of affection create the family "spirit" on a daily basis.

Family life has to be organized: each member has his "place" and all members have to contribute for a well working living together. The main tasks are: shopping, cleaning, cooking, washing up, and driving children to, from and between home, school and friend's homes. A family needs time to relax together, to have fun together, and to experience the world together (e.g. holidays, leisure).

A well working family regularly makes time for talking and listening, sharing daily chores and taking decisions together, and especially resolving the critical incidents of every day life. Each family member wants to talk about what he has done during the day and shows interest in each other's daily life. Every member of the family is special in his own way. All members allow each other to be excited about personal interests. Showing respect and tolerance is a simple but effective rule. Family time also creates a sense of belonging where all members can share ideas, thoughts, and experiences.

All family members need an organized and predictable home environment. The daily chores are shared between father and mother, and the children depending on their age. Children want and need to have a real say in what happens. The right way of communication creates a very special relationship between the family members. Trust and intimacy are vital. A well working family is able to withstand setbacks and crises with constructive attitudes and shared values. All members cope with challenges together.

Routines are the planned and recurring activities that keep the family home running smoothly. Routine provides security and stability. Routines include things that need to be done at certain times (mealtimes, bedtimes, time for shopping and cleaning and washing, regular "play dates", daily hygiene of everybody, reading the bedtime story, house work distribution, setting the table and washing the dishes, hobbies and sport activities, and even the way of greeting and saying "good bye", etc.). Routine makes everyone more organized and less stressed. Routine promotes team work because each member has his responsibility. Routine gives stability, inner security and contentedness.

Rituals help the family members know what's special about the family; e.g. Christmas and Birthday celebrations, social and cultural events, religious celebrations, invitations from the grandparents, cooking a cake on Sunday morning, national and local celebration days. Rituals make family members feel important and strengthen the family identity, partly also a nationality identity. The family also becomes a sense of history and belonging. Rituals together with routines create a family cohesion.

Social activities are another part of the family life, especially keeping in touch with neighbors, friends, sport friends, school colleagues, the children's friends, teachers, and relatives. Social activities enrich a family life and give each member of the family an individual life area for self-expressions and discovering the world.

Family life is not only the most important part of children's lives; it's also the most important part ("home") of the father and mother. The quality of the relationship between the man and woman (father and mother) determines the success of the family life. This relationship also depends on the personality quality and level of the psychical-spiritual development of each partner.

In general, there is an incredible lack of psychical-spiritual maturity and of personality qualities throughout the world. Humans and with that also every family is nowadays exposed to countless influences: media (radio, television, newspapers, magazines, films), internet, advertising, shop-windows offering millions of goods, gigantic offers of toys, electronic games, mobile phones, leisure areas for teenagers (pubs and discos), countless consumer goods, cars, accessories, constantly changing fashion products, etc. The western super-supermarket has destroyed all efforts of parents for a good education of their children. Even small children are already brainwashed and manipulated to consume goods, clothes and shoes, and have as much fun as they can. Violence amongst teenagers and even children at schools and on the streets has increased dramatically. Public schools have become performance fabrics forcing pupils to perform as much as possible – or they fail in school and later in life – also in the family management. Is there hope?

The young generation has lost the minimal respect for their parents, for teachers, for other people, for goods and especially for money. Later in life, the young people get married, have children, have no idea about their grandmother's cooking recipes and can't even cook a normal great meal; and both have no idea about how to manage a family life or how to educate their children. How could they? They can't even manage their own inner life, their relationship, and their real life. They have completely lost the awareness about the family values.

Family values are in great danger!

The basic family management can be compared to a business; but it is much more than this. It has always got to do with intelligence, love and Spirit.

Typical problems in a family life are:

- Family values
- Money management
- Communication
- Decision making

- Household responsibilities
- Family activities
- Social activities
- Individual activities
- Daily routines
- Rituals
- Work (earning money)
- Children's education

25 principles to educate your children

To educate a child is a demanding responsibility. The ability to educate children demands formation. But most young parents have never learnt how to educate their children. Of course they show them how to brush their teeth, wash their hands, how to behave at the table (when eating), and how to keep their bedroom tidy.

A father and mother have an essential influence in the way that their children communicate and cope with a multitude of critical and new normal situations.

A strong educational focus is to give the children a feeling of self-esteem, to give affection and emotional support, to encourage them, and to transmit understanding. Praise promotes learning! Children have to learn the importance of routine and rituals, of contributing in the housework amongst other chores.

A way of educating children is by talking and listening. Talking resolves most situations in a family life. Communication is one of the most important tools for resolving problems in life. Obviously, listening is equally part of talking. "Putting down" communication, threatening and blaming makes your child feel bad, guilty or hopeless.

Criticizing with the right words can help to improve, but can also paralyze learning. The best way is: showing what and why something is wrong because of the lack of efficiency or undesired consequences. Sometimes a certain pressure is necessary; but it can never be the educational key for success. Punishments form part of education; but it must be adequate (appropriate) and never humiliating. Children must get chances to learn by doing. A never-ending fight for control doesn't make a situation better.

Daily routines help set our body and day clock (e.g. bedtime routine). Routines are a way of educating a child about ways to stay healthy (e.g. brushing teeth, washing hands after using the toilet or when coming back home, etc.).

There are many ways to teach children how to manage money. Children have to learn about the importance of the right use of money, mobile phone, internet, etc.

In the industrialized nations already babies and small children, and later all teenagers are exposed to millions of goods and countless possibilities to have fun. Children want to have everything they see with their eyes and can touch with their hands. Parents know very well that nobody can have everything because it would ruin the budget. One has to work for money to get goods, food, and fun. Money can sometimes be an educational remuneration for special behavior or performances, but should never be the norm.

The best way to educate children in a world of countless goods and "offers for fun" is through the way that parents themselves live in this material world. Teaching human values and in general life values has "short legs" if the parents do not live what they teach. The behavior of the parents is the best possible model to provide children with the most important life and human values.

Children copy everything they see in their parents, on the television, on the street, in magazines, in other families, and in friends or other people in general. Children want to explore the world, to try how "it" is, to experience what others have or live. They need to learn how damaging this can become if they do not select with a value orientation.

Most adults have lost the ability to be "strong" and are unable to live a balanced discipline. So, how can they be an ideal for their children? Education includes learning a flexible discipline.

The more that parents live true love as well as themselves in a genuine fashion, the more children accept their words, their rules and values. Strong discipline, efficient working and learning attitudes, together with an understandable and comprehensive explanation, must form part of the children's education.

Parents have an enormous responsibility for the education of their children. But this responsibility has a certain limit. Each child has his own character and always a certain free space to follow the given educational path or to reject it. Each child has its own way and freedom of taking decisions. The environmental influences nowadays are so strong that parents can't protect their children anymore from these manipulations (of information and behavior) and brainwashing forms of marketing.

To give 25 rules for the best way of educating children in a materialistic world, where only life lies, superficiality, money and consumption is valued, and where most people have very low personality qualities and a highly neurotic character (rejecting their inner true world), is like building a house on deep quicksand.

The ultimate hope for fathers and mothers:

There is one rule, only one rule for a good education of your children: educate yourself with a very strong discipline based on your inner Spirit! Acquire knowledge about the inner life of humans and about children's world, and learn the right skills for managing yourself and life itself. Live the path of a personal psychical-spiritual growth together with your partner. Always live love with intelligence and Spirit. This is the best possible foundation of educating your children. But your child will always have the free choice to follow your vivid model, to correct and to improve it, or to reject it in part or completely.

1.12. Discover yourself with dream interpretation

Benefit from the power of your dreams

The inner "Spirit" is the force that creates our dreams, and intelligently composes meditations. The inner "Spirit" is also the source of intuition and inspiration.

→ The Spirit is an informative, organizing and guiding force.
→ The Spirit is the principle of acting in the soul.
→ The Spirit is animating, stimulating, and benevolent.
→ The Spirit is the source of wisdom.

Therefore the Spirit is not a human creation, not a product of culture, but a spiritual psychical function in each psyche (soul, mind) of each person.

The Spirit as the force that creates dreams has some specific characteristics, for example:

- The Spirit knows how and for what purpose he transfers messages to the person.
- The Spirit knows the "Code program" of the psychical-spiritual growing process.
- The Spirit organizes the elaboration of the inventory in the unconscious mind.
- The Spirit knows the paths and steps to a well balanced being and life.
- The Spirit is the source to get information about God and the transcendence.
- The Spirit identifies solutions where people can't find a solution with intelligence.
- The Spirit is the genuine source of each religion, of all religious and spiritual teachings; but this source has been lost centuries and millenniums ago.

Contemplate and use the power of your inner Spirit! And consider this:

1. The inner Spirit is the highest authority and stands above all religions and dogmatic teachings!

206

2. The spiritual consciousness of most people is still on an archaic level! People avoid getting in touch with the Spirit in their soul.
3. Do you have to make your God responsible for everything and ask him for help as a substitute for interpreting your own dreams?
4. God (religion, dogmatism) for most people is a substitute for self-knowledge and self-education! Instead of dealing with dreams people prefer to "ask God" to solve everything.
5. Do you want to grow psychologically and spiritually? Then listen to your inner spiritual power and grow with your inner Spirit!

It is time to really learn how to correctly interpret your dreams!

Dream Interpretation

Let's get straight to the point: We all dream when we sleep. This is extremely important because dreams contain meaningful messages. We all have an inner Spirit in our soul. We can't give orders to this Spirit about what he has to tell us. We also can't form this Spirit in the way we can form our intelligence. This Spirit is transcendental like the soul. At the same time this Spirit is the Spirit of God. – No psychoanalyst, no psychotherapist, and no psychologist would dare to say that.

But I can say it because I have profoundly and minutely explored during 30 years the world of dreams in the context of Individuation (the psychical-spiritual development). I can also say: I have had more dreams about God and Spirit, about the archetypes of the soul, about the human being, and about the meaning of life, than anyone can find in all Holy Books of the history of humanity together. More than a thousand dreams have shown me where humanity and the earth are heading.

The Spirit talks to the person through dreams. The Spirit stays above all religions and above all spiritual concepts. With that the big drama of humanity starts: The religions and the concepts of spirituality have lost the vivid Spirit. They ennoble themselves above the Spirit, with dogmatism, fundamentalism, and abstruse teachings. The thousand spiritual concepts without this inner Spirit are a frightening labyrinth of heterodoxies. A nightmare! Spiritual allurement of human beings! Sects on the level of heaviest neurosis! So what is a religion without this vivid inner Spirit in each human being?

On top of all this, I have consulted countless websites about dreams and dream interpretation. It is unbelievable how sick if not perverse the way they deal with the understanding of dreams is. There are "concepts" of dream interpretation that are more evil than poisonous, nuclear contaminated, stinking pulp.

Some TV reports sometimes argue in the name of science that dreams are nothing other than "brain rubbish". If you want to know what spiritual criminals are, then carefully watch such "scientific" reports and carefully look at the countless self-proclaimed masters of dream interpretation!

The Spirit is part of God, maybe something like the "intelligence" of God. The Spirit permanently gives orientation on the changing realities of mankind and the earth. That means: The Spirit is continuously learning and adapting. Therefore also God is continuously learning and adapting. God orients himself according to the Spirit. Seen from another perspective: what an inefficient Spirit that would be that doesn't learn and adapt anything from what mankind does on earth! What a boring and impotent God that would be that doesn't learn and adapt anything from what mankind does on earth!

Practically, this means: we have to continuously learn and to adapt our perception about ourselves, about human beings, life and the earth. Logically, if dream interpretation shall be correct and also of practical benefit then dream interpretation must be linked with this learning and adaptation process.

How come most people have no interest in understanding the dreams they have every night, or no desire to benefit from these dream messages?

It will rarely come into the mind of a little child that dad and mum learn (must learn, should learn). They simply know everything. And they can also always do everything. How do children deal with the shock, once they become aware of the fact that dad and mum neither have learnt something essential about human being and life, nor have they developed any efficient skills for living? What must young adults think when they see that their parents have learnt nothing or very little about the psychical-spiritual human being and that their parents have learnt nothing or very little about life? Some kids learn, others learn nothing or little and copy the pattern of their parents during their whole life. The Spirit doesn't exist in such a life! This is never a good foundation for a correct dream interpretation!

Fact is: if a person knows 1% about the psychical life, then he can only interpret on a level of 1% or maybe a bit more the dreams he has about this inner life. The following question should be answered honestly: Isn't it fact that most people know less than one per cent about the psychical and spiritual life; and also not much more about life and the world in general?

If God and Spirit are not too lazy to learn and to continuously adapt the permanently changing realities, then it should be self-evident for each person to also learn about the human being and life, and to adapt to the realities. Part of this is that one has to look behind the façades and sceneries. It's also indispensable to always be aware of the dynamic of our zeitgeist (of the archaic human beings): distorting, displacing, embellishing, devaluing, suppressing, repressing, ignoring, intriguing, lying, maneuvering, being in cahoots, and doing everything possible so that the truth can never be detected. Dreams show the real truth if one interprets them correctly! Only very few people want to know the truth about their own being. Therefore, also only very few people want to take dreams seriously. Logically for most people dreams are only "brain rubbish".

In summary, the world of dreams and dream interpretation is not a kindergarten and not a training field for dilettantes and neurotic spiritual masters. Dogmatism and fundamentalism are incompatible with the Spirit and dream interpretation. Correct dream interpretation is demanding and a very serious psychical-spiritual undertaking!

On several online forums, a lot of young people post their dreams and ask for advice, trying to find an orientation to dreams and answers to the meaning of life. I only can recommend to each and every one:

→ Learn a lot about your inner life!
→ Learn a lot about the human being!
→ Learn a lot about the state of humanity and the earth!
→ Learn how to interpret your dreams correctly!

With that you have the best inner guidance and the best spiritual and practical orientation ever existing for mankind: the power of the vivid inner Spirit!

Dreams as the source of life

Do you remember your dreams? Everybody dreams every night. People had always given a high importance to dreams. But today, for most people dreams do not play an essential role for self-knowledge and life.

There are even a lot of people that do not give any importance in thinking and they never reflect upon their thinking.

There are also a lot of people who think dreams are insignificant and they never think about this opinion. Nevertheless, dreams are the most valuable source of life! Why do you reject the power of your dreams for a good life?

Everybody has dreams. Dreams are the most precious source of life. All diverse dream theories have one thing in common: the varied dream images in the shape of human beings or animals, in facts or actions, say something about the reality of the dreamer. Dreams allow us to make conclusions about the dreamer and his life: "Tell me 3 dreams and I can tell you who you are!"

In the ancient world "big dreams" have been considered as messages from God and the Gods. It is not simply an opinion of people from the ancient times, if today they assume that there is a hidden message in dreams.

In essence, all dream theories say that these messages are useful: they inform, counsel, warn, support, promote, heal, develop, evaluate, analyze, and in general they help if a person can't see a path to go forward in life. Dreams also inform about the world, the future, the past, and the transcendental world. That means: An intelligent force in the soul (mind) of each person organizes the dream elements to a message for this person.

Essentially, we correct and extend all well known psychoanalytical and other dream theories: Dreams are the indispensable and with nothing compensable "via regia" (royal path) to the entire psychical-spiritual human being. The psychical-spiritual development ("path") is called "Individuation"; and therefore this growth process is the "royal path" up until the complete self-fulfillment.

- Dreams tell the truth about you, others, religions, ideologies, society, the earth, the future and God.
- 90% of all psychologists, therapists and analysts know a mere 10% about dreams and dream interpretation.
- 99% of all people that interpret their own dreams do it on a level of archaic tools and primitive knowledge.
- You can't interpret dreams correctly without extensive knowledge about the unconscious and real life.
- You need to grow psychologically and spiritually to correctly understand your dreams (and the dreams of others)!

→ Are you against the inner Spirit? You situate your Ego above this spiritual intelligent spiritual force?

Aims of dream interpretation

Dreams help in all matters of life to a good, happy and meaningful life. Dreams indicate the path to the innermost being, to the proper (authentic) psychical-spiritual human being. Dreams support the formation (education) of all psychical forces. Dreams also give an orientation about the external world. Dreams are the door to the psychical and to the spiritual universe.

With your dreams and dream interpretation you want to:

→ Achieve a high consciousness about your being and life!
→ Find the effective orientation for your life!
→ Take the right decision for your happiness!
→ Get advice and suggestions from your inner being!
→ Live correctly with inner freedom and honesty!
→ Live with open, awake and clear eyes!

You have dreams that move you deeply. You feel that your dreams are very important. You want to correctly understand your dreams. Therefore learn the language of the dreams!

Dreams reveal the truth about everything. Comment this statement:

Give some reasons why dreams and understanding dreams are important to all humans:

Manifoldness of dream messages

Dreams contain messages about everything in life, for example.

- Biography (the past)
- Shadows, aspects of personality
- Psychical forces
- Unconscious, complexes
- Nature of drive, sexuality

- Actions
- Aspects of relationships
- Aspects of change
- Self-realization
- Attitudes, beliefs, norms
- Lifestyle, ways of living
- Health
- Archetypes of the soul
- Dangers
- Other people
- Profession, job, work
- Churches, religions, Spirituality
- Society with all its systems
- State of the earth: world and humanity
- Amoral, moral, values
- God and Spirit
- Transcendence (the transcendental world)

The spiritual intelligence (Spirit) in dreams

The "Spirit" is the force that creates our dreams intelligently composing meditations; and is also the source of intuition and inspiration.

→ The Spirit is an informative, organizing and guiding force.
→ The Spirit is the principle of acting in the soul.
→ The Spirit is animating, stimulating, and benevolent.
→ The Spirit is the source of wisdom.

Therefore, the Spirit is not a human creation, not a product of culture, but a spiritual psychical function in each psyche (soul, mind) of each person.

The Spirit as the force creating dreams has some specific characteristics, for example:

→ The Spirit knows how and for what purpose he transfers messages to the person.
→ The Spirit knows the "Code program" of the psychical-spiritual growth process.
→ The Spirit organizes the elaboration of the inventory in the unconscious mind.
→ The Spirit knows the paths and steps to a well balanced being and life.
→ The Spirit is the source for information about God and the transcendence.

→ The Spirit identifies solutions where people can't find a solution with intelligence.
→ The Spirit is the source of each religion, of all religious and spiritual teaching.

Every human has this inner Spirit. Think and use the power of the inner Spirit!

Religion without inner Spirit

Fact is: the Christian religion ignores the dream life of people and the world of dreams in general. They do this although all prophets legitimated themselves with dreams. By doing so, religion ignores the inner Spirit. Religion has no vivid inner Spirit. Fact is also:

→ The inner Spirit is the highest authority and stands above all religions and dogmatic teaching!
→ The spiritual consciousness of most people is still on an archaic level! Most people avoid getting in touch with the Spirit in their soul.
→ Do you have to make your God responsible for everything and ask him for help as a substitute for dream interpretation?
→ God (religion, dogmatism) is for most people a substitute for self-knowledge and self-education! Instead of dealing with dreams people prefer to ask God to solve everything.

You want to grow psychologically and spiritually. Then listen to your inner spiritual power and grow with your inner Spirit! This means: learn to correctly interpret your dreams and use their knowledge!

What is a religion that ignores dreams and dream interpretation? Such a religion ignores the inner Spirit and therefore this religion is "spiritless".

Manifoldness of dream images

We identify the following rough segments of dream images; segments are:

■ Human beings: Body and expressions: mimic, gesture, ways of movements.
■ World of nature: the earth with its basic forces, the entire world of plants.
■ World of animals: everything that anybody knows today.
■ World of objects: basically everything that can be found on earth.

- Activities: any acting, any action, also words and talking.
- Events, incidents: something happened with people, objects, animals, nature, etc.
- Arenas: The place where something happened, is happening, or will happen.
- Archetypes: the numinous, cultural products existing in all variations.

Dream images can contain 3 qualities:

1. Images from the life of a person: the entire personal inventory of life that has a subjective meaning for the person.

2. The symbols: Symbols are those images that in general also form part of the experiences of a person without a personal meaning, but can be interpreted in the context of the general inventory of the world.

3. The archetypes: These are symbols that have a transcendental, not terrestrial meaning beyond the common knowledge. They also do not appear as a habitual object of the culture or as a normal reality. These symbols include for example the circle-cross-mandala, pyramids, a spiritual light, a spiritual fire, a wise figure, an animal with particular qualities, a temple, a mandala, etc.

When interpreting dreams, the following has to be taken into consideration:

- Images with a subjective meaning (through personal experiences)
- Images with a general meaning (e.g. objects of our culture)
- Symbols with a global validity
- Archetypes: Symbols with a specific meaning about the psychical-spiritual life
- Daily actions and rituals
- Language and words

Educational functions of dreams

Dreams contain meaningful messages about the person (that has had the dream), about other people, about facts in the world, and also about the transcendental world. That's why we can benefit practically from our dreams for our daily life.

Dreams:	Describe what you experienced:

inform	
warn	
advise	
support	
promote	
help	
heal	
liberate	
develop	
judge	
analyze	
forecast	

Psychical functions of dreams

→ Dreams have a compensating function that balances the content of consciousness.

→ Dreams have a prospective function, focusing on development.

→ Dreams react on conscious and unconscious realities.

→ Dreams also contain objective information (facts).

→ Dreams show and decisively perform psychical-spiritual processes.

→ Dreams reveal archetypal meanings of the human being.

→ Interpreting dreams includes varied dimensions of meaning.

Dream language

A person has many ways to say something. One can talk loud or accentuated low because the other person doesn't want to listen. Or because of the defense the other person has it is not possible to talk clearly and therefore necessary to make a hint. Sometimes we use an allegory, make comparisons, or considerably exaggerate so that the other person becomes attentive. We all know the difficult circumstance: a person wants to know the truth and at the same time he doesn't want to see it.

Furthermore we use messages ways of warning, explanation, and forecast. We evaluate and judge, and we inform and interpret based on a various points of view.

The force that creates dreams uses this common manifoldness of creating a message as well. The more a person works with his dreams, the more he can experience how the Spirit "talks" with images and sceneries. Everyone can notice that this intelligent power obviously knows more than the "I" can know. The Spirit can also inform about himself and about the spiritual world (the transcendence).

IF YOU LEARN THE DREAM LANGUAGE, YOU HAVE EXTENSIVE ACCESS TO YOUR OWN UNCONSCIOUS, TO THE OWN ENTIRE PSYCHICAL AND REAL LIFE, AND TO THE SPIRIT ITSELF. DREAMS ARE THE DOOR TO THE PSYCHICAL-SPIRITUAL HUMAN BEING.

The power that creates dreams demands: "If you want to communicate with me, then learn to understand me." One becomes competent in this dialogue by being engaged with dreams and at the same time with one's own psychical life.

DO YOU WANT (OR DO YOU WANT TO REJECT) THE ALL-INCLUDING ACCESS TO YOUR UNCONSCIOUS, YOUR ENTIRE PSYCHICAL AND REAL LIFE, AND TO THE INNER SPIRIT?

Dream, Spirit and intelligence

Thinking and reasoning are not in opposition to the acting of the Spirit. Thinking and reasoning are interpolated (integrated) in a superior network with the Spirit.

Expectations of redemption from the other world or for the other world are obsolete concepts. In no way does the concept of Individuation demand blind believing with narrow-minded thinking. People living in the process of Individuation comply with inner dedication and with love, honesty, and Spirit their human being. Dreams show the path.

The "I" of a person manages the process of this psychical-spiritual evolution and his entire life, including the entire psychical organism and the external reality. Apart from using the inner Spirit, this management also demands diverse intellectual activities and a practical form of reasoning.

Remembering dreams

Many people perceive their dream experiences in the same way as they see the external reality: ostensibly, superficially, unilaterally, and related to personal interests. If the attitude and interest in dreams are rather easy and indifferent or even rejecting, the apparently unimportant details of a dream quickly disappear once awake.

But unimportant and marginal details of a dream can have a significant meaning in the context of other elements and with the associations from the person. The stronger the interest in the dream life is, and the more seriously one is elaborating (interpreting) his dreams, the more precisely one can remember his dreams.

Writing down a dream right after waking up can help to remember the entire dream better. Writing dreams down hours later facilitates losing elements of a dream. Sometimes a person remembers more elements of a dream some hours later, half a day or even a day after waking up. Not giving attention to such elements can lead to losing these elements. Such additional elements one often remembers through accidental perceptions during daily activities or even when one talks about a dream with others. Sometimes, when a person repeatedly tells his dreams several times within an hour, he starts to remember more elements.

If a person rarely or even never remembers his dreams, he has a defense, often a complete rejection of his psychical inner life. But we should not forget that in our culture, we don't learn how important the dream life is. A person that doesn't know anything about the dream world and who has never had a chance to find access to it doesn't have an open disposition to remember dreams *per se*.

The more a person knows about the importance of dreams, the more open he is for the message and the easier he can remember dreams. It is very valuable to regularly remember one's own dreams.

Dream Interpretation in 12 steps

The practical dream interpretation proceeds in 12 steps:

1. Write down the dream together with the feelings you had in the dream.
2. Divide the dream into its parts (singular images) and sequences.
3. Especially consider the key images.
4. Identify your position in the dream (The dream-"I").

5. Search for associations: Life experiences, spontaneous reactions.
6. Which psychical forces are focused upon?
7. Which life issues are focused upon?
8. Which other people and specific facts are focused upon?
9. Are archetypes focused or inner archetypal processes in development?
10. Combine your result to a new wholeness-meaning.
11. Compare with earlier similar dreams and dream themes.
12. Expand the dream experience with imagination.

Once you get a result, don't forget to make your practical conclusions.

And in the end you should implement the achieved knowledge into corresponding life situations.

It is always appropriate to be cautious when interpreting dreams because:

> **ONE CANNOT INTERPRET DREAMS BETTER THAN HE HAS KNOWLEDGE ABOUT THE PSYCHICAL AND REAL LIFE. THE MORE A PERSON REJECTS, ALSO TO DISCOVER HIS "DARK SHADOWS", THE MORE HE TENDS TO INCORRECTLY INTERPRET HIS DREAMS. WHAT ONE DOESN'T WANT TO SEE, HE DOESN'T SEE.**

Also in dreams the "spiritual gold" shines only very reticently.

Preparations for dream interpretation

> **THE ONE, WHO ELABORATES HIS DREAMS, FINALLY DOESN'T DEAL WITH HIS DREAMS, BUT MUCH MORE WITH HIMSELF AND HIS LIFE. IN DREAM INTERPRETATION THE PERSON AND HIS LIFE STAYS IN THE CENTER, AND NOT THE DREAM.**

Therefore: There is no extension of consciousness, no healing process, no changes of psychical-spiritual process, and no growth towards wholeness without some activities of the person.

- Interpreting dreams is one thing. To engage in the process of dreams means commitment, seriousness, and readiness for a self-critical view.
- A dream can't take away one's decision and responsibility. This demands ability for conscience and moral responsiveness.
- Without acquiring psychological knowledge, also about the unconscious life, the process of learning and growth cannot be managed. A certain psychological and spiritual knowledge is indispensable.

- Being engaged in one's own dreams costs effort, time, and money. It is certainly appropriate to set according priorities for one's leisure time.
- To follow the dream path demands a certain trust in the power of the Spirit and a binding engagement in the dialogue with the Spirit.
- Success presumes that for the person it is very valuable to get involved with the power of the Spirit, at least as much as the person gives importance to his psychical-spiritual human being and to his life.
- Dream interpretation demands intelligence and reason, balanced with empathy and intuition.

Dream Diary

Keeping a dream diary is an indispensable working instrument for everyone who wants to seriously deal with their own dreams.

It is recommendable to have a small notebook ready on the bedside table, and a pencil. Even in a state of doziness one can write down some keywords or even the entire dream.

After breakfast one can take a quarter of an hour to write down the dream more extensively as well as the feelings one experienced in the dream and the first spontaneous thoughts about the meaning.

It is part of a day time planning to include some time early in the morning for one's own dreams. Maybe one should go to bed half an hour earlier to be able to get up half an hour earlier in the morning.

Dream Protocol

1. Dream: Write the dream down (the dream sequences), also the feelings you had in the dream and the feelings you had after waking up. Also note your position in the dream (e.g. spectator, observer, actively involved).

2. Associations: Memories, thoughts, feelings, facts and spontaneous judgments of the singular images. Give information about people, locations, events and themes that have a specific meaning to you.
3. Personal appeal: Where, what, why, for what and how does this concern you? Interconnect all this with your interpretation.

4. Integrated interpretation: Interpret the key images and then the dream as a whole.

5. Consequences: Psychological, practical (life oriented), moral and spiritual (philosophical) conclusions.

Dream Dictionary

A dream dictionary is never THE interpretation!

Therefore consider the following statements:

→ Nearly all images have more than one meaning; there is an array of meaning.
→ One cannot expect that images in a dream dictionary are exhaustively interpreted.
→ The given information can never be taken as a fixed, irremovable interpretation.
→ The space of the over all meaning gives a surrounding and focusing orientation.
→ Elements of meaning should be managed seriously, but also easily and flexibly.
→ The space of meaning serves as a stimulation to search for more associations.
→ In order to recognize the correct interpretation one always needs the entire dream context.
→ Coherent interpretations are those that the person feels inside and those that match reality.
→ A lot of dream images have the right meaning only in the personal context.
→ Each interpretation has to be connected with the associations of each individual person.
→ If a dream image is not mentioned in the dream dictionary, similar dream images may help further.
→ A dream dictionary is a working instrument, not the interpretation.
→ Dealing with a dream dictionary demands intuitive and creative performance.

2. Knowledge and Exercises for Living Love

The path to love and happiness

Knowledge is power! Incomprehension means powerlessness! Most people know less than 3-5% about their psychical-spiritual being and life. They are at the mercy of the unknown rest. That's like a captain who is only aware of 3-5% of his ship and of the conditions of the passage; the rest he is blindly exposed to. Such navigation must be a nightmare and will surely lead to a catastrophe.

You are the captain of your being and life. Where will this lead if you don't know 95-97% of your being and life and if you don't control it accordingly?

Wake up and live with open eyes!

A saying: Life is the school for a young adult, once graduated from school. But what does life teach people? Do they learn what is really necessary from their life for the personal success and happiness in relationships and self-fulfillment?

Fact is that most people do not learn enough from their life. With that we come to the point: What is essential in learning? Open your eyes and you will quickly see it!

If you never learn about yourself in life, about your way of living, about your partner, about your relationships, about sex, about love and a whole lot more, at the end of your life you basically sacrifice your evolutional chances. Your human being remains unconscious and archaic.

Everybody makes mistakes in life, has failures, difficulties, crisis, pains, and fails even throughout years in everything. That's life and that's "normal". The real problem starts when people don't learn; don't acquire knowledge and skills for living. As a consequence one produces for oneself a life with little consciousness.

Failure, crisis and suffering contain chances: with oneself and one's life to achieve higher aims. Do you want to stick your head into the sand and simply look away? Wake up and live, but correctly!

The problem gets even worse if a person does not want to get to know himself, educate himself, change himself, or grow and develop himself. Self-discovery and self-education is certainly a self-evident pre-condition for all good aims concerning relationships, sex, love, partnership, being a woman / a man, renewing one's life, looking for a partner, etc.

If man doesn't develop himself consciously from his inner being and aiming for a higher quality of being then life forces him to be and to become what the external world forces him to be and to become.

You have the choice: ignorant or clever? Wake up and look at reality! And learn! Think and act according to realities. That means: "to live correctly" and "to love yourself"!

The particular joy of life starts when man can dedicate himself to life and at the same time take his human being and life successfully into his own hands.

With the necessary knowledge of life and a lot of practical exercises you can build up your success in a relationship, creating life and self-fulfillment. This is the path to love and happiness: practice the art to love and love yourself!

2.1. Practice the Art to Love

2.1.1. Create your relationship in manifold ways

Thesis I-1-L1/1.: In a relationship two human beings are face to face with each other. Both have a complex psychical life. There are multiple causes that can produce tensions and conflicts. Everybody can clarify them! Everybody can grow through that. There are several initial stages to improve the quality of a relationship.

Applies to me: 1 = not at all | 2 = somewhat | 3 = frequently | 4 = predominantly | 5 = completely

Rate	Exercise I-1-L1/1.: Me in a relationship. I realize about myself in my actual / past relationship:
	There are a few things going on in my mind that I don't understand well.
	My biography is rather charged and still has its effects on me.
	Certain expressions in front of my partner are / were not constructive.
	Certain patterns of behavior in relation to my partner are / were not well reflected.
	In the past my social system (relatives, friends) influenced my relationship.
	I don't have a strongly balanced life style in living together.
	Sometimes a "shadow" from me breaks through and then a quarrel erupts.
	I have certain small and bigger complexes that disturb certain situations.
	I have a certain tendency to provoke confrontations.

	I have a lack of knowledge and skills for life and relationship.
	The development of my personality is / was hindered in my relationship.
	I can't really live my nature (character as a man / a woman) in my relationship.
	Summarize and write in the field the total of points.

Thesis I-1-L1/2.: Many hopes are connected in a relationship between man and woman: peace, joy, harmony, fulfillment, desire tenderness, love, eroticism, good sex, care, constructive communication, faithfulness, safety, etc. This and much more we can find partnership-like linked with attitudes and behavior.

What have you experienced only slightly or even not at all from the following partnership-like principles in your relationship?

Applies to me: 1 = not at all | 2 = somewhat | 3 = frequently | 4 = predominantly | 5 = completely

Rate	Exercise I-1-L1/2.: Partnership-like principles. I experience (-d) the following partnership-like attitudes in my actual / past relationship.
	Mutual respect of the different nature (character, expression, gender).
	Reciprocity and equality in all life areas.
	Alternating nearness and distance in living together.
	Understanding the differences as well as the common interests.
	Respecting the limits of the other and the world of the other.
	Daily life gets a consciously cared central space in the communication.
	Stimulating love through little attentions.
	No mutual balancing of the mistakes and the undeveloped aspects.
	Reason and intelligence are supportive functions in all concerns.
	Eroticism, being in love and seduction has a place in the usual daily life.
	A high level of self-management (life techniques) on both sides.
	Acceptance of tensions, conflicts and certain risks.
	Mutual acceptance and fulfillment of sexual desire with love.
	Skills and effort to understand the partner and life in general.

	A constructive care of the "inner child" and the weaknesses.
	Mutual creating (developing) of femininity and masculinity.
	Resolving objective matters, interests and aims together.
	Distribution of roles is discussed and accepted; but remains flexible.
	Summarize and write in the field the total points.

Thesis I-1-L1/3.: A successful resolution of conflicts in the relationship demands skills to love and social competences (life techniques).

Manifold situations arise in the daily life of a relationship giving motive to quarrel.

Applies to me: 1 = not at all | 2 = somewhat | 3 = frequently |
4 = predominantly | 5 = completely

Rate	Exercise I-1-L1/3.: Critical situations. Rate what and how strongly arguments and conflicts occurred in your actual / past relationship.
	Not clearly and concretely expressing one's own needs.
	Misunderstandings even in small concerns because of unclear talking.
	Ignoring something to avoid a possible argument.
	Not giving seriousness to one's own feelings and the ones of the partner.
	Talking in unsuitable moments and situations about important matters.
	Not planning / deciding on time what is important and urgent.
	Eating, drinking and watching TV because of frustration or boredom.
	Behaving aggressively to create distance or to drive out (suppress).
	Secretly practiced unpunctuality in order to manipulate.
	Disorderliness indirectly expressing a protest or a provocation.
	Dissatisfaction as a result of a lack of common life aims.

	Financial problems / differences in dealing with money (consumption).
	Neglecting sexual desires (one's own and the ones of the partner).
	Carelessness, coldness, rudeness, negligence, indifference.
	Summarize and write in the field the total points.

Thesis I-1-L1/4.: In order to get success in a relationship, first a common base is needed. Love and the ability to love; as well as (self-) education are also necessary: self-knowledge, knowledge about the human being, forming personality, life learning and Individuation.

Exercise I-1-L1/4.: Find new views and attitudes. Mark what is necessary or especially important to you to give attention to in the daily dealing with relationship problems:

- Talking together is a learning process; e.g. through thinking about talking.
- There is no partnership without strong arguments sometimes.
- Some arguments hide a deficit of living skills and self-education.
- Arguing about banalities arises because of a deficit of conscious self-control.
- The total harmony doesn't exist! It's a serious problem if one is seeking for it.
- Frustration with one's self converts to a frustration in the relationship.
- Dogmas and ideologies are poison for a relationship with self-fulfillment.
- Many problems in a relationship have a lot to do with the whole person.
- Resolving relationship problems often demands also growth of the person.
- Learning and educational processes (reading, courses, etc.) are indispensable.

Exercise I-1-L1/5.: My most important relationship problems are:

Exercise I-1-L1/6.: That's the way I now want to resolve my relationship problems:

2.1.2. Discover being a woman and being a man

Thesis I-1-L2/1.: Man and woman are naturally (substantially) different:

- The psychical life (mind) as a whole doesn't work the same with men and women.
- Female and male roles are not all simply products of learning processes.
- Femininity and masculinity are psychological and biological qualities.
- No man (woman) becomes a man (woman) without the opposite gender.
- Man and woman have the psychical opposite gender as a polarity in their psyche (known as "anima" and "animus").

Exercise I-1-L2/1.: Overloaded experiences. Mark what affects you.

- ☐ I have overloaded and unbalanced experiences about: father / fathers / being a father.
- ☐ I have overloaded and unbalanced experiences about: mother / mothers / being a mother.
- ☐ I have overloaded and unbalanced experiences about: man / men / masculinity.
- ☐ I have overloaded and unbalanced experiences about: woman / women / femininity.

Thesis I-1-L2/2.: Experiences about one's own gender and the gender of the partner not only form the external masculinity (femininity), but also the inner psychical opposite gender pole. This refers to the concept of Individuation, where the inner gender pole of a man is known as "anima" and from a woman as "animus".

Individuation = genuine psychical-spiritual growing process

The more unbalanced the experiences about men and women are, the more unbalanced their inner image is (= anima, animus). With that the development of a person as a man / a woman also becomes unbalanced.

A mature man (and a mature woman) have integrated the female (and the male) concept in polarity to an integrative wholeness. Creating this balanced wholeness is the essential characteristic of a marriage (a firm relationship) between man and woman.

Experiences of the male concept

Applies to me: 1 = not at all | 2 = somewhat | 3 = frequently |
4 = predominantly | 5 = completely

Rate	Exercise I-1-L2/2. A: Male principles. Rate how much you have made negative experiences or had a lack of positive experiences with / about men:
	Spirit as the inner guidance power and source of human values.
	Developing structures as a basic pattern for living.
	Sketch projects to realize being and life.
	Management as a centralizing force in realizing life.
	Orgasmic sex as a lovely integrative experience with love.
	Principles open to life as a foundation for developing life.
	Explorations and discovering as curiosity and pleasure of life.
	Creating (stimulating) incidents and new things in many situations.
	Analytical thinking to understand, transform, and act.
	Rational power to realize life as an expression of responsibility.
	Masculine body and sexuality integrated as a part of self-identity.
	Summarize and write down the total points in the field.

Experiences of the female concept

Applies to me: 1 = not at all | 2 = somewhat | 3 = frequently |
4 = predominantly | 5 = completely

Rate	Exercise I-1-L2/2. B: Female principles. Rate where you have made negative experiences or had a lack of positive experiences with / about women:
	Expressing and living life as a source and expression of human values.
	Care as an expression of responsibility and a way of creating life.
	Nourishing as a law in physical and psychical areas.

	Protecting being and life because values of human beings lie inside.
	Care as an integrative way and expression of realization of life.
	Receiving as an enrichment, to understand and broaden the being.
	Romantic sex as a lovely integrative experience with love.
	Intuitive thinking to understand, improve, transform and act.
	Sensibility to penetrate in being and life, and to understand meaning.
	Emotional power to realize life as an expression of responsibility.
	Integrating the female body and sexuality as a part of self-identity.
	Summarize and write down the total points in the field.

Thesis I-1-L2/3.: The polarity of masculinity and femininity is certainly established naturally in the psyche (mind); but it is also formed by the biography and the living environment through various fragments. The quality of a relationship decisively depends on the way partners deal with this polarity and form, transform and openly develop this polarity for living.

Exercise I-1-L2/3.: Mark how it is with you:

☐ Masculinity and femininity don't mean a lot for my being and life.
☐ Creating a balance between masculinity and femininity is not important to me.
☐ I have only developed very little balance with the opposite gender in my psyche.
☐ Creating masculinity and femininity is not a matter of discussion with my partner.

Thesis I-1-L2/4.: The whole person is acting at all times in a relationship. Both have not well formed masculine and feminine ways of expression. Without a conscious self-education, man and woman mostly have very unbalanced character traits.

Character traits: Weaknesses / unbalanced state

Applies to me: 1 = not at all | 2 = somewhat | 3 = frequently | 4 = predominantly | 5 = completely

Rate	Exercise I-1-L2/4.: Character traits. Rate your weaknesses / your unbalanced state:
	Unbalanced introversion and extraversion.
	Striving for power and dominance.
	Feelings of inferiority, fears (anxiety), depression.
	Exaggerated attitude for order and organization.
	Excessively underlined narcissism.
	Moods, extreme variation of temper.
	Laziness, indifference.
	Nagging, criticizing, condemning judgments.
	Order in housekeeping; correctness in behavior.
	Distribution of roles and work.
	Sexual experiencing and acting, rejecting sexual pleasure.
	Faithfulness and adultery; jealousy.
	Male and female emancipation.
	Adaptation and creative new forming.
	Need of autonomy and liberty.
	Summarize and write down the total points in the field.

Exercise I-1-L2/5.: My most important problems with masculinity and femininity are:

Exercise I-1-L2/6.: My way of better finding my polarity of masculinity and femininity is:

2.1.3. Love and love yourself completely

Thesis I-1-L3/1.: If the partner is the opposite pole in the relationship between a man and a woman, wholeness is created in the person and in the relationship. The psychological compatibility and accommodating spirit of both partners are another part of this wholeness of a person and relationship. Furthermore love wants to realize the being, meaning of life and aims of life as a common solitarian life project.

Real love between man and woman in daily life

Applies to me: 1 = not at all | 2 = somewhat | 3 = frequently | 4 = predominantly | 5 = completely

Rate	Exercise I-1-L3/1.: Foundation in Life. Rate where you see your own weak states, your deficits:
	Highly value the truthfulness of both partners.
	Promote mutual care (forming) of the psychical life.
	Turn towards emotions and interpret these feelings as an important message.
	Face the facts of life with responsibility and awareness.
	Developing (realizing) the potentials and promoting them with the partner.
	To value sensuality and express it in diverse ways with the partner.
	To take arguments seriously and reduce them; reconcile the same day.
	Often wanting constructive talks even with little daily matters.
	Giving high importance to the psychical-spiritual growth and mutually promoting it.
	Giving certain deepness to one's own life and as well to the relationship.
	Being cautious with the own destructive forces of the unconscious.
	Integrating (not suppressing) drive & desire; giving importance, talking about.
	Respecting physical needs (health) and taking care of them.
	Experiencing life time as something valuable and using it in meaningful ways.
	Protecting and promoting the values of being and living together.
	Adapting a lot of knowledge to creating human life with competences (skills).
	Transforming rigid principles and norms in open patterns for life.

	Strengthening decisiveness against everything that could destroy love.
	Developing pleasure in discovering the inner transcendental realities.
	Summarize and write down the total of points in the field.

Thesis I-1-L3/2.: Self-love is the beginning of any love. Love has got to do with having interest, caring, dedicating, promoting, growing, protecting and strengthening. Love begins with turning towards psychical life and integrating it. Forming and protecting one's own psychical life is self-love.

Strengthening for love

Applies to me: 1 = not at all | 2 = somewhat | 3 = frequently | 4 = predominantly | 5 = completely

Rate	Exercise I-1-L3/2.: Strength for love. Rate your qualities:
	I am interested in my inner life and in my whole life.
	I consciously and critically turn towards what I am and live.
	I promote and use my potentials, tendencies and talents.
	I develop my weak and not well formed psychical forces and skills.
	I transform my life forces and life plans into realities.
	I form what is not formed; I also further develop my psychical life.
	I consciously control myself and am balanced in daily life.
	I strengthen my weaknesses; I am regardful with my limits.
	I give importance to my dreams, intuitions and body sensations.
	I am thankful facing life for all that I can live.
	I feel that I am integrated in a transcendental network.
	I take responsibility for my happiness and my acting.
	I act with competences and knowledge in my personal life.
	I can enjoy little things with myself and in my life.
	Summarize and write down the total points in the field.

Thesis I-1-L3/3.: Love between man and woman is not only a psychological matter. Love is stimulated through being addressed from the character (nature) of the other gender and through the archetypal importance of a male-female-relationship. This kind of love promotes the superior wholeness of masculinity and femininity, psychological, physical and practical in life. With such a love man and woman shall find their own wholeness through the other gender.

This unification is of deep spiritual meaning and since the beginning of history one of the highest archetypes; this means: being, path and aim are the same time. The marriage as a bond and way of living *between man and woman* is in that sense archetypal; that means: always valid, always a special meaning of human beings and in this orientation "holy" (means: untouchable and inextinguishable value).

The balance in your relationship

Applies to me: 1 = not at all | 2 = somewhat | 3 = frequently | 4 = predominantly | 5 = completely

Rate	Exercise I-1-L3/3.: Mutual match. Rate how much / how often you experienced this in your actual / past relationship:
	We have some very similar character traits and qualities.
	I am a true friend to my partner when he / she is in trouble.
	In general I feel we are very similar and we really have a lot in common.
	I can live my path of self-fulfillment; nevertheless we are a whole together.
	I feel touched how my partner realizes spiritual values of the human being.
	Our project is to find higher meaning in life; and this is our life project.
	We are peaceful, in our sexual life as well as in all aspects of being and living.
	We are like two instruments playing the same open melody of life.
	In our undertakings we are like companions and accomplices.
	We take the same path and within each of us his own path.
	I feel appealed by the whole nature of my partner – and my partner too.
	We can respect each other in being man / woman with a deep enrichment.
	Summarize and write down the total points in the field.

Thesis I-1-L3/4.: "Do you love me?" is the first question the baby asks mum and dad; it is even a prenatal experience from the fetus. This implies the question after the "me", which means: "especially me; exclusively me as your child". In the relationship between man and woman this question repeats itself on another level every day; and with that often the drama from the childhood.

The complete love between man and woman is a quality that both have to elaborate, to work on; something that is never given naturally. Complete love is an essential aim of marriage.

Applies to me: 1 = not at all | 2 = somewhat | 3 = frequently |
4 = predominantly | 5 = completely

Rate	Exercise I-1-L3/4.: The complete love. Contemplate your state of love for your partner.
	I love my partner with heart, body, mind, spirit and soul.
	I love my partner from the bottom of my being.
	I love my partner with knowledge, wisdom and skills.
	I love my partner will full trust and faith.
	I love my partner with intelligence, reason, intuition, body feelings.
	I love my partner without hidden reserve and unlimitedly.
	Summarize and write down the total points in the field.

Exercise I-1-L3/5.: My love for my partner has some weaknesses:

Exercise I-1-L3/6.: I want to stimulate and deepen my love for my partner as follows:

2.1.4. Enjoy making love with creativity

Thesis I-1-L4/1.: A human being is more than just an apparatus of biological desire. A human being is also a psychical-spiritual nature. Many people mix up sexual desire with love; they think if they possess and satisfy each other physically and if they live together peacefully, they love each other.

Sexual experiences: deficits and unsatisfied needs

Applies to me: 1 = not at all | 2 = somewhat | 3 = frequently | 4 = predominantly | 5 = completely

Rate	Exercise I-1-L4/1.: Sexual experiences. Search for your weaknesses, deficits and unsatisfied needs in your actual / past relationship.
	I feel alienated from my partner in the sexual unification.
	Tenderness as an expression of love is often missed out on.
	I do not recognize my partner as a man (a woman).
	I only experience my partner in sexuality on a physical level.
	I have the impression that I am a sexual object for my partner.
	I think the orgasm is the purpose and aim of making love.
	We don't try to stimulate lust (seduce) and to creatively increase it.
	I don't like the moment of excitement; I feel rather embarrassed.
	For us "Sex = Sex". Love doesn't play an essential role.
	I have difficulty in getting sexual satisfaction; I don't feel comfortable.
	We rarely create an erotic phase before we have sex.
	Summarize and write down the total points in the field.

Thesis I-1-L4/2.: Sexuality is interesting from the beginning of the early childhood; during the whole youth up until the adult age, sexuality plays an extremely important role, as a specific issue (just "sex"). Sexuality also plays an important part in forming the self-identity. In adult age, sex plays nearly a daily role as desire, wish, conflict, and the power of living.

Sexuality is much more than creating lust and orgasm. Accepting sexuality means accepting the nature of the human being with all possibilities of sensual experiences. If somebody really likes sex, he creates a sexual encounter with self-reflection and communication with the partner.
Sexuality and eroticism regularly need creative expressions; and also contemplating and searching one's self and the partner. All sexual problems (as long as they are not medical) have got to do with the whole person!

The sexual biography as the foundation of the actually lived sexuality

Applies to me: 1 = not at all | 2 = somewhat | 3 = frequently |
4 = predominantly | 5 = completely

Rate	Exercise I-1-L4/2. A: Sexual coding. Rate that which concerns you and how much:
	During my puberty sexuality was greatly overcharged with problems.
	I didn't feel comfortable during my first love relationship.
	Experiencing lust and sex is / was often (mostly) mixed with feelings of guilt.
	I had / have special sexual difficulties.
	My first sexual experiences were totally not pleasant.
	In my previous relationship(s) I had very embarrassing sexual moments.
	My previous failure in a love relationship also had to do with sex.
	My (religious) education concerning sex was extremely hostile towards lust.
	My previous partner(s) had serious sexual difficulties.
	I had / have feelings of inferiority in the context with sex.
	I often felt humiliated, depreciated and put down during sex.
	Summarize and write down the total points in the field.

Sexual attitudes

Applies to me: 1 = not at all | 2 = somewhat | 3 = frequently |
4 = predominantly | 5 = completely

Rate	Exercise I-1-L4/2. B: Sexual attitudes. Rate how much you feel concerned.
	I have a relaxed and positive attitude towards sexuality.
	I have a relaxed and positive attitude towards menstruation.
	I have a relaxed and positive attitude towards ejaculation.
	I have a relaxed and positive attitude towards orgasm.
	I have a relaxed and positive attitude towards physical release.
	I have a relaxed and positive attitude towards the (erected) penis.
	I have a relaxed and positive attitude towards the (wet) vagina.
	I have a relaxed and positive attitude towards boobs and nipples.
	I have a relaxed and positive attitude towards my strongly excited partner.

	I have a relaxed and positive attitude towards passionate oral sex.
	I have a relaxed and positive attitude towards seducing my partner.
	I have a relaxed and positive attitude towards sexual manifold creativity.
	Summarize and write down the total points in the field.

Thesis I-1-L4/3.: A human being with his psychical-spiritual wholeness always contributes much more to the sexual play than a simple sexual act. For example: The initiation phase is more than increasing lust, it is a human encounter! Being naked produces more than just lust, it often means being unprotected, sometimes even combined with the fear of being punished, or simply complete dedication.

Sex and experiences as a human being

Applies to me: 1 = not at all | 2 = somewhat | 3 = frequently | 4 = predominantly | 5 = completely

Rate	Exercise I-1-L4/3.: Sex and feelings. Rate what concerns you actually / in the past.
	Whilst experiencing sex I feel vulnerable, sensible, easily offended.
	The sexual encounter produces fear, shame and embarrassment.
	I feel inner closure & blockage from things from the day or from sorrow.
	I have a strong self-control; I feel observed when I have sex.
	I doubt myself; I have feelings of inferiority (physical appearance).
	I have fear that the problems from the past will repeat themselves.
	I feel pressure to perform and fear of not being good enough.
	I feel restraint to tell my partner when I want sex.
	I don't feel well with the shape and size of my penis / my boobs.
	Summarize and write down the total points in the field.

Thesis I-1-L4/4.: Sexual experiencing and acting also include communication; real words or messages expressed in tenderness, kisses, chatting, touching, or eye contact. Therefore sexuality is also a complete sensual experience and forms the self-identity of a person. Symbolic expressions and words during the sexual act move the whole person and not simply the body!

Messages to the love game

Applies to me: 1 = not at all | 2 = somewhat | 3 = frequently | 4 = predominantly | 5 = completely

Rate	Exercise I-1-L4/4.: Communication about sex and feelings. Rate what concerns you actually / in the past.
	How do you feel that? Do you like that? Does this annoy you?
	What do you like? Show me how you like it!
	What / how do you want to do it now? What increases your lust?
	Take your time! It's wonderful to be with you now in that way.
	I would like to try something new. You too?
	What do you especially like on me?
	I love you, your body, and the way you are, also when we have sex.
	Tell me if you don't like something, if something inconveniences you.
	Summarize and write down the total points in the field.

Exercise I-1-L4/5.: What I miss when having sex on the level of love:

Exercise I-1-L4/6.: On the level of the sexual act I have problems with:

Exercise I-1-L4/7.: What I sometimes want my partner to say when making love:

2.1.5. Live your relationship partnership-like

Thesis I-1-L5/1.: There are several possible attempts to avoid arising arguments and conflicts in a love relationship; or to deal with such situations constructively. Both partners jointly determine the conditions and rules for a constructive living together and for a constructive dealing with life matters.

Attitudes about partnership-like living

Applies to me: 1 = not at all | 2 = somewhat | 3 = frequently | 4 = predominantly | 5 = completely

Rate	Exercise I-1-L5/1.: Attitudes for partnership-like living. Search where you see weaknesses, deficits and needs for yourself and for your actual / past relationship.
	Continuous effort to understand oneself and the partner.
	Regularly see the partner in new ways in his being and growing.
	Continuously explain one's own being and growing.
	Mutually promoting and developing being a man / a woman.
	Elaborating and revising the basic values of love together.
	To understand self-management in daily life as a matter of both.
	Creating a home to feel comfortable and where each one has his own place.
	Regularly creating common experiences that bring joy.
	Regularly finding agreements in all matters, also in petty matters.
	To understand and elaborate the common biography of the relationship.
	Forming a couple-identity through the common biography.
	Respecting the fact that both are in permanent development as a personality.
	Continuously learning about psyche, love, emotions, and sex.
	In all areas of living always promote and use creativity.
	Arguing correctly without games of rejection or blocking each other.
	Not mutually balancing the mistakes. To forgive and to reconcile!
	Reducing life lies without reproaching each other; and learning from that.
	Seriously dealing with one's own dreams (that we have while sleeping).
	Giving higher importance to the psychical-spiritual life than to external values.

	Each one practices self-education and personal development in his or her own way.
	Summarize and write down the total points in the field.

Thesis I-1-L5/2.: In a dialogue there are realities which need to be accepted, for example: A complete accord is rarely possible. Talking about talking promotes understanding. One cannot talk better than one perceives, thinks, and has knowledge. Talking is always an expression of a previous thinking and feeling. Communication is a very important way of dealing with realities. Communication is always more human oriented than object-oriented.

Creating communication in a relationship

Applies to me: 1 = not at all | 2 = somewhat | 3 = frequently | 4 = predominantly | 5 = completely

Rate	Exercise I-1-L5/2.: Communication in a relationship. Search for your weaknesses, deficits and needs.
	Objective, informative, precise.
	Transparent, open, not hiding.
	Cooperative, partnership-like.
	Conscious, profound, binding.
	Efficient in time use, organized, systematic.
	Asking, actively and flexibly adapting.
	Prudent, serious, tranquil, decisive.
	Concentrated, conscious, listening well.
	Planned, settled, prepared.
	Summarize and write down the total points in the field.

Thesis I-1-L5/3.: Arguments and conflicts can be avoided or reduced by practical actions. The way a person faces a problem talking to his partner is often more important than the problem (conflict) itself.

Exercise I-1-L5/3.: How do you treat your partner? Mark where you see a deficit for yourself and your relationship:

- ☐ friendly, obliging, benevolent, courteous, respectful
- ☐ honest, authentic, open, without games, fair, just, not ignoring
- ☐ flexible and adapting style (language, behavior) and issue (matter)
- ☐ democratic, partnership-like, cooperative, supportive, tied-up

Thesis I-1-L5/4.: Practical rules of behavior and communication are embedded in a whole complex:

- Accepting the complexity of the psyche (mind), of the psychical-spiritual growth, and of the realities of life.
- Continuously finding and understanding one's self and the partner in the genuine whole being and growing anew.
- Accepting and promoting mutual self-education and life learning.
- A well functioning relationship is decisively based on the forming of the psychical functions (self-education and life learning).
- Self-education doesn't make the relationship good; love is ultimately decisive.
- Love without life learning and without using intelligence destroys itself.

The 12 Rules of partnership-like communication

Applies to me: 1 = not at all | 2 = somewhat | 3 = frequently | 4 = predominantly | 5 = completely

Rate	Exercise I-1-L5/4.: 12 orientations of partnership-like communication. Rate where you see deficits for yourself and for your actual / past relationship:
	Not humiliating, not hurting, not depreciating, and not mocking.
	Not interposing, not exaggerating, and not loosing the tone.
	Discussing matters cooperatively, mutually, complementarily, and together.
	Communication: plain, clear, objective, differentiated, open, direct.
	Listening, understanding, giving weight, selecting, and letting the partner articulate.
	Adequately expressing problems, wishes, questions and feelings.

	Holding and allowing distance and autonomy.
	Respect for the partner as an autonomous person.
	Considering spiritual bonds (e.g. dreams), intuition and inner resonance.
	Considering the physical state of oneself and of the partner.
	Understanding the past as a challenge for learning, and not as a reproach.
	Continuously thinking and renewing values, norms and attitudes.
	Summarize and write down the total points in the field.

Let's be "human":

Misunderstandings are normal. Conflicts and arguments are part of life. Infringing the rules of good communication and of appropriate conducts is human (but should not become a habit!).

Exercise I-1-L5/5.: I recognize a deficit in my way of creating relationships:

Exercise I-1-L5/6.: I will talk to my partner about what we can improve, for example:

2.1.6. Prepare yourself well for love

1. You want to renew your actual relationship. Elaborate the following exercises and show the result to your partner! After that your partner shall do the same and present you his result.

2. You want a new start. You are looking for a partner. You want an ambitious relationship. Elaborating these exercises you prepare yourself for that. Looking for a partner comes later. Consider the exercises especially when making the decision for a partner!

Thesis I-1-L6/1.: The way of living forms in the common frame in which a life with a partner develops.

Exercise I-1-L6/1.: I see my way of living in general as follows:

Mark that which concerns you:

1 = not at all | 2 = a little | 3 = quite a lot | 4 = a lot | 5 = totally

1 2 3 4 5
☐ ☐ ☐ ☐ ☐ Doing active sport
☐ ☐ ☐ ☐ ☐ Consumption of alcohol
☐ ☐ ☐ ☐ ☐ Smoker
☐ ☐ ☐ ☐ ☐ Watching television
☐ ☐ ☐ ☐ ☐ Traveling
☐ ☐ ☐ ☐ ☐ I like cooking
☐ ☐ ☐ ☐ ☐ Going to bars
☐ ☐ ☐ ☐ ☐ Concerts/theatre
☐ ☐ ☐ ☐ ☐ Like discos
☐ ☐ ☐ ☐ ☐ Aesthete, with style
☐ ☐ ☐ ☐ ☐ Social type
☐ ☐ ☐ ☐ ☐ Circle of friends
☐ ☐ ☐ ☐ ☐ Fashion-oriented
☐ ☐ ☐ ☐ ☐ Comfortable clothing
☐ ☐ ☐ ☐ ☐ Energetic type
☐ ☐ ☐ ☐ ☐ Practical type
☐ ☐ ☐ ☐ ☐ Intellectual type
☐ ☐ ☐ ☐ ☐ Artist type
☐ ☐ ☐ ☐ ☐ Business type
☐ ☐ ☐ ☐ ☐ Caring type
☐ ☐ ☐ ☐ ☐ Individualist type

☐ ☐ ☐ ☐ ☐ Suit and tie type
☐ ☐ ☐ ☐ ☐ I like nature
☐ ☐ ☐ ☐ ☐ Animal lover

Thesis I-1-L6/2.: Each person can develop himself; determine his paths and aims with autonomy. Or ignore and reject it. The level and the way of creating this kind of self-forming is that which forms the quality of a relationship.

Exercise I-1-L6/2.: I see myself as a person and my nature in the following way:

Mark that which is important to you:

1 = not at all | 2 = little | 3 = quite a lot | 4 = a lot | 5 = totally

1 2 3 4 5		1 2 3 4 5	
☐ ☐ ☐ ☐ ☐	Experienced in life	☐ ☐ ☐ ☐ ☐	Ambitious
☐ ☐ ☐ ☐ ☐	Peaceful	☐ ☐ ☐ ☐ ☐	Educated
☐ ☐ ☐ ☐ ☐	Optimistic	☐ ☐ ☐ ☐ ☐	Kind-hearted
☐ ☐ ☐ ☐ ☐	Enterprising	☐ ☐ ☐ ☐ ☐	Easy going
☐ ☐ ☐ ☐ ☐	Thoughtful	☐ ☐ ☐ ☐ ☐	Purposeful
☐ ☐ ☐ ☐ ☐	Flexible	☐ ☐ ☐ ☐ ☐	Benevolent
☐ ☐ ☐ ☐ ☐	Self-critical	☐ ☐ ☐ ☐ ☐	Responsible
☐ ☐ ☐ ☐ ☐	Self-assured	☐ ☐ ☐ ☐ ☐	Oncoming
☐ ☐ ☐ ☐ ☐	Tolerant	☐ ☐ ☐ ☐ ☐	Respectful
☐ ☐ ☐ ☐ ☐	Cheerful-vital	☐ ☐ ☐ ☐ ☐	Charismatic
☐ ☐ ☐ ☐ ☐	Sensible	☐ ☐ ☐ ☐ ☐	Open to the world
☐ ☐ ☐ ☐ ☐	Generous	☐ ☐ ☐ ☐ ☐	Circumspect
☐ ☐ ☐ ☐ ☐	Contemplative	☐ ☐ ☐ ☐ ☐	Unconstrained
☐ ☐ ☐ ☐ ☐	Independent	☐ ☐ ☐ ☐ ☐	Creative
☐ ☐ ☐ ☐ ☐	Stable	☐ ☐ ☐ ☐ ☐	Meaning-oriented
☐ ☐ ☐ ☐ ☐	Attentive	☐ ☐ ☐ ☐ ☐	Wise
☐ ☐ ☐ ☐ ☐	Vigilant	☐ ☐ ☐ ☐ ☐	Enthusiastic
☐ ☐ ☐ ☐ ☐	Free-spirited	☐ ☐ ☐ ☐ ☐	Sharpened mind
☐ ☐ ☐ ☐ ☐	Self-confident	☐ ☐ ☐ ☐ ☐	Spiritual
☐ ☐ ☐ ☐ ☐	Decisive	☐ ☐ ☐ ☐ ☐	Open to learn
☐ ☐ ☐ ☐ ☐	Intuitive	☐ ☐ ☐ ☐ ☐	Open for life
☐ ☐ ☐ ☐ ☐	Balanced	☐ ☐ ☐ ☐ ☐	Interested
☐ ☐ ☐ ☐ ☐	Self-strong	☐ ☐ ☐ ☐ ☐	Open for experiments
☐ ☐ ☐ ☐ ☐	Well-read	☐ ☐ ☐ ☐ ☐	Forgiving
☐ ☐ ☐ ☐ ☐	Mentally awake	☐ ☐ ☐ ☐ ☐	Self-determined
☐ ☐ ☐ ☐ ☐	Sympathetic	☐ ☐ ☐ ☐ ☐	Communicative

☐ ☐ ☐ ☐ ☐ Sympathetic mind ☐ ☐ ☐ ☐ ☐ Autonomous
☐ ☐ ☐ ☐ ☐ Caring ☐ ☐ ☐ ☐ ☐ Like being alone
☐ ☐ ☐ ☐ ☐ Unique ☐ ☐ ☐ ☐ ☐ Phenomenal
☐ ☐ ☐ ☐ ☐ Reliable ☐ ☐ ☐ ☐ ☐ Exceptional
☐ ☐ ☐ ☐ ☐ Well cared ☐ ☐ ☐ ☐ ☐ Orderliness
☐ ☐ ☐ ☐ ☐ Honest ☐ ☐ ☐ ☐ ☐ Trustworthy
☐ ☐ ☐ ☐ ☐ Faithful, loyal ☐ ☐ ☐ ☐ ☐ Full of hope
☐ ☐ ☐ ☐ ☐ Lovely ☐ ☐ ☐ ☐ ☐ Compromising
☐ ☐ ☐ ☐ ☐ Authentic ☐ ☐ ☐ ☐ ☐ Able to orgasm
☐ ☐ ☐ ☐ ☐ Transparent ☐ ☐ ☐ ☐ ☐ Attentive
☐ ☐ ☐ ☐ ☐ Humorous ☐ ☐ ☐ ☐ ☐ Entertaining
☐ ☐ ☐ ☐ ☐ Pragmatic ☐ ☐ ☐ ☐ ☐ Hard worker
☐ ☐ ☐ ☐ ☐ Serious-minded ☐ ☐ ☐ ☐ ☐ Sexually natural
☐ ☐ ☐ ☐ ☐ With a clear life path ☐ ☐ ☐ ☐ ☐ Open to grow
☐ ☐ ☐ ☐ ☐ Able to love ☐ ☐ ☐ ☐ ☐ With life aims
☐ ☐ ☐ ☐ ☐ Free in my inner life ☐ ☐ ☐ ☐ ☐ Understanding
☐ ☐ ☐ ☐ ☐ Passionate ☐ ☐ ☐ ☐ ☐ Charitable

Exercise I-1-L6/3.: I have the following conception about the way of living of my ideal partner:

Rate what you expect from your ideal partner:

1 = not at all | 2 = little | 3 = quite a lot | 4 = a lot | 5 = totally

<u>Or renewing the actual relationship:</u>
a) This is how I see my partner.
b) This is how my partner is – or: How I wish him / her to be.

1 2 3 4 5   1 2 3 4 5
☐ ☐ ☐ ☐ ☐ Doing active sport ☐ ☐ ☐ ☐ ☐ Consumption of alcohol
☐ ☐ ☐ ☐ ☐ Smoker ☐ ☐ ☐ ☐ ☐ Watching television
☐ ☐ ☐ ☐ ☐ Traveling ☐ ☐ ☐ ☐ ☐ I like cooking
☐ ☐ ☐ ☐ ☐ Going to bars ☐ ☐ ☐ ☐ ☐ Concerts/theatre
☐ ☐ ☐ ☐ ☐ Like discos ☐ ☐ ☐ ☐ ☐ Aesthete, with style
☐ ☐ ☐ ☐ ☐ Social type ☐ ☐ ☐ ☐ ☐ Circle of friends
☐ ☐ ☐ ☐ ☐ Fashion-oriented ☐ ☐ ☐ ☐ ☐ Comfortable clothing
☐ ☐ ☐ ☐ ☐ Energetic type ☐ ☐ ☐ ☐ ☐ Practical type
☐ ☐ ☐ ☐ ☐ Intellectual type ☐ ☐ ☐ ☐ ☐ Artist type
☐ ☐ ☐ ☐ ☐ Business type ☐ ☐ ☐ ☐ ☐ Caring type
☐ ☐ ☐ ☐ ☐ Individualist type ☐ ☐ ☐ ☐ ☐ Suit and tie type
☐ ☐ ☐ ☐ ☐ I like nature ☐ ☐ ☐ ☐ ☐ Animal lover

Exercise I-1-L6/4.: I wish a partner to have the following characteristics / attributes:

Character traits / characteristics

Mark that which is important to you:

1 = not 2 = little 3 = quite a lot 4 = a lot 5 = totally

1	2	3	4	5		1	2	3	4	5	
☐	☐	☐	☐	☐	Experienced	☐	☐	☐	☐	☐	Ambitious
☐	☐	☐	☐	☐	Peaceful	☐	☐	☐	☐	☐	Educated
☐	☐	☐	☐	☐	Optimistic	☐	☐	☐	☐	☐	Kind-hearted
☐	☐	☐	☐	☐	Enterprising	☐	☐	☐	☐	☐	Easy going
☐	☐	☐	☐	☐	Thoughtful	☐	☐	☐	☐	☐	Purposeful
☐	☐	☐	☐	☐	Flexible	☐	☐	☐	☐	☐	Benevolent
☐	☐	☐	☐	☐	Self-critical	☐	☐	☐	☐	☐	Responsible
☐	☐	☐	☐	☐	Self-assured	☐	☐	☐	☐	☐	Oncoming
☐	☐	☐	☐	☐	Tolerant	☐	☐	☐	☐	☐	Respectful
☐	☐	☐	☐	☐	Cheerful-vital	☐	☐	☐	☐	☐	Charismatic
☐	☐	☐	☐	☐	Sensible	☐	☐	☐	☐	☐	Open to the world
☐	☐	☐	☐	☐	Generous	☐	☐	☐	☐	☐	Circumspect
☐	☐	☐	☐	☐	Contemplative	☐	☐	☐	☐	☐	Unconstrained
☐	☐	☐	☐	☐	Independent	☐	☐	☐	☐	☐	Creative
☐	☐	☐	☐	☐	Stable	☐	☐	☐	☐	☐	Meaning-oriented
☐	☐	☐	☐	☐	Attentive	☐	☐	☐	☐	☐	Wise
☐	☐	☐	☐	☐	Vigilant	☐	☐	☐	☐	☐	Enthusiastic
☐	☐	☐	☐	☐	Free-spirited	☐	☐	☐	☐	☐	Sharpened mind
☐	☐	☐	☐	☐	Self-confident	☐	☐	☐	☐	☐	Spiritual
☐	☐	☐	☐	☐	Decisive	☐	☐	☐	☐	☐	Open to learn
☐	☐	☐	☐	☐	Intuitive	☐	☐	☐	☐	☐	Open for life
☐	☐	☐	☐	☐	Balanced	☐	☐	☐	☐	☐	Interested
☐	☐	☐	☐	☐	Self-strong	☐	☐	☐	☐	☐	Open for experiments
☐	☐	☐	☐	☐	Well-read	☐	☐	☐	☐	☐	Forgiving
☐	☐	☐	☐	☐	Mentally awake	☐	☐	☐	☐	☐	Self-determined
☐	☐	☐	☐	☐	Sympathetic ability	☐	☐	☐	☐	☐	Communicative
☐	☐	☐	☐	☐	Sympathetic mind	☐	☐	☐	☐	☐	Autonomous
☐	☐	☐	☐	☐	Caring	☐	☐	☐	☐	☐	Like being alone
☐	☐	☐	☐	☐	Unique	☐	☐	☐	☐	☐	Phenomenal
☐	☐	☐	☐	☐	Reliable	☐	☐	☐	☐	☐	Exceptional
☐	☐	☐	☐	☐	Well cared	☐	☐	☐	☐	☐☐	Orderliness

				Honest						Trustworthy
☐	☐	☐	☐	☐	Honest	☐	☐	☐	☐	☐	Trustworthy
☐	☐	☐	☐	☐	Faithful, loyal	☐	☐	☐	☐	☐	Full of hope
☐	☐	☐	☐	☐	Lovely	☐	☐	☐	☐	☐	Open for compromises
☐	☐	☐	☐	☐	Authentic	☐	☐	☐	☐	☐	Able to get orgasm
☐	☐	☐	☐	☐	Transparent	☐	☐	☐	☐	☐	Attentive
☐	☐	☐	☐	☐	Humorous	☐	☐	☐	☐	☐	Entertaining
☐	☐	☐	☐	☐	Pragmatic	☐	☐	☐	☐	☐	Hard worker
☐	☐	☐	☐	☐	Serious-minded	☐	☐	☐	☐	☐	Sexually natural
☐	☐	☐	☐	☐	With clear path	☐	☐	☐	☐	☐	Open to grow
☐	☐	☐	☐	☐	Able to love	☐	☐	☐	☐	☐	With life aims
☐	☐	☐	☐	☐	Free inside	☐	☐	☐	☐	☐	Understanding
☐	☐	☐	☐	☐	Passionate	☐	☐	☐	☐	☐	Charitable

Exercise I-1-L6/5.: In no way do I want my partner to have / be / do / wish:

Exercise I-1-L6/6.: Write down 3 points about what has highest importance to you:

2.2. Love yourself

2.2.1. Discover your I and your psychical life

Thesis I-2-L1/1.: Some facts about psychical life are: Nearly everything in life has psychical origins and effects. Each human being has a psychical life. Each person has a lot of singular psychical forces. Everything that man does is linked with his psychical forces. A human being is not determinable without his psychical life. A person never finds his happiness and his authentic self-fulfillment without forming his psychical-spiritual life. Without self-education with Spirit and love there are always unbalanced results with extensive consequences in the life of an individual and in the society.

Lack of knowledge, pre-judgments, thoughtlessness and indifference paralyzes a person, makes him blind and susceptible for manipulations (ideologies, dogmas, consumption, etc).

Applies to me: 1 = not at all | 2 = somewhat | 3 = frequently | 4 = predominantly | 5 = completely

Rate	Exercise I-2-L1/1.: Knowledge, pre-judgments, thoughtlessness. Rate what concerns you.
	So much is going on in my mind that I can't recognize / can't understand.
	If I hear the word "psyche" or "psychological" I turn away internally.
	I feel fear over approaching myself to my inner psychical life.
	I don't know a lot about the psychical life (my own, in general).
	I don't understand what's going on with me / with human beings.
	It's a new idea for me that I can build/form my psyche (mind).
	Self-knowledge sounds interesting, but I don't really want it.
	I have my ideals that lead me; I don't need my "psyche".
	I am sure that I know much more than 3-5 % of my psyche (psychical life).
	I have no need to deepen my self-knowledge.
	I don't think that I have a spiritual force inside.

	I can't imagine that I am dependent through my unconscious.
	Summarize and write down the total points in the field.

Thesis I-2-L1/2.: Probably nearly all men and women know and use a variety of words that have got to do with the psychical life. But most people rarely reflect their system of psychical forces (psyche, inner life, and mind).

Attitudes towards psyche and psychical life

Applies to me: 1 = not at all | 2 = somewhat | 3 = frequently | 4 = predominantly | 5 = completely

Rate	Exercise I-2-L1/2.: State (aims) of development. Rate how much it applies to you.
	I know how I think. I think thoroughly, in networks, creatively and based on knowledge.
	I know my feelings (emotions); I know when and why I have certain feelings; I can deal with it.
	I entirely satisfy my psychical needs; and I satisfy them with reason, love, Spirit, and intelligence.
	I know my ability to love; I know that love is a manifold potential of forces.
	I am aware of my psychical energy. I know how to center and strengthen it.
	I know who I am and what I am; I know my "self"; and I am the captain of my being and life.
	I know my super-ego with the ideals, attitudes, beliefs, values and norms.
	I have a differentiated awareness about what's going on in my head.
	I see clearly what is in my conscience and controls me from inside.
	I have a strong will and clearly reasoned determined wishes. What I want is reflected.
	I am aware about my various mechanisms of defense and I can control them flexibly.
	I consciously control what I integrate from the outside world, having all this later inside.
	My perception is differentiated, long-sighted, and variously interrelated; I am very critical about everything.
	My language is much differentiated and I use my language to deal with my life.

	I do interpret my dreams; I know about the importance of them as a spiritual counselor and guidance for life.
	I utilize daydreaming and fantasies as a creative source to understand myself and people.
	I know my unconscious; I know what kind of inventory is piled up there. Everything is o.k. in there.
	I have a lot of memories and a lot of knowledge about life. I can make use of all this constructively.
	My actions are well reflected (contemplated), well reasoned, and formed widely as skills for living.
	Summarize and write down the total points in the field.

Thesis I-2-L1/3.: The psychical life is a complex and diversely operating inner world. The psyche is similar to the body, like an "organic wholeness". All psychical forces stay interconnected in many active relations. They influence each other, mostly without being perceived by us. We can consider the sum of all psychical forces as the psychical system.

→ We call this reality: **"THE PSYCHICAL ORGANISM"**.

Forming personality

Applies to me: 1 = not at all | 2 = somewhat | 3 = frequently | 4 = predominantly | 5 = completely

Rate	Exercise I-2-L1/3.: Personality aspects. Rate where you see the need of becoming aware and need of forming:
	The actions (behavior) in the external world.
	The psycho-dynamic and its psychical energy. Life energy.
	The "I" and its supportive functions (e.g. will, defense, control).
	The intelligence (from the perception to thinking and learning).
	The emotions (feelings); (the whole spectrum from dedication to rejection of life).
	The needs (psycho-physical, psychical).
	The unconscious, including the conscience.
	The use of the spiritual power in dreams, imagination and contemplation.
	The power of love with all its possibilities to perform.
	The shadows; meaning: the critical traits of the character that sometimes break through.
	Summarize and write down the total points in the field.

Thesis I-2-L1/4.: The mutual influence of the singular psychical forces is varied. No psychical area functions without interconnection with other psychical areas. This inner manifoldness is to most people unconscious, not adequately formed, chaotic, and not really controllable by the "I". In other words: most people are very dependent on the inside; they can't constructively make the most of the singular psychical areas of life and growth; in the absence of knowledge about this inner microcosm most people search for their salvation and fulfillment in the external world.

Exercise I-2-L1/4.: Mark where you strongly see the need to become aware and to form (transform) in the interest of a better controlling and mastering of life:

- ☐ Feelings influence perception, thinking, judging, and conducting.
- ☐ Needs control perception, decision and actions.
- ☐ Perception and conduct are influenced by the unconscious.
- ☐ The unconscious affects the feelings, judgments, thoughts, and actions.
- ☐ The force of love influences emotions, thinking, judging and acting.
- ☐ Dreams produce moods (temper); dream interpretation gives orientation.
- ☐ The psycho-dynamic is formed by thoughts, experiences and the unconscious.
- ☐ The conducts (acts) are influenced by the inner psychical forces.
- ☐ The content of the conscious effects on self-experience and emotions (feelings).
- ☐ Rejection and repression (suppression) charge the whole psychical system.

Exercise I-2-L1/5.: What kind of person am I? How am I? Describe yourself with some short sentences:

Exercise I-2-L1/6.: What kind of person do I want to become? Describe your vision with some short sentences:

2.2.2. Discharge your unconscious mind from ballast

Thesis I-2-L2/1.: The unconscious (subconscious) is something like a vessel: from the prenatal time a human being takes in experiences and these personal experiences remain vivid during one's entire life. Such experiences are always related to situations, it doesn't matter if real or imaginative situations, and therefore they are stored as images. Such experiences always also contain a certain component of meaning and value related to the existence. The unconscious is generally the reservoir of all experiences.

Exercise I-2-L2/1.: The inventories in the unconscious are images with a meaningful content. We can classify diverse charged unities into categories.

Mark that which concerns you:

1 = not at all | 2 = little | 3 = quite a lot | 4 = a lot | 5 = totally

1 2 3 4 5		1 2 3 4 5	
☐☐☐☐☐	Pain	☐☐☐☐☐	Embarrassment
☐☐☐☐☐	Insecurity	☐☐☐☐☐	Offences
☐☐☐☐☐	Failure	☐☐☐☐☐	Strain
☐☐☐☐☐	Shame	☐☐☐☐☐	Punishment
☐☐☐☐☐	Guilt	☐☐☐☐☐	Suppression (repression)
☐☐☐☐☐	Sadness	☐☐☐☐☐	Fear
☐☐☐☐☐	Suffering	☐☐☐☐☐☐	Threat
☐☐☐☐☐	Rejection		

Thesis I-2-L2/2.: All people carry an enormous amount of images with them in their inner world. When a person confronts his past life, he realizes that many memories are emotionally as active in the present, as they were in the past. Once such events or thoughts and activities from the past are experienced again, many of them receive the same psycho-energetic load in the present as they had in the past.

This clearly shows that those past experiences, which were significantly overcharged or positively charged, have the same feelings (emotions) in the present when remembered.

Suffering, embarrassing situations, emotionally intensive thoughts, threatening moments, emotionally impressive incidents, emotional atmosphere in the environment, etc., are still vivid in the unconscious. In that lies the code program of the present life.

The past is the unconscious coding for life

Applies to me: 1 = not at all | 2 = somewhat | 3 = frequently | 4 = predominantly | 5 = completely

Rate	Exercise I-2-L2/2.: Unconscious coding. Rate what could be subliminally vivid in your subconscious:
	Complexes, e.g. painful and unresolved experiences and conflicts.
	Specific life experiences that have got to do with sexual drive.
	Experiencing deficits of general basic psychical needs.
	Feelings of inferiority. Devaluation of one's own being and life.
	Overloaded affective confining bonds from father or mother.
	Tense conflictive interest in myself and in others.
	Cramped unilateral bonds on drives. Wish and rejection at the same time.
	All kind of images about an "I"-ideal; including one-sided positive perception.
	Wishes in all possible directions (allowed, not allowed, fulfilled, not fulfilled).
	Emotional bonds through fear of punishment and therefore fear of life.
	Unresolved feelings of guilt, subjective (imaginary) and objective.
	In general not desired, but pleasant (interesting) sensual experiences.
	"Secret" defense mechanism to hold content from the unconscious at a distance.
	"I"-aspects, not recognized, or rejected (shadows, masks, etc.).
	Severe and unbalanced norms, demands, attitudes, belief.
	Especially difficult child-parent-relations with an ambivalence of rejecting and binding.
	Dogmatic religious images (elements from teaching) and practices transferred as the real truth.
	Summarize and write down the total points in the field.

Thesis I-2-L2/3.: Critical inventories in the unconscious always produce overcharging effects.

Exercise I-2-L2/3.: Mark where you see a need of becoming aware and of reforming (renewing):

Mark that which concerns you:
1 = not at all | 2 = little | 3 = quite a lot | 4 = a lot | 5 = totally

1	2	3	4	5		1	2	3	4	5	
☐	☐	☐	☐	☐	Depression	☐	☐	☐	☐	☐	Dominating
☐	☐	☐	☐	☐	Acting	☐	☐	☐	☐	☐	Fears, anxieties
☐	☐	☐	☐	☐	Always arguing	☐	☐	☐	☐	☐	Sleeplessness
☐	☐	☐	☐	☐	Phobias	☐	☐	☐	☐	☐	Sadism
☐	☐	☐	☐	☐	Aggression	☐	☐	☐	☐	☐	Coercions
☐	☐	☐	☐	☐	Nervousness	☐	☐	☐	☐	☐	Envy, greed
☐	☐	☐	☐	☐	Alienation	☐	☐	☐	☐	☐	Menace
☐	☐	☐	☐	☐	Rage, hate	☐	☐	☐	☐	☐	Migraine
☐	☐	☐	☐	☐	Strong tension	☐	☐	☐	☐	☐	Constipation

Thesis I-2-L2/4.: All unresolved complexes (meaning: complex critical units of any matters) in the unconscious repeat acting in a symbolic way in the present.

A look into the present rapidly leads to the past.

Applies to me: 1 = not at all | 2 = somewhat | 3 = frequently |
4 = predominantly | 5 = completely

Rate	Exercise I-E2-L2/4.: Network of resistance. Rate what concerns you.
	Strong inner bond on de facto far from today yet ended love relationships.
	Strong ambivalent aversion against the opposite gender.
	Clear disinterest in my own feelings and tempers.
	"Shadows" breaking through sometimes (rage, nagging, malicious joy, defiance, etc).
	Hurt and offended self-esteem (e.g.: easily offended, irritated, and vulnerable).
	Strongly focused on consumption, sport, hobbies, materialism, and religious dogmas.

	Indifference towards basic values of human dignity and integrity.
	Little active (or: flooded) awareness about the past life.
	Rational and/or emotional dominance: dominating, controlling.
	Heavy basic attitudes that ignore the inner life.
	Strong and confident people who were rather difficult to bear.
	Exaggerating or diminishing; instead of clearly perceiving.
	An attitude saying that it is best to simply forget about the past.
	Rapidly stubborn, obstinate, thickheaded, defiant, mulish.
	Often insensible, unwilling to listen, unyielding, irreconcilable.
	Little or no need for changes and renewal.
	Strong satisfaction with winner-feeling, control-feeling, dominance-feeling.
	No interest in realizing spiritual values in a relationship and in life.
	Summarize and write down the total points.

Exercise I-2-L2/5.: What would you primordially want clarified and resolved? Describe with some sentences:

Exercise I-2-L2/6.: How do you imagine your psycho-catharsis ("cleaning") of your subconscious? Describe what you first want to do and how you will proceed:

2.2.3. Grow continuously and holistically from inside

Thesis I-2-L3/1.: A person can deny his inner psychical world. Mankind can negate the force of love and compensate in materialistic ways. Human beings can live without communication with the inner Spirit. A person can suppress the inner development. People can destroy and hate all what human beings and human life are. All men can bind on external facts / objects such as goods, power, ideologies, dogmas, laws, leaders (of all kind) as a compensation for self-fulfillment.

Human being with inner life, mind and soul

Applies to me: 1 = not at all | 2 = somewhat | 3 = frequently | 4 = predominantly | 5 = completely

Rate	Exercise I-2-L3/1.: Values. Rate what concerns you strongly.
	Love as a source and power of living, as an aim and value of human beings is important to me.
	Living in an inner communicative connection with the inner spiritual force (dreams) is important to me.
	The intelligence and the power of the inner spirit are also important to me in relationship concerns.
	The inner all-sided balanced development of my human being is in general important to me.
	A new human being against the forces of ignorance, of destruction and hate is important to me.
	Leading back the externally-oriented compensating life to a genuine human being is important to me.
	The balance between inner fulfillment and the demands of the external world is important to me.
	A higher satisfaction with myself and my life is important to me.
	A higher sincerity and honesty towards myself are important to me.
	A critical reflection about the content of the consciousness about me is important to me.
	Summarize and write down the total points.

Thesis I-2-L3/2.: Nothing from our civilization has a value without human beings. A lot is produced (created) without love, without Spirit and without considering the psychical inner world. Human beings also have another possibility, which we can call the "psychical-spiritual evolution".

Exercise I-2-L3/2.: Mark what is important to you:

☐ Integration and far-reaching education of the psychical-spiritual life.
☐ Broadening consciousness about the inner life, especially the unconscious.
☐ Creating order and structure in the psychical system (between all parts).
☐ Spirit as the superior "principle of direction": realizing inside and outside.
☐ Development and growth of all life-oriented inner possibilities and values.
☐ Dedication to the human being and human life based on self-love.
☐ Giving expression to life in interrelation to all psychical forces.

Thesis I-2-L3/3.: Mankind is still at the beginning of the evolutional process. Most people rarely know what of all the vivid psychical realities can actually be formed. Where shall men find answers to their basic questions of the existence if not in their psychical organism and through experiencing the inner psychical-spiritual evolution? Mankind still widely lives at the level of the archaic human being.

Applies to me: 1 = not at all | 2 = somewhat | 3 = frequently | 4 = predominantly | 5 = completely

Rate	Exercise I-2-L3/3.: Human biomass. One's own educational need:
	Negation of the psychical life as the true important life.
	Rejection of the inner Spirit, the educational power of the dreams.
	Restricted by inner (suppressed) conflicts and complexes.
	Living without inner experiences (dreams, meditation, and introspection).
	No holistic growth; exterior-oriented development.
	Little conscious forming of the psyche; predominantly rational areas.
	Defense and suppression of uncomfortable facts as much as possible.
	Living unconsciously, without being aware of the true inner life.

	Tendency to project, identify, and displace realities.
	Establishing life in ideologies, dogmas as a rescuing conception.
	Fixing on material objects, on lust and fun, on external values.
	Undifferentiated experiencing of love, partly as egoism.
	External performances have the highest values: the best, the biggest, the superlative.
	Summarize and write down the total points.

Thesis I-2-L3/4.: Vision: The evolutional human being is a worldwide aim and program of the 21st century: People are psychically and spiritually formed, educated, willing to learn, differentiated, conscious, ordered, structured, balanced, self-controlling, calculable, constructive, many-sided and all-sided developed from the force of the Spirit and love. The first big turning point in a person's life is the knowledge: "I have a psychical inner life." The second big turning point results from the thorough self-consciousness: "I don't want to continue living that way! I want to make more out of my life!" And the third big enlightenment arises after a first touching self-knowledge: "Now I have to work on myself over a longer period of time aiming for the development of a new life with love and Spirit."

Turning point to a new life, to the evolutional human being

Applies to me: 1 = not at all | 2 = somewhat | 3 = frequently |
4 = predominantly | 5 = completely

Rate	Exercise I-2-L3/4.: Turning point to a new life. Rate what you consider to be a special value and what you want to integrate into your personal life culture:
	To accept the entire psychical-spiritual life.
	To become more and more free from inner charges of the past life.
	To create images in the unconscious to constructively/progressively promote life.
	All matters always in communication with the spirit (dreams).
	Regularly gain inner orientation with imagination and contemplation.

	Consciously forming all psychical forces and the whole of the psyche (mind).
	Integration of unpleasant matters despite reasoned rejecting facts.
	Becoming free from projections and identifications.
	Establishing life in the inner life, especially in the power of the spirit.
	Creating relationship and life in general, by respecting the values of the psychological-spiritual growing process.
	Dealing with the worlds of nature and animals with Spirit and love.
	Differentiated development and use of the force of love for everything in life.
	Psychical-spiritual performances have highest value and are signed with love.
	Resolving conflicts with myself, with the partner and with the life.
	Forming a new human being with inner freedom, with dignity and humility.
	Realizing tendencies, talents and potentials through self-education.
	High flexibility and inner freedom towards material goods and superficialities.
	Summarize and write down the total points.

Exercise I-2-L3/5.: The actual state of my psychical-spiritual development and self-education is roughly:

Exercise I-2-L3/6.: With the following activities I want to develop myself to an all-sided balance:

2.2.4. Form yourself and your skills for a good life

Thesis I-2-L4/1.: Personality education is an indispensable condition for any kind of success in life. A life without personality education (regardless of whether one is single or in a relationship) is archaic, unconscious, chaotic, full of failure in small matters; and this makes a person completely dependent on ideologies, dogmas, pre-judgments, institutions, other people, and one's own unconscious.

Pending work in the following areas (aims, ideals).

Applies to me: 1 = not at all | 2 = somewhat | 3 = frequently | 4 = predominantly | 5 = completely

Rate	Exercise I-2-L4/1.: Aims and ideals. Rate what you have to somewhat work in the following areas.
	Differentiated self-consciousness (self-image).
	A clear many-layered consciousness about mankind and the world.
	Consciousness about the transcendental reality through growth.
	A strong, dynamic and positive self-experience.
	Free from rejection and projection; at the same time maintaining a flexible distance.
	A strong, consciously formed and integrated will.
	Balanced self-management in the psychical and real world.
	Completely liberated, elaborated, clarified unconscious life.
	Differentiated perception of the own and alien realities.
	Creative constructive thinking with a clear language.
	Readiness to learn; readiness for changes and extensions.
	Clearly identified basic needs; and a balanced satisfaction of these needs.
	Manifold balanced and cared emotional life.
	Force of love for all life areas, capable of supporting, to put it into action.
	Flexible and vital psychodynamic, free from cramped contradictions.
	Intensive communication with the spirit (dreams, meditation).
	Acting in interconnection with the whole psychical organism.
	Developing the psychical organism in connection with the spirit.
	Living and growing in the direction of the complete self-fulfillment.
	Summarize and write down the total points.

Thesis I-2-L4/2.: The more a person is ready to accept his psychical organism and to understand it as his being, the more he is ready to form it all-sided and balanced. Self-education and Individuation change self-relation, relations to others, to the elements of the life fields, to God and religion.

My actual activities relating to self-education.

Applies to me: 1 = not at all | 2 = somewhat | 3 = frequently |
4 = predominantly | 5 = completely

Rate	Exercise I-2-L4/2.: Self-education. Rate your level of realizing:
	I am open to discover and to see the realities how they are.
	I live in interconnection with my inner growing process.
	I live with a high consciousness towards my inner life.
	Dreams and meditation are my superior instance to create my life.
	I have a high level of inner freedom (unconscious, thinking, attitudes).
	I think, feel and live in the tendency constructively (realizing a "life tree".)
	I expand in quality my knowledge and skills, my life in general.
	I am willing to learn about psychical life and in general I am open to the psychical life.
	My inside (unconscious) is well controllable, predictable, and balanced.
	Through my elaborations of the biography I experience a new life growing inside.
	For me, the force of love is central in everything that I am and live, also in my work.
	My contradictions are diminishing and a balanced wholeness is growing.
	I live in harmony between my inner and my external world.
	I care for my feelings and my psychical needs.
	I deal with transcendental dimensions with reason and objectivity.
	Summarize and write down the total points.

Thesis I-2-L4/3.: Human beings can reject such aims. The decisive pre-conditions are in four areas of interest. Do the people really want a high quality in: knowledge, growth, actions (behavior) and happiness (fulfillment)?

Exercise I-2-L4/3.: Mark what has high importance to you:

- ☐ I am curious and I like discovering. I wish to understand.
- ☐ I experience a need for consciousness. I want to reflect experiences.
- ☐ I want to develop and grow myself and my life.
- ☐ I want to integrate myself, my being and my life; and with that live in evolution.
- ☐ I have a significant drive to create (actions, creativity).
- ☐ I want to expand my life conditions and to utilize the possibilities.
- ☐ I seek and want meaning and fulfillment; I want to live love and Spirit.
- ☐ I entirely want my well-being and inner peace.

Thesis I-2-L4/4.: A natural and undisturbed, not influenced development of a person doesn't exist. Many forces forming a person stay out of his control. Without knowledge and elaboration of the experiences and without a holistic self-education, no self-determination can be realized.

Look at it from another perspective: Without holistic personality education, a human being is what his biography has made of him since the early childhood. He reproduces the patterns of his biography. His unconscious contains the code program for living in the present; and the life in the present forms in the same sense the code program for the future. At the same time with that all suppressed conflicts of the ancestors and all not suitably formed psychical areas are reproduced in the present and in the future.

Exercise I-2-L4/4.: For me the following reasons are especially important. Mark what has high importance to you:

Self-education = Personality education:

- [ ] Creates the competences for constructive, partnership-like relationships.
- [ ] Reduces many risks in the course of life and in the social interconnections.
- [ ] Is adaptable many-sided to be efficient and forms self-identity.
- [ ] Means life knowledge and daily acting, reflected and elaborated.
- [ ] Creates inner security and trust in one's own forces (skills).
- [ ] Is indispensable in all life phases for a substantial self-fulfillment.
- [ ] Integrates a high ethical responsibility for one self, for others, for job, for society.
- [ ] Finally achieve the human being in his deepest psychical-spiritual being.

Exercise I-2-L4/5.: The actual level of my personality education is approximately:

Exercise I-2-L4/6.: I want to achieve the following aims of personality education:

2.2.5. Completely become yourself from your innermost being

Thesis I-2-L5/1.: Today, the standard terms of human education are known: development, deployment, growth, maturity, being in a process, becoming one self, broadening consciousness, self-finding, self-being, self-realization, spiritual development, becoming an adult and so on. Contrary to that we have: Regression, stagnation, reproduction, limitation, lack of freedom, self-alienation, etc. Based on that, we can determine (characterize) with clear terms the process of development and growth with concrete steps.

Becoming yourself from the deepest inner being = Individuation

---

First phase of the psychical-spiritual development (Individuation)

Applies to me: 1 = not at all | 2 = somewhat | 3 = frequently | 4 = predominantly | 5 = completely

Rate	Exercise I-2-L5/1.: Personal development. Rate what has high importance to you:
	To be acquainted with the central psychical forces and discovering them on myself.
	To understand the importance of my biography and to find the access to it.
	Recognizing the complexity and interconnections of my own acting.
	Being able to constructively deal with my own psychical energy.
	To find clarity about "consciousness" with the purpose to handle these realities.
	Building up concrete ideas about the "I" (self) and its control-mechanisms.
	Discovering knowledge about the intellectual functions on myself.
	To recognize the world of feelings, finding access and dealing with them.
	Acquiring knowledge about the manifoldness of the needs through self-reflection.

	Understanding the unconscious as a reality one can systematically transform.
	To understand the way of functioning of the dreams, and find the access to this.
	Understanding love as a decisive life force and highest value.
	Discovering the basic values from the view of the psychical life.
	Improving my way of living with practical self-management.
	To be able to determine small and bigger aims of self-education.
	Discovering masculinity and femininity as roles and as natural being.
	To find clear ideas about intuition, introspection, imagination, contemplation.
	Being able to understand and to practice the first steps of dream interpretation.
	To usefully apply the basic techniques of relaxation.
	To determine and realize the positive values of life.
	Discovering the way of functioning of the spirit and to give importance to this force.
	Taking responsibility for my own acting, life, and my life time.
	Experiencing my own human being in a real and transcendental network.
	To deal with questions of life with meditation and reflections.
	Building up pleasure of life, love to live, hope and trust in life.
	Reflecting, asking, discussing, reasoning about the psychical life and its forming.
	Summarize and write down the total points.

Thesis I-2-L5/2.: We know the psychical organism and its interconnections with the life fields. We know a lot about the way of functioning of the singular psychic forces. If we have a plan, we can organize the process. If we communicate with the inner Spirit, we have the reign over and the guiding principles for the psychical-spiritual evolution.

The practical process is called: **"INDIVIDUATION"**.

Exercise I-2-L5/2.: We divide this process into three phases. Which performances have you already completed? Which ones do you want to elaborate first? Mark what currently applies to you:

1. Phase: Accept, discover, and understand the psychical realities.
1. Phase: Learn the methods to understand and form the forces.
1. Phase: Elaborate the steps till the "birth of the (inner) new human being".
2. Phase: Acknowledge the spirit as the principles for order and guidance.
2. Phase: Transform, strengthen, and develop the singular psychical forces.
2. Phase: Dissolve the inner opposite forces and elaborate an inner unity.
3. Phase: Transform the old norms and rules in favor of the inner Spirit.
3. Phase: Create harmony between inner and external world; love and Spirit.
3. Phase: Fulfill the inner totality and live it by giving real expressions.

Thesis I-2-L5/3.: It's absolutely clear and normal that everybody has defense mechanisms acting against psychical-spiritual growth. The experiences from the past build a decisive rejecting factor. It is also understandable that nobody likes to turn towards his difficult and painful experiences from the past. But it is indispensable!

Critical experiences

Applies to me: 1 = not at all | 2 = somewhat | 3 = frequently |
4 = predominantly | 5 = completely

Rate	Exercise I-2-L5/3: Critical experiences. Rate what you experienced.
	Psychical suffering
	Ignorance, arrogance
	Difficult childhood
	The malicious sides
	Difficult crises, conflicts
	Hard blow from destiny
	Lack of money and disaster

	Deepest disappointments
	Neurotic, unhappy parents
	Repression, dominance
	Misfortune, sadness
	Dogmatic religious education
	Criminal actions
	Injustice, meanness
	Dishonesty, falseness, lies
	Hard challenges
	Failure, breakdown
	Rejection from father / mother
	Punishments, sanctions
	Summarize and write down the total points.

Thesis I-2-L5/4.: No "totality" can exist without the entire psychical organism and without the psychical-spiritual process of Individuation. Without the inner guidance of the Spirit (dreams, meditation) the aim is never reachable. This brings us to the serious question: Where does religion (a spiritual or esoteric teaching) lead us if they ignore the psychical-spiritual life (including the world of the dreams) and the Individuation? Where is the life of our society heading to, if in general everybody ignores the psychical-spiritual life and the Individuation?

Exercise I-2-L5/4.: Mark what you can answer with "yes":

☐ I want to go through this process of Individuation.
☐ I want to form (renew, transform) all my psychical forces.
☐ With that, I also want to strengthen my psycho-energetic structure.

- ☐ I want to become more and more my authentic self by going through this process.
- ☐ I want to discover and utilize all these possibilities.
- ☐ I want the Individuation as a realization of my human being.

Exercise I-2-L5/5.: The actual level of my Individuation is approximately:

Exercise I-2-L5/6.: I want to start this process of Individuation because:

2.2.6. Follow the symbols of the soul to achieve your life aims

Thesis I-2-L6/1. The archetypes of the Individuation are special genuine images of the soul, well known since the beginning of the first cultures. These images are culturally independent image-patterns, most probably first procreated from dreams, from the spiritual source of the soul (the unconscious being). They contain an eternally valid meaning about human being, human life, meaning of life interconnected with the nature of the psyche (soul) and the characteristics of human life from procreation till death; they can never been extinguished. In that sense they are "holy", "untouchable", and valid for all human beings today and in the future.

In apparently common human circumstances an archetypal (eternally valid pattern) meaning is concealed.

Applies to me: 1 = not at all | 2 = somewhat | 3 = frequently | 4 = predominantly | 5 = completely

Rate	Exercise I-2-L6/1.: The high spiritual values. Rate what you feel for you to be a question and an important challenge:
	Procreation: A soul incarnates; a human being and individual becomes part of a community.
	Birth: Being on this earth in full dependency for love, care, education, and becoming a person.
	Being a child: Forming process from the parents, the environment, the culture, etc.
	Adolescence: Discovering one's own being and the world; processes of forming an identity.
	Becoming an adult: The process starting from being a child, from unconsciousness till a consciously formed wholeness.
	The opposite gender: To discover as a real experience, to integrate and to live with.
	Bond between man and woman (marriage): Self-fulfillment through and with the opposite gender partner.
	Polarity of the inner opposite gender (Anima, Animus): Forming the polar balance.
	Inner processes of transformation: psychical forces from old to new, from unconscious to conscious, etc.
	Inner new birth: The elaboration of all psychical areas creates a "new human being".
	Balancing contradictions between the inventory of the unconscious, feelings and intelligence, as well as the inner and

	external world.
	Special qualities (values): Love, truthfulness, purity, stability, hope, etc.
	The Spirit in the psyche: The force that creates the dreams wants to form and guide the person.
	Aim of the psychical-spiritual process: becoming a whole and a totality, a completely integrated human being.
	Special divine vocations (divine services) from the inner Spirit: the wise, priest, pastor, religious teacher, spiritual leader, prophet, messiah.
	God in the psyche (soul): the spiritual sun in the soul; the source of life and creations.
	Summarize and write down the total points.

Thesis I-2-L6/2.: There is an orientation to judge which paths lead to the psychical-spiritual evolution: the methods and the inner experiences in the psychical-spiritual process.

Exercise I-2-L6/2.: Mark where you already have corresponding inner experiences and excellently formed skills:

☐ The wholeness of the psychical-spiritual organism as knowledge and experience.
☐ The methods: dream interpretation, imagination, contemplation, intuitive thinking.
☐ Experiences and handling the psychical energy (e.g. rituals).
☐ The process as a many-sided, graduated, well founded process of transformation.
☐ The meditation (contemplation) about the archetypes and the archetypal dreams.
☐ Archetypal novels (myths, fairy tales, etc.) as a symbolic expression of the process.

Thesis I-E2-L6/3.: Archetypes are instruments that help in finding orientation in the Individuation. Archetypes stimulate forces, growth and development. Archetypes order psychical forces in new structures and new interconnections. Archetypes open and light up new inner realities. Archetypes represent the eternally valid psychical-spiritual process and realities. Archetypes facilitate intercultural communication about these realities. Archetypes also lead to experiences about God. Archetypes are the very old images of a transcendental reality. Archetypes of the soul are also energetic "transformers".

Exercise I-2-L6/3.: Mark the archetypes which especially touch you (a few examples below):

- ☐ Circle-cross-mandala, pentagram, pyramid, square, triangle
- ☐ Chalice, vessel, philosopher's stone, Holy Grail, chalice of the Grail, sword of the King of the Holy Grail
- ☐ King, queen; coronation, "bond" and corresponding insignia
- ☐ Birth, the new human being, a new land
- ☐ Sun, moon, light, source
- ☐ Owl, snake, eagle, lion, tiger, elephant
- ☐ Tree (life tree), garden (paradise)
- ☐ Cottage, house, chateau, castle, temple, "holy" places

Thesis I-2-L6/4.: In all prehistoric cultures, in all religions and spiritual teachings since the ancient times until today, people used and use the archetypes of the soul as instruments (myths). But they have all lost the vivid psychical-spiritual organism and the Individuation. The psychoanalysis still has to learn that Individuation leads also to love, but overall to the Spirit and in the aim to God in the soul (psyche). A spirituality which doesn't teach the Individuation and ignores the dreams as a spiritual guidance of life is merely a seduction of mankind.

Everybody can meditate about the archetypes of the soul and with that experience its meaning. Living in the process of Individuation periodically brings archetypal dreams. A person living in this growing process will get the true answers about the mystery of mankind. – The question is certainly: Does mankind want this? Who wants this today? Do you want this for you?

Exercise I-2-L6/4.: Mark which archetypes (as a theme / pattern of human being) especially address you (a few examples below):

- ☐ Accepting the psychical spiritual inner world: Going on a voyage (long peregrination), going to school.
- ☐ Discovering the psyche (soul): searching for the treasure, investigation of a cave, shadow like persons, going in deep darkness.
- ☐ New birth: Birth of a child, a baby is suddenly there, Christmas, opening something new.
- ☐ Accepting the Spirit: Initiation, consecration, receiving insignia or a new clothing.
- ☐ Transformation: To die, funeral, farewell, coming to a new land.
- ☐ Unification: marriage, embracement with a fairy, entering into a sun, experiencing a special light.

- ☐ New spiritual norms and principles: Insignia of a king, a wise person, a new land, new laws.
- ☐ Harmony interior-exterior, transcendence, melody, a pair of scales, hexagram, light, warmth.
- ☐ Wholeness: Circle, mandala, sun, eternal fire as an ancient source of all life, being in a paradise.

The focus: Analyzing the archetypes of Individuation – especially the aim of human being. Love, unification, Spirit, and God helps to find orientation for the entire human life, for the social life, and also for politics and the economy.

The archetypal process is not only "spiritual". Archetypes also give measures (standards) in quality and quantity, embedded in human life. Archetypes are something like laws and norms for the psychical-spiritual development and at the same time for life realization.

Archetypes demand competences for living (knowledge, skills) and self-management (life learning) from a person. As archetypal symbols they reflect transcendental realities in the psyche (soul) and at the same time realities in the spiritual cosmos (where ever this may be).

Exercise I-2-L6/5.: These archetypal themes produce the following in me:

Exercise I-2-L6/6.: Now I have "archetypal plans" for myself and my life:

3. Methods for a successful Life

The 4 methods for success and joy of life

Realize outstanding visions: Get success and find joy of life! But what are "outstanding visions" in the life of a person?

Not outstanding is: reading nothing, learning nothing, not wanting to know anything about the human being, not having any spiritual aim, not wanting to grow and become more mature, living without spirit, living each day more or less unconsciously, slowly going on with the given facts in daily life, and doing what everyone else does without reflecting what the masses move and what the market of consumption offers. The soul and the life of such a person develop like an apple that is left on the kitchen table for years.

Albert Einstein, C.G. Jung and Sigmund Freud all said: "Stupidity destroys life and earth." – The truth about human beings is always hard! And to achieve outstanding visions is always a bit strenuous. Get success and find joy of life with the right methods!

Firstly: You want professional satisfaction and maybe a professional development, even building up a career. You have your own business and you want to manage it successfully. Money is important to you, but it doesn't mean happiness.

Fact is: a life with very limited means is a continuous plague and an enormous constraint. To act correctly in such a frame is outstanding!

Secondly: You want a happy partnership-like relationship with sexual satisfaction and genuine love.

Fact is: Only very few people achieve and maintain this aim. You must have many skills to successfully achieve such an outstanding happiness. For both partners, marriage is certainly also a challenge, to regularly learn to differentiate and to deepen this high value. This is outstanding!

But if a couple doesn't learn what is necessary, their relationship develops like this apple on the kitchen table. As a consequence these people try to cover this misery with suppressing and ignoring.

Thirdly: You want to find yourself and to realize yourself authentically because you don't like life lies. You want to achieve your entire self-fulfillment. This is a "great work". To get that you must learn. It's never enough to get this happiness with what you learnt at school.

To get success you must learn the appropriate methods. Most people are too indolent – too lazy, too ignorant, too conceited, too stubborn – to make focused efforts for such aims; and they are too avaricious to spend money on that. As a consequence their psyche (mind) develops like this apple on the kitchen table. That's not delightful!

Now you maybe have an idea what we mean with "outstanding visions". It is already outstanding if you learn the basic skills and practice them to fulfill your life happiness. You can achieve all-sided balanced outstanding visions only with the elementary methods.

You have the instruments in your hands to get outstanding happiness and special success with this educational training. Use them and you will always have a delightful apple, to eat such an apple is truly a special pleasure. This is genuine life success and creates joy.

Joy of life is wonderful! Success with yourself and your life is outstanding.

Build up this success in life and find joy of life – and enjoy yourself! The pillars for success and joy of life are the four methods: self-analysis, self-management, dream interpretation, and meditation.

3.1. Analyze Yourself

Considerations about Self-analysis

Surely you sometimes reflect upon yourself. Certainly you want to find more clarity about yourself and your life. You would like to understand yourself. You are looking for your possibilities. You want to start a process to improve. Concerning that you may have some questions:

- In essence, who and what am I?
- How do I live?
- Why do I live just that way?
- What purpose does everything serve?
- Where am I going?
- What do I want from life?
- How do I want to live?
- What is the meaning of my life?
- What can I achieve?
- What can I become?
- How can I realize my potentials?

The issue is about something that concerns you directly, personally and vitally: your psychical life, your life experiences (biography), your aims, your psychical and psychosomatic health, your ability to love, your growth and development. All these matters have an important range, because: your past extensively determines your present. Your present is the foundation for your future. Your future depends also on who you are, how you live, what you want to achieve and what you contribute with your self-education. The way everybody is like, seen from his psychical-spiritual reality and potential, is the starting point and the goal of a broad personality education. In order to promote this process each theme contains many exercises with three practical aims:

- The knowledge about personality education is included in the exercises.
- All exercises assist in finding your own answers.
- Doing the exercises promotes the inner process.

The process of personality education

Personality education has various steps. Everything starts with self-knowledge. Then, one has to acquire psychological knowledge. Additionally one has to learn methods, e.g. dream interpretation, meditation and analytical interpretation.

The objective knowledge becomes alive and gains importance through self-experience. After that one can determine the aims for change. Then, self-education follows. The result is visible in real life. Finally one can check the effects on daily life from what one has learnt. The general aims of personality education are clear. It is about changes, differentiation, growth and development of the psychical forces: feelings, thinking and judging, ego-strength, needs, super-ego (conscience), dreams, subconscious (complexes), will, self-identity, love, skills and much more.

Personality education reaches the whole psyche and the external reality of life.

Personality education with a holistic psychical-spiritual process of growth (called "Individuation") ultimately focuses on the person itself as the main educational goal. In other words: That what everybody is as a psychical-spiritual reality and possibility is the starting point and the aim of personality education. The meaning of life becomes obvious: "My meaning of life is within myself."

Aims of personality education

Personality education has a priceless value. The following list may illustrate this. Everyone can ask themselves if they have an educational deficit. One can determine concrete aims of personality education, based on the knowledge about the psychical organism ("psyche") and the process of Individuation. The foundation lies in the psychical forces and in the way they are formed and the way they act in daily life – and not in ideology, not in metaphysics, not in an esoteric doctrine, not in dogmatism and not in a subjective choice. Essential aims of personality education are:

1. A systematic and comprehensive self-knowledge.

2. A differentiated self-knowledge (self-image).
3. A clear, many-sided consciousness about mankind and the world.
4. A consciousness about the transcendental (inner) world through growth.
5. An experience about the existence within the complexity of inner and external life areas.
6. A firm, dynamic and positive self-experience.
7. Being free from rejection (denial) and projection, but with flexible distance.
8. An open and dynamic integration of all life realities.
9. A strong, consciously formed and integrated will power.
10. A marked self-control within the inner and external world.
11. A completely liberated, explored and understood unconscious life (subconscious).
12. A differentiated perception of one's own and alien realities.
13. A creative and constructive thinking with a clear use of words (language).
14. Openness to learn and readiness for change and development.
15. Realizing clearly identified and well-balanced basic psychical needs.
16. A well-balanced and positively integrated emotional life.
17. Ability to love, loyal and ready to act in all life areas.
18. A flexible and vital psycho-dynamism, free from tense opposites.
19. An intense communication with the inner spirit through dream interpretation and meditation.
20. A daily behavior which is consciously connected with the psychical organism.
21. Developing the psychical organism in the network with love and spirit.
22. To live and to grow towards the highest archetype of mankind.

It doesn't help a lot to say: "I am better from day to day." To live positively is much more than self-suggestion. A positive, conscious and "correct" living is the result of a broad and thorough personality-education.

The process of Individuation

The psyche is a complex organism with many single psychical forces. Psychical forces are the instruments for managing life and mastering the facts of daily life. The psyche as a whole is the value and the goal of human life. The psyche forms the life and life forms the psychical organism from the moment of procreation. Each single force of the psyche is formed by a person's life culture and by self-education. The enormous amount of life-forces influencing and determining the psyche of each person produces manifold contradictory forces in the psychical organism.

No part of the psychical system (e.g. the thinking, the feeling, the basic psychical needs, the subconscious, the force of love) can function reasonably without all the other parts. The "I" (ego) as the control-centre has the duty to mediate between all parts within the system. All the psychical forces can be integrated into consciousness and can be consciously formed and transformed. The transformation and growth of the psyche to a new, harmoniously working whole is called "Individuation".

Individuation in concrete terms means:

- Forming the psychical forces to a constructive ability to live (social competences, life techniques, responsibility for the environment)

- Exploring one's own biography

- Controlling the defense and integration mechanisms

- Exploring and "cleaning" the subconscious (complexes, attitudes, superego)

- Transforming the inner contradictory forces

- Liberation from the generation-destiny

- Unification of masculinity and femininity

- Learning the language of the dreams and meditation

- An interconnected and well-balanced development of all psychical forces towards a wholeness

- Establishing a harmony between the inner and external life

- Realizing an authentic life-culture with love and Spirit

Many women and men can achieve the goal of Individuation. But it is much more important to live in that "bond" with one's own psychical life, to live more and more consciously with regard to the psyche and to growing through learning.

> **The first phase of Individuation – the processes of transformation: accepting the psychical inner world, discovering and understanding the forces; the rebirth of the inner being.**

Initially, in a way of speaking a person first lives without this conscious orientation in his psychical inner life. Most people don't know that they have to discover and to transform their own inner psychical life. They also don't realize in their state of unconscious being that they predominantly live unconsciously. The approach to those inner realities starts with the general personality education.

> **The second phase of Individuation – the processes of transformation: Initiation as an expression of accepting the inner spirit as one's spiritual guidance principal; transformations of all psychical forces ("die and be reborn"), and dissolution of all contradictory forces.**

There comes a time while exploring the inner psychical life, where a person recognizes ever clearer that in dreams and meditations, there is a spiritual force, which guides the process of Individuation. The inner spirit counsels through dreams, analyses situations and produces development (growth). But, does the "I" (ego) want to accept this inner spirit as a higher principle of guidance? While regularly working with dreams and meditation it becomes evident that the inner spirit is transcendental, that means, not sensual, not cerebral-physiological, and not an empirical product of learning processes. The spirit will ask the "I" in dreams: "Do you want me? Do you want to live yourself and your life with me? Do you want to experience the mysteries of human life? Do you want to become what is already based in your psyche as an archetype of the wholeness of a psychical-spiritual person?"

All psychical systems, including the actions (behavior), should now be worked through. This work is like a total renewal of the psyche. All the good forces have to be strengthened. Unformed forces have to be developed. Not well-formed (not useful) forces have to be corrected. The psychical forces have to repeatedly be balanced.

> **The third phase of Individuation – the processes of transformation: from the old principle of rule to a new one; accordance between the inner and external life, and fulfillment of the wholeness of all psychical forces.**

The creation of the personal life areas and the own life culture acquire a completely new expression now. One's life shows the renewed person. With time the new principle of rule assumes a central function in daily life: the intelligence and the mind co-operate with the spirit and the force of love. During the last stage of the third phase a person experiences himself more and more as an inward centered wholeness and unity. The circle is closed, yet open for the external life. The person now becomes a realization of his authentic being. He has found and formed everything that life is inside. The aim (goal) is the fulfillment of the Individuation. A person has found his self-fulfillment. Certainly a person having completed the Individuation process creates a world based on love and truthfulness, on spirit and on an educated many-sided and balanced psychical life.

From the archaic human being to an evolutionary human being

The three-phase model of Individuation expresses two images of human beings:

☐ **The archaic human being**

- Denying the psyche
- Rejecting the inner spirit
- Fixation on dogmas and ideologies
- Troubled by inner conflicts
- Without inner experiences
- Rejection and repression
- Without comprehensive growth
- Live a life in unconsciousness

☐ **The evolutionary human being**

- Living consciously with the psyche
- Communication with the inner spirit
- Individuation as a concept of life
- Order and freedom in the subconscious
- Systematic inner experiences
- Integration and exploration
- A complete and balanced growth
- A life with a broad consciousness

Mankind is living in the ambivalence between the desire to be saved and the banishment of the process of salvation. What does salvation mean? We look at it like this: to be free from an unconscious state of being, free from complexes and life lies, free from neurosis and narcissism, free from discord and from destructive drives, free from materialism, free from illusions about happiness and love, free from egoism, free from the chaos of the unexplored biography, free from a robot-being, free from inner contradictions.

The "salvation" is the process of Individuation, the liberation from an archaic being, and growth as an evolutionary human being until the highest aim: the "individuated person".

3.1.1. Analyze yourself with a model

Thesis II-E1-1-T1: Self-knowledge is the starting point of a balanced development and the door to all truth about the psychical and spiritual human being.

Thesis II-E1-1-T2: A person is not only body and mind, but also his whole life situation and future.

Thesis II-E1-1-T3: If a person has a model about the psychical life, the self-analysis can be objective and differentiated. This is a prerequisite for every holistic self-education.

Exercise II-E1-L1/1: Important terms are: Personality, Psyche, unconscious, inner life, dreams, meditation, etc. What kind of feelings and thoughts do these terms produce in you?

Exercise II-E1-L1/2: Write down some thoughts: "A small self-knowledge has consequences in my life":

Exercise II-E1-L1/3: What I expect from an extensive and thorough self-knowledge in my life:

Exercise II-E1-L1/4: What kind of human being am I? Who am I? Spontaneously describe using 6 keywords:

1)	4)
2)	5)
3)	6)

Exercise II-E1-L1/5: Describe the grade of satisfaction of your complete (self-) image in L1/4:

Exercise II-E1-L1/6: Mark:

I have written in the exercise L1/4 keywords about the following psychical forces (aspects):

A lot   Little   Nothing

☐   ☐   ☐ Control, will, defense, integration, consciousness
☐   ☐   ☐ Thinking, speaking, learning, perception
☐   ☐   ☐ Feelings: of values, lust/reluctance, expression, quality
☐   ☐   ☐ Psychical basic needs (being and growing)
☐   ☐   ☐ Experiences, norms, attitudes, inner conflicts
☐   ☐   ☐ Love: Interest, care, supporting, realization
☐   ☐   ☐ Spirit: dreams, meditation, intuition
☐   ☐   ☐ Psycho-dynamism: stability-instability, strength-intensity
☐   ☐   ☐ Acting: patterns, quality, abilities, repertoire
☐   ☐   ☐ Character: Aspects of the whole person

Exercise II-E1-L1/7: Comment your result from L1/6 concerning self-educational deficit:

Exercise II-E1-L1/8: In general about you as a person. Describe your situation:

a) Age, profession (job), life situation, psychical and physical health, critical actualities, facts, future perspectives (keywords):

b) If I look at my being and general situation, I feel about:

c) What I want to change and extend about my life situation:

Exercise II-E1-L1/9: How I control and manage myself in daily life:

Exercise II-E1-L1/10: My relation to the other gender is:

Exercise LL-E1-L1/11: The psychical reality means to me (importance):

Exercise II-E1-L1/12: My ability to love is:

Exercise II-E1-L1/13: I experience antagonisms and oppositions:
Exercise II-E1-L1/14: My reason and intellect are:

Exercise II-E1-L1/15: My feelings/emotions are:

Exercise II-E1-L1/16: My psychical needs are:

Exercise II-E1-L1/17: My dreams mean to me (importance):

Exercise II-E1-L1/18: My self-realization is:

Exercise II-E1-L1/19: I experience spirituality as follows:

Exercise II-E1-L1/20: What I expect from an extensive personality education:

Summary:

1. What is the most important thing you have learnt from this lesson?

2. What is your most outstanding strength in the subject of this lesson?

3. What is your outstanding weakness in the subject of this lesson?

4. What has touched you most strongly in the subject of this lesson?

5. What is your most important future aim in the subject of this lesson?

6. What is your next step to improve in the subject of this lesson?

7. What are your open questions in the subject of this lesson?

3.1.2. Contemplate yourself holistically

Thesis II-E1-2-T1: Apart from the psyche, a personality is also determined by mind and life style also by the individual links to all life areas.

Thesis II-E1-2-T2: The less the individual components of a person's character are formed constructively, the more risks arise in the course of life.

Thesis II-E1-2-T3: The psycho-vegetative system of a person can decisively influence the quality of life and may hinder self-fulfillment.

Exercise II-E1-L2/1: My self-image as a man (woman) is:

Exercise II-E1-L2/2: My life style is:

Exercise II-E1-L2/3: My relation to my body is:

Exercise II-E1-L2/4: My relation to other people is:

Exercise II-E1-L2/5: My relation to the real life is:

Exercise II-E1-L2/6: My relation to the world of nature and animals is:

Exercise II-E1-L2/7: My life concept (ideals, aims) is:

Exercise II-E1-L2/8: My relation to my psyche is:

Exercise II-E1-L2/9: Evaluate the entire image from L2/1 to L2/8:

Exercise II-E1-L2/10: Dynamic of the character. Mark which aspects of profile are really weak:

☐ Firmness   ☐ Integrity
☐ Self-confidence   ☐ Strength of will
☐ Health   ☐ Ability to perform
☐ Readiness to learn   ☐ Flexibility
☐ Adaptability   ☐ Self-management
☐ Capacity   ☐ Acceptance of living
☐ Self-motivation   ☐ Readiness to perform
☐ Decisiveness   ☐ Emotional stability

☐ Energy, vitality   ☐ Openness
☐ Helpfulness   ☐ Patience
☐ Ability for compromises

Exercise II-E1-L2/11: Mark those aspects of your personality which you express positively:

☐ Solidness	☐ Integrity	☐ Self-confidence
☐ Strength of will	☐ Health	☐ Ability to perform
☐ Body acceptance	☐ Free from fear	☐ Life acceptance
☐ Readiness to learn	☐ Flexibility	☐ Self-management
☐ Ability to adapt	☐ Self-satisfaction	☐ Psychical capacity
☐ Self-motivation	☐ Readiness to perform	☐ Decisiveness
☐ Emotional stability	☐ Energy, vitality	☐ Openness
☐ Patience	☐ Helpfulness	☐ Compromising
☐ Interest in knowledge	☐ Satisfied sexuality	☐ Talents

Exercise II-E1-L2/12: I experience and evaluate the entire image about my personality (from L2/10 and L2/11):

Exercise II-E1-L2/13: Which profile aspects do you experience very constructively in <u>private life</u>?

Exercise II-E1-L2/14: Which profile aspects do you experience very constructively in <u>professional life</u>?

Exercise II-E1-L2/15: Psycho-vegetative dynamism

"Lately I feel": You have the possibility to write down to each keyword a presumed or recognized cause. Mark what and how much overloaded you are:
1 = not at all | 2 = little | 3 = rather a lot | 4 = really a lot | 5 = totally a lot

1 2 3 4 5
☐ ☐ ☐ ☐ ☐ Tense:
☐ ☐ ☐ ☐ ☐ Agitated inside:
☐ ☐ ☐ ☐ ☐ Easily agitated:
☐ ☐ ☐ ☐ ☐ Flabby, inert:
☐ ☐ ☐ ☐ ☐ Capricious:
☐ ☐ ☐ ☐ ☐ Energetically blocked:
☐ ☐ ☐ ☐ ☐ Sleep disorder:
☐ ☐ ☐ ☐ ☐ Diarrhea:

☐ ☐ ☐ ☐ ☐	Constipation:
☐ ☐ ☐ ☐ ☐	Migraine:
☐ ☐ ☐ ☐ ☐	Over-/Underweight:
☐ ☐ ☐ ☐ ☐	Pressure (chest/abdomen):
☐ ☐ ☐ ☐ ☐	Too much nicotine:
☐ ☐ ☐ ☐ ☐	Too much alcohol:
☐ ☐ ☐ ☐ ☐	Palpitation/pain in heart:
☐ ☐ ☐ ☐ ☐	Stomach trouble:
☐ ☐ ☐ ☐ ☐	Diffuse pain:
☐ ☐ ☐ ☐ ☐	Pain in back and neck:
☐ ☐ ☐ ☐ ☐	Aggression:
☐ ☐ ☐ ☐ ☐	Frustration:
☐ ☐ ☐ ☐ ☐	Pessimism:
☐ ☐ ☐ ☐ ☐	Haunted:
☐ ☐ ☐ ☐ ☐	Forlorn/lonely:
☐ ☐ ☐ ☐ ☐	Lack of motivation:
☐ ☐ ☐ ☐ ☐	Lack of inner freedom:
☐ ☐ ☐ ☐ ☐	Boredom:
☐ ☐ ☐ ☐ ☐	Dissatisfaction:
☐ ☐ ☐ ☐ ☐	Hopelessness:
☐ ☐ ☐ ☐ ☐	Sorrow:
☐ ☐ ☐ ☐ ☐	Depressed:
☐ ☐ ☐ ☐ ☐	Inferiority:
☐ ☐ ☐ ☐ ☐	Fear:
☐ ☐ ☐ ☐ ☐	Listlessness:

Exercise II-E1-L2/16: What are the effects of your statements in L 2/14:

Exercise II-E1-L2/17: In my entire image, I want to concretely change L2/14:

Exercise II-E1-L2/18: Give some keywords on how you negatively characterize a person:

Exercise II-E1-L2/19: Give some keywords on how you positively characterize a person:
Exercise II-E1-L2/20: How much real-psychological content do your positive and negative keywords have with which you judge a person?

Exercise II-E1-L2/21: How do you want to support and strengthen the weaknesses of your profile?

Summary:

1. What is the most important thing you have learnt from this lesson?

2. What is your most outstanding strength in the subject of this lesson?

3. What is your outstanding weakness in the subject of this lesson?

4. What has touched you most in the subject of this lesson?

5. What is your most important future aim in the subject of this lesson?

6. What is your next step to improve in the subject of this lesson?

7. What are your open questions in the subject of this lesson?

3.1.3. You are also your biography

Thesis II-E1-3-T1: A person does not only have his authentic biography, but he is also influenced by his biography on a daily basis.

Thesis II-E1-3-T2: Difficult and painful life experiences from the subconscious burden and influence one's life in the present and in the future like a code program.

Thesis II-E1-3-T3: Without wishes and aims for an authentic self-realization, the biography and the life areas will extensively determine the course of life.

Exercise II-E1-L3/1: Mark your <u>weak biographical aspects</u> (experiences you had in the past) and give some concrete keywords:

☐ Rejection:
☐ Rigid care:
☐ Lust denial:
☐ Emotionally burdened home:
☐ Disordered relationship:
☐ Failure:
☐ Rigid norm/principles:
☐ Deficit in basic needs:
☐ Humiliation:
☐ Too low life expectations:
☐ Too high life expectations:
☐ Not much love for life:
☐ Little educational support:
☐ Overemphasis of intellect:
☐ A lot of quarrels:
☐ Material deficit:
☐ Divorce/Separation:
☐ Dogmas, ideologies:
☐ Strong inappropriate punishment:
☐ Denying conflicts:
☐ Little autonomy:
☐ Rude educational practices:
Exercise II-E1-L3/2: Which effects do your weak aspects have?

Exercise II-E1-L3/3: Express an approach how you can (should) change this:

Exercise II-E1-L3/4: List some outstanding **positive** characteristics concerning you to the following themes. Ratings: 1 = positive; 2 = very positive; 3 = totally positive

Themes/areas	Experience, characteristics	Points
1. Parental family		
2. Relationships		
3.Friendship, marriage		
4. Own family		
5. Living		
6. Body, Sexuality		
7. Eating, drinking		
8. Illness, disturbance		
9. School, education		
10. Profession, job		
11. Leisure		
12. Belief		
13. Political activities		
14. Culture		
15. Consumption		
Total points		

Exercise II-E1-L3/5: List some outstanding **burdened** characteristics concerning you to the following themes. Ratings: 1 = burdened; 2 = very burdened; 3 = totally burdened

Themes/areas	Experience, characteristics	Points
1. Parental family		
2. Relationships		
3. Friendship, marriage		
4. Own family		
5. Living		
6. Body, Sexuality		
7. Eating, drinking		
8. Illness, disturbance		
9. School, education		
10. Profession, job		
11. Leisure		
12. Belief		

13. Political activities		
14. Culture		
15. Consumption		
Total points		

Exercise II-E1-L3/6: Concrete conclusions in an overview:

Exercise II-E1-L3/7: Detail some wishes about how you would like to live:

Exercise II-E1-L3/8: New life – Renewal of your life

a) State some wishes on what and how you would like to be and to live:

b) What do you see as a first step to renew your life?

c) What do you see as the next steps in order to renew your life?

Summary:

1. What is the most important thing you have learnt from this lesson?

2. What is your most outstanding strength in the subject of this lesson?

3. What is your outstanding weakness in the subject of this lesson?

4. What has touched you most in the subject of this lesson?

5. What is your most important future aim in the subject of this lesson?

6. What is your next step to improve in the subject of this lesson?

7. What are your open questions in the subject of this lesson?

3.1.4. Recognize your unconscious mind

Thesis II-E1-4-T1: Not clarified and unresolved difficult life experiences operate as unconscious units of complexes and interfere with one's being and daily life.

Thesis II-E1-4-T2: By the effects one can identify the forces of the subconscious. The contemplation about these forces decisively influences the self-renewal.

Thesis II-E1-4-T3: An authentic self-realization is not possible without conscious reflection of one's own defense mechanisms.

Exercise II-E1-L4/1: Development of complexes. Give some keywords concerning you:

1. Painful life experiences:
2. Embarrassing experiences:
3. Suppressing sexual drive:
4. Continuous criticism:
5. Deficit in basic needs:
6. Experiences of fear:
7. Experiences of being lonely:
8. Lies, intrigues, agitations:
9. Guilt feelings:
10. Punishment:

Exercise II-E1-L4/2: How has your personality been formed and developed under these experiences?

Exercise II-E1-L4/3: Signs of unconscious burden.

Rate that which concerns you: 1 = not at all | 2 = little | 3 = rather a lot | 4 = very much | 5 = totally

1 2 3 4 5
□ □ □ □ □ Unsatisfying relationship
□ □ □ □ □ Boring leisure
□ □ □ □ □ Unsatisfying sexuality

☐ ☐ ☐ ☐ ☐ Fear of life
☐ ☐ ☐ ☐ ☐ Strong tension in the relationship
☐ ☐ ☐ ☐ ☐ Feelings of guilt
☐ ☐ ☐ ☐ ☐ Unable to enjoy lust
☐ ☐ ☐ ☐ ☐ Unable to laugh enough
☐ ☐ ☐ ☐ ☐ No or not enough experiences of love
☐ ☐ ☐ ☐ ☐ Unable to be alone
☐ ☐ ☐ ☐ ☐ Strong general/religious norms
☐ ☐ ☐ ☐ ☐ Strong restraint of contact
☐ ☐ ☐ ☐ ☐ No partnership in the relationship
☐ ☐ ☐ ☐ ☐ No time and peace to eat
☐ ☐ ☐ ☐ ☐ No clear own values of live
☐ ☐ ☐ ☐ ☐ Not taking serious one's own feelings
☐ ☐ ☐ ☐ ☐ No positive attitude towards my own body
☐ ☐ ☐ ☐ ☐ Exaggerated hunger for sensations
☐ ☐ ☐ ☐ ☐ Ignoring one's own problems
☐ ☐ ☐ ☐ ☐ No inner orientation (dreams, meditation)

Exercise II-E1-L4/4: List some further burdens you have:

Exercise II-E1-L4/5: Mention with keywords some possible causes of your burdens:

Exercise II-E1-L4/6: How does the dynamic of your defense mechanism work? Mark what you do often:

☐ Transforming into the opposite   ☐ Devaluating
☐ Ignoring   ☐ Suppressing
☐ Projecting   ☐ Displacing
☐ Compensating   ☐ Avoiding behavior
☐ Masks and facades   ☐ Exaggerating
☐ Acting shady   ☐ Intriguing

Exercise II-E1-L4/7: Give 2 concrete examples of defense mechanisms you often use:
Exercise II-E1-L4/8: Give to the keywords (L4/6) a concrete example about your experiences:

Exercise II-E1-L4/9: How do your defense mechanisms affect you, others and the environment?

Exercise II-E1-L4/10: Give some possible alternatives to your defense mechanisms:

Summary:

1. What is the most important thing you have learnt from this lesson?

2. What is your most outstanding strength in the subject of this lesson?

3. What is your outstanding weakness in the subject of this lesson?

4. What has touched you most in the subject of this lesson?

5. What is your most important future aim in the subject of this lesson?

6. What is your next step to improve in the subject of this lesson?

7. What are your open questions in the subject of this lesson?

3.1.5. Form your healthy dispositions

Thesis II-E1-5-T1: A holistic self-experience can be built up positively if one turns to this reality.

Thesis II-E1-5-T2: A fulfilled and successful personal and professional life demands a holistic education towards a healthy being.

Thesis II-E1-5-T3: If you don't want to be dominated by disturbing factors from the environment (life areas), you have to manage them with specific skills.

Exercise II-E1-L5/1: The holistic self-experiencing. Rate your predominant (holistic) self-experiencing on the whole. Give a short comment to each keyword about how this affects you, your fellow human beings and your life. Rate what you feel about yourself and give some concrete keywords:

1 = not at all | 2 = little | 3 = rather a lot | 4 = really a lot | 5 = totally a lot

1 2 3 4 5
☐ ☐ ☐ ☐ ☐ Dull:
☐ ☐ ☐ ☐ ☐ Beautiful:
☐ ☐ ☐ ☐ ☐ Vital:
☐ ☐ ☐ ☐ ☐ With relish:
☐ ☐ ☐ ☐ ☐ Harmonic:
☐ ☐ ☐ ☐ ☐ Cramped:
☐ ☐ ☐ ☐ ☐ Tense:
☐ ☐ ☐ ☐ ☐ Relaxed:
☐ ☐ ☐ ☐ ☐ Nervous:
☐ ☐ ☐ ☐ ☐ Heavy:
☐ ☐ ☐ ☐ ☐ Light:
☐ ☐ ☐ ☐ ☐ Fresh:
☐ ☐ ☐ ☐ ☐ Worn out:
☐ ☐ ☐ ☐ ☐ Comfortable:
☐ ☐ ☐ ☐ ☐ Unpleasant:
☐ ☐ ☐ ☐ ☐ Comforting:
☐ ☐ ☐ ☐ ☐ Tough, hard:
☐ ☐ ☐ ☐ ☐ Cold:
☐ ☐ ☐ ☐ ☐ Exhausted:

☐ ☐ ☐ ☐ ☐ Joyless:
☐ ☐ ☐ ☐ ☐ I am satisfied with my physical appearance.
☐ ☐ ☐ ☐ ☐ I am satisfied with my entire psychical expression.

Exercise II-E1-L5/2: What do you miss in your self-experiencing?

a) I am not happy with my physical appearance because:

b) I am not happy with my psychical expression because:

Exercise II-E1-L5/3: Describe with keywords how your following dispositions are:

1. Accepting life, positive physical feeling:
2. Inner psychical-spiritual forming:
3. Constructive acceptance of masculinity and femininity:
4. Life skills (living competences), Capacity of burden and elaboration:
5. Educating, forming, creating and expressing your potentials:
6. Strive for humanity, meaning and values:
7. Spirituality and its integration into real life:
8. Caring for ecological environment (attentiveness, responsibility, being aware):
9. Using archetypes (prototypes) as a guidepost and source of life energy:

Exercise II-E1-L5/4: What are the consequences if you don't form (educate) your dispositions?

Exercise II-E1-L5/5: Holistic life style. My healthy dispositions are:

4 = very | 3 = preponderant | 2 = medium | 1 = moderate |
0 = little/barely

... Mostly I am aware of what I feel and sense.
... I can represent my opinions and interests.
... I can express bad temper, anger, and rage.
... I can also accept unsettled and strong feelings.
... I like new and also unusual ideas.
... Sometimes I like to be alone and I can occupy myself well.
... I don't have to always solve all problems immediately.
... I can live well, also if everything is not harmonious all around me.
... I care for a continuous life rhythm.
... I control my consumption of tobacco, alcohol, coffee, sweets, and eating in general.

... I can enjoy sex and release completely with orgasm.
... I value time and peace when eating.
... I enjoy my job/work.
... I can deal well with time pressure without running into trouble.
... I experience meaning in my leisure activities.
... My life has true meaning and value.
... I can accept difficult life phases from my past.
... I am confident in my way of creating and mastering life.

Total points: ....

Exercise II-E1-L5/6: Importance of the result by L5/5 for *your work (job)*:

Exercise II-E1-L5/7: Importance of the result by L5/5 for your personal quality of life:

Exercise II-E1-L5/8: Interpret and judge your daily life based on your result of (L5/3):

Exercise II-E1-L5/9: Describe what has an unhealthy and negative effect on you from:

a) Working environment:

b) General life environment:

c) Personal (private) life environment:

Exercise II-E1-L5/10: Mark what you don't consider or don't consider enough:

☐ Experiencing nature
☐ Controlling my feelings
☐ Relaxation training
☐ Making love
☐ Eating culture
☐ Objective self-evaluation
☐ Self-responsibility
☐ Elaborating crises

☐ Light sport (e.g. walking)
☐ Measure in all
☐ Meditation
☐ Balanced attitudes
☐ Healthy environment
☐ Balancing stress
☐ Reducing arguments and quarrels

Exercise II-E1-L5/11: Give 3 ideas how you can improve your body feeling:

Summary:

1. What is the most important thing you have learnt from this lesson?

2. What is your most outstanding strength in the subject of this lesson?

3. What is your outstanding weakness in the subject of this lesson?

4. What has touched you most in the subject of this lesson?

5. What is your most important future aim in the subject of this lesson?

6. What is your next step to improve in the subject of this lesson?

7. What are your open questions in the subject of this lesson?

3.1.6. Form yourself by focusing on aims

Thesis II-E1-6-T1: If the individual psychic forces are not well-balanced and constructively formed, then life tends to become more and more problematical and complicated.

Thesis II-E1-6-T2: A person has to integrate his development into self-management and in doing so needs to proceed systematically. This is the only way to grow from an archaic into an evolutionary being.

Thesis II-E1-6-T3: One has to divide great aims into small aims and to consider all areas, if one wants to grow evolutionary. Self-love demands this.

Exercise II-E1-L6/1: Lack of self-education. Describe with concrete keywords what the state is of your psychical forces. Note below with words like: Will, thinking, feelings, intuition, listening, judging, perception, talking, clarifying, caring, needs, behavior, etc.

1. Undifferentiated:
2. Disordered, chaotic:
3. Not controllable:
4. Not balanced:
5. Not calculable:
6. Destructive:
7. Suppressed:
8. Rejected:
9. Not operational:
10. Unbearable:

Exercise L6/2: Lack of development

a) Describe what is important to you as an entire person with your being and acting in life: developing, differentiating, strengthening, flexibly dealing, control, toughness, etc.

b) What happens with you in the long term if you don't practice any self-education and don't promote your entire development?

Exercise II-E1-L6/3: Concrete aims of self-education
Create a concrete aim of self-education about:

a) Thinking:
b) Feeling:
c) Acting:
d) Perception:
e) Self-control:
f) Relationship:
g) Self-management:
h) Communication:
i) Sexuality:
j) Leisure:
h) Intuition:
k) Self-fulfillment:

Exercise II-E1-L6/4: Mark which <u>formal aspects of aims</u> are very important to you:

☐ Development   ☐ Growth   ☐ Strengthening
☐ Knowledge   ☐ Differentiation   ☐ Flexibility
☐ Harmonizing   ☐ Controllability   ☐ Balance
☐ Bearing strength ☐ Labor skills   ☐ Being aware
☐ Creativity   ☐ Constructivism   ☐ Order

Exercise II-E1-L6/5: Create with the list in exercise L6/4 five examples following the given scheme:

Concrete initial situation:	**Concrete aim**
A force from the psychical organism (thinking, feeling, self-control, perception, acting, etc.). *Choose what is important to you today:*	Acting-orientated description! *Formulate your aim with a keyword or short sentence:*
1)	
2)	
3)	
4)	
5)	

Exercise II-E1-L6/5: What happens if you don't care for your psycho-dynamism?

Exercise II-E1-L6/6: What happens if you don't take your basic needs seriously?

Exercise II-E1-L6/7: Which consequences arise if you let your feelings (emotions) go without control?

Exercise II-E1-L6/8: What remains if you don't live love anymore?

Exercise II-E1-L6/9: Where does it lead if you don't use your intelligence sufficiently?

Exercise II-E1-L6/10: What can you expect if you never clean (elaborate) your unconscious mind?

Exercise II-E1-L6/11: What is the quality of your life without meditation, dreams, and spirit?

Exercise II-E1-L6/12: What happens if you don't take your psychical forces seriously?

Exercise II-E1-L6/13: How is your love and relationship without integration of the psychical life?

Exercise II-E1-L6/14: What is the difference with and without psychical-spiritual development?

Exercise II-E1-L6/15: What happens in the collective in long term if (nearly) all people don't give importance to the psychical life (especially love and spirit)?

Exercise II-E1-L6/16: What happens with you in the long term if you don't care for self-education?

Summary:

1. What is the most important thing you have learnt from this lesson?

2. What is your most outstanding strength in the subject of this lesson?

3. What is your outstanding weakness in the subject of this lesson?

4. What has touched you most in the subject of this lesson?

5. What is your most important future aim in the subject of this lesson?

6. What is your next step to improve in the subject of this lesson?

7. What are your open questions in the subject of this lesson?

3.1.7. Grow continuously and evolutionarily

Thesis II-E1-7-T1: Progression in the human being includes: Objectivity, acceptance, integration, system, order, liberty, spirit, love, life acceptance, dedication, care, balance, responsibility.

Thesis II-E1-7-T2: In the collective unconscious there is something like an "oath" which "obliges" all human beings to believe: "The evolutionary, psychical-spiritual human being doesn't exist."

Thesis II-E1-7-T3: If you want to live an authentic self-realization, then you have to know yourself well and the consequences must lead to concrete actions.

Exercise II-E1-L7/1: Living in the evolution. React with a word or short sentence:

1. I live rooted in my process of development.
2. I live consciously with my inner life.
3. Dreams and meditation are important to me.
4. I have a high level of inner freedom.
5. I predominantly think, feel and live in a constructive way.
6. I am entirely dedicated to life.
7. The power of love is important to me.
8. I can balance my (inner) opposites.
9. I live in harmony with inner life and external life.
10. I consider my feelings and basic needs.
11. I deal with the transcendence with reason (intelligence) and objectivity.
12. Truthfulness and authenticity are very important to me in my life.

Exercise II-E1-L7/2: Interpret the stand / the tendency of your regression-progression:

Exercise II-E1-L7/3: Formulate some measures for a positive further development:

Exercise II-E1-L7/4: Forces against life. What hinders you in the following areas / themes especially realizing an evolutionary human being?

Areas	Hindrances – Forces against
1) Drive to know	
2) Security	
3) Living relationship	
4) Experiencing and living love	
5) Doing business / Earning money	
6) Experiencing joy	
7) Autonomy	
8) Experiencing nature	
9) Safety	
10) Zest for discovering	
11) Calmness	
12) Experiencing God	
13) To have / live a home	
14) Sensual experiencing	
15) Properties	
16) Self-respect	
17) Physical lust	
18) Work and	

performance	

Exercise II-E1-L7/5: Stand

a) Evaluate the level of your authentic self-realization:

b) Your conclusion to an evolutionary human being (e.g.: measures, steps):

Exercise II-E1-L7/6: Realizing human being. Comment on the sentences (L7/4) and their importance to you:

Exercise II-E1-L7/7: What hinders you mostly in realizing an evolutionary human being (see the sentences in exercise L7/1)?

Exercise II-E1-L7/8: Evaluate the level of your authentic self-realization with concrete examples:

Exercise II-E1-L7/9: Your conclusions (e.g.: measures, next steps):

Summary:

1. What is the most important thing you have learnt from this lesson?

2. What is your most outstanding strength in the subject of this lesson?

3. What is your outstanding weakness in the subject of this lesson?

4. What has touched you most in the subject of this lesson?

5. What is your most important future aim in the subject of this lesson?

6. What is your next step to improve in the subject of this lesson?

7. What are your open questions in the subject of this lesson?

3.1.8. Strengthen your ability to love

Thesis II-E1-8-T1: Love wants to develop life, to grow holistically, to live well-balanced, to bond in spirit, to realize transcendence (meaning, values), to build up joy in life, to express itself in the life areas.

Thesis II-E1-8-T2: Self-love is active: interested, dedicated, to promote, to protect, to develop, to strengthen, to activate, to guide, to use, to accept, to educate, to form, to take seriously, to take responsibility, to act competently, to treat with care.

Thesis II-E1-8-T3: Weaknesses are an inevitable part of the human being. But if one doesn't work on them, then self-fulfillment of one's potentials and of one's real life cannot be built up.

Exercise II-E1-L8/1: Love in the concrete daily life. To me, the following aspects of love mean:

1. Accepting my human being and life:
2. Creating my life areas considering the psychical life:
3. Rooting living in the spirit (dreams, meditation):
4. Creating a balanced totality of my person:
5. Entirely integrating the psychical organism into my consciousness:
6. Doing personality education and living psychical-spiritual growth:
7. Developing also an external holistic balanced life:

Exercise II-E1-L8/2: Ability to love. Comment shortly and concretely!

1. I turn towards what I am and live.
2. I promote my talents and potentials.
3. In daily life, I control myself consciously.
4. I give high importance to my psychical life.
5. I deal carefully with my feelings / emotions.
6. I take responsibility for everything that I do.
7. I develop and strengthen my weak forces.

Exercise II-E1-L8/3: Aspects of self-love. Analysis of deficits.
Rate what is right for you:

1 = not at all | 2 = little | 3 = rather a lot | 4 = really a lot |
5 = totally a lot

1 2 3 4 5
☐ ☐ ☐ ☐ ☐ I turn towards what I am and live with concentrated reflection.
☐ ☐ ☐ ☐ ☐ I promote aptitudes, talents, potentials, knowledge, and skills.
☐ ☐ ☐ ☐ ☐ I develop my forces that are weak and not formed enough.
☐ ☐ ☐ ☐ ☐ I use the potential of my forces (life energy).
☐ ☐ ☐ ☐ ☐ I transform the life designs I have.
☐ ☐ ☐ ☐ ☐ I stimulate myself to extend my being and life.
☐ ☐ ☐ ☐ ☐ I continuously form (educate) my psychical life.
☐ ☐ ☐ ☐ ☐ I consciously control myself in daily life.
☐ ☐ ☐ ☐ ☐ I give importance to my psychical life and my dreams.
☐ ☐ ☐ ☐ ☐ I am thankful towards life for what I can live.
☐ ☐ ☐ ☐ ☐ I like putting myself into relation with other people.
☐ ☐ ☐ ☐ ☐ I experience myself as positive part of the nature.
☐ ☐ ☐ ☐ ☐ I feel integrated into a transcendental network.
☐ ☐ ☐ ☐ ☐ I deal carefully with my daily feelings.
☐ ☐ ☐ ☐ ☐ I deal carefully with my physical state.
☐ ☐ ☐ ☐ ☐ I take responsibility for my happiness and for what I do.
☐ ☐ ☐ ☐ ☐ I can also enjoy small things in life and my being.
☐ ☐ ☐ ☐ ☐ I deal in balanced ways with my forces.

Exercise II-E1-L8/4: Evaluate *your weaknesses* in self-love (L8/3). Give some reasons:

Exercise II-E1-L8/5: How can you strengthen the force of your self-love? Give keywords:

Exercise II-E1-L8/6: The quality of my ability to love is shown by the following indicators (give a short example):

1. More extended perception of the psychical and real world:
2. Increasing acceptance of myself, of others and of nature:
3. Increasing spontaneity and authenticity in relationships:
4. A better focus on problems and a flexible way of dealing with conflicts:
5. Bigger distance and yearning for privacy:
6. Increasing autonomy and resistance against external influences:
7. Deeper understanding of emotional reactions:
8. Higher frequency of spiritual and transcendent experiences:

9. Psychical and spiritual openness for relations between people:
10. Democratic and partnership-like structure of character:
11. Strongly increasing creativity:
12. Certain changes in the system of values in favor of the psychical-spiritual life:

Exercise II-E1-L8/7: Where do you see a need for learning and developing? Mark those that apply:

☐ Taking life orientation rooted in the spirit
☐ Acquiring life knowledge and wisdom
☐ Training to form the psychical forces
☐ Taking decisions with love and spirit
☐ Constructive images in the unconscious mind
☐ Being free from inner ties
☐ Forming one's own life plan (concept)
☐ Using archetypes as the forces promoting growth

Summary:

1. What is the most important thing you have learnt from this lesson?

2. What is your most outstanding strength in the subject of this lesson?

3. What is your outstanding weakness in the subject of this lesson?

4. What has touched you most in the subject of this lesson?

5. What is your most important future aim in the subject of this lesson?

6. What is your next step to improve in the subject of this lesson?

7. What are your open questions in the subject of this lesson?

3.1.9. Consider the reasons for Individuation

> Thesis II-E1-9-T1: The alternative to Individuation is: regression, unconscious being, to ignore, without spirit, negation of life, reduction of life, self-alienation, archaism, dogmatism, and fundamentalism.
>
> Thesis II-E1-9-T2: Experiences of the individuation process are: openness, honesty, seriousness, objectivity, authenticity, reconciliation, relief, humanity, self-responsibility.
>
> Thesis II-E1-9-T3: Everyone can find hundreds of reasons against Individuation; and at least one reason for Individuation: the well-balanced development of the psychical-spiritual human being.

Exercise II-E1-L9/1: What do you do for your development? Give some short examples: (e.g.: reading books. Meditating. Reflecting upon feelings. Interpreting my dreams, etc.)

1. Accepting the psychical life: Dedication. Interest. Care. Education (trainings).

2. Discovering, understanding, and analyzing: Curiosity. Searching. Informing. Interpreting.

3. Beginning of a new life (new birth): Protecting. Forming. Letting a new life grow.

4. Acceptance of the inner spirit as a guiding principle: Incorporating the spirit as the guiding force. Experiencing to be all-sided networked. Dedication to this spiritual force.

5. Transforming all psychical forces: Forming, educating. Becoming new. Release the old past, everything that is not successful. Extension.

6. Unification of the opposites: Masculinity-Femininity. Chaos-Order. Being unconscious-Being conscious. Reality-Wish/Ideal.

7. From the old principles to the new principles of government: Living unity. Objective knowledge and wisdom. Spirit above rationality. Spirit instead of "Adaptation".

8. Harmony between internal and external world: Living consciously with the psyche. Self-expression.

9. Execution of the unity and totality: Individuation as an expression of life and realization of God. Promoting evolution.

Exercise II-E1-L9/2: Practical Individuation. Self-education and Individuation:

Rate what you do and how often:
1 = not at all | 2 = little | 3 = rather a lot | 4 = really a lot |
5 = totally a lot

1 2 3 4 5
□ □ □ □ □ Knowing the psychical forces and discovering them on me.
□ □ □ □ □ Understanding the importance of the biography.
□ □ □ □ □ Recognizing the complexity and network of one's own acting.
□ □ □ □ □ Finding clarity in the content of the consciousness.
□ □ □ □ □ Creating a real idea about my "I" and my self-control.
□ □ □ □ □ Discovering the intelligent functions within me.
□ □ □ □ □ Understanding the world of feelings as manageable.
□ □ □ □ □ Discovering my inner needs through self-reflection.
□ □ □ □ □ To understand my unconscious as a reality to explore.
□ □ □ □ □ To understand love as the decisive force of life and value.
□ □ □ □ □ Discovering the basic values from the view of the psyche.
□ □ □ □ □ Seeing the importance of sexuality and its varied ways of living.
□ □ □ □ □ Interpreting health from a holistic point of view.
□ □ □ □ □ To understand partnership-like relationships from inside.
□ □ □ □ □ Discovering masculinity and femininity as roles and being.
□ □ □ □ □ Using intuition, introspection, imagination and contemplation.
□ □ □ □ □ To understand and to practice dream interpretation.
□ □ □ □ □ To apply techniques of relaxation on a daily basis.
□ □ □ □ □ Experiencing myself in the real and transcendental network.
□ □ □ □ □ Experiencing development and extension of consciousness.

Exercise II-E1-L9/3: Your essential conclusions to what you have marked (L9/2):

Exercise II-E1-L9/4: How about your defense against Individuation?

Mark and react with an emotional association (words):

☺ = from that I am relatively free ☺ = yes, moderate ☹ = yes, very much

☺☺☹ I fear my unconscious and my feelings.
☺☺☹ I know myself well; there is nothing much more that I need to know.
☺☺☹ I have family, job, and career. I don't have time for psycho-work!
☺☺☹ I don't have problems. Why should I practice self-education?
☺☺☹ There is nothing to change in my attitudes and beliefs.
☺☺☹ I don't have the energy to pull myself together for daily self-education.
☺☺☹ Reading is tedious; I don't like reading books about psychology.
☺☺☹ I am a simple person; what is there to I learn about my psyche?
☺☺☹ Wisdom is for calm people; I like living and I think rationally.
☺☺☹ I am happy; I don't miss anything. What for is self-knowledge?
☺☺☹ Psychology is for difficult people and only makes life complicated.
☺☺☹ Money determines the future and happiness of people.

Total: ☺ = ...   ☺ = ...   ☹ = ...

Exercise II-E1-L9/5: What do you feel and think about your statements in exercise L9/4?

Summary:

1. What is the most important thing you have learnt from this lesson?

2. What is your most outstanding strength in the subject of this lesson?

3. What is your outstanding weakness in the subject of this lesson?

4. What has touched you most in the subject of this lesson?

5. What is your most important future aim in the subject of this lesson?

6. What is your next step to improve in the subject of this lesson?

7. What are your open questions in the subject of this lesson?

3.1.10. Work methodically and holistically

Thesis II-E1-10-T1: Self-education and Individuation demand intelligence, sense and reason. All work to be done is objective and can be discussed.

Thesis II-E1-10-T2: Creativity is one part of the performance potentials every person has. Therefore, self-education and Individuation demand creativity along with intelligence and reason.

Thesis II-E1-10-T3: The methods of self-education are stimulating, exciting, varied and enormously enriching for the human being and the daily life.

Exercise II-E1-L10/1: Mark what influences you strongly:

☐ Flood of information (media)   ☐ Immense market of books
☐ Zeitgeist   ☐ Social pressure from allover
☐ Consumption offers   ☐ The classical patterns of career
☐ Leisure offers around me   ☐ Fashion trends
☐ The ideals of my parental home ☐ Habits from my youth
☐ Theatre and coulisse   ☐ Ideals in the marketing

Exercise II-E1-L10/2: Mental performances.

a) Describe your mental weaknesses spontaneously and concretely, for example about: clear perception, differentiated use of words, precise thinking, contemplated aims, objective order, logical thinking, detailed facts, reasonable planning, correct sequences, good time organization, awake concentration, fresh memory.

b) Causes for my mental weaknesses are:

Exercise II-E1-L10/3: Mark where your <u>mental</u> weaknesses are <u>remarkable</u>:

☐ clear perception   ☐ differentiated use of words
☐ precise thinking   ☐ well elaborated aims
☐ objective order   ☐ logical thinking
☐ detailed facts   ☐ reasonable planning
☐ correct sequences   ☐ good time organization
☐ high concentration   ☐ fresh memory

Exercise II-E1-L10/4: Comment, explain, and evaluate your statements to L10/3:

Exercise II-E1-L10/5: Creative performances

Describe your creative weaknesses spontaneously and concretely, for example about: Interest in images, remembering dreams, sense colors, experiencing shapes, spontaneous association, creating inner images, experiencing beauty, seeing experiences with the third eye, clear body feeling, good time feeling, a feeling for balance, experiencing totality and unity, interest in creation, power of observation, transforming intuition.

Exercise II-E1-L10/6: Mark where your creative weaknesses are remarkable:

☐ interest in images   ☐ remembering dreams
☐ to feel colors   ☐ experiencing shapes
☐ spontaneous associations   ☐ creating inner images
☐ experiencing beauty   ☐ seeing inner images
☐ clear body feeling   ☐ good time feeling
☐ feeling for balance   ☐ experiencing totality and unity
☐ interest in creating   ☐ power of observation (in life)
☐ transform intuition

Exercise II-E1-L10/7: Comment, explain, and evaluate your statements to exercise L10/6:

Causes for my creative weaknesses are:

Solutions for my creative weaknesses are:

Exercise II-E1-L10/8: Mark your significant deficits:

☐ Profoundly elaborating conflicts and leading them with skills to solutions.
☐ Formulating own attitudes precisely and if necessary revising them.
☐ Revealing masks and facades; finding a clear view for the deepness.
☐ Understanding everything in a complex network and not simplifying.
☐ New learning through systematic and aim oriented reading.
☐ Consciously dealing with life time and one's own forces.

Exercise II-E1-L10/9: The manifold self-education. Mark what applies to you:

5 = totally | 4 = regularly | 3 = often | 2 = sometimes | 1 = seldom | 0 = never/not

..... When I have a problem, I deal with it systematically.
..... I search for the right moment to deal with difficulties.
..... I relax myself with methods (techniques, Mental training, etc).
..... I keep a diary, dream diary, psycho-working diary.
..... I have my "tricks" in order to deal with myself when I am in a bad mood.
..... I know what time of the day I am well disposed for specific tasks.
..... I write down my dreams, interpret them, and make my conclusions.
..... I meditate (imagination, contemplation) with precise rules.
..... I regulate psychical nearness and distance to specific situations.
..... I regularly buy books to widen my horizon.
..... I consciously control myself when I am talking to others.
..... I take my time to reflect my way of living, my thinking and feeling.
..... I consciously form and extend my self-identity as a man (woman).
..... I care for my way of nourishing and in general for my health.
..... Physical self-experience and wellness are important to me.

Total points: .....

Exercise II-E1-L10/10: What do you feel and think now, taking an overview of L10/9? Keywords:

Summary:

1. What is the most important thing you have learnt from this lesson?

2. What is your most outstanding strength in the subject of this lesson?

3. What is your outstanding weakness in the subject of this lesson?

4. What has touched you most in the subject of this lesson?

5. What is your most important future aim in the subject of this lesson?

6. What is your next step to improve in the subject of this lesson?

7. What are your open questions in the subject of this lesson?

3.2. Manage yourself

Considerations about social competences

A great part of our life happens in situations between people: on the job, during leisure time and in the personal relationship. What goes on between people is highly important, and always involves communication. Communication is being, living and acting at the same time.

The more a person is formed holistically, the more successful an interaction is, the easier one can manage the organization and the use of life time and life forces. In an interaction the other person is perceived differently by each participant.

Basic questions about social competences and self-management are:

- How can we create an interaction as constructive as possible?
- How can we guide a dialogue in a way that it becomes a success for all participants?
- How can I respond to a person in order to arrive at a good result?
- What does a partnership-like relationship mean?
- How do I use my time, my forces and all my other resources?
- Which life techniques do I put to use in my life and on the job?
- How do I deal with critical incidents in the best way?
- Which strategies of mastering can help me in difficult conflict situations?

Social competences and self-management are key skills to positively manage the living together and to successfully deal with critical situations. Social competences are connected with the whole person and his abilities to act. Therefore, social competences and self-management are an indispensable part of each complete personality education.

Personality education and life competences

We are all in a psychological and social network. A person has friends or at least some acquaintances. He has his family and his relatives. In his inner life they are all also part of his existence. Each human being also has his relationships in the area of work, leisure and living. Some are married and may have children.

This complex network is the psycho-social space in which we move. Psychical forces are always in action here. Furthermore, there are other issues which arise for self-reflection, e.g.: "I am a "product" of this network".

Leading ideas about personality education

Personality education with social competences and self-management:

- Creates the key skills for life.
- Creates the abilities for constructive relationships.
- Reduces many risks in the personal course of life.
- Enables an optimal way of dealing with the possibilities.
- Produces security and self-confidence.
- Leads to a well-balanced and formed psychical life.
- Is indispensable for an authentic life-fulfillment.
- Integrates high ethic responsibility.
- Is an investment for your future (health, success, etc.)
- Is essential for all professions which offer any kind of guidance to people.
- Reaches the person in his psychical-spiritual being.
- Forms a positive and constructive character.

Personality education includes training the life skills for dealing with psychical life and knowing how to benefit from these forces. If a person can deal with his inner life, he develops a positive self-esteem and self-confidence, which leads to satisfaction, pleasure, life fulfillment and true happiness.

Life demands personality education with training about social competences and self-management for those people who are positively and constructively oriented towards life in general.

The methods of personality education

The methods of personality education are clearly determined. Only a bit of self-reflection and a few lessons do not activate the process. Without profound knowledge, the efforts cannot produce remarkable steps forward. Reading about psychological issues is vital. Thinking is an important factor in self-education. That also includes reflection about the use of words and distinguishing between emotional value judgments and objective statements. Thinking with a fruitful result doesn't happen casually.

For serious thinking one has to sit down. A notebook may help. Writing down allows one to express one's thoughts in written words, which helps to explore them further and helps to reach an aim-oriented analysis. Furthermore, everything that a person learns about self-education has to be applied in real life.

Each psychical sub-system (thinking, feelings, the subconscious, the ego-control, the basic psychical needs, etc.) and especially the behavior (social competences and self-management) have to be explored and worked on using various methods. Some methods are complementary because they focus on different aspects but on the same matter.

Meditation with visualization is an important technique and is connected to:

- With imagination one can explore all psychical and practical life-matters.
- Contemplation allows a person to experience symbols and archetypes, which represent psychical-spiritual processes.
- Mental-training supports the control of thoughts, helps to free the thoughts and aids concentration and a fresh mind in general.
- Introspection focuses more on the various inner emotional impulses: moods, intuitive ideas, self-experience and psycho-somatic reactions.
- Dream interpretation is indispensable for exploring the depths of the psychical life.
- Relaxation techniques help with stress and balancing the energy.
- Checklists and written standard exercises give an orientation to self-education.
- Everybody can learn life techniques and practice them in daily life. Self-management includes numerous practices which have to be exercised in real life situations.

There are more methods which creatively complete the variety, such as: role playing, drawing, discussions, creative activities to express psychical life, the use of technical tools such as video or music. The character of a person may give preference to one or another creative method.

Some people prefer emotional actions. Others favor objective and clear-headed working practices. One person may like to work alone; others need regular support within group work.

Self-knowledge as a part of one's own life culture

The daily activities with all aspects of self-knowledge and self-encounter, of social competences and self-management, make it evident what one knows and doesn't know about oneself and one's life, and what one doesn't know about a better living potential. These activities also heighten the consciousness about one's own rejecting and projecting mechanisms, and furthermore about how the "ego" (the "I") avoids the real life and tries to evade responsibility for a constructive life.

Sometimes one has to admit: "I don't want to see this. It is embarrassing, uncomfortable, troublesome, disturbing, painful and time-consuming."

The dynamics between the conscious and unconscious state of being is a problem of sincerity with oneself: "I want to know more about myself. I want to integrate my realities into my consciousness, and I don't want to continue to function unconsciously. I want to take responsibility for myself and my life." A life without self-knowledge and self-reflection is a life of lies.

Self-reflection forms a picture of oneself as well as one's life: "That is what I am, that is the way I live, and that is my life." This experience stimulates the need to care for and to form (educate) the inner psychical life and the own life culture as a part of one's own being. This is the way psychical life forces become important. They acquire more value. All this is a precondition to build up the force of love. Furthermore, also other people – the life partner, the parents and children, friends and acquaintances – are perceived much clearer with regard to their psychical reality. The psychical reality in general becomes a part of one's own life culture. This is the authentic self-realization.

During the process of self-education it becomes clearer that psychical life is the real human life. This experience activates the inner psychical life. Unrealized realities become an important part of one's own being. Ignored parts receive attention and care. Weakness gets protection and strength. The psychical inner life isn't a "black box" and a dark unreachable mystery anymore. The before unknown psychical forces are now approachable and become an obvious part of the conscious self-control.

More and more often there is every indication that positive and constructive changes occur. The process of the evolutionary growth has started to establish a systematic dynamism. Social competences and self-management are required. Correspondingly one can recognize constructive effects in one's daily life. Thereafter, certain crises, conflicts or disturbances may occur. One person constantly feels stressed. Another person has strong tensions in his relationship or a problem at work. Many people experience their leisure as "empty" time.

Small disturbances concerning the psychical forces can annoy considerably: inhibitions, weak concentration, feelings of inferiority, difficulties with sexual desire, etc. Some smoke or eat too much. The consumption of alcohol may be a bit exaggerated. Or the professional situation may not be satisfactory. Many people have a lack of ideas and initiatives to develop their own life out of the daily routine. The ones, who have children, could make a list of the daily preoccupations. Questions about all these burdens help to meditatively find oneself.

Part of daily life is the various duties, e.g. financial and administrative obligations, such as the rent and insurances. To that can be added: properties, cars, furniture, utilities for hobbies, etc. The way of dealing with all that reflects one's own psychical forces. Life culture in general is an expression of one's own psychical being: housework, cooking, eating, consumption, watching TV, internet, etc. The personal life culture also shows one's self-management. A person is and lives the way he practices social competences and self-management:

→ The way he creates his relationships.
→ The way he speaks and manages a dialogue.
→ The way he responds to others in a conversation.
→ The way he manages himself in a situation.
→ The way he deals with his manifold feelings.
→ The way he lives partnership-roles in his relationship.
→ The way he is able to renew himself.
→ The way he deals with learning difficulties
→ The way he uses his life time.
→ The way he practices life techniques.
→ The way he masters critical incidents.
→ The way he solves problems and conflicts.

Personality education promotes a precise consciousness about oneself, others and life. The self-image becomes more differentiated. The thinking is enriched by intuition. The perception takes on a much better quality. The will is strengthened. The emotional life can be managed reasonably. The psychical needs are recognized and can be satisfied. Projection and rejection are reduced more and more.

Potentials are discovered and can be formed in a useful way for one's own benefit. Adapted strategies to master situations make life more constructive and positive. Certain troubles disappear automatically. Some problems can't even arise. Challenges, crises and suffering can be managed much better.

What is a person without his psyche?

What is life culture without integrating the psyche?

What is self-realization without the psyche?

How is life without social competences and without self-management?

The new life culture integrates one's own and the psychical life of others as an expression of human being.

3.2.1. Manage and control yourself consciously

Thesis II-E2-1-T1: The better the quality of creating an interaction is, the more efficient the proceeding is and the more secure it is to reach the aspired aim.

Thesis II-E2-1-T2: The style of dealing with people in an interaction shows that over 50% in professional and personal life is psychology: as knowledge, theory, opinion, being and acting.

Thesis II-E2-1-T3: The conscious control of communication demands planning and preparation, opening, elaboration of the issue, differentiation and evaluation, decision, guidance of the proceeding, initiation of actions, control, feedback, and measures.

Exercise II-E2-L1/1: That's the way I create <u>my interactions</u> in work, family, relationship, and leisure:
Chose a person/group: .... and mark the characteristics:

☐ objective	☐ slow-clumsy
☐ honest	☐ volatile
☐ conscientious	☐ open
☐ impulsive	☐ time efficient
☐ organized	☐ thoroughly
☐ cooperative	☐ restless
☐ business like	☐ concentrated
☐ competent in the matter	☐ informative
☐ with fear, anxious	☐ consciously controlled
☐ actively adapting	☐ inside not engaged/dedicated
☐ planed	☐ harmonizing
☐ stimulating	☐ indecisive
☐ serious	☐ indifferent
☐ well organized	☐ short/concise
☐ strongly directive	☐ emotionally

Exercise II-E2-L1/2: How do you judge your way of creating interaction?

Exercise II-E2-L1/3: How is the interaction <u>in the company</u> of your partner, and with friends, clients, collaborators?
Chose a person/group: .... and mark the characteristics:

- ☐ friendly
- ☐ communicative
- ☐ taking distance
- ☐ significantly distant
- ☐ flexible in style and matter
- ☐ supporting
- ☐ valuing
- ☐ serving
- ☐ awaiting
- ☐ genuine
- ☐ attentive
- ☐ trustworthy

- ☐ dominant
- ☐ courteous
- ☐ impatient
- ☐ considerate
- ☐ emotional
- ☐ adaptive in style and matter
- ☐ cooperative
- ☐ reinforcing
- ☐ fair
- ☐ reciprocal
- ☐ dynamic
- ☐ informal

Exercise II-E2-L1/4: Interpret your statements:

Exercise II-E2-L1/5: What should you change <u>in the way of creating interaction and keeping company</u>?

Exercise II-E2-L1/6: Mark which rules and principles you don't consider enough:

- ☐ Despite interest, no success with bad (emotional) climate.
- ☐ No success without parallel (mutual) interest in success.
- ☐ Orientation facilitates decisions.
- ☐ Reducing defense: transparency, information, positive attitude.
- ☐ Emotionally strong positive aspects ("anchor") canalize decisions.
- ☐ Consider the state of information and motivation of the other people.
- ☐ Dissonance in style (behavior) slows down.
- ☐ Dissonance in the matter paralyzes (e.g. too high aims, too expensive costs).
- ☐ A wrong point in time can block.
- ☐ Environment-difference hinders (do the right thing in the right place!).
- ☐ Unsettled problems with the other part hinder cooperation.
- ☐ Quality in the relationship determines the perception.
- ☐ Flexibly prepare to find interest and aim (professional, private).
- ☐ "I"-messages (self-presentations) promote the interaction.

(*) Anchor = An image, a theme, a word producing in the other part a positive identification.

Exercise II-E2-L1/7: What are the consequences if you continuously disrespect these rules?
Describe:

Exercise II-E2-L1/8: When you are together with other people and want to talk about important matters, what do you ignore from the list below? Rate:

Mark how much you consider what: 1 = not at all | 2 = little | 3 = rather a lot | 4 = really a lot | 5 = totally / a lot

1 2 3 4 5
☐ ☐ ☐ ☐ ☐ Recognizing style (my style and the one from the other part)
☐ ☐ ☐ ☐ ☐ Understanding the language of the other part
☐ ☐ ☐ ☐ ☐ Seeing through the "game" of the other part
☐ ☐ ☐ ☐ ☐ Recognizing the weaknesses of the other part
☐ ☐ ☐ ☐ ☐ Building up decisions considering matter and resistance
☐ ☐ ☐ ☐ ☐ Creating security and footing there where it is necessary
☐ ☐ ☐ ☐ ☐ To recognize defense of the other part and to understand
☐ ☐ ☐ ☐ ☐ Stimulating life produces a positive climate of the relationship
☐ ☐ ☐ ☐ ☐ Identifying anchor (*) allows us to extend the decision making
☐ ☐ ☐ ☐ ☐ Coaching: serving, supporting, promoting wherever desirable
☐ ☐ ☐ ☐ ☐ Appeal to needs, motive, and product (matter)
☐ ☐ ☐ ☐ ☐ Interpreting state of behavior: defense, readiness for decision
☐ ☐ ☐ ☐ ☐ Recognizing attitudes towards product and reinforcing them
☐ ☐ ☐ ☐ ☐ To reduce hindering habits (behavior, feelings, thinking)
☐ ☐ ☐ ☐ ☐ Promoting self-esteem
☐ ☐ ☐ ☐ ☐ Accepting the other part as an autonomous personality
☐ ☐ ☐ ☐ ☐ Considering arguments (not everything can be argued)
☐ ☐ ☐ ☐ ☐ Let the others participate in the discussions
☐ ☐ ☐ ☐ ☐ Emotions come before arguments
☐ ☐ ☐ ☐ ☐ Find and stimulate common emotional interests
☐ ☐ ☐ ☐ ☐ The HOW: courteous, friendly, fair, restrained
☐ ☐ ☐ ☐ ☐ Being flexible with one's own ideas and proposals

(*) Anchor = An image, a theme, a word producing by the other part a positive identification.

Exercise II-E2-L1/9: What are the effects of neglecting the principles and rules (L1/8) in professional (job, work) settings?

Exercise II-E2-L1/10: What are the effects of neglecting the principles and rules (L1/8) in private and relationship settings?

Summary:

1. What is the most important thing you have learnt from this lesson?

2. What is your most outstanding strength in the subject of this lesson?

3. What is your outstanding weakness in the subject of this lesson?

4. What has touched you most in the subject of this lesson?

5. What is your most important future aim in the subject of this lesson?

6. What is your next step to improve in the subject of this lesson?

7. What are your open questions in the subject of this lesson?

3.2.2. Aim-oriented talking

Thesis II-E2-2-T1: Conveying a message includes: human aspects, knowledge, language and images, non-verbal aspects, ways of talking, and environment.

Thesis II-E2-2-T2: Finding solutions depends on: considering interests and wishes, promoting protection and security, recognizing and reducing resistance, creating a positive climate, stimulating motivation through anticipating aims, etc.

Thesis II-E2-2-T3: Technical aspects optimize success: to give feedback, listening, "I"-messages, open questions, persuade with objective arguments, making an appeal, summarizing, preparing decisions, etc.

Exercise II-E2-L2/1: In general, which facts do you ignore? Mark:

- ☐ In a conversation there are more realities than most people assume.
- ☐ A complete mutual consent is rarely possible.
- ☐ Conflicts, misunderstandings, and arguments form part of life.
- ☐ Talking about talking promotes understanding.
- ☐ One cannot talk better than the way one perceives and thinks.
- ☐ Talking is an expression of previous thinking and feeling.
- ☐ Talking is a very important way of mastering realities.
- ☐ Communication is more human-oriented than matter-oriented.
- ☐ Sensibility, empathy, and intuition are as important as the matter.
- ☐ Infringing the rules of communication is human.

Exercise II-E2-L2/2: Describe the consequences of disregarding these rules:

Exercise II-E2-L2/3: Where do you see your weaknesses?

Exercise II-E2-L2/4: You have to discuss an important matter, about a matter in the professional field or private life. Write down 1-2 keywords or respond with a short sentence to each statement:

Your matter to discuss:

1. Preparing the dialogue:
2. Where do I start?
3. How do I create a comfortable relationship?

4. How can I reduce insecurity and fear on the other part?
5. Where am I flexible in the aim-orientation?
6. Providing knowledge:
7. Providing skills:
8. Providing attitudes:
9. Power-talking (reinforcing the other part):
10. Recognize anchor (a positive key word) by the other part and talk about it:
11. Connect the anchor of the matter with the anchor from the other part:
12. Directly addressing needs of the other part:
13. Indirectly addressing (secondary) needs of the other part:
14. Recognizing annoying factors and eliminating them:
15. Planning and controlling of the proceeding:
16. To find the right moment:
17. Adjust mutual interests:
18. Recognize defense/resistance:
19. Reducing defense/resistance:
20. Contemplate about arguments around the positive value:
21. To further develop arguments around a plea:
22. Recognizing steps of changes:
23. Consciously care for a style of communication:
24. Creating positive projections (identification):
25. Asking questions to make the other part listen:

Exercise II-E2-L2/5: Mark how you will talk with your partner (friend, girlfriend, boyfriend) when you have a quarrel or conflict, and want to resolve it:
Mark the way you will talk and how you will do that: 1 = not at all | 2 = little | 3 = rather a lot | 4 = really a lot | 5 = totally / a lot

1 2   3 4 5
□ □ □ □ □ convincing
□ □ □ □ □ motivating
□ □ □ □ □ encouraging
□ □ □ □ □ evaluating/judging
□ □ □ □ □ manipulating
□ □ □ □ □ elating
□ □ □ □ □ dominating
□ □ □ □ □ competing
□ □ □ □ □ inducing
□ □ □ □ □ listening
□ □ □ □ □ provoking
□ □ □ □ □ harmonizing
□ □ □ □ □ conducting

□ □ □ □ □ creating comfort
□ □ □ □ □ giving orientation
□ □ □ □ □ understanding
□ □ □ □ □ giving decision support
□ □ □ □ □ showing interest
□ □ □ □ □ creating an anchor
□ □ □ □ □ using an anchor
□ □ □ □ □ reinforcing
□ □ □ □ □ cooperating
□ □ □ □ □ asking
□ □ □ □ □ rivaling

Exercise II-E2-L4/6: Your conclusion to improve the situation (relationship):

Exercise II-E2-L2/7: Note those keywords from L2/5 where you are especially strong in your professional life (or: in your relationship):

Exercise II-E2-L2/8: Note those keywords from L2/5 where you are especially weak in your professional life (or: in your relationship):

Exercise II-E2-L2/9: Your conclusion to improve the situation (work, job)

Summary:

1. What is the most important thing you have learnt from this lesson?

2. What is your most outstanding strength in the subject of this lesson?

3. What is your outstanding weakness in the subject of this lesson?

4. What has touched you most in the subject of this lesson?

5. What is your most important future aim in the subject of this lesson?

6. What is your next step to improve in the subject of this lesson?

7. What are your open questions in the subject of this lesson?

3.2.3. Consider the rules while talking

Thesis II-E2-3-T1: The levels of orientation in the control of communication are: person(s), issue, communication techniques, decisions, knowledge, the way of creating the dialogue, and actions.

Thesis II-E2-3-T2: The other is a human being with thoughts, emotions, needs, resistance, interests, knowledge, experiences, abilities (skills), and weaknesses, conscious or unconscious aspirations.

Thesis II-E2-3-T3: Taking into consideration the ethical roles in a dialogue improves the chances for success and also benefits all participants.

Exercise II-E2-L3/1: Mark what you want to consider for orientation in a dialogue because it is important to you:

☐ Direct clear information
☐ What has to be done
☐ Objectivity with a certain distance
☐ Experiencing emotion
☐ Experiencing security
☐ Reducing fear
☐ Fast solutions
☐ The special aspects of the matter
☐ Uniqueness of the opportunity
☐ Future benefit
☐ Service, help, support
☐ Critically evaluating pleas
☐ Strengthening self-image
☐ Factor of time for decision
☐ Arguments and not emotions

☐ Strong guidance
☐ Why something has to be done
☐ The effects of an act
☐ Proceedings
☐ Details
☐ Alternatives/options of choice
☐ Repetitions, aid to memory
☐ Personal benefit
☐ Emotional support for decision
☐ Immediate benefit
☐ Reactions to a style of talking
☐ Comfort
☐ To truly help the other part
☐ Discharge of sorrow
☐ Efficiency

Exercise II-E2-L3/2: Give an argument why orientation in a dialogue is important:

a) Style of dealing with each other:

b) Listening:

c) Experiencing:

d) Questioning:

e) Considering habits:

Exercise II-E2-L3/3: Where do your weaknesses lie within the following cases?

Posture: open, resistance, informal, formal; Breathing: relaxed, tense; Abdomen: lax; Way of talking: Tone, speed, rhythm, smoothness; Language: keywords, words from the real life of the other part.

Exercise II-E2-L3/4: What have you neglected until today about the partner-orientation?

Showing interest in the other part (situation, thoughts, needs, and possibilities): questioning, listening, expressing understanding; repeating, considering the steps of remembering (short time storage: 10 sec.; some words and short sentences, short time memory: 1-2 days, 7-9 words).

Exercise II-E2-L3/5: What do you feel about "creating visions"?
Creating visions: Using slightly emotional (not too strong!) colored images; Anticipating the future of the matter; building up a mental film with elements from the other part; presenting an image as experience; Images: clear, colored, positive, future-oriented, bright, clear shapes.

Exercise II-E2-L3/6: Give an example of how you create information:
Stimulating senses with words and images: Senses: taste, see, listen, smell; sense of warmth, sense of touch, state of muscles, gravity; creating in a network and step by step, facilitating repetition.

Exercise II-E2-L3/7: Formulate to "serve" an instruction or an advice for a collaborator or friend:

Explaining: (giving orientation); transmit constructive attitudes; giving support for decisions; supporting emotionally; appealing: doing something to make something happen.

Exercise II-E2-L3/8: My conclusions to my weaknesses:

Exercise II-E2-L3/9: I respect the following moral rules. Rate!

Rate how much you respect the rules: 1 = not at all | 2 = little | 3 = rather a lot | 4 = really a lot | 5 = totally a lot

1 2 3 4 5
☐ ☐ ☐ ☐ ☐ Not to humiliate, not to hurt
☐ ☐ ☐ ☐ ☐ Listen, empathize, understand
☐ ☐ ☐ ☐ ☐ Not to exaggerate / not to trivialize
☐ ☐ ☐ ☐ ☐ Adequately expressing feelings
☐ ☐ ☐ ☐ ☐ Not interrupting
☐ ☐ ☐ ☐ ☐ Hear out what the other party has to say
☐ ☐ ☐ ☐ ☐ Consider questions and wishes
☐ ☐ ☐ ☐ ☐ Allow autonomy
☐ ☐ ☐ ☐ ☐ Mutually communicate
☐ ☐ ☐ ☐ ☐ Expressing respect with a certain distance
☐ ☐ ☐ ☐ ☐ Not to coax, but persuade

Exercise II-E2-L3/10: What are the consequences if you don't respect these rules (L3/9)?

Exercise II-E2-L3/11: Your conclusions from L3/9:

Summary:

1. What is the most important thing you have learnt from this lesson?

2. What is your most outstanding strength in the subject of this lesson?

3. What is your outstanding weakness in the subject of this lesson?

4. What has touched you most in the subject of this lesson?

5. What is your most important future aim in the subject of this lesson?

6. What is your next step to improve in the subject of this lesson?

7. What are your open questions in the subject of this lesson?

3.2.4. Strengthen yourself for interaction with others

Thesis II-E2-4-T1: The weaknesses in self-guidance are: 1) the mental level; 2) the level of the issue and of the procedure control; and 3) the level of abilities (skills) for innovation (changes, developments).

Thesis II-E2-4-T2: In a constructive communication a person has to guide himself: regulate, coordinate, plan, organize, concentrate, be attentive, control, enforce aim setting, and take decisions.

Thesis II-E2-4-T3: Emotional comfort, positive attitudes and being aware of meaning and transparency promote (support) success in a dialogue and in all kinds of processes for finding *solutions*.

Exercise II-E2-L4/1: My <u>strong</u> abilities to find orientation are:

☐ Concentration	☐ Attentiveness	☐ Flexibility
☐ Motivation	☐ Alternatives	☐ Ability to adapt
☐ Ambition	☐ Interest	☐ Reinforcement
☐ Self-confidence	☐ Ideals	☐ Thinking

Exercise II-E2-L4/2: How do you improve your weaknesses?

Exercise II-E2-L4/3: My <u>strong</u> abilities to control (manage) are:

☐ Determining aims	☐ Directing	☐ Giving content
☐ Decision	☐ Enforcing	☐ Regulating
☐ Coordination	☐ Concentration	☐ Planning
☐ Control	☐ Organization	☐ Networking

Exercise II-E2-L4/4: How do you improve your weaknesses?

Exercise II-E2-L4/5: My <u>strong</u> social competences (skills) are:

☐ Cooperation
☐ Promoting development
☐ Objectivity/Competences
☐ With attitudes of love
☐ Setting boundaries towards others

□ Independence
□ Founded in the inner spirit
□ Selecting, giving the right weight/importance
□ Balance: Will-situation

Exercise II-E2-L4/6: How do you improve your weaknesses?

Exercise II-E2-L4/7: Evaluate with points your perception in interactions: Perception of interaction in:

□ working place
□ relationship

My perception is: 5 = very; 4 = preponderant; 3 = moderate; 2 = partly; 1 = little

Quality	Points
vague, diffuse, nebulous	
undifferentiated	
superficial	
unilateral, partial	
rejecting, suppressing	
habitual	
rigid, fixed	
nearsighted	
emotional	
With vague sensation of values	

Total points: ....

Exercise II-E2-L4/8: Conclusions and consequences in some short words:

Exercise II-E2-L4/9: Mark your empowerment-deficit; circle of persons:

Work Leisure Love

□	□	□	Propensity or renewal
□	□	□	Optimism
□	□	□	Actively participating
□	□	□	Leasing and adapting

☐	☐	☐	Further education
☐	☐	☐	Life quality
☐	☐	☐	Autonomy
☐	☐	☐	Success
☐	☐	☐	Clear field of activity
☐	☐	☐	Motivating, aim-anticipation
☐	☐	☐	Diversification
☐	☐	☐	Flexible working aims
☐	☐	☐	Ideas, aims, visions
☐	☐	☐	Information
☐	☐	☐	Appreciation
☐	☐	☐	Transparency (matter, proceeding)
☐	☐	☐	Co-determination
☐	☐	☐	Life philosophy
☐	☐	☐	Physical state
☐	☐	☐	Living conditions
☐	☐	☐	Partnership
☐	☐	☐	Leisure activity
☐	☐	☐	Joyful satisfaction
☐	☐	☐	Team work

Exercise II-E2-L4/10: Mark your <u>deficit</u> concerning ability and consideration:

☐ Organizing	☐ Clarifying	☐ Discussing
☐ Directing	☐ Deciding	☐ Informing
☐ Planning	☐ Controlling	☐ Delegating
☐ Coordinating	☐ Initiating	☐ Promoting
☐ Stimulating	☐ Rectifying	☐ Selecting
☐ Evaluating		

Exercise II-E2-L4/11: Look back over the last days and weeks. Try to identify the variety of your emotions / feelings. Comment in words:

Positive feeling:	Frequency, weight/importance: (in words)
Being happy	
Trust	
Peace	
Hope	
Truthfulness	
Love	
Dedication	
Security	
Joy	

Satisfaction	
Wholeness	
Meaningfulness	

Negative feelings:	Frequency, weight/importance: (in words)
Unhappiness	
Distrust	
Strife	
Hopelessness	
Negation	
Hate	
Aggression	
Insecurity	
Sadness	
Dissatisfaction	
Inner disruption	
Meaninglessness	

Exercise II-E2-L4/12: Formulate 3 acting suggestions about what you can do to improve your negative emotional state:

Summary:

1. What is the most important thing you have learnt from this lesson?

2. What is your most outstanding strength in the subject of this lesson?

3. What is your outstanding weakness in the subject of this lesson?

4. What has touched you most in the subject of this lesson?

5. What is your most important future aim in the subject of this lesson?

6. What is your next step to improve in the subject of this lesson?

7. What are your open questions in the subject of this lesson?

3.2.5. Respect the principles of partnership

Thesis II-E2-5-T1: Partnership tends to establish a balance in issues and persons: Masculinity, femininity, psyche, sexuality, power, self-esteem, communication, interests, housekeeping, etc.

Thesis II-E2-5-T2: The formal principals of partnership are: Flexibility, reciprocity, respect, exchange, cooperation, constructiveness, love, integration, distribution, promotion, and objectivity.

Thesis II-E2-5-T3: Embarrassing, delicate and sensitive incidents which are not dealt with tend to hinder and block the full development of a relationship in the present and in the future.

Exercise II-E2-L5/1: Mark what you consider very consciously in living with your partner partnership-like today (or: in the past):

☐ Integration of the biography of each other
☐ Sexuality with love and joy
☐ Constructive communication
☐ Cooperative distribution of housekeeping
☐ Flexible dynamism of power
☐ Mutual enrichment of forming self-identity
☐ Respecting femininity and masculinity
☐ Exchange and inner bond to personal growth

Exercise II-E2-L5/2: What can / could you not accept enough or live in the relationship with your partner (today / in the past) from the following aspects:

Mark what you value:
1 = not at all | 2 = little | 3 = rather a lot | 4 = really a lot |
5 = totally a lot

☐ A mutual openness for the life of both partners can also contain conflicts.
☐ Partners respect each other in their differences (character, gender).
☐ Reciprocity and equality are taken as basic principles.
☐ Nearness and distance are a normal part of living together.
☐ The biography of both partners is as important as the self-identity.
☐ Partners agree on their differences and the things they have in common.

- [ ] Partners respect the limits of the other and the world of the other.
- [ ] Love in a partnership has to be continuously formed.
- [ ] In a partnership both discuss common daily matters and concerns.
- [ ] In a partnership the mistakes are not mutually balanced.
- [ ] Intelligence and reason are supportive; but don't guarantee love.
- [ ] Eroticism and being in love have a place in the normality of the daily life.
- [ ] Partnership-like love includes tensions and risks.
- [ ] Mutual satisfaction of sexual desire deepens the partnership.
- [ ] The partners do not possess each other in the totality of their being.
- [ ] Mutual dependence of sexual satisfaction is not against autonomy.
- [ ] The ability to love includes the ability to understand (can be difficult).
- [ ] Every few years self-identity changes on both sides.
- [ ] Partners mutually form femininity and masculinity.
- [ ] Elaborating the unconscious mind is partly a common work.
- [ ] Together, the partners orient on their dreams, intuition and meditation.

Exercise II-E2-L5/3: Write down some consequences for necessary "renewals":

Exercise II-E2-L5/4: Give an answer to the following sensible questions about partnership:

1. What have I learnt from my previous partner(s)?
2. Which experiences are still embarrassing / uncomfortable when remembered?
3. Which conflicts have I had in previous relationships?
4. What have I been told about sexuality?
5. How do my first sexual experiences affect me when remembering them?
6. What have I always liked about my previous partners?
7. How have I reacted in the past about having children and contraception?
8. What has strongly hurt me in sexual behavior and experiences?
9. What importance do I give to faith and being with the partner, also in difficult times?
10. What do I especially like on the female / male body?
11. What have I never dared to talk about with my partner?
12. What have my partners expected from me in the past?
13. How have I discussed conflicts with my previous partners?
14. Which attitudes, laws, and prohibitions about sex have I experienced in the past?
15. Which feelings and ways of experiencing have I had about self-satisfaction?
16. Which was one of the most beautiful sexual experiences in my life?

17. Which sexual pre-judgment have I (had) about women / men?
18. What was my physical ideal of the desired partner?
19. Which were the most embarrassing sexual experiences?
20. Which qualities do I wish for in my partner?
21. Which were the most wonderful non-sexual experiences with my partner(s)?

Exercise II-E2-L5/5: From all these statements what do you now conclude for yourself?

Summary:

1. What is the most important thing you have learnt from this lesson?

2. What is your most outstanding strength in the subject of this lesson?

3. What is your outstanding weakness in the subject of this lesson?

4. What has touched you most in the subject of this lesson?

5. What is your most important future aim in the subject of this lesson?

6. What is your next step to improve in the subject of this lesson?

7. What are your open questions in the subject of this lesson?

3.2.6. Renew yourself

Thesis II-E2-6-T1: The ability for innovation can be improved by: trial, new approaches to problem solving, creative implementation, addressing the patterns of interpretation, concernment and nearness to life.

Thesis II-E2-6-T2: Optimal learning is connected with: 1) Perception and experience; 2) Language and communication; 3) Aims, values, plans; and 4) Understanding with thinking and valuing.

Thesis II-E2-6-T3: Learning through motivation happens on a personal level (own interest) and on an objective and future oriented level which, with concrete issues, produces motivation in the present.

Exercise II-E2-L6/1: Which is your strength of renewal? Mark:
Mark what is right for you: 1 = not at all | 2 = little | 3 = rather a lot | 4 = really a lot | 5 = a lot / totally

1 2 3 4 5
□ □ □ □ □ I think all-embracing.
□ □ □ □ □ I like decisiveness for new tasks.
□ □ □ □ □ I have a high level of energy.
□ □ □ □ □ I have a realistic view.
□ □ □ □ □ I spend time analyzing problems.
□ □ □ □ □ I do not think ideologically.
□ □ □ □ □ I am far-sighted when taking decisions.
□ □ □ □ □ I am not afraid of making mistakes.
□ □ □ □ □ I am open to learn in daily life.
□ □ □ □ □ I can accept unsolved situations.
□ □ □ □ □ I am concentrated, but easy in my self-control.
□ □ □ □ □ I feel free from dogmatic thinking.
□ □ □ □ □ I am not really opportunistic.
□ □ □ □ □ Not everything has to be calculable for me.
□ □ □ □ □ I am flexible in traditions.
□ □ □ □ □ I like developing new ideas for my daily life.
□ □ □ □ □ I am able to feel fascinated by something.
□ □ □ □ □ I can bear frustration.
□ □ □ □ □ I also have a sense of humor.
□ □ □ □ □ Irrational matters do not easily unsettle me.

□ □ □ □ □ I look at the big picture without loosing the details.
□ □ □ □ □ I interpret in manifold ways.
□ □ □ □ □ I can decompose into smallest elements.
□ □ □ □ □ I recognize aspects of values.
□ □ □ □ □ I can deal with dissonance and disharmony.
□ □ □ □ □ I can also accept difficult human situations.

Exercise II-E2-L6/2: What are the effects of your weaknesses (L6/1) in daily life / in your job?

Exercise II-E2-L6/3: Learning effectively is something that needs to be learnt. What do you conclude for yourself?

Exercise II-E2-L6/4: How important is "always learning in all areas of life and work" to you?

Exercise II-E2-L6/5: How is your self-realization if you don't learn anything?

Exercise II-E2-L6/6: Search for your learning difficulties! Mark what burdens you:

1 = not at all | 2 = little | 3 = rather a lot | 4 = really a lot | 5 = totally a lot

1 2 3 4 5
□ □ □ □ □ General reluctance to learn
□ □ □ □ □ Lack of motivation to learn
□ □ □ □ □ Not many explored reasons for learning: Why this? Why now?
□ □ □ □ □ No zest for discovering, little curiosity in new matters
□ □ □ □ □ Intellectually not really accessible (it must be concrete)
□ □ □ □ □ Doubt in the meaning of learning
□ □ □ □ □ Easily evaporated interest, strong ephemeral attentiveness
□ □ □ □ □ Little confidence in my own ability to learn (thinking)
□ □ □ □ □ Little confidence in my own ability to evaluate / judge
□ □ □ □ □ Resistance against effort and discipline
□ □ □ □ □ Afraid to form my own opinions and hypotheses
□ □ □ □ □ Few experiences about taking responsibility in learning
□ □ □ □ □ Stress in learning. Stress through learning
□ □ □ □ □ Difficulties in concentration
□ □ □ □ □ Too often copying what others are saying instead of thinking
□ □ □ □ □ Lack of ties for my own acting
□ □ □ □ □ Too heavily burdened with problems and conflicts
□ □ □ □ □ Heavy experiences from my school time

☐ ☐ ☐ ☐ ☐ Devaluating the necessity of life long and extensive learning
☐ ☐ ☐ ☐ ☐ Little tolerance of frustration
☐ ☐ ☐ ☐ ☐ Unable to suffer in understanding / expressing verbally
☐ ☐ ☐ ☐ ☐ Hardly pressed from general dissatisfaction and reluctance
☐ ☐ ☐ ☐ ☐ Continuous retention of my own life forces
☐ ☐ ☐ ☐ ☐ No planned way of dealing with pauses and varieties
☐ ☐ ☐ ☐ ☐ Indecisiveness in determining aims and path
☐ ☐ ☐ ☐ ☐ Strong dominance in utilitarian thinking
☐ ☐ ☐ ☐ ☐ Not giving importance to knowledge / life knowledge
☐ ☐ ☐ ☐ ☐ Not ready in acquiring new attitudes and values about matters

Exercise II-E2-L6/7: Favorable learning dispositions. React emotionally with a short evaluating word:

1. Opinions and attitudes for learning, principally ready to learn:
2. Ability to organize learning situations and to manage them:
3. Interest in knowledge and creativity in the field of the psyche:
4. Perseverance, endurance and ability to concentrate:
5. Clear perception, spiritual / mental presence and perspicacious thinking:
6. Positive acceptance of life problems and challenges:
7. Readiness to recognize and understand the psychical realities:
8. Interest in a differentiated development and growing process:
9. Dedication to values such as truthfulness and love:

Exercise II-E2-L6/8: As a consequence formulate 3 good solutions:

Summary:

1. What is the most important thing you have learnt from this lesson?

2. What is your most outstanding strength in the subject of this lesson?

3. What is your outstanding weakness in the subject of this lesson?

4. What has touched you most in the subject of this lesson?

5. What is your most important future aim in the subject of this lesson?

6. What is your next step to improve in the subject of this lesson?

7. What are your open questions in the subject of this lesson?

3.2.7. Use your time efficiently

Thesis II-E2-7-T1: Everyone has at least a quarter of an hour a day for self-education. Per week this makes: 105 minutes, per year 5,460 minutes = 91 hours. In 40 years this is an immeasurable capital for the evolutionary psychical-spiritual development!

Thesis II-E2-7-T2: The three questions of time use and time control are: 1) What for? (Importance, urgency, value, purpose, aim); 2) How? (Strategy, management, overview, will, procedure); and 3) Power? (Self-esteem, energy, condition of health, stress, flexibility).

Thesis II-E2-7-T3: If it is important to reach valuable aims in life (e.g. relationship, profession, further education, hobbies), then happiness can be built up with an efficient time management.

Exercise II-E2-L7/1: Write down your daily use of time in minutes (week retrospection):

... Travel to work
... Reading books
... Household
... Chatting
... Telephone
... Curiosity for incidents
... Searching for stuff
... Watching TV
... Waiting
... Making a decision
... Traffic jam/ - light
... Cooking
... Paperwork
... Money planning
... Visits
... Short visits to bars
... Discussions
... Eating
... Unplanned shopping
... Doing the dishes
... Playing games

... Reading newspapers
... Professional lecture
... Further education
... Hanging around
... Listening to music
... Hobbies
... Decorating
... Small shopping spree
... Physical experiences
... Psychical strengthening
... Dream interpretation
... Keeping a diary
... Collecting information
... Meditation
... Experiencing nature
... Relaxation
... Relationship / Love
... Preoccupied

Exercise II-E2-L7/2: Your conclusion:

Exercise II-E2-L7/3: Write down what you spontaneously feel about the following questions:

1. What do I want to talk about on the phone and how long do I want to listen?
2. Do I really have to go shopping with the car 5 times a week?
3. Do I really want "this"? Does "this" have to be right now?
4. Do I really have to know that much about people I don't know?
5. What have I gained for my life from these TV-shows?
6. What do I talk about with my colleagues at work?
7. Do I plan new projects by searching for information (work, leisure)?
8. Do I sufficiently plan changes or do I start "just like that"?
9. Do I consider my feelings (intuitions) when I want to realize something new?
10. What do I do when I am driven by boredom and lack of drive?

Exercise II-E2-L7/4: Give a spontaneous association (verbal reaction) to the following principles of a constructive time management.

1. Planning the day in the morning (handling something, proceeding, time frame)

2. Retrospection in the evening (What have I finished? When do I have to do "this"?)
3. Planning the week ahead every Sunday (rough distribution of each day)
4. Setting weekly and daily aims (big, medium, small aims)
5. Weekly retrospection every Saturday (done, not at all done: causes?)
6. Preparing and evaluating important phone calls
7. Check lists (e.g. for travelling, shopping, all the small things)
8. Identifying the importance and the urgency
9. Sometimes pauses are important: for a short mental training
10. Getting an overview of proceedings and managing / talking about
11. Biorhythm: What do I like to easily do at which time of the day?
12. Time distribution: 30% planning; 60% realization; 10% evaluation
13. First exploring "new areas"; then collecting information
14. First reducing anger and then starting to deal with the matter (by talking about it)
15. New situations: Benefit from experiences from others and first elaborate this
16. Elaborate structured preparation, execution, and evaluation

Exercise II-E2-L7/5: What is indispensable for your time planning? Make a list:

Exercise II-E2-L7/6: Formulate some concrete conclusions for your time planning:

Summary:

1. What is the most important thing you have learnt from this lesson?

2. What is your most outstanding strength in the subject of this lesson?

3. What is your outstanding weakness in the subject of this lesson?

4. What has touched you most in the subject of this lesson?

5. What is your most important future aim in the subject of this lesson?

6. What is your next step to improve in the subject of this lesson?

7. What are your open questions in the subject of this lesson?

3.2.8. Apply life techniques

Thesis II-E2-8-T1: The characteristics of life techniques are: order, planning, structure, clarity, overview, determination, self-management, seriousness, controlled speed, exact aims.

Thesis II-E2-8-T2: Integrating mental techniques in one's own life culture grants the best chances for a development towards gain, success and happiness; on the level of profession, relationship and leisure.

Thesis II-E2-8-T3: The network of success includes: self-management, social competences, personality, private life, self-profile, fitness, empowerment, sources of ideas, and strategies for problem solving.

Exercise II-E2-L8/1: How consciously do you apply life techniques? Give keywords:

1. Principles of small steps
2. Elaborating information
3. Dosing amount and intensity
4. Self-management by learning
5. Thinking positively with intelligence
6. Diligence and effort
7. Controlling perception
8. An all-sided networked thinking
9. Giving constructive meaning in an extended context
10. Living the human being

Exercise II-E2-L8/2: Answer with a short sentence; not with "yes" or "no".

1. Do you concentrate on the result of your acting?
2. Are you ready to invest time and work for your life wishes?
3. Have you explored the way of your thinking and judging?
4. Have you determined aims and taken responsibility for success?
5. Do you try to resolve problems objectively and with intelligence?
6. Do you distinguish between importance and urgency?
7. Have you calculated your time demand for a decided matter?
8. Does your time planning leave space for unexpected incidents/matters?
9. Do you know what you should omit in important situations?
10. Ask yourself: "Is this the best use of my time?"

11. Do you have a sane self-confidence?
12. Do you give high significance to your needs and desires?
13. Do you take responsibility for your feelings?
14. Do you trust your strength and do you consider your weaknesses?
15. Are you aware that perfectionism can hinder efficiency?
16. Do you have the courage to act and do you dare to deal with something new?
17. Do you have the habit to postpone pending tasks and duties?

Exercise II-E2-L8/3: Application of life techniques:

Rate what you consider and do: 1 = not at all | 2 = little | 3 = rather a lot | 4 = really a lot | 5 = totally a lot

```
1  2  3  4  5
□  □  □  □  □  Finding and considering positive images
□  □  □  □  □  Constructive thoughts also in small daily matters
□  □  □  □  □  Relaxing your thinking, 2-3 times daily
□  □  □  □  □  Liberating images through meditation
□  □  □  □  □  Creating mental distance if you are fixed too much in thoughts
□  □  □  □  □  Dissolution of opposites through meditative elaboration
□  □  □  □  □  Getting rid of suffering through elaboration
□  □  □  □  □  Resolving conflicts through clarification and right attitudes
□  □  □  □  □  Practicing mental fitness
□  □  □  □  □  Caring for a positive physical relationship
□  □  □  □  □  Considering the world of meanings
□  □  □  □  □  Giving importance to positive life acceptance
□  □  □  □  □  Satisfying needs with intelligence and at the right moment
□  □  □  □  □  Reducing stimulators; do not empathize with everything
□  □  □  □  □  Contemplated life rhythm, also in professional situation
□  □  □  □  □  Living health holistically; psychically as well physically
□  □  □  □  □  Understanding life/existence intellectually and intuitively
□  □  □  □  □  An integrated thinking between intelligence and spirituality
□  □  □  □  □  A linear-synthetic elaboration (thinking in network)
□  □  □  □  □  Considering the biorhythm, especially for special work
□  □  □  □  □  Inner distance to other people and alien life matters
□  □  □  □  □  Delimiting and managing the themes in discussion
```

Exercise II-E2-L8/4: Interpret your potential of a psychical mastering of difficult situations:

Exercise II-E2-L8/5: Your conclusion in one sentence:

Summary:

1. What is the most important thing you have learnt from this lesson?

2. What is your most outstanding strength in the subject of this lesson?

3. What is your outstanding weakness in the subject of this lesson?

4. What has touched you most in the subject of this lesson?

5. What is your most important future aim in the subject of this lesson?

6. What is your next step to improve in the subject of this lesson?

7. What are your open questions in the subject of this lesson?

3.2.9. Clarify critical incidents and situations

> Thesis II-E2-9-T1: An action contains various system components: action, aim of acting, value, situation of acting, life area of the action and the acting person, as well as the psychical organism of the acting person(s).
>
> Thesis II-E2-9-T2: In daily life various actions are "critical", that means: delicate, disagreeable, unclear, conflictive, insecure, disturbing, encumbering, embarrassing, painful, tense, etc.
>
> Thesis II-E2-9-T3: Critical life situations are part of each person: life with the partner, knowledge and education, culture and leisure, profession and working place, consumption and money, life area, spiritual basic questions as well as social life.

In daily life, many activities are "critical"; that means: delicate, uncomfortable, unclear, conflictive, insecure, molesting, burdening, embarrassing, painful, tense, etc.

Exercise II-E2-L9/1: Mark in which form you have experienced "critical" activities / situations:

1. ☐ The acting contains a decision problem.
2. ☐ There is a difficulty to act because of a lack of acquired skills.
3. ☐ The effects are different from the expected ones.
4. ☐ Unexpected and undesired side-effected were arisen.
5. ☐ The aims are not achieved with the activities.
6. ☐ The environment sets limits to act.
7. ☐ The psychical life produces limitations or has annoying effects on the activities.

> View: "critical" is what **I** do (act, react) in a situation, in front of a critical action of another person. *And not the negative/problematic acting from this other person!* The initial stand to analyze the solution of a problem is on YOUR side!

Exercise II-E2-L9/2: Find examples from your daily life (personal or job related). First shortly describe the situation and then in which way this is "critical" for you:

Example:	
It is critical because:	
Example:	
It is critical because:	
Example:	
It is critical because:	
Example:	
It is critical because:	

Exercise II-E2-L9/3: Resume what you in general feel as highly "critical" in an overview.

Exercise II-E2-L9/4: Fill in the standard-protocol with keywords/short sentences.

Analytical protocol: My "critical incident / situation"

"Critical" means: insecure, uncomfortable, delicate, conflictive, tense, embarrassing, weak, molesting, burdening, painful, failure, difficult to take decisions, need of renewal, etc.

Take an example from daily life and elaborate following the scheme:

1. The situation of incident: What happened? What occurred?

2. The behavior / action in the critical situation: What have you done? Who has done what?

3. Life systems/ environment systems: How was the environment? What has had an effect on the event / incident?

4. What (and in which sense) do you feel as "critical" (which aspects)?

5. Prospective: What are your ideal wishes / changes / aims?

6. Where is the start for solutions? What is the first step for a solution?

Summary:

1. What is the most important thing you have learnt from this lesson?

2. What is your most outstanding strength in the subject of this lesson?

3. What is your outstanding weakness in the subject of this lesson?

4. What has touched you most in the subject of this lesson?

5. What is your most important future aim in the subject of this lesson?

6. What is your next step to improve in the subject of this lesson?

7. What are your open questions in the subject of this lesson?

3.2.10. Benefit from strategies for solutions

Thesis II-E2-10-T1: A strategy is connected with: life areas, psyche, related persons, interactions, actions, action areas; the past, present and future.

Thesis II-E2-10-T2: Everything starts with the person: Intelligence, needs, emotions, psycho dynamism, readiness to learn, creativity, self-esteem, self-guidance, and the integration of dreams (messages in the dreams).

Thesis II-E2-10-T3: Success in life happens through: having an aim, define the path, procuring the instruments, learning the skills, dealing with difficulties with competences (skills).

Exercise II-E2-L10/1: Where do you see your weaknesses concerning a competent mastering of life? Check from the list below!

☐ Give attention to what it is thinking about!
☐ Give importance to sorrow and deal with it!
☐ Find the reasons of fear, of a lack of self-confidence!
☐ Be aware of what produces emotions; focus on these influences!
☐ Deal with unsettled matters with a time plan!
☐ Clarify your lack of competences and improve by learning!
☐ Examine your explanations, especially also your style of explanations.
☐ Examine and change your attitudes if necessary!
☐ You can be satisfied with your performance if you achieve 80-90% quality!
☐ See the positive aspects of challenges and moderate your demands!
☐ Do not give unilateral importance to economical and business success!
☐ Regularly practice critical self-reflection; and enjoy life!

Exercise II-E2-L10/2: Describe your deficit in pre-dispositions for happiness and life fulfillment using keywords:

1. Working techniques, self-management
2. Objective competences, development of talents
3. Social competences, communication
4. Personality, life culture
5. Balanced private life
6. Fitness, psychical and physical health
7. Further education, counseling, coaching
8. Strategies for resolving problems, readiness for renewal

9. "Empowerment", self-motivation
10. Information, also informal tips
11. Sources of ideas, support for creations / activities
12. General superior strategies for actions, aims of life

Exercise II-E2-L10/3: Draw an image about your desired "success in life" (life aim):

Exercise II-E2-L10/4: What have you done till today for your success in life (life aims)?

Exercise II-E2-L10/5: What more can you do to achieve your aims for life?

Exercise II-E2-L10/6: Positive and negative ways of mastering.
Rate how much you consider the following statements:
1 = not at all | 2 = little | 3 = rather a lot | 4 = really a lot |
5 = totally a lot

1 2 3 4 5
☐ ☐ ☐ ☐ ☐ Positive re-interpretation
☐ ☐ ☐ ☐ ☐ Being aware of ignoring perception
☐ ☐ ☐ ☐ ☐ Personal engagement
☐ ☐ ☐ ☐ ☐ Rationalizing, getting back to reality
☐ ☐ ☐ ☐ ☐ Finding information
☐ ☐ ☐ ☐ ☐ Recognizing projections
☐ ☐ ☐ ☐ ☐ Giving new importance to values
☐ ☐ ☐ ☐ ☐ Understanding somatic reactions
☐ ☐ ☐ ☐ ☐ Giving the right importance and not trivializing
☐ ☐ ☐ ☐ ☐ Confidence in one's own acting
☐ ☐ ☐ ☐ ☐ Integrating instead of suppressing
☐ ☐ ☐ ☐ ☐ Contemplation of the self-control
☐ ☐ ☐ ☐ ☐ To face instead of running away
☐ ☐ ☐ ☐ ☐ Flexible adaptation to a situation
☐ ☐ ☐ ☐ ☐ Controlling reactions of fear and depressiveness
☐ ☐ ☐ ☐ ☐ Focus instead of deflect
☐ ☐ ☐ ☐ ☐ Expressively accepting a situation
☐ ☐ ☐ ☐ ☐ Tackle instead of fatalism
☐ ☐ ☐ ☐ ☐ Being aware of the limits of one's own capacities
☐ ☐ ☐ ☐ ☐ Being flexible instead of abandoning aims and expectations
☐ ☐ ☐ ☐ ☐ To grab support and chances

☐ ☐ ☐ ☐ ☐ Remain with the matter, not to displace to compensation
☐ ☐ ☐ ☐ ☐ Aim-oriented self-suggestions (mental-training)
☐ ☐ ☐ ☐ ☐ Decomposing actions and planning instead of postponing
☐ ☐ ☐ ☐ ☐ Express feelings with measure
☐ ☐ ☐ ☐ ☐ Concretely formulate hope / optimism instead of giving up

Exercise II-E2-L10/7: Comment your marks:

Exercise II-E2-L10/8: Which "critical" elements apply to you: often / very often:

☐ My acting does not produce what I wanted to achieve.
☐ I hope my acting has better results in the future.
☐ My actions result in tense situations.
☐ I don't know for what reason I act in a certain way.
☐ I act without knowing exactly why I act like that.
☐ I wish to better understand my acting.
☐ I feel insecure in my acting.
☐ I always act in the same way as in the past.
☐ In different situations I would like to be able to act in other ways.
☐ I can't decide how I have to act.
☐ My way of acting continuously produces conflicts.
☐ I feel that my actions are sometimes without motivation.
☐ I don't really act consciously in the things I do.

Exercise II-E2-L10/9: Where do you see necessary changes for improvement?

Summary:

1. What is the most important thing you have learnt from this lesson?

2. What is your most outstanding strength in the subject of this lesson?

3. What is your outstanding weakness in the subject of this lesson?

4. What has touched you most in the subject of this lesson?

5. What is your most important future aim in the subject of this lesson?

6. What is your next step to improve in the subject of this lesson?

7. What are your open questions in the subject of this lesson?

3.3. Interpret your dreams

Considerations about dreams and dream interpretation

All theories about dreams accept that the dream messages are useful: they inform, give advice, warn, and help further when the thinking doesn't have access anymore. That means: an intelligent spiritual force creates the dreams and forms them to a meaningful structure.

Dream messages inform about:

- One's own psychical life
- The inner psychical life of other people
- The external world (politics, culture, state of the earth, institutions, etc.)
- One's own external life (actions, life culture, life themes, etc.)
- The external life of others
- The transcendence and the mystery of the being
- Death, the eternal life and the meaning of life

Dream interpretation is always based on knowledge about the psychical and real life. Generally, the more one knows about the psychical life and the life of mankind, the more differentiated the results of the dream interpretation will be. A life with dreams promotes the evolutionary human being.

> Therefore dreams are the "royal path" to the psychical-spiritual being. Therefore the Spirit as the transcendental force in the psyche is above every religion.

To be able to interpret dreams correctly is as helpful as thinking. Therefore:

→ Learn to interpret your dreams correctly!
→ Learn the language of your inner Spirit!
→ Live and grow with your dreams!

Dreams

Everybody dreams and the dreams have always been understood as important.

However, just like there are people who consider thinking to be unimportant; and who never reflect upon their thinking, there are also people who believe that their dreams are rubbish and they never think about this attitude.

Nevertheless, dreams are the most important source of life! It is well known in general that already in ancient "great dreams" were valued as messages from God. It is not simply an opinion of people, if many say that dreams contain a message. We call the psychical force which creates dreams, the "inner spirit".

Some dream theories may be one-sided, but all theories have one fact in common, that dream images and symbols – like figures or animals, facts or actions – inform us about the reality of the dreamer. We can draw conclusions from a dream about the dreamer and his life: "Tell me three dreams and I will tell you who you are!"

Dreams help us in all matters of life to achieve a good, happy and fulfilled life. Dreams indicate the path to the inner psychical life, to the true psychical-spiritual being. Dreams support the forming of all psychical forces. Dreams also give an orientation in the external reality. To write down one's dreams in a dream diary is an indispensable practice in the basic work of self-knowledge. However, it is not sensible to start with complex interpretations. In a first step it is enough to get a general view over several months.

• What are the main figures and the main themes in the dreams?
• What are the objects and actions?
• What relations to daily life and to the past can be identified?

The elements of dream scenes are like the beginning of a thread. If you pull this thread, then you'll be automatically led to yourself. Nevertheless, one has to keep an eye on the fact that one can interpret dreams only as well as one has knowledge about the variety of one's own life and the psychical forces. Dreams are an essential door to self-experience. The profound and complete personality education and the Individuation always require the consideration of dreams. In personality education the whole human being is focused upon, and therefore also his dream life.

The language of the dreams

You want to understand a person: What does he mean? Why does he speak like that? What makes him live the way he does? The more you know about the psychical life, the more you can recognize it.

The more a person knows about those realities, the more resources he has to understand a person. Dream interpretation is also based on the knowledge about the psychical and real life.

A person has various ways to communicate. One can speak very loud or distinctly low because others don't want to listen. Or one makes an allusion because it is impossible to speak directly about the matter due to the rejection mechanism of the other person. Some people speak in allegories, make a comparison or exaggerate extremely with the intention of producing attention. It is well known that this is a difficult matter: A person wants to know the truth but in fact he doesn't want to see it.

The force that creates the dreams uses the same manifold possibilities to create a message from this wealth in human life. The more a person works with his dreams, the more he can experience how the inner spirit is "speaking". Everyone can observe that this intelligent force obviously knows more than the "I" can know. The spirit can also "speak" about himself or about the spiritual world (the transcendence, God). The only true source that can give everybody an orientation about his psychical-spiritual being and development, is the inner spirit. This spiritual force in the psychical organism is the "architect" of the dreams.

The essence of a new dream theory

The eight essential theses about the spirit in the soul – developed by Dr. Edward Schellhammer – provide the foundation for a new dream theory:

1. The Spirit guides a person trough dreams and meditation.
2. The Spirit creates the dreams and meditations with intelligence.
3. The Spirit works within and around us like a cosmic energy.
4. The Spirit has its own language with images, symbols, archetypes and words.
5. The Spirit knows the inner process of growth much better than each theory.
6. The Spirit has its own system of norms and values.
7. The Spirit also has an extra-sensorial perception: clairvoyance and prescience.
8. The Spirit is an assimilating force; e.g. experiences, suffering, grief.
9. The Spirit is a transcendental force in the human's inner life; not simply a brain function.

10. That's why the Spirit stands above every religion and every political ideology!

Everybody can learn the language of the dreams just like they can learn a foreign language. Learning the language of dreams, results in access to the inner spirit and ability to comprehensively explore one's own psychical life. Dreams are the door to the psychical-spiritual human being and to the spiritual universe!

Practical dream interpretation in 12 steps

The dream creator invites: "If you want to communicate with me, then learn to understand my language!" One becomes competent for this dialogue by getting involved with one's dreams and at the same time with one's psychical life. For that purpose we give a short guide:

First: Put the single images in a context of experiences. The essential question is: What comes into my mind regarding that association? Then, focus on the general symbols; e.g.: What does a snake mean, a burning house, flying in the dream, to lose a tooth, miss the train, etc.? For that purpose it may be helpful to browse through some dream dictionaries, and to learn more about the diverse, often contrary, meaning of a thousand and more dream symbols. Exploring the wide range of meanings helps to find the right meaning of a dream image in the context of the dreamer and his life. But a dream dictionary is only an auxiliary means to determine the field of the manifold meanings of a symbol.

Second: Dreams speak in allegories, make allusions, exaggerate or understate, displace certain elements, "speak" loud or especially low; they make jokes and comparisons, produce a strong emotion along with the message, etc. One has to explore in each dream which kind of "speaking" is meant with the images and actions, since the way the dream is created (speaking with images) also forms the message.

Third: One has to explore the direction of the purpose in a dream: Does the dream want to inform? Is it an explanation or an opening to a new life issue one has to reflect upon? Does the dream develop a future perspective? Does the dream demand to explore some life experiences? Does it concern something critical or even dangerous? Does the dream deal with attitudes, inner conflicts or real behavior (actions)? Has it got to do with life experiences one has to work out or with preparations regarding the future?

The 12 steps of dream interpretation are:

1. Write down the dream and the feelings you had.
2. Break up the dream into its pieces (singular images) and sequences.
3. Especially consider the key images in the scenario.
4. Identify your own position in the dream (the "dream-ego").
5. Look for associations (experiences, thoughts, feelings).
6. What types of psychical forces are being addressed?
7. Which themes of life are being addressed?
8. Which other persons and facts are being addressed?
9. Are there any archetypes or inner archetypical processes which are topical?
10. Connect your result with a whole new meaning.
11. Compare with dreams and themes of dreams you had before.
12. Develop the dream experience with imagination (meditation).

After going through these steps don't forget to draw your personal conclusions. Finally, put the found knowledge into practice in daily life.

A certain self-critical prudence when interpreting dreams is always reasonable, given that one cannot interpret one's dreams better than the amount of knowledge about the psychical and real life one has. Beware: The spiritual "gold" in a dream in most cases doesn't shine!

The dream report

Practice your dream interpretation according to the following report:

1. The dream

Precisely write down the dream (the dream sequences) as well as your feelings in the dream and after the dream upon awakening. Describe your position in the dream (e.g. observing, acting).

2. The associations

Formulate your associations to every single image (as far as possible): memories, thoughts, feelings, facts, spontaneous judgments and interpretations, etc. Also jot down some personal information which may relate to the dream images (e.g. persons, places). Put the elements of the dream, the whole dream and your associations together to shape a new whole.

3. The concern

Where and what may it be about. How does the dream affect you? Connect this with your interpretation.

4. The whole interpretation

Interpret the key images and then put the pieces of the interpretation together to form a new whole.

5. The conclusions

What psychological, (life-) practical, ethical and philosophical conclusions may result from the interpretation?

3.3.1. Interpret dreams with the right attitudes

> Thesis II-E3-3-T1: The interest and attitudes towards dreams influence the ability to recall dreams.
>
> Thesis II-E3-3-T2: One often has dreams which include some concrete elements from the day before or from the days before. But this doesn't mean that day-residues are "rubbish" from the brain. Dreams always contain a message.
>
> Thesis I-E3-3-T3: One has to learn the dream language like a foreign language. Without learning the dream language, one would not gain a broad access to the psychical-spiritual life.

→ For this unit you need some of your dreams. Keep a dream diary and write down your dreams for the next 10 days.

● In this lesson you get a first orientation in the subject of dreams; and not about dream interpretation!

Exercise II-E3-L1/1: How many dreams can you remember a day / a week?

Exercise II-E3-L1/2: How do you experience the effects of your dreams as much as you can remember them or know at least that you have dreamt?

● Attitudes towards dreams influence the ability to remember them.

Exercise II-E3-L1/3: Describe your previous attitudes towards dreams, dream theories and dream interpretation:

● Knowledge about dream interpretation influences the ability to remember dreams.

Exercise II-E3-L1/4: Using 3 sentences formulate what you know about dream interpretation:

● External stimuli are seldom a cause for dreaming in the sense "this was only because …"

Exercise II-E3-L1/5: Can you remember a dream having elements of an external stimulus (e.g. a noise, a cold airflow, a leg not covered, an uncomfortable sleeping position, an urge to urinate, the numb arm, etc.)? Describe:

● "Remains" of the day in a dream can refer to a range of possibilities. This does not mean that the element from that day ("a remain") is related to what happened the day before.

Exercise II-E3-L1/6: Can you remember a dream with "remains" from the previous day? Describe:

Exercise II-E3-L1/7: Give 2 examples about a very short dream you had (e.g. one image, one word):
Exercise II-E3-L1/8: Give an example of a short dream you had (a short scenery):

Exercise II-E3-L1/9: What is the difference between a short dream and a long dream?

● You have to learn the language of the dream like a foreign language. If you don't learn it, you will never have an extensive access to the psychical and spiritual life.

Exercise II-E3-L1/10: Describe with a short example your experience in the following:

1. I have read books about dreams and dream interpretation.
2. I have participated in a course / seminar about dreams and dream interpretation.
3. I have learnt how to interpret dreams.
4. I talk with others about my dreams.
5. I sometimes want to dream about a matter / concern, for example:
6. I keep a dream diary; and this in the following way:

7. I consider my feelings in dreams and also the subsequent emotional state during the day.
8. I wake up without an alarm clock so that I remember my dreams better.
9. When I wake up at night because of a dream, then I write the dream down immediately.
10. I take small fragments from dreams I remember into consideration. Sometimes they follow me the whole day.
11. I have a balanced life rhythm and I feel it helps with remembering
12. I meditate about my dreams.
13. When I have drunk too much alcohol, then my ability to remember dreams is reduced.
14. I sometimes take medicine to relax and sleep better; but then I remember my dreams much less.
15. In general I conclude from 1) to 14):

Summary:

1. What is the most important thing you have learnt from this lesson?

2. What is your most outstanding strength in the subject of this lesson?

3. What is your outstanding weakness in the subject of this lesson?

4. What has touched you most in the subject of this lesson?

5. What is your most important future aim in the subject of this lesson?

6. What is your next step to improve in the subject of this lesson?

7. What are your open questions in the subject of this lesson?

3.3.2. Learn the language of the Spirit

Lesson II-E3-2

Thesis II-E3-2-T1: The spirit guides a person through daily life as well as to his psychical-spiritual being, to his happiness and to his self-fulfillment.

Thesis II-E3-2-T2: Dreams have the function to guide a person, to give an orientation in all the fundamental questions (issues) of existence, such as death, God, the transcendental life, the meaning of life, destiny and fate, etc.

Thesis II-E3-2-T3: If a person wants to benefit from his dreams, he has to contribute: with engagement, will, seriousness, thoroughness and readiness to learn, etc.

● Dreams help in all matters / concerns of life to a good, happy, and meaningfull living. Dreams indicate the path to the genuine innermost psychical-spiritual being. Dreams also give an orientation about death, essential questions about human existence on earth, the trenscendence, God, meaning of life, spiritual values, etc. Dreams are the door to the psychical and spiritual universe!

Exercise II-E3-L2/1: Describe how you have experienced the spiritual power of the dreams:

1. The Spirit guides a person through the dreams.
2. The Spirit is the force that "intelligently"constructs dreams.
3. The Spirit acts with its psycho-energetic power.
4. The language of the Spirit is: Images, symbols, archetypes, and language.
5. The spirit knows the program of the inner growing process better than any theory.
6. The Spirit has his proper system of norms and values.
7. The Spirit also contains parapsychical abilities (extra-sensorial perception).
8. The Spirit has a powerful ability to elaborate, e.g. life experiences, suffering.

• Dream theories evidently presume that the meassages are useful: they inform, counsel, warn, and help where thinking doesn't have any access.

Exercise II-E3-L2/2: What do you concretely expect from this spiritual power for your life?

Exercise II-E3-L2/3: I guess that a dream wants to tell me something, because:

Exercise II-E3-L2/4: I feel that I should interpret my dreams, because:

Exercise II-E3-L2/5: My dreams have helped me a lot, for example:

• The Spirit gives a complete orientation about the psychicl-spiritual being and growing, and about life in general.

Exercise II-E3-L2/6: Give some keywords where you feel addressed:

1. A dream clarifies and organizes all important inventory of my life.

2. A dream promotes solutions for diffficult situations.

3. A dream promotes my psychical-spiritual education and development.

4. A dream opens the access to the sources of the mystery of human being, to Spirit and God.

5. A dream helps for ordering and cleaning (elaboration) life and mind.

6. A dream supports and helps to understand one's own being and life.

7. A dream informs about other people and external realities.

8. A dream shows danger, warns, and advises to be cautious and vigilant.

9. A dream gives creative tips for matters of life.

10. A dream has healing effects.

● If you do nothing with your dreams, you can't live from the bottom of your innermost source of life.

Exercise II-E3-L2/7: Describe your previous activities with dreams:

1. I experience obligation and seriousness to critically deal with my dreams.
2. I react to dreams with diligence and responsibility.
3. I can interpret my dreams with meditation.
4. I know that I schould profoundly elaborate certain dream messages.
5. I acquiere knowledge to better understand dreams as well as myself.

6. I take time for my dreams and I give the necessary priority elaborating them.
7. I am confident that my dreams guide me well.
8. I experience dreams as an engagement for inner dialogue.
9. I give high importance to dreams, because:
10. I know that dreams expect an entire self-education from me.
11. I am patient with elaborating dreams.
12. I don't immediately expect a concrete result from my dream interpretation.
13. I understand dream interpretation as an intellectual work with intuition and introversion.
14. I use dream dictionaries, because:
15. I feel the occupation with my dreams is a long term process.

Summary:

1. What is the most important thing you have learnt from this lesson?

2. What is your most outstanding strength in the subject of this lesson?

3. What is your outstanding weakness in the subject of this lesson?

4. What has touched you most in the subject of this lesson?

5. What is your most important future aim in the subject of this lesson?

6. What is your next step to improve in the subject of this lesson?

7. What are your open questions in the subject of this lesson?

3.3.3. Understand images, symbols, and archetypes

> Thesis II-E3-3-T1: Dreams include various different realities and areas of life. Thus, it becomes clear that a person lives, acts and reacts meaning-oriented with regard to reality and spirituality.
>
> Thesis II-E3-3-T2: Each dream symbol refers on the one hand to meaning, that means: psychical forces, personality, actions, behavior, life issues; and on the other hand to an imminent quality: value, state, importance, etc.
>
> Thesis II-E3-3-T3: The characteristics of a creation with images and scenes may indicate that something is bizarre, confusing, risky, mysterious (holy, archetypical value), etc.

Exercise II-E3-L3/1: Dreams contain totally different segments of images. Give 2-3 examples to the segments of images (keywords).

1. People: Body, expressions; facial expression, gesture, ways of moving around.
2. World of nature: The earth with its natural forces, the entire world of plants.
3. World of animals: Everything that a person knows today.
4. World of objects: All kind of "things" we can principally find on this earth.
5. Actions: A behavior, an activity, also communication and singular words.
6. Incidents/events: Something happens with people, objects, people, animals, nature, etc.
7. Theatres: Places where something happened, happens or will happen.
8. Ancestral images: Something numinous (mysterious, spiritual); present as good of a culture.
9. Themes: Sex, violence, aberration, danger, discovery, relationships, work, etc.

● Dream images are copies if they represent something that exists in reality.
Exercise II-E3-L3/2: Give 5 examples from your dreams:

● A symbol refers to something in the psychical life, in behavior (action), in events (incidents), and in the reality in general. Therefore a symbol has an immanent meaning.

● First we have to find the correct correlation of the meaning: psychical force, personality, activity, incident/event, fact, etc.

● Then we determine the quality: meaning, value, moral, truthfulness, benefit, purpose, importance, brisance (explosiveness), actuality, the "critical" aspect, etc.

Exercise II-E3-L3/3: Elaborate the meaning correlation and the quality:

Symbol	Meaning correlation	Quality determination
1) Tree, half side without growth (dead)		
2) Dog, skinny, barking		
3) Teeth falling out		
4) Car, inability to drive		
5) An unknown aggressive person		
6) Burglar in the bedroom		
7) Missed train		
8) Flying without falling		
9) Standing in a dangerous versant		

● Bizarre, analogical, confusing, displaced, intricate, meaningless images say that something is just like that. Examples: low ceiling, aslant floor, magic marsh, a too big finger, disturbances of rooms, etc.

Exercise II-E3-L3/4: Give 5 examples from your dreams and try to find the meaning and quality:

Bizarre image	Meaning correlation	Quality determination
1)		
2)		

3)		
4)		
5)		

● "Critical" aspects in images, sceneries and actions say that something is critical; e.g. conflictive, unregulated, messy, tense, dangerous, not functioning, defective, blocked, inhibited, dissonant, unrealistic, unhealthy, etc.

Exercise II-E3-L3/5: Give 5 examples to that and try to find the meaning and quality:

Critical element in an image	Meaning correlation	Quality determination
1)		
2)		
3)		
4)		
5)		

● Archetypes are fundamental prototypes (paradigms) about psychical forces, the entire person and the psychological-spiritual process of changes and growth. Archetypes are dynamic, creative, energetic, growth-oriented, demanding (calling).

Exercise II-E3-L3/6: Find the meaning and quality to the following examples:

Pattern: A rotten apple in the dream.

Meaning correlation: An apple stands for lust, pleasure, something fine and healthy. The quality judgment "rotten": Something is rotten and in that sense absolutely not fine and healthy!

Archetype	Meaning correlation	Quality determination
1) Birth; a baby is here now		
2) Being at a source		
3) An owl is calling:		

"Come! Follow me!"		
4) Getting / Seeing a mandala		
5) Being on a journey		

Important: Most images in dreams are not fully and clearly determined and like a copy of a reality. Mostly they are linked with actions, incidents, events, circumstances, arenas, etc.; and these contexts themselves create a specific relationship.

Exercise II-E3-L3/7: How do you feel about the distinction of meaning-correlation and quality-determination?

Summary:

1. What is the most important thing you have learnt from this lesson?

2. What is your most outstanding strength in the subject of this lesson?

3. What is your outstanding weakness in the subject of this lesson?

4. What has touched you most in the subject of this lesson?

5. What is your most important future aim in the subject of this lesson?

6. What is your next step to improve in the subject of this lesson?

7. What are your open questions in the subject of this lesson?

3.3.4. Interpret with varied references

Thesis II-E3-4-T1: To relate a dream image to real life (psyche, situations), the dreamer has to react with associations (spontaneous ideas).

Thesis II-E3-4-T2: There is knowledge from the very old times in fairy tales, myths and "holy books". There are dream-images and dream scenes (actions), which relate to that knowledge.

Thesis II-E3-4-T3: Unknown figures in most cases represent one's own unconscious and unknown personality aspects (repressed traits of character). These are mostly aspects which are not well-formed; sometimes also positive traits (skills, talents) the dreamer is ignoring and repressing.

● The real associations. They relate to something real that has been experienced. The meaning is something real.

Exercise II-E3-L4/1: Take some dreams. Chose 2 images. Then formulate your spontaneous real association.

Dream image	Real association

● The interpreting associations. They relate to a spontaneous unconscious meaning. Such expressions are: thoughts, judgments, conclusions, evaluation of a sensation, an intellectual comment, a joke, etc.

Exercise II-E3-L4/2: Take some dreams. Choose 2 images. Then formulate your spontaneous interpreting association.

Dream image	Interpreting association

● The sublime (spiritual) associations. That means: religious themes, spiritual ideas, and fundamental questions of life (existence), moral and esthetic judgments.

Exercise II-E3-L4/3: Take some dreams. Choose 2 images. Then formulate your spontaneous sublime association.

Dream image	Real association

● The catharsis associations. They express an "Aha-expression" ("I see"), a clarifying emotional reaction, an inner liberating experience.

Exercise II-E3-L4/4: Take some dreams. Choose 2 images. Then formulate your spontaneous catharsis association.

Dream image	Catharsis association

● The amplifications. They extend and deepen the understanding relating to something from fairies, myths, legends, religious narratives, classic scenes from novels, ideals, etc.

Exercise II-E3-L4/5: Try to amplify the following dream images with a corresponding context.

Dream images	Amplification
1) A wise person gives me a Circle-Cross-Mandala. This is my "compass". I shall go my path now.	
2) I am coming to a temple. It's said that inside they do "cleanings". I don't know if I want to enter.	

3) I am in a house. There is a closed room. A housekeeper says that I should never enter into this room.	

● Interpreting on a subjective level means that an unknown person in a dream expresses one's own personality aspects.

Exercise II-E3-L4/6: Take some dreams. Choose 2 images of an unknown person. Then formulate your spontaneous subjective association about the person.

The unknown person in the dream	Interpretation

● Interpreting on an objective level means that a known person in a dream expresses this person. The dream tells us something about this person or about the relationship to this person.

Exercise II-E3-L4/7: Take some dreams. Choose 2 images of a known person. Then formulate your spontaneous objective association about the person or relationship to this person.

The known person in the dream	Interpretation

● "Anima" means the female pole in the psyche of the man and "Animus" means the male pole in the psyche of the woman. Anima and Animus are the opposite gender pole in the psychical organism. The development of a woman conditions the maturation of the Animus; the development of a man conditions the maturation of the Anima. Anima and Animus are formed with complex inner images through life experiences.

Exercise II-E3-L4/8:
To women: Describe an unknown male dream figure in a dream (2 examples).
To men: Describe an unknown female figure in a dream (2 examples).

Interpret the quality of the meaning (2 examples):

The unknown figure in the dream	Interpretation

Summary:

1. What is the most important thing you have learnt from this lesson?

2. What is your most outstanding strength in the subject of this lesson?

3. What is your outstanding weakness in the subject of this lesson?

4. What has touched you most in the subject of this lesson?

5. What is your most important future aim in the subject of this lesson?

6. What is your next step to improve in the subject of this lesson?

7. What are your open questions in the subject of this lesson?

3.3.5. Recognize your position in the dream

Thesis II-E3-5-T1: If the dreamer is in an observer position in his dream, the meaning focus is on the fact that one has to learn something about what one sees. It is often about a collective matter, or sometimes it shows a future perspective (destiny).

Thesis II-E3-5-T2: The feelings one has in a dream form the dream message.

Thesis II-E3-5-T3: The active action of the dreamer often reflects a lack of skills, or a demand to act in real life, or shows: "See: you can do it!"

● The meaning of the individual elements composes together form the dream message.

Exercise II-E3-L5/1: Take a dream with elements of images in the same scenery, but from their appearance do not fit together. Find the network of the meaning.

An example: I am in my room from my childhood. My father (who passed away long ago) is here. A professionally successful colleague of mine, talks with my girlfriend in the living room. The furniture is the one I actually have in my apartment.

Orientation for the interpretation: The past still lives in the present through the father and the life culture from that time. Context: Relationship and success.

a) Give an example:

b) Interpret the meaning-network:

● The dynamic of the energy (intensity of the experience) holds an aspect of the message.

Exercise II-E3-L5/2: Describe a dream you experienced very intensively. Interpret your experience.

a) Give an example:

b) Interpret your emotional experiencing:

• Dream-"I": The dreaming person is not in the dream. What has this got to do with me?

Exercise II-E3-L5/3: Give an example with a short interpretation.

a) Example:

b) Interpretation:

• Dream-"I": The dreaming person (as the dream-"I") is only observer in the dream. Learn from what you see!

Exercise II-E3-L5/4: Give an example with a short interpretation.

a) Example:

b) Interpretation:

• Dream-"I": The state and expression (power) of the dream-"I" is the message.

Exercise II-E3-L5/5: Give an example with a short interpretation.

a) Example:

b) Interpretation:

• Dream-"I": The action (ability to act, ability to master, resistance, integration) of the dreaming person (the dream-"I") is the essential message.

Exercise II-E3-L5/6: Give an example with a short interpretation.

a) Example:

b) Interpretation:

• PSI-Phenomenon: The dream informs about something the dreaming person can't know. (PSI: Parapsychology, extra-sensorial perception)

Exercise II-E3-L5/7: Give an example with a short interpretation.

a) Example:

b) Interpretation:

Exercise II-E3-L5/8: How do you feel about the variety of the logic of the meaning-relations?

Exercise II-E3-L5/9: Dream interpretation also gets an orientation with the characteristics of the components: network of the meaning, energy, dream-"I", actions, and PSI-facts. What do you feel and think about this?

Summary:

1. What is the most important thing you have learnt from this lesson?

2. What is your most outstanding strength in the subject of this lesson?

3. What is your outstanding weakness in the subject of this lesson?

4. What has touched you most in the subject of this lesson?

5. What is your most important future aim in the subject of this lesson?

6. What is your next step to improve in the subject of this lesson?

7. What are your open questions in the subject of this lesson?

3.3.6. Evaluate the ways of image creations

> Thesis II-E3-6-T1: Dream images and dream scenes include a message through the emotions they produce.
>
> Thesis II-E3-6-T2: Dream images and dream scenes include a message through strange and bizarre presentations (displacements, mixtures).
>
> Thesis II-E3-6-T3: Dream images and dream scenes include a message through positive and negative, mythical or religious facts.

● Micro-structure = Ways of creating: The micro-structure of a dream consists of the manifoldness of the singular images and scenarios. These ways of creating already contain a meaning or at least an indicator where and how a meaning is to be found from their characteristics. The dream language (presentation of images and symbols) is as manifold as the use of language in life, in literature, in art, and in painting.

Exercise II-E3-L6/1: How do you talk in delicate situations? For example:

1) If the other part does not want to listen:

2) If the other part has resistance:

3) To get attention:

4) When you judge:

5) To indirectly warn:

6) If the other part doesn't want to listen to the truth:

● A person forms and expresses a message in different ways depending on the conditions given by the receiver. The dream creating instance uses the same variety in constructing a dream message.

● The ways of creating: Dream images and dream scenarios are created in a way that this way of creating already contains intention, information, message, and tendency.

Copy: Objectively it's like that! It's really about this.
Exercise L6/2: Give an example from a dream.

Hint: Look at it precisely!
Exercise II-E3-L6/3: Give an example from a dream.

Disfiguration: There is something completely disfigured and has to be put / seen the right way.
Exercise II-E3-L6/4: Give an example from a dream.

Intensive experience: Important. Meaningful.
Exercise II-E3-L6/5: Give an example from a dream.

Causal: Mixture of times with "critical" (moral, conflictive) elements.
Exercise II-E3-L6/6: Give an example from a dream.

Compensating: Correct, change, balance, and give the right dimension (weight, height).
Exercise II-E3-L6/7: Give an example from a dream.

Contrast: Shows what surely is not like that, but completely different.
Exercise II-E3-L6/8: Give an example from a dream.

Ways of talking: Images are translations of ways of talking.
Exercise II-E3-L6/9: Give an example from a dream.

Reduction: Important. Essential. Characteristics.
Exercise II-E3-L6/10: Give an example from a dream.

Secondary elaboration: Creating scenes and morals.
Exercise II-E3-L6/11: Give an example from a dream.

Reversion: Focus on the opposite!
Exercise II-E3-L6/12: Give an example from a dream.

Compacting (condensing): It's compact / dense! Recognize the concentrate!
Exercise II-E3-L6/13: Give an example from a dream.

Comparison: Search for your position!
Exercise II-E3-L6/14: Give an example from a dream.

Mixture: It's mixed. Divide into pieces!

Exercise II-E3-L6/15: Give an example from a dream.

Displacement: Something is displaced. Put it the right way.
Exercise II-E3-L6/16: Give an example from a dream.

Judgment, evaluation: That's how it is psychologically, spiritually, morally.
Exercise II-E3-L6/17: Give an example from a dream.

Games with words and figures: A game. Think a bit about it!
Exercise II-E3-L6/18: Give an example from a dream.

Lucid dream creations: Special way to make realize something. "Thank goodness!"
Exercise II-E3-L6/19: Give an example from a dream.

Exercise II-E3-L6/20: The exercises L6/1 to L6/19 show enough reasons why one should use dream dictionaries very carefully. The superficial way many people interpret their dreams (and dreams from others) is obvious! Such thoughtless piece of work can produce heavy damages! Express yourself to that:

Summary:

1. What is the most important thing you have learnt from this lesson?

2. What is your most outstanding strength in the subject of this lesson?

3. What is your outstanding weakness in the subject of this lesson?

4. What has touched you most in the subject of this lesson?

5. What is your most important future aim in the subject of this lesson?

6. What is your next step to improve in the subject of this lesson?

7. What are your open questions in the subject of this lesson?

3.3.7. Identify the focus of the dream message

Thesis II-E3-7-T1: Dreams inform and explain aspects of all realities of mankind; that means: they not only inform about the psychical life.

Thesis II-E3-7-T2: Dreams seize and promote the whole life from the dreamer with all his individual life-areas.

Thesis II-E3-7-T3: Dreams promote the evolutionary psychical-spiritual human being, confronting the dreamer with its characteristic realities.

● The dream is the indispensable, through nothing replaceable 'via regia' (royal path) to the entire psychical-spiritual human being up to the highest possible psychical-spiritual level of development.

● This means: A dream message can contain everything that concerns the psychical-spiritual and natural human being; and everything that surrounds a person in the world. All psychical forces and all natural needs and desires, however they are formed by an individual (efficient or not), can be content of a dream message.

● Everything that surrounds a person real, near and far away, can become a theme in a dream. Dreams can present a complete life reality to a person with the purpose to elaborate it. Dreams can focus on everything concerning our being and life!

Exercise II-E3-L7/1: Take some dreams. Collect from them the themes of the messages as far as you can recognize or guess them. Make a list of the themes with the appropriate keywords:

1)	6)
2)	7)
3)	8)
4)	9)
5)	10)

● We classify the themes with the following 6 groups. Note examples (keywords):

1) The own psychical organism:

2) The psychical world of other people:

3) The own external life:

4) The external life of others:

5) The transcendence and God:

6) The external general world:

● Dream messages contain: The past, present, future, and eternity.
Exercise II-E3-L7/2: Give a dream image or a short dream scene to that.

● Dream messages contain everything about: Psyche, personality, and character.
Exercise II-E3-L7/3: Give a dream image or a short dream scene to that.

● Dream messages contain everything about: Body, nature of drive, instinct, and sexuality.
Exercise II-E3-L7/4: Give a dream image or a short dream scene to that.

● Dream messages contain themes such as: Behavior, life style, and relationship.
Exercise II-E3-L7/5: Give a dream image or a short dream scene to that.

● Dream messages contain the fundamental themes of life from the procreation until death.
Exercise II-E3-L7/6: Give a dream image or a short dream scene to that.

● Dream messages contain themes such as: Changes, development, expansion and growth or stagnation and regression.
Exercise II-E3-L7/7: Give a dream image or a short dream scene to that.

● Dream messages contain themes such as: Potentials, abilities, talents, life aims, and potentials of living, destiny and designation.
Exercise II-E3-L7/8: Give a dream image or a short dream scene to that.

● Dream messages contain themes such as: Positive, critical and dangerous situations, arenas and events in life.
Exercise II-E3-L7/9: Give a dream image or a short dream scene to that.

● Dream messages contain themes like: Money, goods, values, resources, nutrition, and materials of all kind for life realization.
Exercise II-E3-L7/10: Give a dream image or a short dream scene to that.

● Dream messages contain themes such as: The world, the world population, and the society (community) with all the possible part-systems and institutions.
Exercise II-E3-L7/11: Give a dream image or a short dream scene to that.

● Dream messages contain themes such as: Schools, education on all levels and kinds, and also job, work, and working place.
Exercise II-E3-L7/12: Give a dream image or a short dream scene to that.

● Dream messages contain themes such as: All possible positive and negative ways of experiencing all kind of thinkable life situations.
Exercise II-E3-L7/13: Give a dream image or a short dream scene to that.

● Dream messages contain themes such as: Spirituality and religion in teaching and practice, esoteric and transcendence, moral and ethic.
Exercise II-E3-L7/14: Give a dream image or a short dream scene to that.

Exercise II-E3-L7/15: For you, what are till today the most important dream messages you were able to understand / to get?

Summary:

1. What is the most important thing you have learnt from this lesson?

2. What is your most outstanding strength in the subject of this lesson?

3. What is your outstanding weakness in the subject of this lesson?

4. What has touched you most in the subject of this lesson?

5. What is your most important future aim in the subject of this lesson?

6. What is your next step to improve in the subject of this lesson?

7. What are your open questions in the subject of this lesson?

3.3.8. Interpreting dreams by proceeding step by step

Thesis II-E3-8-T1: The interpretation of dream images and symbols is only the first step to get to the dream message.

Thesis II-E3-8-T2: By exploring the result of the interpretation of images and symbols with systematic questions, the message is connected with the life areas and with the dreamer's patterns of life.

Thesis II-E3-8-T3: By broadening the process of interpretation with the model of the psychical organism and the process of personality development, one gets a better orientation for self-education and Individuation.

Step one: The actual dream interpretation.

- The dream document with experiences, structures and creations.
- The key images and symbols (actions, incidents, places, etc.).
- The dream-ego: Position and expressions.
- Associations: real, interpretative and spiritual spontaneous reactions.
- Personal appealing based on associations and questions.
- Complete interpretation: putting the parts of interpretation together.
- Conclusions: each interpretation comes to some personal conclusions.

Exercise II-E3-L8/1: I have elaborated this first working proceeding the following way:

Step two: Ask questions systematically, creatively and with an aim orientation. Then finish off with systematic questions about: persons, actions, events, world of nature and animals, objects, places, mysterious elements, facts.
Exercise II-E3-L8/2: I have elaborated this second working proceeding the following way:

Step three: Psychological, practical exploration of a dream.
Go over a dream from a psychological point of view: The actions. The psycho-dynamics. The "I" and its associate functions (will, control and defense mechanism). The intelligence performance. The emotions. The needs. The unconscious. Spirituality. Love. The process of Individuation.

Exercise II-E3-L8/3: I have elaborated this third working proceeding the following way:

Exercise II-E3-L8/4: I have taken consequences from my dreams in the past:

☐ Taking a decision.

☐ Controlling activities with more concentration.

☐ Learning for new ways of acting.

☐ Elaborating the biography.

☐ Acquiring knowledge.

☐ Revising the way of living.

☐ Regulating matters.

☐ Changing fundamental attitudes and beliefs.

☐ More vigilance and clear-sightedness.

Elaborating dreams with a dream protocol

Exercise II-E3-L8/5: Take a short dream you had recently. Elaborate this dream with the following protocol.

Dream protocol. Essential theme:
.... **Date:** ....

---

1. Dream: Exact description without any interpretation.

2. Dream experience: The emotional experience during and after the dream, even the day after.

3. Key-images: Singular images and scenarios presented as a unit.

4. Dream-"I": Position, emotional/physical state, expression, ability to act.

5. Associations: Personal experiences, spontaneous thoughts, spiritual context.

6. Feeling to be intrigued: Identifying the concrete anchor giving this feeling.

7. Entire interpretation: Putting together the meanings and qualities to a message.

8. Consequences: Self-knowledge, Individuation, decisions, activities, future orientation.

Summary:

1. What is the most important thing you have learnt from this lesson?

2. What is your most outstanding strength in the subject of this lesson?

3. What is your outstanding weakness in the subject of this lesson?

4. What has touched you most in the subject of this lesson?

5. What is your most important future aim in the subject of this lesson?

6. What is your next step to improve in the subject of this lesson?

7. What are your open questions in the subject of this lesson?

3.3.9. Systematically ask questions

Thesis II-E3-9-T1: Asking questions about the indicated life reality supports knowledge about practical life issues.

Thesis II-E3-9-T2: By asking questions related to an event, scene or place in a dream, one broadens the point of view about the complexity of the reality.

Thesis II-E3-9-T3: The meaning of the world of nature and animals in dreams is so varied that asking various questions may help to identify the network of meaning with the dreamer.

● Questions form the viewing angle. This helps to precisely identify the images and events in the dream, and the dream as a whole.

● Questions allow a precise relation of the dream theme with the dreaming person and his life.

● Elaboration with aim-oriented questions corrects and broadens the interpretation, first of all directed to life practice.

● Persons in the dream

Exercise II-E3-L9/1: Give a dream example. Then ask questions.

● Actions in the dream
Exercise II-E3-L9/2: Give a dream example. Then ask questions.

● Events in the dream

Exercise II-E3-L9/3: Give a dream example. Then ask questions.
● World of nature in the dream
Exercise II-E3-L9/4: Give a dream example. Then ask questions.

● World of animals in the dream
Exercise II-E3-L9/5: Give a dream example. Then ask questions.

● Objects in the dream

Exercise II-E3-L9/6: Give a dream example. Then ask questions.

● Theatre/arena in the dream
Exercise II-E3-L9/7: Give a dream example. Then ask questions.

● Mystic elements in the dream
Exercise II-E3-L9/8: Give a dream example. Then ask questions.

● Singular themes in the dream
Exercise II-E3-L9/9: Give an example from 3 dreams. Then ask questions.

Summary:

1. What is the most important thing you have learnt from this lesson?

2. What is your most outstanding strength in the subject of this lesson?

3. What is your outstanding weakness in the subject of this lesson?

4. What has touched you most in the subject of this lesson?

5. What is your most important future aim in the subject of this lesson?

6. What is your next step to improve in the subject of this lesson?

7. What are your open questions in the subject of this lesson?

3.3.10 Interpret psychologically and practically

Thesis II-E3-10-T1: The psychological exploration of a dream can broaden the field of meaning in such a way that it creates the need for changes (self-education).

Thesis II-E3-10-T2: The more precise one can relate the dream message with psychical forces and patterns of behavior, the more concrete one can determine practical conclusions.

Thesis II-E3-10-T3: If one can exactly identify the unconscious issues of the dream message, it is easier to determine what one has to explore in one's subconscious.

● **Proceeding:**

Through the psychological and life-oriented practical elaboration of dreams the meaning of a symbol is related to the psychical life, the actions and the real life.

● **Actions**

Exercise II-E3-L10/1: Describe an action. Comment with psychological interpretation and evaluation.

● **The psycho-dynamic (vitality, power, feeling, basic mood, etc.)**

Exercise II-E3-L10/2: Describe an experience about the dynamic. Comment with psychological interpretation and evaluation.

● **The "I" and its supporting functions (will, control, defense, integration)**

Exercise II-E3-L10/3: Describe what you recognize about this. Comment with psychological interpretation and evaluation.

● **The intelligent performances: Thinking, learning, language, perception**

Exercise II-E3-L10/4: Describe an appropriate scene. Comment with psychological interpretation and evaluation.

● The feelings

Exercise II-E3-L10/5: Describe the feelings in the dream. Comment with psychological interpretation and evaluation.

● The needs

Exercise II-E3-L10/6: Describe the needs you identify in the dream. Comment with psychological interpretation and evaluation.

● The unconscious

Exercise II-E3-L10/7: Describe dream images that represent inventory of the unconscious mind. Comment with psychological interpretation and evaluation.

● The spirituality

Exercise II-E3-L10/8: Describe a dream image that shows religious (spiritual) aspects. Comment with psychological interpretation and evaluation.

● Love

Exercise II-E3-L10/9: Describe a dream image about love. Comment with psychological interpretation and evaluation.

● The process of Individuation

Exercise II-E3-L10/10: Describe a dream scene showing a theme in the process of Individuation (development, growth). Comment with psychological interpretation and evaluation.

Exercise II-E3-L10/11: How do you evaluate (judge, value) your knowledge and your skills to elaborate a dream psychologically and practically (life oriented)?

Exercise II-E3-L10/12: What are your conclusions from L10/11?

Summary:

1. What is the most important thing you have learnt from this lesson?

2. What is your most outstanding strength in the subject of this lesson?

3. What is your outstanding weakness in the subject of this lesson?

4. What has touched you most in the subject of this lesson?

5. What is your most important future aim in the subject of this lesson?

6. What is your next step to improve in the subject of this lesson?

7. What are your open questions in the subject of this lesson?

3.4. Meditate correctly

Considerations about meditating correctly

If we know where we want to get with meditation and if we proceed methodically, then meditation is extremely enriching.

Meditations serve very different purposes

- Imagination about the psychical life and for solving problems.
- Mental Training for relaxation and to strengthen concentration
- Contemplation to experience the meaning of symbols and archetypes.
- Clairvoyance to understand people and psychical realities.
- Regressions until the prenatal time to explore the biography.
- Imagination about dreams to revive and explore a dream.
- Healing meditation for oneself and for others.
- Precognition about one's own life and about society.

Meditation is an aim-oriented visualization, a practice of self-reflection, a state of contemplation. Meditation means a thoughtful reflection and experience about the inner being. Meditation opens the inner source of life. Meditation is also a conscious inner dialogue with the inner spirit. Meditation strengthens a person in his inner being. Meditation gives life to creative forces, promotes intuition and creates an inner experience about meaning and value. Meditation is indispensable for discovering the "other reality". Meditation is the door to true spirituality. Thus, meditation is helpful for one's self-education, for understanding the psychical-spiritual human being, for the development of one's personality, for success in life and also in the job.

What is meditation? What is the purpose of meditation?

Meditation is visualization. We presume that in the visualization the same intelligent force acts as in dreams. Thus we can use this spiritual force as an aim-oriented tool. If we know what we want to achieve with a meditation and if we proceed correctly, then meditation is extremely enriching. The complete and well-balanced education of the psychical life demands meditation. Without meditation and dream interpretation the subconscious can never be explored completely. Meditation is indispensable for the Individuation process. Meditation is an inner visualization and an aim-oriented work with inner images.

The five basic questions of meditation are

1. What do we want to achieve? Determination of aims. Reasoning.
2. With which images (symbols) do we want to work with? Determine instruments.
3. How do we actively create the visualization? Operations. Procedure.
4. How do we proceed with the interpretation? Interpretation.
5. How do we apply the result in daily life? Conclusions for life.

There are several preconditions required in order to meditate successfully:

☐ Readiness to learn   ☐ Realistic expectations
☐ Willingness   ☐ Ability to concentrate
☐ Seriousness   ☐ Sincerity / Honesty
☐ True interest   ☐ Power of imagination
☐ Self-confidence   ☐ A positive attitude
☐ No religious position   ☐ Free from fundamentalism

Imagination

During visualization the same intelligent force as in dreams is active. With imagination one can relax, find new strength, prepare solutions for problems, free the mind from thoughts, understand other people, find the meaning of life, explore dreams, discover reasons for suffering and difficulties, explore the subconscious and much more.

Imaginations are for example:

- "I want to see the state of my needs. I imagine: my needs are represented as animals on a farm."
- Which masks does one put on, and what is concealed behind the mask? In an imagination one can look into a mirror, and question the masks and the faces which appear. These can be visualized as animals, figures of fairy-tales or real faces.
- One can go in a store room and explore one's biography there (stored in boxes and on shelves), and then create order with visualization.
- Or, one can go down to the cellar and find one's repressed life forces there: the child, unused forces, dusty laws, hidden plans for life, etc.

> **Imagination is the way of meditation with the purpose to explore, to understand and to renew (form) the complete psychical and real life.**

Mental-Training

This is a way of meditation to relax the mind and body. Purposes are:

- Clearing the mind (brain)
- Finding peacefulness
- Letting go of thoughts
- Building up energy
- Focusing energy towards an aim
- Finding concentration
- Establishing balance of nearness and distance
- Releasing external bonds
- Exploring the past day
- Preparing the coming day

Contemplation

In the contemplation we work with general symbols and archetypes. Archetypes are related to general patterns of psychical forces, to processes of psychical transformation, to fundamental life themes, to meaning and essential values, and to the transcendental reality. Archetypes are e.g.: the pyramid, Mandalas, sun, figures such as the old wise man (woman), etc. General symbols reflect the concrete basic themes of human existence, which concern all of us. General symbols are images from the real world: house, car, birth, marriage, child, old man, dog, mother, father, etc. These symbols express the essential real life themes of everybody. Example of contemplation: Try to visualize a night sky with various stars. One star comes nearer and nearer, then stays as a little sun in front of you. The light of this sun shines agreeably warm into the body, until the whole body from head to feet and hands is full of light-energy. After that, ask this sun: "Who are you?"

Contemplation gives us access to the "mystery" of mankind.

Archetypes of Individuation

The archetypes have a key function in the process of individuation. Mandalas represent the higher unity and wholeness; create focus and a new orientation. Let's pick out two symbols (archetypes) which have taken a high importance in the western history to express the psychical-spiritual evolution: "The Holy Grail" and the "Circle-Cross-Mandala" (also called "life symbol").

The "Grail" is the "philosopher's stone". The occidental tradition also speaks about the "cup", the "emerald" or the "Jewel". The "Grail is the vessel of transformation"; it also means the "spiritual human being". The Grail is an allegory for the highest psychical-spiritual development and therefore the supreme mystery of the human being. Psychologically we can interpret the stories of the "Holy Grail" as an inner process of transformation. The inner spirit is the guiding force through that process, which creates the dreams and composes the imagination to informative messages. On that journey a person has to give up a lot. But he gets back everything in a new form: This is the process of "dying and being reborn" until the new wholeness is completed.

The circle-cross-mandala has a history which dates back to the ancient Egyptian high culture. The wheel of the sun is probably the first symbolic representation of the mystery of mankind. Drive and spirit, psyche and terrestrial life, earth and sky, wholeness and centeredness, masculinity and femininity are realities connected with that archetype (symbol). The wheel also represents, according to the ancient tradition, the circle-movement of reincarnation, in other words: the inner rebirth from the archaic human being to a new evolutionary human being. This archetype also represents the sun and with that also the transcendence.

The Grail and the life-symbol both essentially comprise the same theme: the inner psychical-spiritual human being. We can thoroughly understand the process and the aim of Individuation only in relation to this archetype.

If words, such as psychological terms, cannot capture the essential facts, the symbol can talk and express the meaning for a deeper understanding. One has to close one's eyes and meditate about this archetype; that's the way to understand, in the case where words can't help for an authentic understanding.

Examples of application of meditation

1. Relaxation, balance and centering of energy
2. Self-strengthening, renewing the energies
3. Being conscious of one's daily life style
4. To understand relationships
5. Developing solutions for new challenges
6. Clarifying difficulties and conflicts
7. Understanding psycho-somatic suffering
8. Getting rid of painful past experiences
9. Understanding dreams

10. Exploring all inner elements of the conscience
11. A conscious dealing with emotions (feelings)
12. Dealing with one's own needs
13. Strengthening will and ego-control
14. Recognizing projections and identifications
15. Using intelligence consciously
16. Broadening the perception
17. Understanding the mystery of mankind
18. Recognizing the state of the earth from a spiritual point of view
19. Identifying and understanding one's own destiny
20. Planning and realizing the path of Individuation.

To broaden one's self-experience

In reality, one can understand another person only if one contemplates the other person under the perspective of his life-experiences. The biography forms a person. The biography is a part of the present existence of a person: "I am my living past." The lived past is the code program for the life in the present and the future. We can explore and change this inner living reality with meditation. From this we draw some special questions for self-knowledge:

➔ How does the past – the lived life – influence the present?
➔ How do the last days and weeks come to mind?
➔ Which memories often come back into the present?
➔ How does looking back upon the past including childhood affect me today?
➔ Which prominent life experiences form the self-identity?
➔ Which perspectives on the future are already manifested in the present?

Meditating correctly – The general rules

➔ Determining what one wants to achieve: knowledge, changes, consolidation.
➔ Determining the images and symbols for meditation.
➔ Letting the course of visualization develop aim-oriented, passively or actively.
➔ Exploring the meaning; interpreting the result, like a dream.
➔ Draw conclusions for one's life and try out results in real life.

The procedure: Sit down comfortably in a chair. Close your eyes. Relax 1-2 minutes: release the thoughts and breathe deeply. Then say for example: "I want to see inner images, which show me: That's me!" You can work with an imaginary mirror.

In the imagination you see various faces in that mirror. Then, let the "film" develop during around 2 minutes without controlling too much. Concentrate on what you can visualize clearly or vaguely.

Make your first meditative exercises short. Stop the "film" if you experience a flood of images. Don't force images to come. If nothing happens, concentrate on your feelings and your floating thoughts. After the exercise write down your experiences. And then interpret the result of your meditation.

3.4.1. Meditate in the appropriate manner

Thesis II-E4-1-T1: Aims of meditation are: Relaxation, renewing life energy, understanding psychical life and realities of life, problem solving, explore the unconscious, promoting healing processes, investigating the mystery of the human being.

Thesis II-E4-1-T2: Constructive meditation consists of: specific images and symbols, creating the process of visualization, roles of interpretation and formulating consequences for daily life.

Thesis II-E4-1-T3: Nothing speaks as truthfully as the inner spirit who creates the dreams and organizes the events in meditations with intelligence, provided that one meditates correctly.

● Meditation is visualization and an aim-oriented operating with inner pictorial ideas. The 5 basic questions of meditation are:

1. What do you want to achieve? Aim determination. Reasons.

2. Which images and symbols do you want to work with? Operating instruments.

3. How do you actively create the inner pictorial events? Operations. Proceeding.

4. How do you proceed with the interpretation? Interpretation.

5. How do you transform the result into your life? Consequences in real life.

Exercise II-E4-L1/1: Several conditions should be considered to get real success with meditation. Mark your dispositions for meditation:

☐ Readiness to learn
☐ Realistic expectations
☐ Strength of will
☐ Ability to concentrate
☐ Seriousness
☐ Honesty
☐ Genuine inner interest

☐ Ability to visualize
☐ Self-confidence
☐ Positive elemental attitudes
☐ No opposite religious position
☐ Free from fundamentalism

What do feel about these pre-conditions?

Exercise II-E4-L1/2: What is "meditation" in your opinion?

Exercise II-E4-L1/3: In your opinion, how do we have to meditate "correctly"?

Exercise II-E4-L1/4: In your opinion, for what purpose can we meditate in your opinion?

Exercise II-E4-L1/5: Does a person need "meditation"? Give reasons:

● Aims of meditation: Health, self-education, healing, transcendental experiences, etc.

Exercise II-E4-L1/6: What do you expect from meditation?

● The more intense an inner visualization is the stronger the effect on the psyche and body.

Exercise II-E4-L1/7: Describe your experiences with an example:

● The message (meaning) from an image in the meditation is based on the characteristics of the inner spirit (similar to dreams) if we consider the rules for creating a meditation.

● The interpretation of a result of meditation proceeds like with dream interpretation. Be cautious: There is always a tendency to see what one wants to see in a meditation.

Exercise II-E4-L1/8: Mark what is the case for you. Comment and explain:

☐ I don't have important meditative experiences; reasons are:
☐ I practice meditation often / sometimes / rarely in the following way:
☐ I mainly worked with the following images and symbols:
☐ I interpreted my meditations with the following criteria:
☐ Meditation has helped me. For example:
☐ I have learnt the following from meditation for my life:
☐ I have taken decisions from meditation. For example:
☐ I have the following questions about meditation:

Exercise II-E4-L1/9: What do you expect from meditating? Describe concretely:

Summary:

1. What is the most important thing you have learnt from this lesson?

2. What is your most outstanding strength in the subject of this lesson?

3. What is your outstanding weakness in the subject of this lesson?

4. What has touched you most in the subject of this lesson?

5. What is your most important future aim in the subject of this lesson?

6. What is your next step to improve in the subject of this lesson?

7. What are your open questions in the subject of this lesson?

3.4.2. Practice visualization

Thesis II-E4-2-T1: Imagination means meditating about psychical life, biography, daily behavior, life issues and life problems.

Thesis II-E4-2-T2: By practicing imagination, you actively and consciously create the course of images (film); you can explore complexes and conflicts, and find solutions.

Thesis II-E4-2-T3: The active communication with the inner spirit takes place through meditation (images, visualization) and that's the way to form wisdom.

● Imagination is meditating about the psychical life, the biography, the acting, the life themes, for problem solution, etc. In the imagination we work with images which can represent the matter. For that we can stipulate about the use of symbols:

Real theme (elements from):	Images, symbols, scenes (etc.):
The psychical life as a whole	Instruments / orchestra
The self-system (I, ego)	Captain with a boat / on the steering wheel
The needs	Animals on a farm
The feelings (emotions)	The color spectrum
The intelligent functions	A computer
The unconscious (mind)	A store room / a grot
The love	The eternal fire / the sun
The Spirit	Owl / a wise person
Individuation	Journey, expedition
The psychical totality	The circle-cross-Mandala

Exercise II-E4-L2/1: Construct 3 examples to themes and (meditative) images:

Real Theme	Appropriate (convenient) images
1)	
2)	
3)	

● For each way of imagination apply: Formulate questions – Determine images and symbols – Find orientation in the psychical system and / or in the matter:

Exercise II-E4-L2/2: Give examples of questions that you meditated over:

Exercise II-E4-L2/3: Until today, my psychical themes for meditation have been:

Exercise II-E4-L2/4: Until today, my life themes ("matters") to meditate over have been:

Exercise II-E4-L2/5: Create 3 meditations:

The question for the meditation The theme/matter for the meditation	The inner pictorial language Images - Symbols - Archetypes	The psychical sub-system The life system The themes
Example: My depression. Why am I depressed (aggrieved) again and again without any apparent motive?	Example: I carry a backpack; open it, look what is inside, and I can find what is depressing me.	Example: Needs, feelings, thoughts, ideals, memories, wishes, events, etc.
1)		
2)		
3)		

● Operations - Changes. The aim is: searching, finding, integrating and elaborating ignored and suppressed psychical forces.

Exercise II-E4-L2/6: Elaborate as given. First relax 2 minutes.
a) Chose the specific psychical forces and a symbolic image to that:

Psychical force:	

Images::	

b) Imagine for around 2-3 minutes. Describe your pictorial experience:

c) Interpret the experiences. Formulate a consequence:

● Self-discovering: Visualize a mirror and look into it; you can recognize your faces. Go in a store room and you can find your biographical inventory. Go in a house and you see your way of living. Etc.

Exercise II-E4-L2/7: Elaborate as given. First relax 2 minutes:

a) Chose the specific psychical forces and a symbolic image to that:

Themes to discover:	
Scenery:	

b) Visualize for 2-3 minutes. Describe your pictorial experiences:

c) Interpret what you experienced. Formulate a consequence:

● Operative symbols. The way we can elaborate problems.

Exercise II-E4-L2/8: Elaborate as given:

a) Create a reconciliation of any kind of conflictive situation that you had in the past (or currently):

b) With a magic stick, open a room in your cellar (your complexes are stored inside):

c) Integrate a person helping you in a difficult situation (a wise person, a friend):

d) What are the effects of these meditative-operative actions?

Summary:

1. What is the most important thing you have learnt from this lesson?

2. What is your most outstanding strength in the subject of this lesson?

3. What is your outstanding weakness in the subject of this lesson?

4. What has touched you most in the subject of this lesson?

5. What is your most important future aim in the subject of this lesson?

6. What is your next step to improve in the subject of this lesson?

7. What are your open questions in the subject of this lesson?

3.4.3. Benefit from the power of mental-training

Thesis II-E4-3-T1: Mental-Training helps to sort out and to deal with the events from the past day.

Thesis II-E4-3-T2: Mental-Training helps to relieve a burdened mind, to find concentration, and to create free space for new issues.

Thesis II-E4-3-T3: The force of visualization produces a renewal, building up your life-energy.

● Mental-Training is a way of meditation with the purpose of mental relaxation.

Aims of Mental-Training are:

- To empty the mind
- To find peace (calmness)
- To release inner tension
- To release thoughts
- To center energies
- To focus energy on an aim
- To find concentration
- To create a mental border to others and the world
- To release mental ties with the external world
- To elaborate the passed day
- To preview the day
- To renew life forces

Exercise II-E4-L3/1: Until today, how have you tried to achieve such aims? Describe:

● Systematically establishing calmness

Exercise II-E4-L3/2: Concentrate on your physical state and say while you visualize: "The face is soft ... released ... warm ... calm ... loose ... relaxed". And continue with all parts of the body: neck, shoulder, chest, arms, hands, stomach, back, legs, and feet. Result:

- Psycho-hygiene in the evening

Exercise II-E4-L3/3: Go over the past day: Concretely focus in fast and slow motion. Concentrate on important moments. In the end put away the "film". Result:

- Preparing the day

Exercise II-E4-L3/4: Go over the coming day: Concretely focus in fast and slow motion. Concentrate on important upcoming moments. Find positive attitudes. Result:

- General catharsis and strengthening

Exercise II-E4-L3/5: Call a light (a sun). The sun is here as big as a football. The suns rays fill your body with energy. Result:

- The general standard exercises

Do the following exercises, each for 3-5 minutes (chose one; or all, but not all one after another. Pay attention to the easy approachable motives.

➔ In the future, create your own varieties!

Exercise II-E4-L3/6: Empty your head. A vessel sits on the floor next to your feet. Imagine you have a hole in your forehead and the weight in the head comes out and falls into the vessel. Result:

Exercise II-E4-L3/7: Release thoughts: Thoughts are like clouds, clouds are coming and going, more and more the sky becomes blue. Result:

Exercise II-E4-L3/8: Find distance to everything that happens in your head: Make a boat trip on calm flowing water in a green area. Leave people behind and all matters on the edge. Result:

Exercise II-E4-L3/9: Protect yourself from external influences: Put a glass wall between you and the world; create a scene with a protecting distance (for example a hedge, a fence, etc.). Result:

Exercise II-E4-L3/10: Silence: Sit in a pyramid with the life symbol on top – like a sun radiating in the center. You are sitting in the light beam. Result:

Exercise II-E4-L3/11: Strengthen your life forces: Sitting by an oak, leaning against the trunk. You become unified with the oak. You feel the energy of the oak entering into your body, back, and abdomen. Result:

Exercise II-E4-L3/12: Reduce nervousness: A glass (vessel) slowly fills with water; at the same time the more water that enters into this glass (vessel), the more inner calmness grows. Result:

Exercise II-E4-L3/13: What do you feel and think about such meditations?

Exercise II-E4-L3/14: What happens with you if you never practice mental-training?

Summary:

1. What is the most important thing you have learnt from this lesson?

2. What is your most outstanding strength in the subject of this lesson?

3. What is your outstanding weakness in the subject of this lesson?

4. What has touched you most in the subject of this lesson?

5. What is your most important future aim in the subject of this lesson?

6. What is your next step to improve in the subject of this lesson?

7. What are your open questions in the subject of this lesson?

3.4.4. Explore spirituality with contemplation

Thesis II-E4-4-T1: Contemplation is the kind of imagination by which you can explore the basic issues of the psychical-spiritual personhood.

Thesis II-E4-4-T2: The general symbols of contemplations are the archetypes; universal symbols with eternally valid meaning.

Thesis II-E4-4-T3: The psychical-spiritual issues of human beings are always part of the Individuation process.

● Contemplation is concerned with the fundamental themes of the human being in a general way and especially with the archetypal processes of the Individuation.

Exercise II-E4-L4/1: What are you interested in concerning the fundamental themes of human being? Formulate 2 questions:

● The proceeding of the contemplation is similar to the imagination (visualization).

→ **Do not make the exercises one after another.**

Exercise II-E4-L4/2: Imagine you go on a world journey discovering the "mysteries" of (human) life. A boat is ready for you. Pack your stuff. The journey starts now. Result and consequences:

Exercise II-E4-L4/3: Imagine a wise person (a wise man or woman). Tell the person that you want to know more about the life of the soul. Ask what you have to do for that. Result and consequences:

Exercise II-E4-L4/4: Imagine a simple Mandala (a quadrate with a circle and a cross, with rosettes if you like). You know: This represents the "totality" (completeness). Talk to the symbol, ask the symbol to transform in a way that it represents your actual psychical-spiritual level (state)! Result and consequences:

Exercise II-E4-L4/5: You receive a transparent ball, like a little sun, as big as a tennis ball. This is your inner life source. Do something with this ball! Result and consequences:

Exercise II-E4-L4/6: Call the "circle-cross-Mandala". Take it in your hands. Ask in the meditation: "Let me experience (feel) what I can do with you". Result and consequences:

● Contemplation about archetypes

This is the simplest way of contemplation. Call a corresponding symbol and ask it: "Please, act upon me in a way so that I can understand what you mean." Or: "Please transform into another symbol (image) in a way I can understand you."

Exercise II-E4-L4/7: Owl

Exercise II-E4-L4/8: Elephant

Exercise II-E4-L4/9: Cup (chalice)

Exercise II-E4-L4/10: Death

Exercise II-E4-L4/11: Birth, new life (a baby)

Exercise II-E4-L4/12: Your spontaneous reactions to such archetypal images:

● Contemplation about archetypal processes

Exercise II-E4-L4/13: Imagine you go into a process of transformation (changes) and renewal. Ask what can happen with you and what will be the effects. Result and consequences:

Exercise II-E4-L4/14: You decide to precede the inner growing processes (Individuation). You accept the inner spirit as your authority of guidance. Call in the contemplation a wise person (man or woman) and ask: "I want to go through the archetypal processes." – What happens now in the meditation? Result and consequences:

Exercise II-E4-L4/15: Do you want to form a "new human being" from the depth of your soul? Yes, and then imagine you go in a sanctuary and explain your readiness. You will be guided directly into the first starting proceeding. Let the images flow. Result and consequences:

Exercise II-E4-L4/16: If a human being doesn't want to practice such meditation, what remains of him? What is the difference (doing it or ignoring it)?

Summary:

1. What is the most important thing you have learnt from this lesson?

2. What is your most outstanding strength in the subject of this lesson?

3. What is your outstanding weakness in the subject of this lesson?

4. What has touched you most in the subject of this lesson?

5. What is your most important future aim in the subject of this lesson?

6. What is your next step to improve in the subject of this lesson?

7. What are your open questions in the subject of this lesson?

3.4.5. Practice meditative regressions correctly

Thesis II-E4-5-T1: Regression means that one can, in a meditation exercise, return to the past, back to the prenatal time revive it and, if necessary, work out the critical experiences.

Thesis II-E4-5-T2: The regression exercises serve as a first approach to train your retrospective and meditative skills. This way the past emotional experience seems like yesterday.

Thesis II-E4-5-T3: Everything that happened in the past up to the prenatal time is stored in the brain (mind). That forms the foundation of how one is as a person, how one thinks, feels, values, reacts and lives.

● Regression means: Roll up the whole past through meditation (biography until the prenatal time) with the purpose of experiencing special moments again as well as to elaborate experiences.

● The psychical processes start to be formed from the moment of procreation: VERY IMPORTANT!!!

● The following exercises aim to provide a first insight into different life phases. Do each exercise for a maximum of 3 minutes. Stop the meditation after 2-3 images. Never force images of a past time. Stop the regression when the images become too intense or overwhelming.

The following exercises allow a first entry into varied life phases. First, train by remembering without any elaboration and without deepening the experiences. Therefore: Do the exercises shortly (maximum 3-5 minutes) and stop after a first result. If you can't visualize any memories, be patient and repeat these exercises periodically.

Proceeding:

1. First do a short relaxing exercise to direct concentration towards your inner life.

2. Suggestions: "Time is unimportant. The space around me is unimportant. I am going back into my past life now. I am reaching for the time when … Now the pictures from that time are coming to the surface."

3. Look at the images and scenes. Call other images. Then go a bit further back in time (e.g. 20th birthday), etc.

4. Finish the exercise with these suggestions: "The images withdraw more and more now. Slowly the present time becomes more and more important. I can feel the space around me now. The present is back now."

5. Breathe deeply. Open your eyes. Move your arms and legs.

6. Describe the result of the regression exercise.

● **IMPORTANT: It is not recommended to practice intense and long regressions to the early childhood and the prenatal time without professional guidance!!!**

The following exercises: In each exercise only call 3 images from the chosen time (past moment)!

Exercise II-E4-L5/1: Regression to the past days

Exercise II-E4-L5/2: Regression to the past months

Exercise II-E4-L5/3: Regression to the time around a year ago

Exercise II-E4-L5/4: Regression to the time around 5 years ago

Exercise II-E4-L5/5: Regression to the period of your adulthood

Exercise II-E4-L5/6: Regression to your youth

Exercise II-E4-L5/7: Regression to your childhood

Exercise II-E4-L5/8: Regression to your early childhood

Exercise II-E4-L5/9: Regression to the prenatal time (only with professional guidance!)

Exercise II-E4-L5/10: Find, overview and summarize the result. Describe with keywords:

a) What are the key-images?
b) What are the essential themes?
c) How have you experienced these moments emotionally?

Exercise II-E4-L5/11: Why have these images arisen and not others? Try to understand these images as "messages", and interpret: they all want to say something to you. What do these images want to say to you?

Summary:

1. What is the most important thing you have learnt from this lesson?

2. What is your most outstanding strength in the subject of this lesson?

3. What is your outstanding weakness in the subject of this lesson?

4. What has touched you most in the subject of this lesson?

5. What is your most important future aim in the subject of this lesson?

6. What is your next step to improve in the subject of this lesson?

7. What are your open questions in the subject of this lesson?

3.4.6. Elaborate aspects of your life experiences

> Thesis II-E4-6-T1: One can focus the regression on specific life issues to better understand the corresponding experiences.
>
> Thesis II-E4-6-T2: One can work with imagination on critical situations from the past, sorting them out makes us free from them.
>
> Thesis II-E4-6-T3: Embarrassing and delicate (critical, difficult) experiences in the past bind the issue and fixate the Ego onto the learned patterns of reaction.

> ● **Do not work out very painful life experiences without professional support!**

● You can do these regressions theme-oriented. In each exercise only call one theme. It is important to keep the time proceeding; in other words: do not jump from one time moment to any other (up and down and up again in the time scale).

Example "father experiences": Step by step call scenes where your father plays an important role, where these experiences have formed something in your mind: start with the last years and then go back periodically until your childhood. Choose themes:

Exercise II-E4-L6/1: Theme: Mother experiences

Exercise II-E4-L6/2: Themes: Religious experiences

Exercise II-E4-L6/3: Themes: School and learning experiences

Exercise II-E4-L6/4: Themes: Quarrel and conflict experiences

Exercise II-E4-L6/5: Themes: Sexual experiences

Exercise II-E4-L6/6: Themes: Love experiences

Exercise II-E4-L6/7: Themes: Friendship experiences

Exercise II-E4-L6/8: Themes: Experiences about lies, intrigues, meanness, betrayal in trust, etc.

Exercise II-E4-L6/9: Themes: Embarrassing and lasting uncomfortable experiences

Exercise II-E4-L6/10: Themes: Experiences of all kind of pain

Exercise II-E4-L6/11: Themes: Experiences that have formed your being a man / a woman

Exercise II-E4-L6/12: Themes: punishment experiences (active punishments, silent rejection and ignoring, etc.)

Exercise II-E4-L6/13: Summary.

Write down your general impression (positive, negative, similarities, variations):

Exercise II-E4-L6/14: What do you feel and think now, that you are always also your biography?

Summary:

1. What is the most important thing you have learnt from this lesson?

2. What is your most outstanding strength in the subject of this lesson?

3. What is your outstanding weakness in the subject of this lesson?

4. What has touched you most in the subject of this lesson?

5. What is your most important future aim in the subject of this lesson?

6. What is your next step to improve in the subject of this lesson?

7. What are your open questions in the subject of this lesson?

3.4.7. Explore other realities meditatively

Thesis II-E4-7-T1: Clairvoyance is a specific kind of directed imaginary intuition about alien psychical and real matters and realities.

Thesis II-E4-7-T2: The interpretation demands consideration for one's consciousness about oneself and furthermore demands in-depth psychological knowledge.

Thesis II-E4-7-T3: There is often a resistance to accept that what one sees in a meditation is a direct symbolic expression of the focused issue.

Important: Clairvoyance as imagination shows an unknown reality with one's own images. One can run great risk to mix own material with alien material, or to project material from one's own subconscious onto a place or other person. Therefore, be cautious with your interpretation!

● Clairvoyance is meditation about other's psychical, institutional or objective facts without having a direct access to these realities. Instead of asking "Who am I?" we can ask: "Who is Mr. X (Ms. Y)?" The inner perception is able to see other people's psychical-spiritual realities.

● Nothing remains hidden to the "third eye". Distances are unimportant. Sometimes it's enough to know the person's name, a photo, a piece of clothing, or holding a letter in the hand, and we get access with extra-sensorial perception to the psychical-spiritual reality of this person. Such objects that create access to a person para-psychologically are called "conductors". The time is also relative. We can also see into the past, e.g. the childhood, of a person, or see in an unknown house how people live there or lived there before.

● The main difficulty is the interpretation of the images we experience in the meditation. Here we have to confront the same problems that we also have with dream interpretation and imagination in general.

We see unknown realities with our images.

We can run the risk of confusing own matters with matters of the other person, projecting something that is not there. Or we simply have resistance to accept that what we see, expressed in a symbolic way the reality from this other person (or institution, or place). The correct interpretation demands being fully aware of one's own consciousness, biography, unconscious mind, and especially one's own level of psychical-spiritual development.

• The general rule is: The more a person has progressed in his Individuation, the clearer and more precise this person sees realities and can therefore correctly interpret them.

Exercise II-E4-L7/1: You can explore this educational program. Visualize into the practical program and study manuscripts. Then ask your inner Spirit: "What happens with the people that do this program? Where are they guided to with the Individuation?

Exercise II-E4-L7/2: Go to an astrologer. Proceed like L7/1:

Exercise II-E4-L7/3: Visit an esoteric institution you know. Proceed like L7/1:

Exercise II-E4-L7/4: Go to a catholic church. Mass is being held. Proceed like L7/1:

Exercise II-E4-L7/5: Do you know an ill person? Visit this person. Ask your inner Spirit why this person is ill.

Exercise II-E4-L7/6: Visit a place from where you want to know how they live there.

Exercise II-E4-L7/7: Visit a place from where you want to know how the energy is there.

Exercise II-E4-L7/8: You want to know how the childhood of another person was. Call this person and go with him to his childhood.

Exercise II-E4-L7/9: You want to know how your friend (boyfriend, girlfriend) feels at the moment. Visit this person. The man (woman) shows you what depresses him (her) at the moment.

Once you have done these exercises, contemplate as follows:

What was your motive for this meditation?

What is the exact practical purpose of this meditation?

What does the meditation result say about you?

What will you do with the result of the meditation?

Exercise II-E4-L7/10: Review: Evaluate your experiences with the meditations, and mark the appropriate box:

I experience:	always	mostly	often	sometimes	seldom
No images					
Vague shadow-images					
Blurry images					
Vague ideas					
Clear spoken sentences					
Too many images					
Overflowing images					
Floating disorder					
Very real, concrete images					
Fabulous, magical images					
Without emotion, feeling					
Emotionally very intensive					
Very strange images					
But without understanding					
With a clear understanding					

Exercise II-E4-L7/11: Conclusions. Write down what has to be done now:

Summary:

1. What is the most important thing you have learnt from this lesson?

2. What is your most outstanding strength in the subject of this lesson?

3. What is your outstanding weakness in the subject of this lesson?

4. What has touched you most in the subject of this lesson?

5. What is your most important future aim in the subject of this lesson?

6. What is your next step to improve in the subject of this lesson?

7. What are your open questions in the subject of this lesson?

3.4.8. Elaborate your dreams meditatively

Thesis II-E4-8-T1: In an imagination one can visualize and revive each dream scene or dream image and in doing so, gain a better understanding.

Thesis II-E4-8-T2: In a meditation each image, each symbol, each archetype, each action and each data from a dream can be investigated meditatively to understand the meaning.

Thesis II-E4-8-T3: The meditative finishing-off of a dream can help to find solutions which are not clearly indicated in the dream. One can also bring an open dream situation to a positive end.

● We can elaborate dreams with meditation. Each image and symbol, each archetype, each action, and each fact in a dream can be explored to get the meaning.

● We can start visualizing the dream and experience it again. In this way we can learn to understand each image.

● Additionally we can introduce new figures into the dream. We can put a light where it is dark and obscure. We can open closed doors. We can talk to unknown persons: "What do you want from me? What are you doing here? Who are you?" We can also introduce a wise person and ask: "What does this scene show me? What does this dream image show me?"

● Or we can change and extend a scene in the meditation. With that we can master critical moments, find solutions for a problem, and transform images that we do not understand into other images. With this kind of active imagination the meaning of a dream (the dream message) becomes clear. We can also put chaotic scenes in order, or close an open scene. The effect is relieving. Imagination is an important support in the elaboration of dreams.

Exercise II-E4-L8/1: Choose 5 key-images, actions or scenes from different dreams. While meditating ask about the meaning.

● Identifying a person: Often it is unclear what a known or unknown person in a dream means. In the imagination you can ask questions: What are you doing here? What do I have to do with you? What do you want from me? Etc. Take 2 dreams.

Exercise II-E4-L8/2: A known person. Describe the person and his action in the dream.

Exercise II-E4-L8/3: An unknown person. Describe the person and his action in the dream.

● "Critical" situation in a dream (accident, fear, danger, violence, etc.)

Exercise II-E4-L8/4: Choose 3 complex "critical" situations from different dreams. Meditatively go into the difficult situation. Ask about the meaning of this situation. Find a solution.

Exercise II-E4-L8/5: Meditation as a supportive instrument for dream interpretation: What have you experienced and learnt now?

Exercise II-E4-L8/6: What are your difficulties doing these exercises?

Summary:

1. What is the most important thing you have learnt from this lesson?

2. What is your most outstanding strength in the subject of this lesson?

3. What is your outstanding weakness in the subject of this lesson?

4. What has touched you most strongly in the subject of this lesson?

5. What is your most important future aim in the subject of this lesson?

6. What is your next step to improve in the subject of this lesson?

7. What are your open questions in the subject of this lesson?

3.4.9. Benefit from the energy of healing meditation

Thesis II-E4-9-T1: Colors produce an effect on the psyche and the body corresponding with the symbolic meaning of the color.

Thesis II-E4-9-T2: Healing meditation is a way for recognizing the causes of a disorder or suffering. In case that the psyche or certain behavior is the cause, you can recognize them.

Thesis II-E4-9-T3: Healing meditation means: Activating the life energy with inner images (visualization) in order to revitalize, strengthen, heal (cure) etc. for oneself or for others.

● **Healing meditation is not a substitute for medical help!**

● Spiritual healing: Meditative and aim-oriented activation of life energy with inner images to revitalize, strengthen, and self-healing (etc.) for you and other people.

● Colors in the meditation have an effect on the psyche and body corresponding to its symbolic meaning.

Exercise II-E4-L9/1: Ask contemplating: Which color now has a good effect on my psyche and body? – Which color do you see now? How is the color portrayed in the meditation?

Exercise II-E4-L9/2: Let this color be effective on your body and psyche.

Exercise II-E4-L9/3: Try to understand the effect of each color. (Don't do all colors at the same time, do one after another; Chose a color and do the next color a bit later):

Blue: Yellow: Violet: Red: Green: Brown:

● You can use the psychical and spiritual forces to activate and strengthen healing processes in meditations.

Exercise II-E4-L9/4: Call the healing force of the soul. A figure appears. Present your concern, for example: "I can't sleep; help me"; or: "I often have headaches" (pressure on my chest, constipation, high blood pressure, heart pain, allergies, etc.) "Why do I have these disturbances? What shall I do?"

Exercise II-E4-L9/5: Organ meditation. Call the sun and let the sun radiate through your open hands into your entire body. Imagine all parts of your body and organs until the singular cells. Imagine: in each cell there is a little sun and activate the program for health". Result:

Exercise II-E4-L9/6: Sit into a pyramid full of light. Stay some minutes.

● There is a spiritual sun in the spiritual universe, in a certain way the universal eternal force of life (life energy). Many people call this the "divine source". We teach that the human being has this sun in his soul ("inner being"). We can use this energetic force of the spiritual sun for healing processes.

For the following exercises you have to choose a partner. This person shall sit 3 meters from you or even in another room (distance is principally unimportant), relaxed and in meditative attitude. Then start with the following exercise.

Exercise II-E4-L9/7: Sending the sun. You sit comfortably. Take a meditative attitude (inside-oriented concentration). Close your eyes. Hold your hands open. Call the sun – as big as a football –, take this sun into your hands, and then send the sun to the partner next to you as described above, with the idea, the sun shall "clean" the entire body of this person, making everything light, giving warmth, strengthening, in general bringing peace and love. During this, try to see this person (visualizing) or to feel his presence. Repeat this action 3-5 times very slowly.

a) What do you feel while sending the sun to the exercise-partner?

b) What is the result on your exercise-partner (having received the sun)?

● Everybody sometimes has some kind of a problem, an inner pain, a real suffering, a painful conflict, an unsolved inner matter, etc. The psychical-spiritual energy of the sun can have releasing effects, introduce healing processes, and stimulate hope and confidence for a good solution.

With such healing meditation we also have to consider that psychological causes and varied ways of living can cause illness.

Change the role now. The passive person: Sit around 3 meters away from your exercise-partner (or in another room; distance is not important), remain relaxed with a meditative attitude. The acting person proceeds the following way:

Exercise II-E4-L9/8: Sending the sun theme-oriented. This exercise has the same proceeding as exercise L9/7. Concentrate mentally on your exercise-partner. He may be consciously or unconsciously not really well at the moment; he may be sick or has any inner pain. Visualize this person. Ask what preoccupies him. Say: "I want to see now the causes of your suffering". After some first images calling the sun, send the sun 3-5 times slowly to the person, with the wish the sun may activate healing forces, make the reasons aware, showing a path for solutions, and also have an effect where the causes are.

a) The experience of the acting person (sending the sun):

b) The experience of the passive person (receiving the sun):

Summary:

1. What is the most important thing you have learnt from this lesson?

2. What is your most outstanding strength in the subject of this lesson?

3. What is your outstanding weakness in the subject of this lesson?

4. What has touched you most in the subject of this lesson?

5. What is your most important future aim in the subject of this lesson?

6. What is your next step to improve in the subject of this lesson?

7. What are your open questions in the subject of this lesson?

3.4.10. Meditate about the future

Thesis II-E4-10-T1: The force of the spirit can see tendencies of a development. In the meditation one has to consider that the meditative scene may reflect a subjective opinion first, and that the meditative result refers to the person who is meditating (knowledge, resistance, antipathy, values, patterns of life concept etc.).

Thesis II-E4-10-T2: If you want to know if it is worthwhile to integrate a role model as life guidance, the meditative precognition exercise can clarify it. During meditation, one can often see the basic tendencies of a future development, always represented in a symbolic way.

Thesis II-E4-10-T3: We can not foresee facts when the forces (the conditions) producing these facts are not yet in the present or not 100% sure to exist in the future.

● The capacity of people for extra-sensorial perception like clairvoyance and precognition (= foresight, future sight) are different, but basically always given. The ability to get success depends among others on the ability (experience) to meditate.

● The power of the inner spirit is able to represent the focused future correctly. But we have to consider that the spontaneously appearing images can first and foremost express a subjective supposition. Furthermore the images are always created in relation to the meditating person (knowledge, resistance, aversion, patterns of values, etc.).

● Furthermore we have to be aware that each precognition principally has certain limits. It's not possible to preview something if the causal forces (the conditions for effects) are actually still not present. Apart from that we always have to calculate with unforeseeable incidents ("imponderables"). These imponderables always have a significant effect in the future development.

● In such meditation you mostly see some basic tendencies of future developments, in most cases always symbolically (!!!), seldom in concrete singular facts, seldom with a precise time table, mostly in a general motto: "If everything continues like today, then ...".

● The exercises for future views have to be done the same way as meditation / imagination.

Your own future perspectives

Exercise II-E4-L10/1: If I continue living like today, how will my life be in 5, 10 or more years? Result of the meditation:

Exercise II-E4-L10/2: How can I take these developments into my own hands, correct them where necessary, and guide them with responsibility towards a good path and good aims?

The future perspectives of another person

Exercise II-E4-L10/3: Choose a partner for the exercise. Practice the exercises like L10/1 as a way of extra-sensorial perception. If he/she continues living like today, how will his / her life be in 5, 10 or more years?

Exercise II-E4-L10/4: How can he / she take these developments into his/her own hands, correct them where necessary, and guide them with responsibility towards a good path and good aims?

The future perspectives of society

Exercise II-E4-L10/5: If the people in Northern Europe (or chose another continent) continue living like today, how will their future be in 5, 10 or more years?

Exercise II-E4-L10/6: How can these people take these developments into their own hands, correct them where necessary, and guide them with responsibility towards a good path and good aims?

The future perspectives of Christianity

Exercise II-E4-L10/7: If Christianity continues living (teaching and acting) like today, what will the future of this religion be in 5, 10 or more years?

Exercise II-E4-L10/8: How can these churches tackle these developments, taking into their own hands, correcting where necessary, and guide them with responsibility towards a good path and good aims?

The future perspectives of humanity

Exercise II-E4-L10/9: If the people worldwide continue living like today, how will the future of humanity and the earth be in 5, 10 or more years?

Exercise II-E4-L10/10: How can the people worldwide take these developments into their own hands, correct them where necessary, and guide them with responsibility towards a good path and good aims?

General overview

Exercise II-E4-L10/11: Summarize the result of these exercises about the collective:

Exercise II-E4-L10/12: What importance does this kind of (extra-sensorial) meditation have?

Exercise II-E4-L10/13: What do you conclude for the capacity of such meditations?

Exercise II-E4-L10/14: Write down your critical thoughts about your result:

Summary:

1. What is the most important thing you have learnt from this lesson?

2. What is your most outstanding strength in the subject of this lesson?

3. What is your outstanding weakness in the subject of this lesson?

4. What has touched you most in the subject of this lesson?

5. What is your most important future aim in the subject of this lesson?

6. What is your next step to improve in the subject of this lesson?

7. What are your open questions in the subject of this lesson?

Made in the USA
Charleston, SC
09 October 2012